A Secretly Handicapped Man

a Memoir by
NORBERT NATHANSON

North Wind Publishing
Brewer, Maine

North Wind Publishing
P.O. Box 3655
Brewer, ME 04412
northwindpublishing.com
info@northwindpublishing.com

All photographs courtesy of the author

Text set in Times New Roman
Cover by Jared L. Nathanson
Printed in the United States of America

ISBN: 978-0-9895689-1-3
Library of Congress Cataloging-in-Publication Number: 2013944439

To Barbara, Jessica and Jared

Contents

FOREWORD

One of my earliest memories is mother directing me not to tell the neighbors about my father's legs. I was 3 years old, playing on the front lawn in Schenectady with my sister. We were constantly reminded that we were not to talk about my father's secret that, in our suburban 1970's American life, he walked with a prosthetic leg below each knee.

We never told anyone. It wasn't the world's biggest secret, nor was there any shame or scandal, but it was my father's desire. In my mind he was, and is, tough, self driven, and capable, and the least disabled person I've known, but unable to recognize and enjoy his achievements.

It was only in college that I realized how much his story defined us all, how proud and in awe I was of him, and how angry and confused I was to be prevented from expressing my pride in his accomplishments. Born with severe disabilities in a time of great inhumanity and economic ruin, he spent a third of his life enduring ridicule and pity, underestimated by both his community and colleagues. In a world that had no room for him, he demanded space for himself. From working class beginnings in Depression Era Pittsburgh, he fought past class barriers at college and into the burgeoning field of early television. Here, denied entrance to the main stream and facing constant rejection and prejudice, he nevertheless worked successfully with some of the foremost innovators in the field. After being perceived for more than 30 years as a "cripple," walking with a short awkward gate, conspicuous in any public place, attracting unwanted and unavoidable attention and constantly in pain, he then experienced a miracle. Modern advances in medical science provided him a new façade. Artificial legs and feet normalized his height, gait, and appearance and facilitated a privacy he had never known. No longer a public spectacle, he was free to enjoy anonymity, but the memories of years of prejudicial treatment did not disappear behind his new façade.

As society slowly redefined its prejudicial view of people with disabilities, my father enjoyed a now protected privacy. With disabilities now hidden, he did not venture to share his story, fearing that disclosure could invite return of discriminatory treatment he had previously experienced. He became involved with helping to tell the story of disabled people and was active in their search for independence, but he never fully understood the accomplishments of the person he had been and was now, an experienced, driven television executive, educator, outdoorsman, sailor, carpenter, and fisherman, enjoying the peace that being out of the spotlight of public stigma offered him.

Growing up in his world, I knew him to be a compassionate man, a leader, a capable person. It has always been a wonder to equate his physical disabilities with his actual capabilities. I've frequently reflected on what he has overcome. It was not easily done. Through sheer force of will he forged a life, accepting his triumphs as unremarkable, normal, effortless, never defining himself dramatically and never perceiving himself as disabled. He is a survivor, and his survival is a triumph, his entire life a victory. In later life, he enjoys privacy and lack of attention, and remains dissatisfied with his accomplishments, believing them to be minimal. He is unable to envision them as I do, as trophies. For him they were merely steps along the way.

The battles that formed him were costly. Had he not been strong, he would not have survived, and the armor that was his protection and the means for accomplishment still hangs on him today, secretly ready.

I see his triumph as my own. He is a source of great strength to me, an important part of the center of my being. His armor gives me toughness. His victory gave me existence.

Although he will never understand it, he is remarkable . . . as is his life.

—Jared Lucas Nathanson

INTRODUCTION

The years of my lifetime have witnessed numerous public protests in the United States seeking equality in some form. Among these are the Labor union struggles of the early and mid century, the broad based human rights movement of the 60s, and the Gay Rights and Women's Rights movements which are not yet fully resolved

In the 1970s a national movement of disability rights groups was generated by long overdue and unsigned implementation regulations for physical access to public buildings and education (Rehabilitation Act of 1973, PL 93-112, Section 504). Demonstrations, in ten cities across the nation failed to capture the support of non-disabled groups and were generally failures except for one organized and directed at the Berkeley Center for Independence, Berkeley, CA. It became the nucleus of a national independent living philosophy that ultimately resulted in the Section 504 regulations being signed. At no time, however, has there ever been a broad-based public movement to equalize rights, privileges and opportunities for persons with disabilities.

Since World War II, the medical industry, in both its noble and commercial efforts, has achieved great scientific advancements in treatment and prevention, but has inadvertently fragmented the disabled community according to disability, thus creating a system of specialized disability organizations, none of which have sufficient numbers to create a critical mass, and which vie with one another competitively for political and funding support, thus precluding the possibility of a constituency of sufficient size to bring about successful political and civic progress in recognizing the problems of the disabled and ensuring their equality of good life and opportunity.

This book documents the efforts of one person with physical disabilities to live, work and pursue a career in American society from the mid 1920's to the early 90's. It is my story. In the space of seventy years I was variously labeled as crippled, deformed, handicapped and disabled, more recently as a person with disabilities, and currently as physically challenged. The evolving choice of epithets traces the gradual changes in societal perceptions, but all these terms have a common theme; they designate someone who is different.

Exclusive labels, even when given a positive spin, reveal real societal attitudes. If one is a member of a minority, one becomes used to the subtle and not so subtle discrimination practiced by the majority, often unknowingly, against members of various minorities. Race, religion, ethnicity, gender, sexual orientation, physical, developmental and emotional disabilities are all sources of vulnerability. Differences are manipulated by various sectors of the society to accommodate their own interests. Over time, these discriminatory practices build up a sea of frustration that, at the flash point, can result in violence.

I began to write during my last period of unemployment when my potential for rehire had been diminished by age and limited professional visibility. I was depressed, angry, and exasperated by the difficulties I had experienced during much of my working life as a result of being disabled. I was very near the flash point, but lacking a viable target at which to strike, I began to write. I wanted my children and others to recognize the difficulties persons with disabilities encounter in their effort to live and have a career in this society.

Initially my intent was to symbolically strike out at those whom I perceived to be members of the alleged conspiracy that had prevented me from achieving my goals. Subsequent re-employment, and eventual retirement dissipated the anger that had motivated my early efforts. For fifteen years my writing lay abandoned. Ultimately, in the security of retirement, I was able to begin again, in a somewhat more philosophical vein.

The reader may experience my story as a "Perils of Pauline" saga, or perhaps, "a tale of sour grapes." I admit my own contribution to some of my difficulties, but why things happened the way they did, what aspects can be attributed to disability, personality, inexperience, or incapability is a matter for conjecture. Certainly disabilities contributed to the series of adventures that, in some ways, reads as a continuous cliffhanger.

When I read Erving Goffman's book, "Stigma," in 1963 at the age of thirty-seven, it had a profound impact on me: it provided a rational perspective and understanding of a lifetime of experiences. Goffman explained society's expectation that the stigmatized individual should cheerfully and unselfconsciously view himself as normal, but carefully absent himself from situations wherein society at large would regard him as uncomfortably abnormal. Thus the unfairness and pain of having to carry a stigma would never discomfit those without stigma; they would never have to strain their limited tact and tolerance, and could remain relatively uncontaminated by intimate contact with the stigmatized.

As I aged, Goffman's theories brought my social and professional experiences into sharp focus. In re-living those experiences I have elected to occasionally cite Goffman because I believe he provides credible explanations and clarity for my experiences, and conversely, my experiences appear to illustrate his theories.

It is to be hoped that my journey may provide an opportunity for individuals with disabilities, care givers, those with a disabled family member, as well as "normals" to clarify their respective perspectives or better their situations by providing an inside look at a life of one who has experienced many subtleties of discrimination, including the ways the disabled must accommodate the normal, and the roles that upbringing, attitude, and tenacity play in opening up opportunities in areas that may otherwise appear impregnable. There have been many changes in societal perception of disabilities since the years of my youth, but there is still a long way to go to insure that people who are different are afforded respect and opportunity equal to that enjoyed by those without disabilities.

Discrimination directed against the young boy or girl of today is capable of diminishing the hope, happiness, security, and success of the man or woman of tomorrow. The situations pass; the scars remain.

....

Note to Myself. Nov. 5, 1960

"Last Wednesday I was thirty-four years old and it seems important to put my thoughts down on paper so that I can know, as time passes, where I am heading. Since last May, when I first decided to explore the medical and physical rehabilitation program recommended by Dr. Russek, little else has been on my mind. I have found, however, that the prospect of surgery and the following rehabilitation is now less of an issue to me than is my concern over when it is to be done. My mind has kept jumping from one aspect of my anticipated hospitalization to another, but invariably my thoughts focused on the problems I'd encounter walking on artificial legs, or, in fact, getting around without them in emergency instances. I am convinced that in such cases my capabilities would be no less effective than they are now. In fact, it's reasonable to assume that meeting emergency situations would be easier in the future than it is now. Actually, I believe that this is going to be good for me in all aspects and I look forward to getting it over with. The negative and positive aspects of the pending rehabilitation program seem to balance out to the point of neutrality. The quid pro quo is, very simply, the traumatic experience of surgical amputation vs. the will to function and appear normal. The former is something no rational person approaches without some degree of trepidation; the latter something no disabled person does not dream about."

A Secretly Handicapped Man

son to be examined. Before that, my advice was always to leave well enough alone. So far I've been able to do anything I needed to do." Russek studied me. "And what prompted you coming here at this time?" I responded, "Well, my current job was funded by a grant and now it's over. I always have difficulty finding jobs, and I've just learned about the Institute, so I thought it might be a good time for another diagnosis." Russek asked me to remove my shoes, which I did and he stared, shaking his head slowly. "Do you have much pain?"

"Yes, quite a bit. I'm fine when I start out in the morning, but I can't go too long without having pain."

"What do you do then?"

"If I can sit down, I do, otherwise I just keep going."

"Were you in pain when you entered here?"

"Yes."

"You didn't indicate it."

"I've learned to keep it under control."

The examination proceeded and I noticed, as we talked and Russek looked, touched and probed, that he seemed totally amazed that I was as active as I was, and able, at the age of thirty-four, to still function. He approached the situation tentatively. "What is it that you think you would want done about your situation?"

"I really don't know. I have no idea what possibilities might exist."

"Do you think you might want to consider surgery?"

"If that would provide some improvement, I suppose so, but I have no idea what that involves."

Russek leaned back in his chair and gave me a long, serious look. "You know, the reason you have pain is that, for many years, your weight has been concentrated on a very few square inches of bone at the bottom of your legs. You have no arch or spring mechanism to absorb the shock. You have insufficient area to which to distribute the weight. In short, the ends of your legs are severely overloaded. Here on the left leg you're bearing your weight directly on the bottom of the tibia on less than four square inches of area." He pointed to the left foot. "You see here, you've built up a callous to protect the end of the bone. Notice that with the constant beating over the years, the bone has begun to spread. It's the same kind of thing that happens if you pound on a stick with a

....

hammer. Notice also that it's cyanotic, it has a bluish tinge. That's because there is an insufficient blood supply to this area and insufficient flesh there." He leaned forward and said very softly and earnestly, "I believe I can help you. You are very fortunate that you have been able to function for such a long time and right now you are in no immediate danger, but if this situation continues, now that you're thirty-four years old, you will eventually develop some vascular problems and that could well complicate your situation and probably require your legs to be amputated at the level of the knee. If that were to happen, it would be very unfortunate because right now you have two good functional knees. Might you be willing to consider amputation?"

Amputation? That was a frightening word. It had never entered my mind that I'd be asked such a question. I was shaken. "That's a frightening thought. Can you tell me more about what you're suggesting?"

"Yes of course. For many years the artificial leg worn by a below-the-knee amputee has been a heavy cumbersome affair that has a shell, or socket into which the leg fits, and an arrangement of stainless steel rods which form a hinge which permits the leg to flex and provides stability. This is in turn laced to the upper leg and strapped to the waist. One of the reasons you've never been advised to pursue this matter previously is probably due to the weight and awkwardness of the available prostheses. Ironically, you have more mobility now, despite your pain, than you might have had with such a prosthesis. However, a couple years ago at the University of California, Berkeley, a new, fiberglass leg was developed which is uniquely made for your situation. This new leg is designed to distribute your weight here," Russek grasped both my legs in his hands, fingers stretched around them just below the knees where the bone begins to narrow, as if he were holding a glass. Russek pushed upward. "That doesn't hurt, does it?" It didn't. "That's how you'll bear weight in a prosthesis which will be held on by a light weight leather strap around your leg above the knee with another strap to a belt around your waist worn under your clothing. Your legs would be amputated about six inches below the knee. The artificial legs would look perfectly natural and your knee action would be unimpeded. You would be able to stand and walk, probably much longer and farther than you can now and

1

Decision

"I've decided I want to go ahead."

I'd finally said it. A half hour ago I was still undecided, weighing the pros and cons, but now I had just agreed to have both of my lower legs amputated below the knees. I took a deep breath. It was really going to happen. Dr. Russek smiled, "In that case there's someone I want you to meet."

******

I was teaching three courses at New York University's Washington Square Campus as an adjunct professor; directing University closed-circuit instructional television courses; completing a Master's Degree in Communications; living on meager earnings in a small efficiency apartment in West Greenwich Village; and had been trying, for more than a year with no success, to find a full-time job somewhere in the television broadcasting industry. Unfortunately, in spite of my eternal optimism, my general appearance, given my highly visible disabilities, had proven to be an insurmountable obstacle in my search for employment, and I had reluctantly concluded it was directly preventing my being given serious consideration. In addition, the exhausting and painful walking and standing necessary for job hunting in New York City was beyond my sustainable limits. I was thirty-four years old and at a cross-roads.

My Master's thesis was an experiment: a series of programs that attempted to teach deaf youngsters by television—no one had ever attempted it before—and it was sufficiently newsworthy to have justified an article in the *New York Times* which had, to my surprise, been picked up by the *London Times*. I was in need of $3,000 dollars to record the lessons for further study, but unsuccessful in finding a grantor. In my search for funding, however, I'd

•••

discovered an organization that, although unable to fund my project, had aroused my personal interest.

During World War II, Dr. Howard Rusk, an Army Air Corps physician, had created new and unique physical/surgical rehabilitation procedures and products that had enabled many wounded soldiers to return to active duty. After the War, Arthur Hays Sulzberger, publisher of the *New York Times*, had offered him space for a weekly column on health issues. Rusk had used the column to generate support for what had ultimately become the Institute for Physical Medicine and Rehabilitation in the New York University Medical School. The Institute provided civilians the kinds of services Rusk's military programs had provided for soldiers. I knew little about the actual work done at the Institute, but it occurred to me given my stalled career, that as many years had passed since I'd had any assessment of my disabilities, IPMR might perhaps have someone who could evaluate my condition or advise me of any new medical developments that might be of value to me.

I phoned the Institute, explained my inquiry, and my call was forwarded to the appropriate office. No matter how many times I've later recalled that moment, I'm unable to dismiss the perception that fate intervened when my call was answered by the Chief of the Institute's Rehabilitation Service, Dr. Allan Russek, who was in charge of the Institute's wide range of rehabilitation services and personally possessed unique expertise in the development and fitting of prostheses for amputees. He listened as I briefly outlined my life and condition, and then suggested, "It might be a good idea for you to come in for a visit so we can see firsthand what your situation is, then perhaps we can talk about what possibilities might exist for bettering it." A week later, on arriving at the Institute at 34th Street and 1st Ave on Manhattan's East Side, I was shown into Dr. Russek's office.

Russek was a tall man of ruddy complexion, with a bit of a stoop. His kindly expression and sad eyes were both gentle and thoughtful and his professional composure when we met did not hint at his actual feelings on seeing me, but I sensed that my appearance surprised him. I was unaware of it at the time, but my situation proved to be, for Dr. Russek, quite special. He was both amazed and intrigued. He invited me to sit and I reviewed our brief phone conversation, "Since I've become an adult, I've had no rea-

without pain. Your normal height would be a bit taller with prostheses, and your condition would be stabilized. Development of vascular disease would be prevented."

Was it actually possible that my situation could at long last be improved? I became overwhelmed with seemingly unrelated thoughts, remembrances of happiness, of pain, of thoughts long relegated to a back corner of my mind as being completely impossible. Now it was all tumbling back into the open. Russek was telling me that my impossible, repressed dreams were indeed possible. I had already reluctantly, but pragmatically accepted the idea that I would live out my life alone, without companionship of wife or parenthood. I had made that analysis, then put it out of my mind and gone on with my life. Emotionally I yearned for the companionship that I witnessed daily in the lives of others around me, but intellectually I had concluded that there were very few women who might possibly find me of interest and the odds were that I would never find them. After all I was thirty-four years old and apart from a brief relationship at the age of nineteen, for which I had been unprepared and inexperienced, there had been little else. I had thought it through time and again and always came to the same conclusion: It was how it was going to be and I would live with it. I had locked my dreams away behind a thick wall.

Now a jagged crack had just appeared in that wall and behind it was a dammed up flood of emotions and dreams that I had tried so valiantly, or had it been foolishly, to repress? All those emotions now began bursting out of that remote corner of my being, growing and expanding like a genie out of a bottle, and engulfing me with visions of a future about which I had long ago ceased to dream. My exuberance could not be contained. My thoughts flew, bounding and stumbling over each other, a montage of flashbacks, of my twisting and squirming trying to get out of the spotlight of people's stares, my constant pain, lack of employment, and nonexistent social life. Now I had a momentary vision of myself standing in the midst of a crowd of people: no one staring; I was standing there at ease and I wasn't in pain. I appeared to be as normal as everyone else.

This all went through my head in a matter of seconds and just as quickly my thoughts returned to the reality of Russek's office. It was a wonderful idea, but it could never happen. I looked at him.

"What you're talking about would have to be a very expensive undertaking," I said, "I don't see how it could be possible. I don't have any money." Russek smiled, "If you decide to go ahead with this, I don't think you'll have to have any money." He was saying it could actually happen?

"I have to think about it, Dr. Russek. It's a big decision."

"Of course, we'll talk about it again."

A few weeks later, at Dr. Russek's invitation, I visited with a group of his medical students who were studying orthopedics. The visit confirmed my feelings that Russek believed my situation to be an unusual case. He again asked me to remove my shoes as he explained my medical condition to the student physicians.

Russek's suggestion remained on my mind constantly, but I wasn't yet ready to commit myself. I had always been a risk taker. Now I was being offered a risk beyond imagination, a chance to realize my ultimate dream. Whatever the downside, I could not bring myself to believe that it could be worse than my current situation. I called my parents and explained the situation to them. Their reactions, like my own, were a mixture of joy and fear; joy at hearing that there was finally a possibility for my condition to be vastly improved, something none of us had dared to think about, and fear of the unknown: perceived risks and procedures I must undergo.

The physical distance separating me from my parents would prevent their being as closely involved in this undertaking as they wanted to be. For thirty-four years they had carried the burden of my disabilities on their consciences. They had brought me into the world and thus believed it was their responsibility to do everything possible to remedy the physical inadequacies I had endured since birth. However, as Dr. Russek had explained to me, only recently had new options developed. Their questions were the same ones that had already gone through my mind. What might happen if everything did not go as expected; if my legs were amputated and the prostheses didn't function — how would I get around — would I have to use a wheelchair for the rest of my life? For me, hope overrode doubts of each fear. My father's response was typical and predictable. "It sounds wonderful, something we've always wished for, but we don't know anything about that sort of thing. You know more than we do. You do what you think is best." Mother echoed that feeling: "Oh, it would be so wonderful if it could really happen. Are you sure you want to do it? Are you certain it will be all right?" I assured them, as best I could with the information and knowledge I had, which was limited, that the doctor had assured me that everything would be fine.

In his office again, Russek introduced me to Irving Weissfeld. Mr. Weissfield, a soft spoken, middle aged Jewish man of short stature, was a case worker for the New York State Office of Vocational Rehabilitation which was the agency that could make it possible for me to have the surgery and to be fitted with artificial limbs. In short, if approved, OVR could underwrite my entire rehabilitation. From the conversation between the two men it was obvious that they had worked together on a number of occasions and respected one another. "This is a unique and special case, Irving. You must get full approval for everything we need. It has to be complete," Russek stated very seriously. "I understand, Alan," Weissfeld replied, "but you know there's no precedent for underwriting a complete rehabilitation when there is no immediate medical need."

This was a matter of considerable importance. A primary consideration in underwriting an OVR rehabilitation service, was that the assistance must enhance the recipient's ability to be employed and become more independent. At the time it was OVR's practice to provide assistance to those who, because of their disabilities, were essentially non-functioning, dependent persons who could not afford their own care. I, on the other hand, was essentially fully functioning and completely independent and, although I was only marginally employed and about to become fully unemployed, I had savings in the grand amount of $500, a used car, and the furnishings of a one-room rental apartment. The crucial portion of the appeal for underwriting was Russek's argument that although at the moment the applicant was not in a critical situation, in a matter of a year or two he would be, at which time rehabilitative efforts would offer fewer opportunities for success than they did at the present time. That placed the argument into the category of preventive rehabilitation, and preventive rehabilitation per se was unprecedented in OVR's rehabilitation funding policies.

I was now becoming acutely aware of Russek's professional as well as personal interest in my case, but still didn't fully understand the reasons. I didn't realize then that Russek's response to my situation was a very singular one, a unique challenge. In his daily practice he faced problems of how to facilitate the greatest possible salvage of bodily functions to maximize the restoration of capabilities and functions that had been lost due to trauma and disease. In each instance the post-rehabilitation condition, in even the most successful cases, resulted in a lesser capability or function than had been present prior to the affliction. My situation was just the opposite. My successful rehabilitation would create function and capability that was vastly improved over that which previously existed. My situation was that one- in- a- million occurrence which offered Dr. Russek an opportunity to use his skills to make whole and more capable, a body that had always been incomplete and disabled. Russek viewed the situation as one that not only provided a great opportunity, but also enormous professional and human satisfaction. I perceived it as a potential miracle.

2

The Way It Was

God, how it hurt. I walked along at my usual slow pace. Every time either foot touched the ground it felt like needles stabbing into the bottom of my leg and traveling like inverted lightning upwards. I concentrated on keeping moving, knowing that at the end of the next block I could sit down on a stoop and wait for the trolley. It was a cool day in late September, school had let out a half hour before, and so far I had navigated only two of the three-block trek to the streetcar line. Before I reached the end of the first block, my clothes were soaking wet under my lightweight jacket. I had acquired the ability to endure the persistent pain and continue with whatever physical activity was at hand without revealing my discomfort, but I could not prevent the perspiration.

Finally, into the last block, I had to pass the high wooden fence and that always required extra self-control. Just keep going, don't look at them, maybe today they'll forget about me. I looked straight ahead. No such luck. They were there, waiting for me, two little boys, probably five or six years old. As I approached they climbed up the inside of the wide board fence and sat precariously on the two by four top rail. "Here he comes. Hey, Mum, here he comes." I was their treat for the day as I continued my tortured walk, slowly approaching them, trying to ignore them, my lower legs five inches shorter than the norm, my left foot pointed to the left at a right angle to my body, the right one angled to the right and my only hand, the left one, holding my books against my chest aided by my right arm which ended short of the wrist. "Look how funny he walks. Hey, Mum, see him?"

Mum's face appeared above the fence line, staring as one with her two ignorant offspring. I plodded along, looking everywhere but in their direction, refusing to let them know that I noticed. As I passed by I could hear them scrambling down off the fence, the

11

....

screen door slamming as Mum went back into the house and the childish chatter slowly faded away. With a sigh of relief I rounded the corner, waited for a car to go by, crossed the street and sat down heavily on a three-step wooden stoop near the trolley stop. Slowly I lifted my feet off the ground, one leg at a time, to relieve the pressure. The right foot began to have a series of spasms, like knives piercing my flesh. The left one thumped as the blood returned to the minimal tissue in my misshapen overburdened feet. Slowly, the pain subsided. Being careful not to bear weight on them, I rested my feet once again on the concrete pavement.

I mopped my forehead and neck with a handkerchief, flexed my back muscles to relieve a cramp, leaned back against the house, shut my eyes and waited for the trolley, hoping it would be late. Eventually it would come. I'd wait until the last moment, timing my movements carefully to prevent extended standing, and get up from the stoop just in time to get on the trolley. It was the way the day was managed: planning every movement; the standing and walking times; the rest stops; pacing myself every minute of the day. The intense pain of standing and walking began to ease and as it did I began to relax.

Today wasn't such a bad day; most days weren't. I didn't really think about the pain; pain was a given and I was too busy with logistical problems, how to get from where I was to the next place I was supposed to be. Being promoted from sixth grade elementary school to seventh grade junior high school had changed my entire life.

November 2 of 1938 was my twelfth birthday and the following January I finished the 6th grade. A big transition awaited me, physically and logistically, since Latimer Junior High School wasn't even in my neighborhood. Spring Hill, where I lived and attended grade school, was physically removed from the rest of Pittsburgh's North Side.

Spring Hill was a community of middle European born immigrants, working-class homeowners who were respectable, law-abiding, mind-your-own-business types. The standard joke at City Hall when there was a need for money was "Send the tax bills to Spring Hill and they will be paid promptly." Our community was situated on the top of a cluster of hills accessible by only two routes; the main one the southern slope where the electric streetcar ran to the end of the line, just a block from my house. The "back of the hill" was a steep one lane road winding down the west side of the hill only inches from an extremely steep drop off.

Latimer Junior High School, at the edge of the main North Side business section of Pittsburgh on the flat plain adjacent to the north bank of the Allegheny River, was in a completely different type of neighborhood. Latimer was approximately one and one half miles from the grade school. To get there, one had to walk down the hill on the main street, and then three city blocks to the school. In elementary school, I had been one of a bunch of neighborhood kids who walked to and from school most days, though Mother would more often than not drive me to and from school whenever the car was available. Dad too, tried to accommodate whenever possible. On such occasions, one or more friends might ride along. Thus, I was a part of the childhood goings and comings that surrounded the school experience. Going to Latimer changed all that. Going to Latimer was a big deal, for everyone. It was growing up. And "walking the hill" was an important part of that big deal. It was during that walk to and from school that the day's events were discussed, friendships made, plans consolidated for after school activities, and tentative "boy-girl" relationships of the early teens that would develop further in high school, were begun. I wasn't able to be a part of it. My disabilities made the walk a physical impossibility. I either had to be driven or take the trolley at the bottom of my steep street, and then either make two transfers, or walk three blocks.

The junior high school itself, on Tripoli Street, three blocks away from the streetcar line, was an old four story, yellow brick building, built soon after the turn of the century in what, at the time of construction, had been a middleclass neighborhood. Two blocks west a park bordered a line of elegant, but weathered townhouses, reminders of the once bustling city of Old Allegheny. The once resplendent townhouses, adjacent to the newly relocated Allegheny General Hospital on North Avenue, had long since been converted to doctors' offices with second and third story rental apartments. Two blocks to the south the local North Side business district extended for seven or eight blocks from Chestnut Street on its eastern boundary to Federal Street at the west. Latimer lay three blocks north of the approximate center of this east-west axis in a working class neighborhood. Adjacent blocks comprised a variety of two and three story brick or clapboard houses fronting directly on brick sidewalks. Hidden behind them were tiny yards and garages accessed by a system of back alleys. Between the business district and the Allegheny River, blocks of deteriorating, worn frame houses and industrial shops, plagued in the spring by flooding, served as homes for day laborers, drifters and homeless. At the Western end of the North Side, on higher ground, were the remaining, once stately homes of the post Civil War industrial barons, mansions that were now decaying boarding houses, funeral homes and commercial establishments. Still further west were neighborhoods of middle European emigrants who worked in the steel and rolling mills, construction industries and fabricating shops.

These neighborhoods on the banks of the Allegheny and Ohio rivers differed from Spring Hill by having a distinct inner city flavor. Spring Hill, Troy Hill, Mount Troy and Fineview, neighborhoods that bordered the City to the north, each occupied its own distinct grouping of hilltops, separated from the others by valleys, distance, and elevation and possessed an ambience of a small town residential neighborhood. Children from these strongly ethnic neighborhoods: German, Russian, Finn, Croatian, Slovakian, Greek, Italian, and African American families came to the junior and high schools with family customs and disciplines intact. "Bad" or non-conforming kids were few and had low visibility.

The school's physical design was a four floor rectangle, twice as long as wide, each floor featuring a wide central hallway on either side of which were four classrooms. Shops and cafeteria were in the basement; my homeroom, Room 134, was on the first floor. My daily schedule was strenuous: English on the second floor, electric shop in the basement, geography on the third, science on the fourth, and art back on the second. I climbed or descended stairs between classes seven times a day and twice more to go to lunch. Fortunately, class changes were quick, and although five minutes was allowed, I could usually do it in less time. The routine was consistent and I had identified rest stops.

******

The trolley was late. That was good. The longer I could rest on the stoop, the easier it would be to walk home when I got off the trolley. Although there were many times when I wished I were not different, I never dwelt on it. I was what I was. I was a fatalist; I didn't waste my energy on wishing for miracles. As I sat on the stoop awaiting the trolley, one of my earliest memories came to mind. It was of kindergarten. It was a difficult time for me then, but on reflection, it was much more difficult for my parents, especially my mother, who was the one masterminding my growing up. Masterminding precisely describes her actions, seeing each new problem as it developed, or before it developed, and creating solutions. I was one of a kind, the only physically handicapped child in the school with the exception of a boy subject to epileptic seizures, but unless he was having a seizure he was quite normal. I was different all the time. I understood that people like myself were perceived as "cripples", but Mother was always ahead of the times. "You're not crippled, you're handicapped," she'd say. So, when kids, and sometimes grown-ups, would say, "Hey, you're crippled" or "How'd ya get so crippled?" or "Hey, whattzamatter with your legs? You crippled?" I'd say, "I'm not crippled, I'm handicapped." And they'd look at me and say, "Whaddaya mean handicapped? What's handicapped? You're crippled! That's what ya are!" Adults, with surprising frequency, would just smile and I always had the impression that they had no idea what I was talking about; the distinction I made had no meaning for them. I wasn't certain it had meaning for me either, but it did for my mother. Whatever the words, I was aware that everybody knew what I was and I guess I did too. In any event, I remember the day in kindergarten when, because I was experiencing unbearable pain, I took off my shoe. Taking a shoe off wasn't a big deal. When it was naptime, all the other children took off their shoes and lay down on the floor on large pieces of rag paper, the teacher drew the blinds and we were all supposed to sleep. I never took my shoes off at naptime. I never took my shoes off anytime, except for that one day. But when someone takes off his shoe and he has no foot, that's cause for real excitement, even for the teacher. I'm certain that the kindergarten teacher, Mrs. Miller, a lovely lady, remembered that day to the end of her life, because she was suddenly faced with the same problem that I had. I wasn't able to put my shoe back on— and she couldn't either. The primary, functional reason that I never took my shoes off when not at home was that at five years of age,

••

and with only one hand, I was unable to put them back on again. Mother put them on for me each morning. Mother had also instilled in me by the age of five (and probably much earlier), the belief that I had no need to share any details of my disabilities with anyone, no matter who they were or what they asked. My answers were, "I'm handicapped." and "It's none of your business" and that served to dispel or at least put off the most curious. Now Mrs. Miller was faced with dealing with a classroom full of children who all wanted to see and who were astonished by what they saw.

To say that I had no feet would be only partially correct. Certainly, in terms of what is generally considered to be a foot, I had none. I had been born with severe deformities of both lower legs. At the end of each leg where the ankle, arch, heel, instep and toes would normally be, there was only a misshapen mass of bone and tissue, sans ankle, heel, arch, etc. that terminated, on each "foot" in a single toe. Since the physical configuration of each foot did not therefore conform to either the shape or volume of a normal foot, but was considerably smaller, it was necessary to use prosthetic devices in order to fill out the shape of the shoes. These devices were hand-carved of cork, sanded smooth, padded with cotton and covered with chamois cloth, the outside shaped to fill out the shoe and the inside hollowed out to fit the irregular shapes of my inadequate extremities. The term given these rudimentary prosthetic devices was "forms." The myriad of chemical and plastic materials of custom specified resiliency and density available at the close of the century were unknown in the 1930s. Each time my shoes were used it was necessary to place new, dry cotton in the forms. Its shock-absorbing properties lasted only until perspiration soaked the cotton at which point the cushion disappeared. Lacking muscular and skeletal engineering structure of arches to disperse weight and absorb shock, my weight would bear down directly on the small end of my tibia and I would experience pain. At the age of five I hadn't yet learned to endure the pain that resulted from being tightly laced into the prostheses which never fit exactly, hampered circulation, and which were always in need of adjustment. Standing and walking exacerbated the discomfort. On the day I removed my shoe in kindergarten, I was just a five-year-old who couldn't endure the pain and so removed the cause of it. Mrs. Miller was in a quandary. She couldn't leave me there as the center of attraction, and she couldn't help me. She took one look at my "foot" and was overwhelmed. She made a courageous attempt to replace my shoe, as I tried to guide her, but soon realized that it would not work. She phoned my mother who came to school, put my shoe on me, thanked Mrs. Miller, and took me home.

It wasn't the end of the matter. After school that day the event followed me back to my neighborhood. Albie Weiss, who was in my kindergarten class, had had a glimpse of my foot and went home full of exciting things to tell. It wasn't long before his older brother Herman knew all about it and only a few moments more to make getting a look at my feet a top priority. By that time, word had spread to several of the neighborhood kids. I remember that afternoon, sitting on the curb in front of the Martin house at the top of the street. There were several kids, Mike Bikel, Bud Klehm, Al and Hermie Weiss, and a few others gathered around, all intent on one thing. "Norb, let me see your foot. Take your shoe off. Do you really have only one toe? Lemme see." And then Hermie saying, "If you take it off, I'll put it back on for you," to which, having learned from my kindergarten experience, I responded with a series of "no's" until I realized it wouldn't stop them and I finally went home.

It is perhaps a commentary on the nature of the neighborhood, the time in which I grew up, and the prevailing values, that my refusal to comply with my playmate's requests was sufficient to quell their ardor; there was never any threat of their physically having their way. It could have been easily accomplished. Fortunately, at the time, in my working class, predominately Catholic, middle European neighborhood, families exercised strong parental control over their children. Every adult knew every child and no childish behavior ever went beyond the level of mischief. The excitement of that day was no doubt the main topic of conversation at the dinner tables of my kindergarten classmates that evening, but being a neighborhood in which families didn't intrude on the privacy or the problems of others, the children were probably told to mind their own business and "Let the boy alone." In any event it was the last time I took off my shoe in public and the kids never bothered me about it again.

Although very young at the time of this experience, it left a lasting impression. Even at such a young age, I understood that I was an object of curiosity and my presence could invariably generate a variety of reactions, from astonishment, or sympathy, to curiosity, or sometimes open revulsion. I couldn't change it; it wasn't something I could do anything about; I just had to learn to endure it.

In junior high school I became a member of a student body that comprised a range of adolescents representing a full spectrum of physical and social maturation; and although my maturation was not the slowest, it was certainly very low on the general maturation timetable. I was again fortunate to find the environment essentially benevolent. I was assisted by the teachers wherever possible and was never accosted by fellow students with the single exception of an experience in the school's basement restroom. I had been on my way to lunch in the cafeteria in the school basement and decided to stop at the boy's lavatory. There I found myself alone with two students that I didn't know. They looked at me and the one nudged the other, "Hey kid, what the hell's the matter with your legs?" Usually I'd say, "It's none of your damn business" or try to ignore it. I'd never been physically abused, but this time I sensed something different about the situation if only because the boy's lavatory was off in the corner of the school basement and I was alone with two strangers, so I played it to stall. "What do ya mean?" I said.

"What's wrong with your legs? What you got wrong with you?"

"Nothin's wrong with me. That's the way they are."

I began to sense an awareness of being trapped and started to move toward the door, but they cut me off. I backed up to the wall and they closed in. "What are you, some kind of wise ass? You want me to show you what it is to be a wise ass?" In an instant things had changed. It was clearly a no win situation. I had done nothing to motivate their hostility, but for whatever reason I was suddenly facing it. Fortunately, a well-muscled student whom I didn't know suddenly walked in, and sizing up the situation in a glance, confronted my would-be aggressors saying, "Leave him alone." With quick thanks I took the opportunity to get out in a hurry and into the midst of the students that I knew for the rest of the lunch period. I didn't tell my mother. The incident had scared me, but I couldn't tell her about the two kids. It would have worried her.

One day, my math teacher, Miss Edith Skarinski, who also taught typing, beckoned me after class and asked, "Do you plan to go to college?"

"I think so."

"Would you like to learn to type?"

The thought of actually typing had never entered my mind; typing was a two handed activity. The idea seemed to make little sense to me, but my teacher said, "I know of a man who types with one hand and can type as fast as most people can type with two. If you'd like to learn, I would be happy to teach you. There are some typewriters that have a left-handed carriage return and we could probably find one for you to practice on." "You really think it's possible?" I asked. "Of course, if you're willing to practice. You could come in here a half hour early every morning and stay a half hour after school and I think you'd do fine. Why don't you talk it over with your parents and let me know." My mother instantly recognized the worth and generosity of the idea and within a few weeks Miss Skarinski had found a used L.C.Smith typewriter with a left-handed carriage and my father managed to find $25 to pay for it. Thus began a two-year regimen of morning and afternoon practice under Miss Skarinski's generous direction and additional practice at home. Using S, F, H, K and L as my home keys, I was able, with some finger stretching, to cover the keyboard with one hand and was ultimately able to type twenty-six words per minute.

As a result of sensitive and caring teachers, my informal and unofficial mainstreaming continued through the secondary school years, but I had virtually no contact with classmates outside of school. My after school hours remained parochially in my own neighborhood with neighborhood friends. Scholastically I managed to maintain an above "C" average, but increasingly the energy necessary for physical endurance began to take a toll, and although my mother was ever present, pushing for me to earn higher grades, the combination of my social, physical and intellectual immaturity permitted me only to be above average, but not at the top.

I enrolled in electric shop, sheet metal shop and wood shop and was disappointed that I was unable to take machine shop as well. I had used basic tools almost from the time I could lift them: hammers, saws, files, pliers, vices, etc. I started at an early age to build model airplanes and was skilled at cutting, gluing and fitting

••

together the fragile parts of the flying models. In electrical shop I learned to do bell and light wiring, solder and tape splices and staple them down in acceptable fashion on work boards; in tin shop I used the brake and the roll, cut tin with a tin snips, soldered joints and hammered rivets. I made a cookie cutter and a small scoop. In wood shop I was occupied with the use of the crosscut and rip handsaws, wood plane, scriber, try square, rasp and sandpaper and learned to stain, varnish and paint. My finished products were a water-pump lamp, a doorstop, and an oak footstool. Apart from the discomfort of standing, my disabilities were never a problem for such work. I was always able to figure out a way to use each tool, even the ones designed for right-handed use.

As I grew older it became apparent that most reactions to my disabilities were casual and although there were exceptions, few people would go out of their way to pursue their curiosity beyond the casual level. I also quickly learned that the more of myself I revealed, the more curiosity and interest I aroused. I don't remember thinking about it in my early years, but I was aware that, conspicuous as I was, it was important to make every effort to make myself as physically inconspicuous as possible, and to try to be as normal as possible. Into my adult years, I was never able to reach the point, even in the presence of friends, of feeling comfortable removing my shoes, or even my pants, which revealed my misshapen legs. I was always concerned that such an action would invite inquiry and I developed such antipathy to any concentration of attention to my disabilities that I avoided it at all costs, in all probability complicating my life rather than simplifying it. In later years I often asked myself if perhaps life may have ultimately been easier had the ignorant curiosity of casual acquaintances or strangers been simply obliged.

******

The streetcar arrived. I got up from the stoop and made my way up the car's high steel steps. The conductor, foreign born from middle Europe, worked this shift every day. His speech evinced a remaining accent and as he called out the streets at each stop he had a tendency to say "straight" instead of "street." He greeted me, "How ya doin today?"

"O. K."

"Been waitin long?"

"About ten minutes."

"Couldn't be that long. I'm only three minutes late. Accident other side of the bridge." I smiled as I remembered his favorite joke. When asked by a small child or a cautious adult, if it was safe to put a foot on the trolley rail, the conductor would say, as he pointed to the overhead wire, "Sure it is, as long as you don't put your other foot on the line up there." I took a seat near the front on the right side and the car started up the long hill. By sitting on the right I could see my friends as they were walking up the hill on the sidewalk. I relaxed in the woven wicker seat. At this time of day there were not many people in the car, only a few women and older men coming home from shopping. It was too early for those whose workday at the Heinz Pickle factory ended at 4 o'clock and anyway, most of those workers walked up the hill like my classmates. As the car proceeded up the hill a line of students became visible strung out along the hill, walking home, boys and girls, singly and in groups, enjoying the walk, socializing, talking about what had happened that day, what they would do in the evening and with whom, and when and where they would meet for the morning walk to school. Looking at them, one group after another, I wondered what they were thinking and talking about and thought how nice it would be, to be able to walk with them, to be a part of the discussion, to share that daily experience, but I knowingly passed it off as an activity that was quite beyond my physical capability. I never rationalized the situation. It wasn't a case of convincing myself that what I couldn't have, I didn't want. I desperately wanted to be able to walk home from school with my classmates, but I understood that it wasn't possible.

The trolley car was a double ender. It had a driver's seat and controls at each end. Outside, at each end on the roof were the trolleys, long springy metal arms with little wheels on the ends that rode along the overhead electric wires through which the car received its power. At the end of the line, the tracks just stopped. The conductor went outside to lower the trolley and hook it under the fastening on the roof. Then he returned and transferred his driving controls from one end to the other and reversed the seat backs. At the other end of the car he again exited the car to unhook the second trolley and raise it to the power wire. Then, checking his watch, he re-entered the car and set off on his next circuit.

Certain conductors, as they got to know us, allowed us to ride free into downtown for a movie. Sometimes, on a chilly or rainy night, when we had nothing to do and it was too early to go home, a conductor might let us sit in the trolley and ride the round trip down into town, a twelve minute ride one way, and then back home again. On a cold or rainy evening we'd sometimes ride four trips. Most often, however, we'd pass the idle time just loafing at the end of the line.

At the end of the working day when the car was packed with neighborhood men returning from the mills, the conductors were in the habit of stopping the car several feet short of the end of the tracks with the doors exactly aligned to the entry of Suckitt's Saloon. There were three concrete steps from the sidewalk to the door of the saloon and our favorite game was to hassle the men as they made their exit from the streetcar to the saloon for their customary beer or boilermaker before heading home. For us it was a game. How many steps would it take from the streetcar to the saloon?

"Here it comes.

"Bet they make it in four steps.

"Count 'em." As the first man's foot hit the sidewalk there was a chorus of "One" and then, as he climbed the steps it was "Two, three, four, made it!" and, as other men followed, the chorus continued, at times taking on the semblance of a musical round as the men, now noticing us and realizing we were taunting them became agitated, changed the pace of their walking to throw off our counting, and responded: "Get outta here you little shits, Go on home." Amid much catcalling and laughing, everyone was ready to run in case one of the men got really mad. For us it was simple fun, trying to get a rise out of the men; for the men, however, it was a comment on their behavior, on the need they had for that drink after a day's labor, that brief respite before once again facing the burdens of wife and home and children. The end of the day was also suppertime for us and soon our mothers' voices would ring out calling our names and the fun was forgotten as we all disbanded.

We'd be back again after supper, and as the warm summer evenings grew dark, the gang congregated at the end of the line. Josie

Eichleman's candy store was just across the street from the saloon and her husband John, although blind, frequently tended store. The candy store was a sacred place free of any mischief. Nobody ever tried to outfox John, who would unerringly make the correct change for any purchase. Here one could find a five-cent ice cream cone or Popsicle, a nickel candy bar and in the summer a frozen Powerhouse bar or Milky Way that Josie had placed in the ice cream freezer until it was hard as a rock and took a long time to eat.

******

Halfway up the hill on the trolley line there was a siding that allowed the descending trolley car to pass the one that was upward bound. While the car waited for the other car to come down, I saw several of my friends walking by. One waved. That was Albie from a few houses down the street. "You gonna be out later?" he called.

"Yeah, come on up."

"O. K., see ya." Albie turned as another boy gesticulated and started to laugh. The others laughed too. I wondered about the laughter. Sometimes I'd get that uncomfortable feeling that they were laughing at me. I experienced that kind of behavior on occasion with strangers. My mother's reaction was that it was ignorance, "You have to ignore it," she'd say. But even with my friends, I was never certain how they felt about me. It was not until much later in life that I realized the most detrimental aspect of my disabilities was not my physical anomalies, but the fact that, because of them, I had been isolated from the all-important, social intercourse of the early teens and much of the social and work activities of early adulthood.

My mind flashed ahead and I thought about how, in a few minutes, I'd get off the trolley and trudge the long steep block home, the next to the last house at the top of the hill. Then I'd take off my shoes and Mother would massage my legs while I laid down on the couch and let the strain of the day slowly dissipate. Maybe, with clean stockings and fresh cotton in my shoes I'd go outside for a while and hang out with Albie.

Now, as the trolley approached my stop, my mind replayed the day's events. I had left the house early, walked next door, and rapped on Aunt Lil's door. Aunt Lil was my mother's oldest sister. Never divorced, she lived alone for many years after her husband Oscar, a skilled calligrapher, left her. I never knew just why Oscar left or where he had gone; I barely remembered him. Aunt Lil was a slow and indecisive woman. She was an excellent seamstress who sewed alterations on expensive furs at the Palace, a well-known Pittsburgh fur store. Overweight, she had difficulty walking, and her son, Walter, would pick her up at the bottom of our steep street where the trolley ran, and drive her to work. Walter never drove up the steep street to pick up his mother; she had to walk down. Moreover, Walter was subject to narcolepsy and extremely difficult to awaken in the morning, so he frequently arrived late. After Aunt Lil had finally opened her door that morning and went through the ritual of rearranging her coat and her purse and finally fumbled the key into the door to lock up, we started to walk down the street. I always took it easy walking, being careful to place my feet down softly so the pain wouldn't begin too soon. I hoped the cotton would last a bit longer this morning, maybe till third period. Then I'd have a chance to rest again. By the time we reached the trolley line however, I was beginning to feel some discomfort, so I sat on the low stonewall in front of the old, now closed grocery store, and rested. Riding with Walter was a choice. It wasn't a good choice, but it was the most efficient. I could take the trolley, which meant taking a roundabout route which necessitated getting transfers and using three trolleys, but to do that I'd have to leave home at least 45 minutes earlier and would have to stand and wait three times, once for each trolley, and standing was even more painful than walking. If I rode with Walter, he'd drop me off at the bottom of the hill and I'd then have to walk only the three blocks to school. Although it would have taken him only five minutes to detour from his route and drop me off at school, the offer was never forthcoming and it was ironic that he was responsible for my walking rather than having Dad drive me both ways.

Nobody in the whole family recognized just how difficult and painful it was for me to walk so much. It had been my first semester at Latimer in the seventh grade and Dad had just begun a new store window decorating business. Because Dad's customers owned stores in a number of outlying small towns around Pittsburgh, he tried to schedule his work so that he could drive me to and from school and still tend to his business. Our old car was no longer dependable and in order to ferry me to and from school and meet his business obligations, Dad needed a more reliable car. He didn't have the money to buy another car so my mother asked her sister, Aunt Kate, and Aunt Lil's son, Walter, if they could lend Dad and her a few hundred dollars and they agreed. When Dad, whose auto dealer friend offered a good deal, enabling him to buy a new car for about $600 instead of another used one, they went into a jealous rage. "Who do you think you are? We (Aunt Kate and Uncle Al) don't even have a car and you borrow from us to buy a new one? How the hell do you get the nerve? Are you some kind of a big shot?" There was a violent argument at the house one night that ended with Walter screaming at Dad, "You can go to hell!" Mother decided she had had enough of the situation with her family; she asked my Dad to return the car. "Look Sam, one way or another we'll get along and Norb will be all right. It'll be difficult for him for a while, but he'll manage. Just take the car back and we'll give them their money back and we'll be free of them and I'll never ask any of them for another thing ever again." When Mother asked Dad for something, anything, he always obliged. The car dealer proved to be a real friend. He returned the money and they in turn returned the borrowed funds to Aunt Kate and Walter and there was no new car; there was no family car at all. Dad now had to take buses and trolleys to work appointments. And now Walter was giving me a ride in the morning, and I still had to walk three blocks morning and afternoon.

One cold and snowy winter morning Walter dropped me off and I was trudging along on the uneven, snow packed sidewalk of the first block, hard pressed to differentiate between the pain and the cold. I heard a car horn, but head down, examining the sidewalk to determine where to place my feet, I was reluctant to break the rhythm of my pace. When the horn persisted, right beside me, I turned to see the driver beckoning to me. "Where ya goin? School? Latimer? Want a ride?"

"Yeah. Sure. Thanks."

I climbed into the warm car. The man smiled at me. "Cold out there this morning."

"Yeah."

"You walk this way every day?"

"Yeah."

"It's a long walk."

"Yeah."

"I've seen you walking a couple of times." "Thought you might like a ride."

"Yeah, Thanks. I appreciate it." The warmth felt good as it began to creep into my legs. That morning mother had suggested that I wear my flannel pajamas under my pants and tuck the bottoms into my socks. I had some doubts about trying it. I didn't want to be embarrassed, but it did help to keep out some of the cold. The three blocks went by quickly and my rescuer asked which door I entered. "Tripoli Street, but you can drop me off anywhere."

"No. I'll take you around the corner to the Tripoli Street door." "I don't come this way every day, but when I do, if I see you, I'll give you a ride."

"Thanks again, see ya."

When I told mom she was concerned. "What did he say? What did he look like? Where was he coming from? What did he ask you?" I didn't understand her concern. All I could think about was the possibility of riding those three blocks instead of walking. That would have been great, but I never saw the man again.

******

When the trolley stopped at my street I eased myself down the steps and onto the sidewalk, waited until the trolley had moved on and crossed the street. I liked the way the street looked, rising up so steeply from the tracks. I always felt that living on a hill beat living where it was flat. There were so many things to do on a hill that you couldn't do on flat land and I couldn't think of anything that could be done on flat land that you couldn't do on a hill. My street had a pitch of about twenty-five degrees and my house was almost at the top. I looked up the steep Belgian block street, remembering coming down it on a bicycle. It made you give some thought to what you would do if the brakes failed, and they sometimes did, from overheating. Pushing the bike back up the hill when you were tired was something else, but I loved the hill. It wasn't too long since the WPA had re-paved it. The Dads of a few of my friends' were on the work crew. They removed the Belgian blocks, graded the steep incline, set in new hand-hewn granite curbstones, then re-laid the Belgian blocks so they were straight and even. Finally, they reset all the brick sidewalks in a herringbone pattern which prevented them slipping on the steep grade.

There were fifty families who lived on the street before WWII. Mother's sister, Aunt Ann, her husband Steve, and their daughter, Lillian, occupied the second floor and third floors of our house. After the war, when the guys all came home from the army, the street became jammed with cars. Before then, the only vehicles to use the street were my dad's and uncle's, the milkman, the bakery truck, and the fruit and vegetable hucksters in old straight body van type rigs. The garbage wagon was pulled by a team of horses and they managed even in the snow. Since the street was a dead end there was no through traffic; it was perfect for sled riding. We started at the top of the street, and continued to the streetcar tracks that cut across it on a 45-degree angle at the bottom. The old Flexible Flyers were the favorite sleds because they were easily steered. The condition of the street would get better, icing up as the sled riding continued. Ten or fifteen kids would make the track slick in a short time, requiring a heavy coating of ashes for the length of four or five houses to bring a sled to a stop. In those days, in Pittsburgh, the common winter heating fuel was coal, and everyone dumped ashes in the street when there was snow so the produce hucksters and milkman could get up the street. If there weren't enough ashes there was always a homeowner who would provide some if asked. Further up the track, where the riders didn't want ashes, there was always the one grump who would throw his ashes in the middle of the track, just when it was getting fast. The reaction to that was to shovel the grump's ashes onto his sidewalk, shovel new snow on the track and get on with the sled riding.

I became aware that, on my sled, I could do anything that any of my friends could do with theirs and, I came to realize, because I had to think about everything I did, that I could sometimes do some things better, or quicker, or could refine it a bit more. On reflection, the sled, my first vehicle, was an equalizer, as were cars, horses, boats, and airplanes in later years. All the pain, discomfort and even the dread of hauling the sled back up the hill after the run disappeared when I was flying down that hill.

• •

Dragging my sled and myself back up the hill after the ride required the utmost energy and control. Sometimes, I'd plop myself down on the sled of one of the older boys in a teasing manner and sometimes, in deference to my disabilities, they'd pretend they didn't notice. Several of the older boys were accommodating in that way, for a short distance. Once in a while, on a clear cold night, grown-ups would come out to go sled riding with the kids. It was always a very special occasion when Dad would go with me, because then I'd have a ride both ways. I remember the crispness of those winter nights, snow crunching under boots, the slippery sound of the slick runners whispering as I flashed down the street and the harsh, rasping sound as the runners hit the heavy ashes at the bottom, sparks flying, and came to a stop, then the peaceful joy of those few precious seconds, lying there on the sled and looking back up that terribly long steep hill.

******

I started walking slowly up the street, taking it easy. I could stop anywhere along the block to rest. Every house on the right side of the street, where the land was lower, had a stoop. On the left side, where the houses sat up high above the street, each had a long flight of concrete steps leading up to the front door and many had front porches. There were only two houses with front porches on my side of the street, our house and the one next door. A few doors from the bottom of the street on the left side was where the Steiger family used to live. The older son was in the penitentiary for robbery and the younger one, Harry, seemed to be headed in the same direction. One day Harry came home with a horse, leading it with a tether. When his mother saw it, she screamed at him, yelling, "What in hell is wrong with you?" Harry, with the tether in his hand, said: "He followed me home."

The Martins weren't unfriendly, but kept to themselves. They attended the same church as my mother, originally the German Evangelical Protestant Church, later the Congregational Church, where Louis Martin and I had been confirmed together. The Confirmation party at the Martin house had been fun. We played Spin The Bottle, me for the first time, and I had the thrill of kissing my first unrequited love.

* * * * * *

******

The street was steep and I had to lean into the grade as I continued trudging up the slope. Halfway up was Klehm's house on the right, next door to Weiss.' Across the street lived the Marty's and Schrott's, and on the level section at the very top of the street was the Martin house. My house was the second from the top. Beyond the Martin's the level section continued for two hundred feet and then ended. Perpendicular to the end of the street was a chain link fence running across the street, separating it from St. John's Cemetery. The pipe and screen gate in the fence at the street's end had long since been broken and hung only from its bottom hinge, permitting easy entry to the cemetery. Just down the hill to the right of the gate were the graves of my mother's father, mother, uncle and brother. The twin granite headstone on my grandparent's grave was sculptured with a double curved top, originally a polished surface, now dulled and worn from the weathering of years. Occasionally, Mother would walk over to the graves with a rake and sickle and cut and rake the grass and weed the planted beds, lovingly arranging the little plants known as hen and chickens that bordered the graves. Sometimes on special occasions she'd place fresh flowers from her garden on the graves.

******

I arrived home from school earlier than those who walked. The streetcar ride was usually faster. I reached my house and walked down the side path, down the first four heavy sandstone steps, then two, then three more along the pre-cast concrete slab walkway, and finally onto the back porch and into the basement kitchen. Mother was there, beginning preparations for supper. "Like something to eat? I baked some cookies." My little brother, Wayne, bright, handsome, fully formed with an athletic build and eight years my junior, was playing in the yard with a neighbor's child. "Yeah, I wanna sit down first." I sat at the table and she placed a glass of milk and a plate of cookies in front of me. I melted into the chair, untied my shoes and let them drop to the floor. Mother would see to it that my brother didn't bring his friend in the house while I was resting. I rubbed my feet and stretched my legs and rubbed one leg against the other, heaving a sigh of relief. My left leg thumped from a muscle spasm and made me jump. The milk was cold and I was thirsty. Mother brought me a dry shirt and I peeled off the sweat sodden one I was wearing. It was good to just relax completely. I closed my eyes. "How was the day?"

"It was O. K."

I ate some cookies and drank the rest of the milk. The pain in my legs subsided and I was now thinking about what I might do until suppertime. It was a nice day and I wanted to be outside. I put clean cotton in my shoes and I put them on, ready for after school play. They felt good. I had no pain.

I grabbed an apple and went out to sit on the front porch. Across the street the tree and brush covered hill rose sharply from the street to its crest several hundred yards higher up. It had been my favorite playground for as long as I could remember. Just over the brow of the hill were the tanks, two massive round, steel plate water tanks that were part of the Pittsburgh water system, built to attain a water level and provide the pressure needed for distribution. The tanks were forty feet high, fifty feet in diameter, and open at the top. A steel ladder extended from the top rim to within seven or eight feet of the ground. Only once had I climbed the ladder and looked down into the water that filled the tank to about ten feet from the top. I was scared. I didn't like it at all and Mikey, who was behind me at the time, was pushing and telling me to straddle the 12 inch wide steel plate which formed the rim so he could get up there too. No way was I going to sit on that rim so I squeezed over to one side of the narrow ladder and let Mikey climb up. He threw a leg over the foot-wide rim, swung both legs back and forth, and looked at me, "Wassamatta, you scared?"

"No, I just don't wanna sit up there."

"You're scared, That's what."

I was scared, but I wasn't going to admit it. I climbed down the ladder and shimmied down the tree limb we had leaned against the side of the tank to provide access to the ladder's lowest rung. Two of the other boys climbed up and all three sat straddling the rim. Mikey boasted, "I caught a catfish in here a week ago."

"Baloney. There ain't no fish in there."

"Sure there is, it's just river water."

Nobody had ever seen a fish caught in that tank.

Climbing the tanks wasn't the only challenge in the neighborhood. There was danger aplenty, just waiting to be discovered. One Fourth of July Fireworks aftermath is a good example. Every year the American Legion Post would sponsor a spectacular aerial fireworks display on the hill (we called it "the Mountain") that was behind our house and a block away. Our back yard and the rear, flat roofed portion of our house provided box seats for the display. On the day following the great event, I walked over on the hill as we always did on the day after, to see what could be scavenged from the previous evening's show. I was lucky. I found a package about a foot long and six or seven inches in diameter, wrapped up in heavy paper and sealed with heavy tape. A kid from a nearby neighborhood found an American flag and a parachute from an aerial flare. I took my package home intending to take it apart at my leisure to see what was inside. I was sitting with it on the porch when my Uncle Steve came home from work and saw me with the package. "Whattaya got there?

"It's a thing I found"

"Where ja find it?"

"Over on the hill. It's left over from the fireworks last night."

"Lemmesee it."

I reluctantly handed it over. I would rather have taken it down to the cellar and taken it apart. Uncle Steve hefted it in his hands and turned it over and over. He began to gingerly unwrap the one side where the remains of a twist of heavy paper was sticking up. Pretty soon I heard Uncle Steve whisper "Jesus Christ!" as he pulled out of the paper package a small piece of copper tube about an inch and a half long and a quarter of an inch thick and held it up between his thumb and forefinger. I reached for it but my Uncle pulled it away. "You know what this is?" "No." I answered. "It's a nitroglycerin cap," Steve said, pointing to his other hand, to the place where his forefinger should have been, but where there was only a large scar. "That's how I lost my finger. I found one of these beside the railroad track and I hit it with a hammer." He tore the paper a bit further, enough to reveal the insides. "You know what that is?" I looked closely at what appeared to be several lengths of greasy broomsticks covered with sawdust and shook my head. He looked at me sternly, "Its Dynamite. That's eight sticks of regular Dynamite. That's what makes the big bang in the fireworks. The nitro cap sets it off and the whole thing blows up. I'll take care of this." Uncle Steve took the explosives and put them in the trunk of his car. I sat there stunned. I'd been carrying dynamite and nitro-glycerin around most of the day.

******

Mikey, Bob, Jim, Buddy and two others, came up the street, one of them swinging a baseball bat. "Wanna play some mush ball?" "Sure." "Can we use your ball?" Mush balls were the balls of choice on the steep street where we played most of the time. The same size as a softball, but softer and having a raised seam on the outside, a mush ball couldn't be hit as far as a softball and could be caught easily without stinging your fingers. It was rare that any-one broke a window and the neighbors were used to having us play ball in the street. "I'll get it." I went inside to get the ball while the boys jostled one another around on the sidewalk and porch.

Usually, when we had an uneven number we played "One out, the catcher's in", rotating positions, the last position before becom-ing a batter, was catcher. I loved to play, but I was a slow and painful runner and I rarely got a hit. Now, just rested from a tedious and physical day, I didn't want to push myself too far. I came out of the house and threw the ball to one of the boys. They immedi-ately spread out across the street throwing it from one to another. "There's seven of us," I said: "Why don't you pick sides and I'll pitch for both sides." That way I wouldn't have to bat and run bases. It wasn't the first time I'd done it; the boys were used to it. They quickly agreed and selected teams and we started. I liked to pitch and was pretty good at it. With slow ball pitching, which we always did, I was able to put the ball pretty close to where the batter wanted it and I came to know each boy's weak spot. My greatest joy came when I struck a boy out. I couldn't do it as often as I was convinced I could, because the kids would start yelling at me. "C'mon, Let him hit it.

"I'm putting it right over the plate."

"Naw, you ain't. You're trying to strike him out."

So what I had to do, and I had to be satisfied that that was all I could do, was pick my spots and then concentrate on striking out this one or that one, but never the same boy twice in succession.

My successes were private ones that I could never share with my friends, but I did develop an expertise.

After playing for a half hour my legs began to hurt and I didn't want the pain to build up as it had earlier, so when two of the boys had to leave for supper, I said I would stop pitching and sit down and watch. The game lasted only another few minutes until the voices of mothers of the other boys were heard calling them for supper. I took the ball and sat on the porch. I hoped Dad would be coming home soon instead of working late.

"Mom, is Dad comin home for supper?"

"Yes he is, he should be here very soon."

After supper I did my homework. I didn't have very much. Math and English were the most difficult. Dad was a math whiz, but I hadn't inherited that skill. My brother had. I had a difficult time with math, beginning when I'd had to learn the multiplication tables. English was different. I loved to read or write, but found the complexities of grammar and syntax difficult and at times virtually impossible to understand. After supper it was time for the radio shows, "Jack Benny," "Red Skelton," "Fred Allan," and then bed at about 10 o'clock. At the rear of the house, over the basement kitchen, Mother had made a bedroom for my brother and me. Next to it, in the middle room, was my parents' bedroom and the front room, off the entrance hallway at the front of the house, was the living room with a large bay window opening onto the large front porch. In the winter, open-faced Reznor gas stoves without flues, dangerous at best, heated our bedroom and my parent's bedroom. The living room heater had a flue. The open gas stoves created moisture and on very cold winter days, it would create a layer of ice on the inside wall of our bedroom. Downstairs in the basement kitchen, a flat top coal stove provided heat and an enameled metal gas stove was used for cooking and baking. Each morning Mother would get up an hour before anyone else, go down to the kitchen and start a coal fire so that by the time I had to get ready for school, the kitchen was the warmest room in the house. Two steps up at the rear of the kitchen was the basement which housed a large coal burning convection furnace which could heat the whole house, but when Aunt Ann and Uncle Steve moved in upstairs and the Depression set in, they stopped using it because, although Steve never missed a day of work, my father and mother couldn't afford to share the cost of the coal, so each family had a coal burning stove in their respective apartments and two separate gas and electric meters were installed.

I lay on my bed. My brother was asleep in the twin bed beside me. The sheets were pulled tight and had no wrinkles. It was always a wonderful feeling to slide in between the cool sheets and then let my body warm them up. Laying there my body felt fine, there were no aches or pains. I thought how wonderful it would be if I could feel like this all the time. I thought about how it must be for the other kids who were able to run and jump as much as they wanted; how it would feel to jump down from even a two or three foot height and not have any pain. I shivered as I imagined how painful it would be if I tried it.

3

Sam and Louisa

Louisa Frederica Haisch was next youngest of her siblings, four sisters and a brother. Born on Christmas Day in 1900, she delighted in her years in elementary school, and eagerly looked forward to attending high school. In the German, Hungarian, Austrian, Polish immigrant community of Spring Hill on Pittsburgh's North Side, Louisa worked after school assisting her mother in their small neighborhood butcher shop which her father, Gottlieb, had established on the ground floor of their small house. She had quickly learned the different cuts of meat, how to tell if a chicken was a fryer, boiler or roaster, and even to slice the meats, sausages and wursts. Gottlieb Haisch, a descendent of several generations of German Lutheran farmers and wagon makers in Stuttgart had, in his successful effort to avoid conscription into the Kaiser's military, begun his American journey as a wagon driver. In a subsequent job at the Oswald & Hess meat packing house he used his farm learned skills to slaughter, skin, and quarter beef and pork, and learned new skills of making sausage, blood pudding, and wiener snitzel. Industrious, he reasoned that if he could perform these tasks successfully for the packing company, he could also do it in his own shop with the help of his wife, Catherina. Catherina Unfall, who had emigrated alone to America to seek work as a household servant, was quite willing to assist Gottlieb by tending the shop while he continued his daily job at the packing house. During World War I, their older children, Lillian and Katherina, both masterful seamstresses, and Ann, were all married. Son Carl, having learned his father's skills, was in France serving as a butcher in the Army, and being otherwise occupied in the Meuse-Argonne. Margaret, the youngest, impatient to earn money, quit school and found office work, leaving Catherina alone in the store except for Louisa, who regretfully had to quit school to provide assistance to her mother.

Catherina, although having no more education than her husband, was blessed with greater sensitivity and awareness of the substance and nature of her environment. She understood Gottlieb's personality traits and had no difficulty managing, with considerable finesse, his sometimes obstreperous behavior in the house. Unlike Gottlieb, she was soft spoken, tactful and perceptive with an intelligence that directed her actions in a manner that made her much appreciated as both the proprietor of the neighborhood meat market and a presence in the community. Although a perceptive and knowing observer, alert to every nuance of behavior, she always presented a calm and accommodating facade to the customers. Of her six children, only Louise and Katherine inherited her sharp and penetrating awareness and sound judgment; the others more closely resembled the less sensitive, self centered and stubborn behavior of their father. For Louisa, who spent many hours during her teens and early adulthood in close proximity with her mother, Catherina was an oracle, an example, and a mentor who made a lasting impression. From her, Louisa learned to observe the broader picture, to identify relationships and characteristics of people and events, to deal with people gently while studying them closely, and to anticipate, sometimes even predict their actions, particularly if they were children.

Gottlieb was a boastful man. His demeanor was more suitable for the rough and noisy environment of the slaughterhouse than the peaceful neighborhood butcher shop. Not unfriendly, he was gruff, highly opinionated, and enjoyed being important. In his household, he was uncompromising, expecting complete obedience. At his dinner table, everyone ate what Gottlieb wanted to eat and children sat until they emptied their plates. His word and his opinion were law and could not be challenged, but as the children grew, they devised numerous ways of circumventing his expectations. He enjoyed walking through his back yard, surveying the onions and tomatoes and beans and beets which Louisa and Catherina had labored planting and tilling and weeding, tasks in which Gottlieb never participated, but if a neighbor happened to pass, he would immediately call to him saying, "How do you like my garden? Look at my tomatoes."

The Haischs were friendly with their next door neighbors, the Guidicis, an Italian family who like themselves were immigrants.

Mr. Guidici made wine in his cellar every year in a large wooden tub, and the entire family would take turns stomping the grapes, resulting in several barrels of strong Chianti that he always shared generously with Gottlieb. Gottlieb's ethnic affinity, however, was for beer, taken with a frequent shot of whiskey, and he enjoyed drinking, too often in excess. His capacity for wine, however, was limited and he inevitably encountered difficulty with the Guidici wine. His tendency to drink it like beer resulted in his becoming both drunk and sick, and when drunk, frequently loud, coarse and sometimes belligerent. On one occasion, after having had too many drinks, he precipitated a loud and furious argument with Catherina in the butcher shop, and began bellowing about shooting (who or at what was unclear). It angered Louisa who, in her teens, had become increasingly disgusted with her father's behavior. Louisa ran upstairs to where she knew he kept a revolver, and grabbing it, ran down again to the butcher shop. Racing into the room where her father was still shouting threats, she waved the gun around and yelled: "If there's any shooting to be done around here, I'm going to do it!" Gottlieb was thunderstruck. He shut up and sat down.

Sam Nathanson's ethnic environment was quite different from Louisa's. It is difficult to identify two ethnic groups of the time that had less in common, and more social, religious and cultural barriers between them than Sam's Russian Jewish heritage, and Louisa's German Lutheran one. Sam's childhood was spent in Pittsburgh's Lower Hill District, an ethnic community of Eastern European Jewish immigrants located adjacent to the wholesale business district that was shuttered on Saturdays, the Jewish Sabbath, but open for business on Sundays when Jewish small stores' proprietors located in various industrialized areas surrounding Pittsburgh came to replenish stock for the coming week. In his small storefront tailor shop, Sam's father, Nathan, specialized in making men's pants

Following the death of his first wife Rivka, Nathan had immigrated from the Ukraine with four children to Baltimore, Maryland, following his eldest son, Max, who had preceded him by two years. Max was in process of learning the clothing manufacture trade, and immediately found jobs in it for his father, brothers and sisters. In Baltimore Nathan met and married a Russian immigrant Jewess, Sophie Halpert, who bore him a girl, Sadie, and a boy,

Samuel. In a few years the family followed Max to Pittsburgh, where Sophie gave birth to Sylvia. By the time Sam was old enough to begin school, his eldest half-brother Max , ever seeking new opportunities, had moved on to Cleveland, Ohio, and begun his own business that eventually became a major men's clothing manufacturer with more than twenty retail stores. Sam's two other half-brothers, David and Morris, followed Max to Cleveland and linked their livelihood and families' futures to Max's success. As he became his family's most successful member, Max enjoyed his new affluence and importance to the extent of dropping his given name in favor of his initials, M. J. which he felt was more in keeping with his stature as a successful American businessman. Sam's mother, although she had close relationships with her step-children until the end of her life, was closer to her three American born children, all of whom remained in Pittsburgh. Nathan, busy with his tailor shop and second family, was also active in the affairs of his synagogue, Shaare Tefila, known variously as the Russian Shul or the Little Synagogue. He was its president when, on the first day of Rosh Hashanah, on Oct. 2, 1913, he was stricken with a massive heart attack at the synagogue where he died, and was carried home by members of his congregation. Sam was thirteen.

Sam possessed an innate facility with numbers, a natural sensitivity and appreciation of the arts, and an athlete's precise control of his body. In his teens he was a regular participant in athletic events, playing basketball and running track at the Settlement House located in the area, winning several ribbons for his track performances. A quick study and a risk taker, neither long-range planning nor plodding were his forte'. He was a young man in a hurry to be somebody, to be rich, to make his mark. He left school early and found work, initially as a clerk and then as an accountant within the Jewish business community. As a young man, he drifted from job to job, picking up skills in retail selling. He also had an intense interest in dancing and took every opportunity to watch traveling dance acts in theaters, memorizing their performances and practicing the steps. In his eagerness to become a success, he decided that his dancing skills were sufficiently expert to attempt a career as a dancer and without notice to family, departed to Boston to make his debut in show business. On learning of his actions, the family was sufficiently upset to dispatch one of its own to Boston to bring him home with the promise that his Uncle Nathan would pay his tuition to a business school.

It is probable that it was not the promise of business school that dissuaded Sam from pursuing his show business interest; it is more likely that in the short time he had been in Boston he had already had some indication that making a career as a dancer might be much more difficult, arduous, and less glamorous than he had anticipated. But business school did not hold him; his interest was in making an easy dollar. With the advent of prohibition, easy dollars beckoned in the illicit trade of alcoholic beverages and he dipped his toe in those adventurous waters. Fortunately, his involvement was short-lived and as he remembered, "It was the kind of activity that, once a person became deeply involved, it was extremely difficult to get out of it." Before that happened, however, to the relief of the family, he found work as a salesman in retail clothing and shoe stores.

In the course of working in retail stores' seasonal sales, he discovered a need for free-hand brush lettering, and began to teach himself, initially with speedball pens and then with lettering brushes, to create posters, sales signs and price tags needed for a sale, and he had an affinity for the work. It came easily to him; his employers welcomed his new skill, and were willing to pay for it. With practice, he became adept at extremely fast, high quality brush lettering. As both salesman and sign painter, his days were full, and his evenings were all his own, for dancing.

******

With World War I ended and Carl safely returned, times were good for the Haischs; Gottlieb sold the butcher shop and bought a bigger house, Margaret worked as a secretary, and Louisa, now freed of the butcher shop, kept house for her parents. Because sisters Kate and Lil were both accomplished seamstresses, Louisa and Margaret, who still lived at home, wore the latest style custom-made dresses for only the price of the fabric. Catherina subsidized their stylish shoes and Louise and Margaret were free to explore the social worlds of the 20s.

Large traveling bands were the rage and the major entertainment was ballroom dancing. Everyone rejoiced that the war was over, the flapper age had begun, and crowds danced at the large downtown hotels, the West View Amusement Park outside of town, and at private clubs. Young adults from all parts of the city whose social, economic and ethnic milieus had little or nothing in common met and became acquainted on the dance floors. It was inevitable that somewhere in that mixture of city-wide social, sensual exuberance, Sam Nathanson, whom everyone agreed was an unusually expert dancer, would ask Louisa Haisch, who was equally as graceful, to dance.

Sam met Louisa —now Americanized to Louise—at one of the many dances they both attended, each with their own group of friends, but it was not long before Louise and Margaret—now Marge—both Christian women from Pittsburgh's North Side, had become involved in a youthful Jewish social group from Squirrel Hill, a more affluent and burgeoning neighborhood of small businessmen and entrepreneurs located far off on the other side of the city. Sam's interest in Louise was immediate, direct, and focused; he was in love. Louise's was less so. Sam wanted Louise and marriage; Louise was not certain. Each was aware of the religious conflict a marriage between them could entail. Neither was intimidated.

As first generation Americans in the free and tempestuous twenties, both were determined to live their lives as they wished. Neither was so seriously dedicated to their respective religions as to preclude determining their own actions. For Sam, his religion was not a factor as far as his relationship with Louise was concerned. He was Jewish. He observed the Holy Days and he made his living in the Jewish business community. Beyond that, he ignored religion, content with the knowledge that if Louise consented to become his wife, nothing else mattered—not his family, his friends or his religion. Louise also had few worries concerning religious aspects of such a marriage and was confident that her family would accept Sam as her husband. She simply wasn't yet certain she wanted to marry him.

Sam's sisters on the other hand were distraught. Sylvia and Sadie were active in the social circles into which Sam had introduced his intended bride and her sister, Marge. Sam's relationship with Louise was the talk of his Jewish community. Although his sisters had no personal dislike of Louise—they barely knew her, or many other Christians for that matter—the idea of an interfaith marriage in their family both frightened and embarrassed them.

In their community it simply didn't happen. If it did, how would they be perceived? How could they live with a Christian sister-in-law? They felt compelled to prevent it, but how? With this thought in mind, Sylvia, who believed the potential social calamity to be extremely serious, encouraged Sadie to discuss the matter with Louise and convince her to stop chasing Sam, to allow him to get on with his life as a Jewish man. Sadie dutifully took up the challenge and arranged to have a talk with Louise. However, when Sadie talked with Louise and suggested that Louise give Sam up, Louise's response was, "I'm not holding him, and I'm not chasing him. He's the one who's decided he wants to marry me. I haven't made up my mind. You had better talk to him." Talking to Sam, of course, was impossible; he wouldn't discuss it. He had indeed made up his mind and as far as he was concerned, it was no one else's business.

Ultimately, Louise succumbed to Sam's pleading. They decided to marry, but had only two hundred dollars between them. Louise went to her mother with their dilemma, "Sam and I have two hundred dollars. If you will permit us to live here with you, we will take a few days for a honeymoon. If not, we will use the money to rent a place and buy some furniture." Catherina's response was immediate and affirmative: "You'll live here." Accordingly, on September 3, 1925, before a Justice of the Peace in the courthouse in Pittsburgh, Sam Nathanson and Louise Haisch were married.

Now they were faced with informing Sam's mother of their marriage. They met with her at her home in Squirrel Hill, the predominantly Jewish section of the City, where she lived with Sam's sister Sylvia, and her husband, Jack, and told her their happy news. Sophie Nathanson was not happy, but she was gracious. She knew a fait accompli when she saw one, and when she had digested the news, which obviously had not come as a surprise to her since it had been a widely known topic of discussion both in the family and within the Jewish community, she wished them happiness and then asked Louise directly: "Will you consent to marry again in the temple in a Jewish ceremony?" Louise responded just as directly: "No, I'm sorry, but Sam has not asked me to become a Jew and I have not asked him to become a Christian, so I cannot do as you ask." And there began a relationship of respect and understanding between the two women which existed until Sophie's death, and with Sam's sisters ever after.

Sam and Louise drove to Conneaut Lake, ninety miles north of the city, for a brief honeymoon. Their informal pre-nuptial agreement concerning religion was simple; Louise would raise the children in her religion and Sam would continue to celebrate his. They would all participate in the festivities and holidays of both religions.

As a married man, and subsequently as a father, Sam had an ebullient, optimistic, light-hearted manner, always ready to try something new or different, to take a risk, totally convinced that whatever it was and whatever the odds, "things would work out." He was dedicated wholly and unflinchingly to his family, and could not perceive any member of his family ever doing wrong. His belief was literal, and he was ready to put his life on the line for what he believed.

Louise, by comparison, was reserved, slower to become enthused, a realist in matters of everyday life, but liberal in terms of other peoples' rights. She believed that everyone should be content to live with what they had and should not always be looking for ways to have more. Her ability to assess people's actions and motivations was superb. She never missed even the slightest nuance of what was happening around her, and was not deluded by empty talk or social gossip. She quietly penetrated gossip and social repartee and examined what lay underneath. She listened politely and participated, while at the same time taking measure of the person, less interested in what someone said or did than in understanding the type of person who would say or do it. She frequently appeared to know what was in other people's minds before they did themselves. With children particularly, she was always a few seconds ahead and almost invariably moved quickly to redirect their actions before they themselves had a chance to move. She would watch quietly to see how a youngster was going to test a situation, "Now watch," she would say, "He/she is going to do this or that." "You can just see their little mind working on it." She was invariably correct.

For Sam, living in Gottlieb's house was not an enjoyable experience. Having grown up in an ethnic Jewish environment, he soon learned that, quite apart from religious differences that were easily resolved between he and Louise, living in a Gentile household with a stubborn, overbearing father-in-law nevertheless posed a variety of irritants and problems. Gottlieb expected that when he was ready to sit down to dinner, the meal would be ready on time and everyone would be there, awaiting his pleasure. Catherina, of course, knew his routine and schedule and delivered his meals on time. Sam's retail store work schedule did not coincide with Gottlieb's early morning start and early afternoon finish at the meat packing company. Sam would often arrive late for dinner that had at times been delayed for a few minutes awaiting his arrival or begun without him, in either case resulting in Gottlieb's displeasure. In addition, the food served in a German Gentile house was a cuisine quite different from that served by Sophie Nathanson from her kosher kitchen on Tilbury Street in Squirrel Hill. Sam was used to and enjoyed his mother's Eastern European cuisine. Although he had no reluctance to eating non-kosher food, he was not used to sauerkraut, blood pudding, pickled pig's feet and sauer brauten and so, when he arrived home after work and was offered one of these dishes, he forced himself to eat some lest he be greeted with Gottlieb's, "What's the matter? It isn't good enough for you?" Gottlieb's reactions, however, were never in any way anti-Semitic; he didn't care about religion, he just didn't like being inconvenienced.

Until he was able to earn enough to move with his wife into their own quarters, Sam was willing to endure anything in order to have Louise. No matter what the ordeal, in his view she was worth it.

4

The Early Years

I was born a healthy baby on Nov. 2, 1926 at St. John's Catholic Hospital on Pittsburgh's Northside. My mother had experienced an uncomfortable pregnancy during which she had suffered extreme back pain, and my delivery, a breech birth, necessitated the use of forceps and involved many hours of labor. Ultimately my birth was a severe shock to my parents because I lacked a right hand and both of my lower legs and feet were not fully formed. In telling me of my birth Mother always had great praise for her doctor, saying, "Doctor Liebold came into my room. He was so gentle and hopeful. He held my hand and told me of your deformities and then he said, 'He is a beautiful and a healthy baby. He will grow up normally and will be active." Then the nurse, a nun, brought you in to me and also praised your beauty, saying "He is a lovely child."

My father arranged for my bris to be held at the hospital and invited his Jewish friends to serve as a minyan. A Rabbi performed the circumcision. It was the first time such an event had occurred in that hospital and the nuns and doctors all came to witness it. Grandmother Haisch was deeply troubled by my deformities, and although she welcomed and loved me and her pity knew no bounds, she was unable to imagine how I could possibly fare in the world, envisioning my disabilities as being impossible to overcome. That worry and concern weighed heavily and constantly on her, and in later years Mother always believed that my birth might well have hastened Grandmother's death a year later.

When the news of my birth became known there were some insensitive and even vehemous reactions. Interfaith marriages were almost non-existent in the 1920s. Some believed them to be sinful and to be ultimately avoided, others viewed my birth as a judgment:

"She made her bed, now let her sleep in it," and from those with anti-Semitic feelings, "That's what she gets for marrying a Jew." There were also those who somewhat grudgingly viewed such marriages as courageous, but found the depths of their own courage challenged by the example. Although such comments were never made directly to my parents, ignorance and vindictiveness was expressed to some who had close relationships with them. Within the family, however, among both the Nathansons and the Haischs, there was nothing but sympathy, hopeful wishes and support.

The question foremost in the minds of Mother and Dad was, "What can be done to better the baby's physical condition, namely his legs and feet?" Dr. Liebold, mother's physician, called in Dr. Heberling and his associate Dr. Silver, both orthopedists. Dr. Heberling was very positive in his prognosis: "The child is fortunate in his misfortune. His knees are normal and the lengths of his lower legs, from the knees to the end of the legs, are equal. With some inventive prosthetic development I believe he will be able to wear regular shoes and will walk and be able to function very well". The absence of the right hand is of minimal concern. He will be able to do anything he desires to do with only one hand. It will not hinder him. They all were agreed that for the moment, however, there was little to do except give me the opportunity to cope and see what I could do for myself.

When I was nine months old Dr. Heberling performed minor surgery on my right foot, which had a single toe turned back and under like a finger in a closed fist. The muscle that held the toe in position was snipped and the toe stretched out to full length permitting the foot to develop in a manner that would be more supportive for walking. A second operation was required a short time later to complete the stretching. No corrective surgery was indicated for the left foot, the single toe of which unfortunately faced to the left at a right angle to its normal direction. With apparent disregard for my disabilities, I grew and performed and responded like any other baby: sitting up, crawling, turning over and speaking. When, at ten months, I showed signs of pulling myself up to stand, Dr, Heberling advised putting on a pair of booties filled with cotton and permitting me to do as I pleased. To everyone's joy, I stood up and walked at eleven months.

....

During my second year I was very physically active and when the time came for me to wear a more substantial shoe the problem of prostheses had to be addressed. Plaster casts were made of my extremities on which my weight rested when I stood. Among my earliest remembrances is the experience of having a large wad of cotton with a gob of wet Plaster of Paris pressed against the bottom of my foot and held until it set. Using these initial castings as molds, a prosthetist made plaster replicas of my feet. These were then used as models to determine the shape and depth of depressions that fit my feet. Pieces of composite cork were then hand carved to replicate the models and the exteriors of the cork were shaped to fit into the shoes. The myriad of chemical and plastic materials of custom specified resiliency and density available at the close of the century were unknown in the 1930s. Each time my shoes were used it was necessary to place new, dry cotton in the forms. Its shock-absorbing properties lasted only until perspiration soaked the cotton at which point the cushion disappeared. The completed prostheses, termed "forms," were covered with cotton and soft chamois cloth and forced into the shoes. Additional padding was applied to the tongue of the shoe to fill the remaining empty space between my foot and the shoe. When I walked, due to the position of the left toe, the left shoe faced left and the right side of the shoe faced forward.

The doctors advised my mother that she should massage my left leg daily, gently, but firmly, and attempt to exert twisting pressure on the leg in hope that over time it would alter the direction of the toe and make it point in a more forward direction. Mother would say, "The doctor said we should do this," as she massaged my leg and twisted it, but this bit of medical advice proved to be little more than a placebo in which Mother could temporarily place her hope. The assumption that by periodic manual manipulation, the lower extremity of the tibia, the major weight bearing lower leg bone, could be twisted ninety degrees from the upper portion, was a wholly unrealistic proposition. For a time my mother did massage my leg and for a longer time talked of what the doctors had said, but she never fully believed it, she just went through the motions. In her own mind she came to the conclusion that the suggested outcome was not possible.

It became apparent in the first few years that as I grew, it was necessary to repeat the plaster cast process and to have new cork forms fabricated. The process, implemented initially by a pros-thetist at the hospital, was expensive. My Uncle Al had a solution; he would make them himself.

Uncle Al was a quiet, portly man of average height with a cer-tain elf like quality enhanced by a rounded body, thinning white hair, twinkling eyes, a sense of quiet humor, and a soft passivity in stark contrast to his wife Kate's warm and loving, but sharp, Major Domo like domination of her husband and her household. Uncle Al fascinated me with stories of collecting wild cherries and elder-berries for jams and wines, hunting squirrels, rabbits and deer, and tent camping in the wilds.

Al obtained several samples of manufactured cork of various densities from his brother who worked for the Armstrong Cork Company. Finding one that he believed suitable, he made his own tools for cutting the cork, and then carved a set of forms which proved to be functional and useable, indeed identical, to those made by the prosthetist.

As I grew, Uncle Al continued making new pairs of forms for me as needed and as my weight and activity increased. The cork, under the pressure of perspiration and use, would eventually decay and disintegrate causing the forms' function to be minimized and my shoes to become misshapen. Each time new forms were made they had to be fitted into a new pair of high rise blucher style shoes, the new leather serving as a reinforcement to hold the forms in shape. Uncle Al would sculpture the cork blocks to fit into the shoes at his leisure, but it was always necessary, in the final phases of hollowing out the forms to the correct size and shape to fit my legs, for me to sit with Uncle Al for an afternoon to fit and refit as the work progressed and until I decided they felt comfortable. Lit-tle by little, as I gained knowledge of tools and perfected my model airplane building skills I began to assist Uncle Al in the annual form making sessions, initially sanding the cork surfaces until they were smooth enough to slip into the shoes and later fine tuning the depressions in the cork to fit my feet using the home made scrap-ers Uncle Al had created for that purpose. By the time I was fifteen or sixteen I was ready, with cork supplied by Uncle Al, to attempt making my forms myself and I was pleased that my first pair served me quite well. From then on, until I was thirty-four, when-ever new forms were needed, I made them myself.

Unfortunately Al, whose warm and gentle demeanor never varied, was a drinker, and every Friday when he received his pay as a coil winder at the Allis Chalmers Transformer plant, it was his practice, as he walked home along East Street, to stop at one of several saloons for a shot and a beer that led to another and another. On many paydays he arrived home well after dinnertime, frequently with the needed assistance of a friend or neighbor. As the years passed and his drinking increased, Katherine knew that, if he were to come home, she would have to fetch him and so she would go from bar to bar until she found him and led him home. He never complained; he was always sweet, calm and sorry, but he never changed, and one night he died in the street on his way home from a saloon.

******

I was just five years old when I began attending kindergarten for a half day. My unusual appearance generated much interest on the part of the other children, but was soon dissipated. They quickly became accustomed to me, and my participation in activities was not limited. Indeed, every effort was made to see that I was included in all class activities.

I was not quite six years old when I began first grade. School began in September and I would turn six in November, so the principal permitted my early enrollment. Spring Hill School was an old school, even in 1932 when I arrived. It had an open central hall with a classroom on either side of the entry. The second floor had five classrooms. The first grade, Miss Hunter's domain, was on the first floor.

The front of the classroom featured a blackboard and a large wooden teacher's desk. The cast iron rococo bases of the student desks, bolted to the floor, had wooden box tops with a lid that covered a book storage area and provided a slant top writing surface. A small glass inkwell with a cork top which, when needed, was filled from a large bottle by the teacher, rested in a circular hole on a narrow, level segment at the front of each desk.

When I sat at my desk in the first grade, my feet did not reach the floor. Since the shapes of my feet were amorphous, unlike the contours of a normal foot and much smaller, they were held tightly between the dense cork forms and the cotton padded leather tongue of the shoe, and my high top shoes had to be worn tightly laced to preclude their falling off. With the shoes tightly laced, circulation in my extremities, less than normal at best, was additionally impeded, causing a kind of burning pain. I would frequently experience this pain when just sitting, particularly if weight was not bearing on the shoe. In an attempt to alleviate my pain I would minutely twist my foot around inside the shoe and sometimes force my pencil between the lacings and with the end massage my foot. Once again Uncle Al had a solution. Using two wooden Velveeta cheese boxes turned upside down and stapled together, he made a small platform about 4 inches high which when placed under the desk, served as a foot rest. It enabled me rest my feet on the "floor" permitting me to exert pressure on the shoe thus gaining some movement between the foot and the form and alleviating the discomfort.

First grade was exciting. There were books to read and new songs to sing. The writing lessons were tedious, and it was necessary to learn the precise procedure. We were taught that our metal pen points were precious, and we were cautioned to take care of them. We kept them in the desk, and each time we had a penmanship lesson, I would take a pen point out, insert it in the holder, open the inkwell, and position the cork on a specific part of the desktop. Those whose ink supply was low would raise their hands and the teacher would go around the room with a large inkbottle and pour ink into the wells. We were counseled to never dip the pen too far into the ink, as it would result in blotting, and the teacher would put only a small amount of ink into the inkwells making it virtually impossible to overload the pen. Nevertheless, inkblots were a regular part of our writing lessons.

All writing was done on lined paper. The teacher would specify how many lines to use, "Now class, we will use three lines, that is two spaces," she would say, "The capital letters will use two spaces and the lower-case letters will use only one space. We are going to write a line of capital A's, then a line of small a's, then b's. Now remember to keep your hands and elbows loose. I want to see your arms moving in a nice easy flow. Ready now? All right, begin, capital A, capital A, capital A." Our arms would move in unison as the teacher established the beat.

The functional design of a quill pen requires that it be used in a motion that draws the point away from the line it is scribing, thus allowing pressure on the point to vary, spreading the points of the nib changes the width of the line. When writing left to right with the right hand, the pen is always ahead of the line, moving away from it and pointing back to it. Unfortunately, my only hand was the left, and in the left hand the pen is pushed into the line instead of being pulled away from it so it had a tendency, in the hands of a novice, to stick and dig into the paper. With a bit of experimentation, I devised a way to make it work. Tilting my paper far to the left and turning my hand around so it was above the line being written, rather than below, as were the other children's, the pen point was in a position to function without digging into the paper. I was essentially writing upside down.

"Now we're going to do the free hand exercises, the circles and the verticals. We'll do twenty and then shift, ready now, circles first, one, two, three." Writing sessions always ended by putting the cap on the inkwell, using our individual four-inch square of cotton cloth to wipe excess ink from the point, removing the point from the holder and putting them both away inside the desk. Using the pen required extra thought and a lot of practice, but, I noticed, when the papers were hung up at the front of the room, although mine wasn't the best, it wasn't the worst either.

In reading and singing I had few peers. My reading skills were beyond my grade; I had a good singing voice and could commit songs to memory easily. In physical education class, I wasn't required to do all the exercises that the class did, but was welcome to do as many of them as I wanted and I usually did more than was expected. Some things I couldn't do, such as run races, or play ball, but the teachers always made a point of including me in the activity, if only to act as scorekeeper.

For boys, one of the most sought after jobs at the end of the day, primarily because it meant getting out of the classroom five minutes early, was dusting erasers, a job that consisted of taking the six or eight blackboard erasers outside to the front of the school and, with one in each hand, smacking them together until the chalk dust was gone, usually ending up on the dust remover. With only one hand, it was not an easy job to do, but it was a privilege and when it was my turn I was not about to pass it up. Nor did the teacher deny me the chance. I took the erasers under my arm, chalk dust all over my shirt, and walked outside. I put one eraser on the ground and smacked it with another and when I had finished, I took an eraser and cleaned up the residue on the ground, then, smacking that eraser on another a few times I headed back to class, satisfied that I had done the job at least as well as some of the other boys.

Mr. Shartung, the school principal and the teachers, both separately and collectively, provided the support that made it possible for me to be integrated into the dynamics of the elementary school process, to participate and be included and accepted without becoming an object of mischief or discrimination. In the early 30s, long before the term "mainstreaming" was used to refer to the practice of placing children with disabilities in regular classrooms thereby permitting their participation in a natural growth experience, I was informally mainstreamed by ad hoc cooperative efforts. The support of my teachers and the benign environment they established on an informal basis was a major factor in reinforcing the self-confidence and reliance that my mother had set in force when I had first begun to exert my physical capabilities.

My mother's point of view was demonstrated one snowy day, when a neighbor said to her, "I was watching your son this afternoon and do you know what he was doing with his sled?" Mother's reply was: "Don't tell me. I don't want to know. I'd only worry and he's going to do it in any event." She never forbade me, or even warned me against doing anything physically challenging, nor was there ever a suggestion that anything in my life should not be attempted or could not be accomplished. In her perception, I had a handicap; I would overcome it.

On most days Mother or Dad would drive me to school in the morning, pick me up to go home for lunch, and then drive me back again for the afternoon session. Although I was never aware of it, during the Depression my father was having a difficult time finding work. Until he got his business going in my high school years, maintaining a car was an unaffordable expense that my parents endured, except for my beginning junior high school years, primarily to enable me to be driven to and from school. Dad would leave the car at home whenever possible so Mother could drive me back and forth. Only in later years did I discover that, during the

Depression, she was daily confronted with the dilemma of deciding whether to spend her few pennies on a loaf of bread, a bottle of milk, or a gallon of gas.

In the winter I stayed at school at lunchtime. I would eat my bacon and peanut butter or baloney sandwich in an unused classroom on the second floor, sit at the window and drink a bottle of milk given to me at school, and wait for my friends to return after lunch. When they arrived, I'd go outside for the few minutes of play before afternoon classes began.

After school was playtime and I was as active as any of my playmates. We played cowboys and Indians, built roads and garages for our toy cars and played all the usual games. Jumping rope and playing hopscotch was particularly painful for me and I couldn't bear it for long, but whenever the game was being played, despite the pain, I was a part of it. I learned how to jump up and come down as softly as possible, using my knees as springs in order to minimize the impact on my feet, which helped, but never solved the problem. It was painful, but I did it anyway.

My physical coordination was exceptional and I could do, at least for a short time, almost everything other kids could do. I became expert at analyzing the challenges so that when I tried something I was successful. When I faced a physical challenge that I thought I couldn't do successfully, I would not attempt it. On rare occasions I was even able to out-perform friends. To compete at anything I had to be able to think it through and perform better, but I also learned that if a person with disabilities achieves higher than a person without disabilities, it sometimes results in reactions that are unexpected or negative.

******

When I was in the third grade Mother gave birth to a second child. For eight years following my birth, she had feared that my abnormalities might be a genetic flaw and she doubted that she would have the strength and will to handle two children with disabilities. When she finally decided to take the risk, however, her pregnancy, although beginning with some apprehension and trepidation, proved to be uneventful, resulting in the birth of a healthy baby boy normal in all respects. My brother, Wayne, was an undemanding child, particularly in his early life, and left Mother free to continue to provide me the support needed as I began to approach puberty. In her later years she worried that she had been neglectful of Wayne in order to provide more care for me. "Wayne was never a care or bother," she would say, "He almost seemed to raise himself," inferring that she felt she had, in some ways, been deficient in the distribution of her love, affection and support between her two sons, while at the same time wondering how she could have done things any differently.

At ten or eleven I was able to play touch and even tackle football with friends on one of the nearby sod fields and I enjoyed being in the thick of the action. I couldn't run much, but I enjoyed the tumble of tackling, and I was good at throwing passes, so I was invariably the one who threw passes to my teammates who were doing the running. As for the pain in my legs, I would drop down on the sod and rest frequently on my knees while the boys were coming back for the next play. In this manner I could keep going indefinitely, not without pain, but with frequent relief and unlimited determination. Before puberty, despite my disabilities, there was a certain amount of day-to-day physical contact between my friends and me, the usual rough and tumble of young boys, in which I was able to give as good as I took. The onset of puberty, however, in addition to intensifying the physical differences between my peers and me, also brought about a role change. A few of the boys younger than me became physically superior to me and it was occasionally important for them to direct their newfound prowess at an older, but weaker peer. Such occasions were not physical in the sense of being beaten up, but were small humiliating actions wherein one is physically forced to give ground one way or another. I was never physically beaten by anyone; there always seemed to be a kind of protocol that dictated that nobody actually harm me. It didn't mean, however, that when one or several of the kids were feeling physical and showing off their strength, I would be exempted from the casual punching and slapping that was a natural aspect of adolescent male behavior. I received a punch on the arm or leg just like the next guy and if I hit back, which I sometimes did, I'd get another harder one. I soon learned to take the punch without fighting back even though rage boiled inside me. There were no winning situations for me in that

physical adolescent, world. Meanwhile my own physical maturation evolved at a snail's pace.

Emerging maturity, however slowly it progressed, was a
tumult of emotional and intellectual confusion that was subliminally pitted against the ever-present stress induced by the tardi-
ness of my physical development. Just prior to beginning junior
high school, the discomfort and strain of my physical condition
resulted in behavior that worried my mother sufficiently to seek
medical advice. In the attempt to seek comfort from the incessant
pain in my right foot, I had developed the habit of kicking at any
solid object I happened to pass. I never missed a telephone pole or
a concrete stoop. One small kick jostled my foot within the tight
bonds of the prosthesis and stimulated the blood circulation. At
the same time I also developed an unsightly habit of repeatedly
opening my mouth as wide as possible resulting in deep bleeding
cracks on my lips. Even the varied ointments applied by my
mother seemed to have little effect. Mother was convinced that I
had developed a serious condition, then called St. Vitus Dance,
that manifested itself in uncontrollable jerky and awkward movements. The doctor's diagnosis was stress resulting from the combination of physical discomfort and nervous tension at the time
of approaching puberty.

In the fall of my twelfth year I began attending weekly evening
sessions for the coming year's confirmation class, a group of five
boys and five girls with whom I had attended Sunday School at
the German Evangelical Church. The informal evening meetings
constituted my first experience at social intercourse with girls my
age in other than the classroom and I found it enjoyable. I found
less rewarding *The Ten Commandments, The Apostles Creed, The
Doxology, The Books of the Bible,* and ritualistic aspects of church
services that we had to memorize and recite together while Reverend Giese, our instructor, already beyond his middle years, would
occasionally doze off. My involvement pleased my mother. For
me, I could as easily do it as not, and although we never discussed
it, I wondered what relationship it had to my Jewish father. On confirmation day, the pastor, at the altar, examined the confirmees and
for the benefit of the congregation each was asked one question.
Turning to me, the Pastor asked, "What is time?" I responded, as I
had been taught, "Time is the stuff of which life is made" which

brought a chuckle from the congregation. Later that day, the Confirmation party at the Martin house had been fun. We played Spin The Bottle, me for the first time, and despite some embarrassment, I had the thrill of kissing my first unrequited love.

Grade promotion procedures at the end of school semesters was such that on a given day, classes would march as groups to their new classroom. When it was time to be promoted to the third grade, two classmates and I were told to go, not to the third grade room but to the fourth. We were puzzled, and didn't realize that on the basis of our knowledge levels, we were being given a double promotion, moving from the second to the fourth grade. Two years later I was in the sixth grade, preparing to make the big move from elementary school to junior high school, and one year younger than my fellow students.

A new bicycle became a passport to new activities. It was a standard single-speed Schwin with double crossbars enclosed by side panels with batteries for a small headlight mounted on the front fender. Without ankles, the positioning of my shoes on the pedals and the fact I had only one hand on the handlebars constituted a tenuous situation, but it didn't stop me. I was unable to stand up while pedaling, limiting my ability to negotiate even small upgrades, but I had no delusions as to my physical capabilities on the bike. It became a veritable flying carpet, extending the range and frequency of my perambulations and providing me a convenient seat wherever I happened to be.

The shopping area closest to Spring Hill was a strip near the junior high school that consisted of several blocks of numerous retail stores: clothing, shoes, jewelry, furniture, hardware and pawn shops, many owned by Jewish merchants, most of whom my father knew. One of my friends was in the habit, as were his father and mother, of referring to the various neighborhood business establishments, even in conversations with me, as "Harry the Jew, Sam, the Jew, the Jew clothing store," or "The Jew jeweler." It was common among my neighbors and friends, when they had made a purchase of which they were proud, to say, "I Jewed him down," or "I Jewed down the price." "Jewed" became a functional verb replacing "bargained." On such occasions those present would grin and look at each other out of the corner of their eyes as they watched for my reaction and shrugged their shoulders as if to say, "If he doesn't like it, screw him." I couldn't fight them although I would have liked to do so on many occasions. Never, however, did I respond to these references to my father; I did my best to ignore them.

I did become aware, however, of the fact that people treated Dad and me with a façade of politeness, even friendliness, that in moments of anger, dissatisfaction, or jealously, was forgotten, revealing anti-Semitism. My neighborhood was predominately Catholic. My mother and I were Protestant and my father was the only Jew in the whole of Spring Hill. Anti-Semitism lay not too far below the surface of the polite neighborhood demeanor, but it nevertheless existed among the immigrant families that populated the area. On a face-to-face basis, and in large measure due to the respect in which the Haisch family and particularly Mother and Grandmother were held, Dad was treated with friendliness and respect. He even pitched for the softball team of the Brotherhood Association of Mother's church. But the real perceptions and attitudes of the neighborhood families were, on more than a few occasions, revealed by their children.

Many, perhaps most of the neighbors, were above such action; some were not. It was not unusual, if I became involved in a dispute, to be called "Jew boy." It confirmed my deeply seated feelings that I did not share the same degree of membership in my group as did the others. Many years after becoming an adult I was given insight to a more substantive and deeper psychological and sociological explanation for such behavior. My wife, then completing an M.A. in Sociology, handed me a book and said, "You need to read this." The book, *Stigma,* by Erving Goffman, provided a new perspective, a rational and understandable explanation for my experiences of the past, and a warning about my expectations for my future.

According to Goffman, since the time of the ancient Greeks, societies have been guilty of identifying, sometimes by physically branding, persons who are different in appearance, have individual character flaws, or are of a race, nation or religion, traits that can be transmitted through lineages which are disfavored.[1] The stigmatized person is then constrained to accept society's decreed rules of

---

[1] *"the Ancient Greeks [...] originated the term stigma to refer to bodily signs designed to expose something unusual and bad about the moral status of the signifier. The signs were cut or burned into the body and advertised that the bearer was [...] a blemished person, ritually polluted, to be avoided, especially in public places."* Erving Goffman, Stigma (Englewood Cliffs, NJ: Prentice-Hall, 1963), p. 1.

behavior for the stigmatized. Unknowingly, I possessed two of the three societal stigmas that Goffman describes;[2] both my body and my father's religion contaminated me. Although I had become astutely aware of the physical barriers I faced as a disabled person, in my ignorance I had assumed that discriminatory acts I had experienced were simply manifestations of personal likes and dislikes, not societal ones. Goffman's assertions stunned me. I had no understanding of the broad societal implications of Goffman's theories, or how my personal experiences related to them. Indeed, I never suspected that society might expect me to act in prescribed ways or to assume a prescribed role, and had never done so. I was concerned pragmatically with the "here and the now." Although my body had significant disabilities and my physical movements conveyed a visual perception of distorted motion, inside it where I lived, I experienced my actions as being as fluid and supple and as coordinated as an athlete's. And yet I knew that my every action was a dichotomy between my feelings of sensory and physical movement, and my actual appearance as seen by others. Despite my disabilities, and even when my pain was greatest or hopes lowest, I never felt that I was different from any of my acquaintances. Although totally aware of my deficiencies, I did not perceive myself as disabled and thus had never accepted nor even been aware of the role that, according to Goffman, society had proscribed for me.

Unaware of alleged societal restraints, I unwittingly went to great lengths to reject or ignore them. No matter how difficult the activity, I was always ready to try whatever anyone else tried, and most of the time I succeeded. In my teenage years and later in adult life, as the maturation process widened the physical capabilities gap between my acquaintances and myself, my major competitive asset became my quick wit and active verbal response. Verbally and argumentatively, I was louder and quicker and made up in verbiage what I lacked in physical prowess, in some cases resulting in minor physical retribution. When physical strength was the determining factor, however, and in many instances it was, I understood I was the weakest and I didn't push my luck. As my social relations became increasingly limited, I became conditioned to being

---

[2] *"[...] first there are abominations of the body—physical deformities. Next there are blemishes of individual character [...] Finally there are the tribal stigma of race, nation, religion, the latter being a stigma that can be transmitted through lineages and contaminate all members of a family."* (Goffman, p.4)

a loner; I took my lumps and kept quiet, knowing that direct reaction would only encourage more severe hurt. As time passed, I began to find my satisfactions in areas other than my childhood environment.

******

If my Confirmation party had awakened in me an anticipation of growing up, it was graduation from the sixth grade and the move out of the neighborhood into junior high school that presented the first major departure from the secure academic world where I had spent my grade school years. In junior high school I became a member of a student body that comprised a range of adolescents representing a full spectrum of physical and social maturation; and although my maturation was not the slowest, it was very low on the general maturation timetable. I was again fortunate to find the environment essentially benevolent. With the single exception of the experience in the basement restroom, I was never accosted by fellow students and was assisted by teachers wherever possible.

5

Outside Looking In

Junior high school brought a number of friendly relationships. I attended home basketball games and a few after-school dances, but I never danced. I didn't know how, had no female friends to teach me, and was intimidated by the thought that if I didn't dance well, my failing would be attributed to my disabilities. With so many able-bodied boys to dance with, I hardly expected that girls would have an interest in me, and rather than be rejected, I did not venture forth. I became increasingly aware that fellow classmates, both boys and girls, appeared to be much more mature than I was or than I felt. They were growing up; I felt I was being left behind. The girls, now with budding breasts, and many much more developed with adult hairdos and cosmetics, looked like grown women. From my vantage point in gym class where, in lieu of participating in the physical workouts and games, I passed out towels as the boys came from the showers, I could see that most boys my age had impressive body and muscle development and much body hair. These physical changes in my body had not yet begun.

I had no direct knowledge of the variety of social activity and involvement occurring in and after school. Overheard comments suggested that many, if not all of my schoolmates, were regular participants in these activities. It was apparent to me, from behavior and snatches of conversation between boys and girls, that many friendships extended beyond the school day and many of my classmates were already embarked on experimentation with adult sexual behavior that they would perfect as they matured. I was increasingly aware that I was not a part of these activities and unable to envision how I might gain access to them.

I often thought about how girls perceived me and those thoughts engendered acute awareness of my appearance. There was little I could do to change it, but I tried. I had my mother lengthen my pant legs to partially cover my misshapen shoes. As I traveled home from school, between trolley stops, I studied my reflection in store windows, experimenting with my gait to see if it could be made less noticeable. I began holding my right arm at my side and just a little to the rear so that someone approaching me in front could not see that I had only one hand. I tried to meld all of these actions into a choreography of objective movement calculated to diminish my obvious differentness, but although my efforts were valiant, none made any significant change in my appearance, and I ultimately realized that I had to live in this body and make the best of it.

As my friends now walked to and from school, their independence grew and their geographic horizons expanded. In the neighborhood of the school, bordering on a commercial area, were two movie theaters. It became a regular Saturday afternoon entertainment for kids in my neighborhood to go to a movie. Having decided which movie they wanted to see, they proceeded to walk to the theater. By prior agreement, I would take the streetcar, which required that I use three streetcars, obtain two transfers, and then walk a short distance to the theater to meet them. Calculating as best I could the time it would take them to walk, I would plan to meet them at the theater. As can frequently be the case with a group of young boys, however, in the course of conversations and horseplay that occurred during their walk, the group's plans could be changed, sometimes by a decision to go to a different theater, to a later showing, or, if the inducement were strong enough, to cancel the movie and embark on a totally new adventure. Accordingly, I would frequently find myself at the chosen theater only to learn that my friends had arrived early and were already inside, or were late, or never arrived, and after having this experience a number of times, I realized that my friends had little concern whether or not I was with them. I began to go to the movie by myself. I could easily go to larger theaters downtown by taking only one streetcar that delivered me right to the theater. It wasn't as much fun as being with friends, but I could make my own choices and set my own schedule. It was the beginning of my independence.

After school and in the evenings I was still able to participate in the informal "hanging out" on the neighborhood stoops, at the drugstore, or at the end of the trolley line. With a bike, my perambulations had expanded and my friend Marty and I frequently traveled around together on my bike with me sitting on the crossbars and Marty pedaling. I was particularly conscious of the physical changes that had occurred between my friends and myself when one night Marty decided, on a whim, to ride me on my bike up to my house at the top of our steep street. Taking "s" turns up the three-car wide Belgian block street, gaining six or seven feet at each turn, Marty pumped the bike with both of us on board all the way to the top without a stop.

Marty was of medium height, slightly built, but rangy, strong as an ox and totally without fear. His open and friendly manner hid a pugnacity which could come quickly to the fore. He was constantly on the alert for a dare, a threat or a snub, and quick to respond. The size of a potential opponent never deterred him. On the dance floor, if another boy cut in on him, there were certain to be words, always with a smile, but with cockiness and challenge. If it happened repeatedly, there was an altercation. There were frequent occasions when, with a certain assurance that because of my disabilities I would not be struck, I stepped between Marty and the would-be opponent just moments before the fists flew and talked Marty out of the situation. Invariably the other fellow would be more quickly inclined to forget the matter. When fisticuffs did appear to be the course, at the last moment Marty would remove his upper denture plate and with a big grin say, "Hold this for me," and then turn to begin battle. Win or lose, his dentures were the first thing he asked for when the fight was over. He enjoyed the fighting so much that he decided to try it in the ring. With the help of another of our neighborhood crowd who had already fought several successful amateur bouts as a featherweight, Marty began training. A few months later he had his first three-round amateur fight and was barely able to last the three rounds. In addition to being exhausted, he received a beating and decided to end his career as a boxer. It didn't alter his attitude.

Marty's strength and endurance on the bicycle, although he never owned one, was prodigious. One summer evening when several boys with bikes were gathered in front of the drug store with nothing to do, someone suggested we all ride out to the North Hills Dairy, some fifteen miles north of the city, for a milkshake. The trip required traversing a number of dark country roads on which the wartime traffic was light. The debate waged back and forth as each boy contemplated how much he wanted to exert himself on the warm evening. I sat on my bike, watching and listening, aware that it wasn't something I could do. Three of the boys were inclined to go, but there was no leader to initiate the action. Marty had no bike, but his interest was aroused, and always impatient to be doing something, he turned to me and said, "C'mon, let's go. You sit on the crossbar and I'll pump." "Out there and back, and up the hill?" I responded. "Sure, I promise you, you won't have to walk. If I can't pump you up the hill I'll push you." Marty's interest convinced the other boys, so I removed my sweatshirt, wound it around the crossbar to provide a bit of padding for my lean posterior, jumped on the crossbar and off we went. The round trip took more than three hours and Marty pumped the single speed bike up and down hills with a strength and energy that was amazing. Although I walked a bit, I needn't have, but I thought it only fair. It was a trip that I could never have attempted; Marty had done it without concern, carrying my extra weight.

******

School friendships continued into high school where tentative, experimental adult behavior of junior high became adult behavior of young men and women more sure of themselves. Boys and girls had a familiarity with each other outside the classroom that was foreign to me. It appeared to me that everyone was dating and they talked of parties and picnics and who liked whom.

At long last my body began to physically respond to my years, but my social maturity lagged far behind. Classmates were friendly and I fit well in the in-class activity. After class it was different. I had to accept that in one important aspect, my physical body, I was indeed different and, it occurred to me, below par. I had a desire to participate, to have a friendly relationship with a girl of my age, but in the teen-age world of physical development where the attitudes clearly demonstrated Darwin's theory of survival of the fittest; the competitive emphasis was on attractiveness of physical form and beauty. My features were not unattractive, but physically I was completely outclassed. I reasoned that any girl, given the options of many physically complete young male specimens from which to choose, was unlikely to give a second glance to someone with only one hand, abbreviated legs and deformed feet. Missing from my life were the small intimacies, teasing by-play, for instance, that a girl had a crush on a boy or vice versa, which happened regularly among my classmates. I was never the object of such a tease, however, and it dawned on me that in their minds I was not a participant in this game. They could not envision me in such circumstances, not even to tease me, and so involuntarily, and certainly without malice, they excluded me. Although physically highly visible, I was socially invisible.[3] What I did not comprehend was that, having been denied the benefit of the social by-play in which my friends had been engaging for the past few years, I was untutored in social behavior. Distanced from the mainstream of social intercourse of my milieu, my growth and maturation was retarded. I had only conjecture and second-hand observations from which to learn. It took time for me to recognize that, although I was treated politely and with great friendliness, I had become somewhat of a mascot rather than an actual member of the group. That recognition didn't come easily; I fought it. I tried to do all the things that the other boys did, but was eventually forced to recognize that my relationships with girls was quite different from those of other boys. Throughout adolescence, therefore, in order to not be rejected, I choose to not make advances. I kept my interest in the opposite sex to myself.

Extracurricular social life in high school was active, varied and focused on sports, student government and academic preferences, i.e. Latin Club, Music Club, Math Club, etc. I didn't fit into any of the categories. Academically I maintained a respectable, average place, occasionally making the honor role. Physically and socially, my world was limited to in-class contact with other students before and during classes. I would join a group that was just casually conversing and I was welcomed, but invariably it became too painful to continue standing, and I was forced to leave early to find a place to sit down, thus missing critical parts of conversations, or opportunities to participate in spur-of-the-moment activities. At the end of the day I was usually exhausted and learned early the old axiom,

---

[3] ...where the infantiley stigmatized manages to get through his early school years with some illusions left, the onset of dating or job-getting will often introduce the moment of truth. (Goffman, p-33)

"Out of the room, out of the deal." Outside class, because walking and standing was required, and events like football games were a mile from school, I was unable to participate. Although I never realized it, each effort to socialize, in addition to the day-to-day physical activity of getting to and from school and from class to class, sapped energy that might have been more productively used for improving academic performance.

One day, in art class, Marjorie, the girl who sat in front of me and with whom I always had enjoyable and sometime teasing conversations, turned around and said, "So and so is having a party Saturday night, would you like to go?" Marjorie was a pretty girl, very fully matured, the type of person any fellow would be proud to be seen with, but I didn't know if she was asking me to simply come to the party, or to take her to the party, and I hadn't the faintest idea as to how to find out. My mind raced. I would love to go to the party, but I was scared stiff. Saturday night? I had no way of getting there, wherever it was. I couldn't drive. I couldn't walk. I didn't know what streetcar to take. I'd never attended a party. What would I say to my parents? Dad would probably offer to drive me. I couldn't let that happen. How to answer this pretty girl who sat smiling at me? I offered some lame excuse. What an embarrassment. How dumb. " I'm sorry, maybe another time?" she offered.

"Yeah." Of course there was never another time and I never learned what motivated the invitation.

Despite lack of involvement, the high school years were not without interest. The general ambiance of friendliness in home-room and classrooms made school enjoyable. Knowing the football and basketball stars as fellow classmates in algebra and Spanish classes provided a special perspective. I secretly wished to be a class officer or a member of this or that committee, but was never nominated and had no idea how to make my interests known.

It was in my first year in high school when in the tenth grade that the accident occurred. Ever alert to ways that would save a bit of painful physical effort, I had developed an unusual, but effective way of descending the tiled steps between floors of the school. The placement of the banister enabled me to balance my right elbow on it and agilely launch myself, with an energetic jump, down the stairs. I would ride the banister with my elbow for most of the distance of ten or twelve steps to the landing between floors, walk across the landing and then ride the banister down the remaining flight of steps to the next floor.

One day however, something went awry and as I landed on my right foot I experienced a slash of severe pain, and clutching my foot and fighting back the tears, tumbled right into the arms of an upperclassman who picked me up and carried me bodily to the principal's office. My mother was called and came for me with the car. It was the beginning of a seven-week period of intermittent, but severe pain. A single trip to the doctor resulted in my leg being taped into what the doctor believed to be an appropriate position, but which later proved to be one that increased the discomfort rather than relieving it. Surprisingly, no x-rays were taken.

In the following weeks my leg, just above the foot, would be painless one moment and in the next a muscle would involuntarily spasm causing extreme pain. The spasms of the muscle were clearly visible on the surface of the skin and each spasm sent unbearable pain shooting up the leg and into my body. The only relief came from my mother's grasping the leg and muscle very tightly, physically restraining the spasms until they subsided. The medical care and advice provided during this time left something to be desired, but the experience once again awakened my parent's interest in what might be done to improve my physical condition, but the doctor's answers were essentially the same. "Leave well enough alone. He's getting along well."

Because I accepted Mother's advice that it was not necessary to reveal the specific nature of my feet, visits from neighborhood friends were not encouraged during my incarceration when I was unable to put on my shoes. I spent the weeks through late winter and early spring alone, doing schoolwork that had been sent to me, and fighting boredom by building model airplanes. The senior boy into whose arms I had fallen was a warm, sensitive and friendly fellow who called periodically to see how I was coming along, and, after I was well enough to put on my shoes, but still unable to bear weight, he occasionally stopped by to say "Hello." Once or twice, when I was finally able to stand again, he came to the house in the evening in his convertible with his girl friend, and took me out for a ride and a snack. On my return to school he would, on occasion, drive me home. Those evening rides in the company of a guy and

• •

his girl were my first experience "going out" for the evening in a car with persons my own age. They both treated me as a friend and the context and experience was new and exhilarating. My foot healed, I made up my academic work and received passing grades, but I had to stop sliding down the banisters.

******

At sixteen my greatest desire was a driver's license. I studied my father's driving for months, asking questions and conducting mental dry runs while sitting in the driver's seat parked in front of the house. I analyzed every motion as Dad or Mother drove the family car, a 1941 Plymouth with a standard transmission, one of the first with the gearshift mounted on the steering column. That new innovation made it possible for me to drive. As I studied the car, I projected in great detail each of the actions and accommodations necessary for me to adapt my physical self to this inanimate machine. I visualized how my arm would grasp the steering column mounted gearshift, and, since my legs below the knees were shorter than normal, how my feet would fit onto the pedals and how the seat should be adjusted.

The routine was imbedded in my mind. A few days after my sixteenth birthday, my learner's permit in hand, Dad was ready to take me out for a first driving lesson. I asked his permission to start driving right there in front of the house. That he did not refuse the request was an indication of the respect he had for my understanding of both my capabilities and limitations. Without hesitation, I started the motor, released the parking brake, put the car in gear and drove it down the steep street for my first lesson, manual clutch and all. I knew that to pass the test I had to be better than the average person, because I would be scrutinized more closely. As I drove that first time, my father, familiar with my determination and skill, was nevertheless surprised. Only a few weeks later, on the first attempt, I passed the driving test. Acquiring a driving license widened the scope of my activities. Permission to use the car for an evening or occasionally on a weekend for a full day gave me an exaggerated sense of importance and independence, as well as a false sense of belonging. Being the first of my friends to have that privilege made it even more so. It was an opportunity to explore.

Being mobile without having to painfully walk and stand was a new experience and an enormous change in my life. Like the vehicles that had preceded it, the automobile gave me the means to move from place to place comfortably; it offered physical mobility that my body did not provide. As I grew older other vehicles: boats, airplanes, iceboats, and even horses each expanded my capabilities to enjoy new experiences and the broad scope of movement without discomfort. I experimented with each one, amazed and gratified at being able to do things and go places not previously possible. My "equalizers" in a world that was otherwise only painfully accessible, provided freedom of movement, speed and exhilaration otherwise unattainable. With them, I could perform competitively in any activity that did not require standing and bearing weight on my legs and feet. With an auto available I was able to explore areas further from home, go fishing with friends, or in season, squirrel and deer hunting. My friends were avid, aggressive hunters who left no bush or clump of brush unexplored in their relentless search for rabbits, grouse, pheasants and squirrels, impossible activities for me. With them, however, I would drive upstate to a large oak woods where the walking was easier and the pace slower, and while they ranged far and wide, I would find a sheltered spot beneath a pine tree, gather dead branches and boughs for a comfortable seat and quietly wait with my scope equipped 22. caliber rifle for squirrels to appear. We also spent many days at a nearby lake in a rented, sturdy clinker built double-ended boat with two rowing positions. We'd row far out amid the numerous tree stumps that drifted about on the upper reaches of the flood control lake and fish for bass and perch and crappies, and when the day was done, if the wind was in the right direction, we'd mount one oar vertically in the boat's bow as a mast, attach an old blanket to it and sail back to the dock. Benny, Marty and I eventually became a regular threesome and my having a car available brought me into the social world of the late teens in full force, but as I would learn, for the wrong reasons. We were soon acquainted with numerous fellows and girls, some of whom we knew from school or the neighborhood, and others we met at dances. I still did not dance and now, well in my late teens, was reluctant to appear as a beginner when most of the others were already skilled. That I lacked this skill was well known, but publicly attempting to acquire it required a more confident and secure person than I was. For one already set apart easily by physical characteristics, attempting graceful physical movement is a formidable undertaking, particularly when there is always that unuttered but agonizing thought, "Who will want to dance with me anyway, and why should they?" I sat on the sidelines, talked with the fellows and girls who weren't on the floor, and watched everyone dance. I didn't dance, but I was there, where I had never been before.

Both Marty and Benny had left school in their early teens and were working, Benny collecting $90 per week as take-home pay in 1942, an impressive amount for a person who had left school at the age of 15 and could barely read and write. Marty, after working at what he called the rag factory, a business that collected old rags and then sorted, baled and sold them, found a job at a local dairy where he worked the swing shift from week to week.

Marty was gregarious, always looking for something new or daring. At fourteen, lying about his age, he had joined the National Guard where he met for drills once a month and went to camp for two weeks in the summer. His interest, everywhere we went, was to meet new girls and "score," and although his success rate wasn't outstanding, his manner was charming and what he lacked in finesse he made up in boldness and fearless audacity. Through Marty we met girls and if Marty's newest interest had friends, and they always did, we would all have dates.

I was happy, at long last, to be a part of the social whirl, but wise enough to know that the girl who happened to be my date was not there because I was her first choice, but rather as a favor to her friend who was with Marty. In fairness, there were many times when the girls were, like me, pleased to go for a ride or a movie just to have something to occupy their evening. I was the one with access to a car, however, and that was special. I knew enough to not press my attentions, so while others were usually engaged in exploring how far their dates would go in necking and petting, I reverted to my skills of singing and joking.

A persistent and recurring fantasy I had as a teenager was to be a pop singer. I wasn't alone in that dream. In my fantasy I would have artificial legs, and prophetically, I envisioned them as a pair of boot-like affairs into which my legs would fit, and instead of bearing my weight at the end of them as I actually did, my legs would be held tightly suspended just below the knees, my prosthetic feet would appear normal, and my lack of a hand would make no difference. Popular music in my teen years was mostly ballads. The stars were: Frank Sinatra, Perry Como, Nat King Cole, Bing Crosby, Vaughn Monroe, and Tony Bennett. It all seemed so easy. My voice was one physical characteristic that had no disability. It wasn't perfect, but my second tenor was better than most of my friends. I knew all kinds of songs: pop songs that everyone knew; old songs I'd learned from Dad and Mother; and novelty songs including Spike Jones' *Chloe* with all the effects, Phil Harris' *Darktown Poker Club*, and Johnny Mercer's *Surprise Party*.

When singing started I was in the middle of it. Someone would usually ask, "Hey, do the one that . . ." and off I'd go. I was background music for everyone else's amourous experiments. On a hayride , a wiener roast, at a party, even though I had a date, and I frequently did, my date didn't have to avoid necking with me, I didn't take a chance of being refused. On occasion I thought I should have been more aggressive, but the thought of being rejected was painful, and so I sang. I was probably my own worst enemy in that I permitted my self-esteem and confidence to be undermined. Other guys could have a date and if the gal wouldn't kiss them they just laughed it off, but if it happened to me I KNEW it would be because of my disabilities. I was ready to settle for what I could get, however, so if a girl was willing to go out with me for an evening, to be with the crowd—there were a number of girls that I was too timid to ask—I didn't push it. My singing and joking were so fast and so agile that I could keep things going for a considerable time.

Underlying these actions was always the hope that, as so frequently happened with my friends, a girl would find me attractive and would be motivated to become a bit intimate. From time to time that dream would focus on a particular girl, but the dream remained unfulfilled despite the fact that, on occasion, I did have a date with one of those girls. In the company I kept, I was the court jester; my routines eased my presence and masked my lack of romantic involvement.

I found one girl particularly irresistible. Marty's cousin, Helen, was a uniquely beautiful brunette and an excellent jitterbug dancer who attended the same local dances I did. Marty's overriding interest in her friend, Rosie, resulted in dates for us when my dad's car was available. Inevitably, I became infatuated with her and she, being friendly and sympathetic, but having no personal interest in me, would agree to double dates for Marty's benefit. The dates most often consisted of an evening's drive with a stop for a snack at a barbecue or roadhouse.

One summer evening, Marty and I were at a loss for entertainment and he said, "Let's go to Helen's." I wanted to go, but Helen lived down off the Hill and I didn't have the car. "C'mon, we'll take your bike and I'll ride you home." I let myself be convinced. Marty went into the drug store and called Helen. "She's home. She's ironing. She said to come on down." With the two of us on the bike we had a wild ride down the long Spring Hill to the East Street valley and Howard Street. She was still ironing and not dressed up. Marty was not a naturally agile dancer, but wanted desperately to dance well and at his request, Helen stopped ironing and began teaching Marty new steps. In a few minutes the phone rang and answering it, Helen became very excited. "Its Eddie! He's home on leave. He wants to go out." Marty's immediate reaction was, "Can Rosie go too?" "I don't know, I'll call her" It was wartime and a sailor friend home on leave was an attraction for any high school girl. I couldn't compete with that. All of a sudden I was invisible. I was completely forgotten in the excitement that followed as arrangements were made for Helen to get dressed, Eddie to come over and Rosie to accompany them as they went out for the evening in Eddie's car. My only hope at that point was that Marty would think about my having to push the bike up that long hill and I waited, hoping that he might suggest that maybe the bike could be held on the running board of Eddie's car and they would give me a lift, but the suggestion never came. I was too proud to ask. Eddie arrived and soon he, Helen, Marty and Rosie were dancing to the music of *Hamp's Boogie Woogie.* I said my goodbyes, and struggling the bike down the narrow stairway that Marty had so easily carried it up, I rode the few blocks to the backside of the hill, dismounted and began the long, painful push home. I was completely distraught. It hadn't been a date. We had just informally dropped in. Events just happened.

As I pushed the bike up the long hill, all of the circumstances that surrounded my social existence, factors with which I was familiar and with which I dealt every day in my attempts to be a part of the teen-age social life that surrounded me, were suddenly brought into a sharp focus. The tears streamed down my cheeks as I pushed the bike up the steep hill. At first I was angry, but the more I thought about it, the more I knew that those four people had not meant to cause me any pain or discomfort; they were each just selfishly pursuing their own interests and caught up in the excitement of the moment. I had never even entered their thoughts. What I had to accept was that my providing a car for our collaborative enjoyment on frequent occasions had been the admission ticket to the social company of my friends. My mind searched back over the list of my acquaintances, male and female and I wasn't able to identify a single one I could believe desired my company. There was no evidence that among the various girls I had dated, there was any one who had had any interest in me at all. I concluded that there was no reason for the girls to go out with me when there were so many other more attractive guys around. Without a car I would not have been included in any of the social activities in which I had been marginally involved. I desperately wanted to be a part of the social scene, but in doing so I had allowed myself to be used.

The realization hit me with great force. It was not only having been used that hurt me. I realized that although I could easily discontinue the arrangement, if I did I would no longer be included in the social events which I enjoyed. By the time I reached home, sweating, in pain, and both physically and emotionally exhausted, I had reached a decision. I would no longer allow myself to be used even if it meant being alone. I understood that one didn't have to be in love or be loved in order to go to a movie or out for a drive, just having company was worthwhile and everybody was trading off in one way or another. I decided that in the future I would take my pleasures when I could, but I would not buy them. The following evening I told Marty exactly how I felt and that it was no longer going to be the way it had been. He was contrite. He had not perceived the situation in exactly the same way, and did not fully comprehend its seriousness from my point of view, but he understood I was upset, and promised to not take advantage in the future. We remained friends, and dated together and had good times, but I never forgot that night.

••

As I grew into young manhood I was increasingly conscious of my appearance and how I attracted the stares of strangers. My overriding goal was to minimize my visibility and blend into my surroundings as unobtrusively as possible, an impossible task. I yearned for anonymity, but it was not possible to hide; I was noticed everywhere I went. My physical appearance communicated to strangers a lack of capability and facility that was at odds with the character and potential of the person who lived in my body and I was determined that I would not be perceived as one who was unable to function or cope or who required assistance.

Most people, after overcoming the initial shock and/or curiosity at first seeing me, were motivated to help. They erroneously assumed, on the basis of their visual assessment, that I needed help to do a variety of mundane, everyday things and were invariably surprised at the realization that I didn't require assistance. My independence was unlimited, frequently to the point that those who would like to have helped me in a gracious and genuinely helpful, but frequently patronizing manner, were taken aback at my refusal of aid. I was adamant and constantly at work at it. Before anyone could ask, "Can I help you?" I had already accomplished whatever it was that prompted the offer and the Good Samaritan was awarded a look, not always with a smile, but with a firm "No thank you, I believe I can manage." Most often, the offer to assist died incomplete on the person's lips as they saw what they perceived to be the need for assistance disappear. Ultimately my independent attitude became such a driving force in my life that those who had occasion to be with me frequently, including friends from childhood, learned not to offer assistance, and I never asked for it.

It is perhaps ironic that even my father ran afoul of my independence on occasion, a problem that became a standing joke between us. Experience had taught me that my disabilities, particularly when discovered by other diners in restaurants, could sometimes generate either impolite stares or on some occasions, obvious revulsion. Accordingly, whenever I dined at a restaurant with my family, since I used my right arm to effectively hold a knife while I cut my meat or to hold the bread as I buttered it, I would always take a seat that placed me in a position of least visibility to other diners. Each time we entered a restaurant and were shown to our table, my father, thinking only of my comfort, would invariably delay our being seated while he asked me where I preferred to sit. It was only with great difficulty that I finally convinced him to ignore the problem, that I was always thinking ahead and planning my actions accordingly. "Dad, as soon as we enter I know exactly where I'm going to sit and I assure you I will arrange to sit there. I will be way ahead of you. You don't have to worry about it. As a matter of fact, I don't think it's possible for you to stop me from sitting just where I want to sit."

My independence was, nevertheless, an exhausting process; it required planning every move as far ahead as possible. It was necessary to stay one step ahead of everyone, in thought, intent, and ultimately deed. Because my tolerance for standing and walking was extremely limited, I always projected the logistics for even a simple activity like attending a performance. I estimated the time for every move, where to park, where to walk and when to arrive, in order to assure that I would not be caught in a situation that would require unanticipated standing or walking which would cause additional pain. While others could casually stroll to an event or stand in line without concern, I had to be certain that I would be on my feet no longer than it was absolutely necessary. In order to accomplish this, I constantly assessed all of my alternate options, planning how I could take advantage of them while maintaining the appearance of being as natural and casual in the situation as was everyone else. Without question, my physical stress might have been alleviated by accepting assistance or letting it be known that a specific activity was difficult, but the independence I had learned at my mother's knee, and my life experience that had generated a determination to never rely on others no matter what the consequences, were so powerful that I was unable to permit myself to be placed in a position where I would be the recipient of such assistance. Illogically, I used my refusal of assistance to prove that I was not disabled.

My indomitability no doubt ultimately worsened my situation, for in numerous instances, had I requested it, assistance of the type that could have eased my daily stress would have been forthcoming. I would not, I could not, ask. Stemming from my earliest years, concealment of all aspects of my disabilities had become an integral part of my life, approaching almost a kind of martyrdom or masochism. My disabilities were physical only. I perceived them as my personal, private problem and I was determined I would live my life in spite of them and without assistance, so I concealed my pain from even my closest associates and I maneuvered the logistics of my life to minimize my energies and discomfort. When that was not possible I simply bore the pain, which, as I reached maturity, increased in proportion to my increased activities.

6

Inclusion, Exclusion, Discovery

The City of Pittsburgh Board of Education conducted a special Saturday morning program known as Tam O'Shanters, for children who showed exceptional talent in art. While still in the sixth grade, I was invited to attend. On Saturday mornings during the school year I attended a class of approximately two hundred children that met in the Carnegie Museum from nine until noon to draw with colored pencils and pastels among the varied exhibits under the direction of art teachers, James Fitzpatrick and Henry Steffens. Each year I was invited to return; my participation continued until I entered college.

The instructor selected several student drawings each session as examples and showed them to the class at the beginning of the following week's session, commenting on their fine points. Occasionally, one of my works was selected for this honor. In the fourth year I was promoted to the painting class that met on a balcony in the museum overlooking the Greek sculpture exhibition. Each student artist had his/her own easel, gouache paints, brushes and a water pot and we produced one or more paintings, related to an assigned theme, on large sheets of gray rag paper. As before, the instructor would select several works as examples or to demonstrate a point and again my work was occasionally chosen.

Saturday mornings, Mother would drive me to art class, and while I was in class, she took my brother to the story hour in the main library within the museum building. In the course of numerous visits we all became intimately familiar with the library and museum and it was a regular procedure to return home with books. I had no one to lead me to the classics, but I read all the popular adventure stories, westerns, sea stories, and exploration and fantasy books.

Mother encouraged my expanding my world by traveling alone, so by the time I was in junior high school and going to school on the trolley, I used my student pass to go to and from the art classes by myself. The museum was located in Pittsburgh's cultural center surrounded by the city's finest public park, the University of Pittsburgh's stately sixty story Cathedral of Learning, the then fashionable Scheneley Park Hotel, and Forbes Field, the home of Pittsburgh's baseball and football teams. On the hill behind the University's skyscraper was Pitt Stadium, where University home games were played. Following my art lesson on those Saturdays when the Pitt team was playing a home game, I rode the streetcar five blocks, enjoyed a hamburger and a milkshake for a quarter at Isaly's ice cream store, and then trudged several blocks up the hill around the huge oval wall of the stadium to the end zone entrance where, for the student price of twenty-eight cents, I was admitted to the game. For a few years I saw almost every home game, sitting alone on a woolen blanket encased in a seat cushion carrier until it got too cold, and then wrapping myself up in it. Despite cold or inclement weather, rain or snow, I always stayed for the entire game and afterwards retraced my steps down the hill and rode the three streetcars home. It was with a sense of one-upmanship that I related pertinent comments to neighborhood friends about this or that game I had seen. During the same years boys and girls could see the Pittsburgh Pirates baseball games at Forbes Field for the same price and my friends had great interest in seeing them. I went to one game to see the Pittsburgh Pirates, but was not as thrilled by baseball and never accompanied them again.

During my last year of high school, the last year of my involvement in the Saturday Art Program, the advanced classes were conducted in the Art Department on the campus of Carnegie Tech where I was hoping to be accepted as an undergraduate. Sculpture class, in which I was enrolled, was held in a dungeon like room in the Sculpture Department in the school basement. We sat closely packed on either side of long tables in a low ceilinged room where we worked with plastilene, a plastic, non-hardening clay.

The class was an unusually enjoyable social and aesthetic experience. We were all high school juniors and seniors, most of us planning to attend college to study art, and there was exhilarating collegiate intercourse. While taking this course in the winter of 1943-4, I submitted my application to the Painting and Design Program in the Art School at Carnegie Tech.

Incoming freshmen had a choice of three majors: drawing, painting or sculpture. My most recent Saturday morning class was an exciting new experience for me and I had developed a considerable interest. With little thought and no understanding as to how such training might enable me to earn a living, and lacking advice from anyone knowledgeable, I chose sculpture.

Due to participation in the Saturday classes, I wasn't required to take technical tests for admission, but my high school Math and English left something to be desired. In the spring of 1944, therefore, I was informed that I would be accepted as a freshman for the fall semester depending on the results of academic tests, to be taken during the summer. At seventeen, while others my age were going to summer camps or working summer jobs, I was still a part of the family vacation plan, which was a two-week cottage rental on a lake one hundred miles north of Pittsburgh. The announced dates of the academic tests were in conflict with our second vacation week, so I planned to drive the family car home, stay overnight, take the test the next day and then drive back to the lake.

It had been my practice since early childhood, when at home and not expecting visitors, to frequently remove my shoes in order to ease my discomfort. I was able to move about the house on my knees with great agility. Years of such activity had developed calluses on my knees and had never resulted in any problems, but unfortunately, during the first week at the lake, I developed what proved to be an infection of the bursa of my left knee. In a matter of hours, the knee was so swollen that I could not bend it or walk. I was taken to a local doctor who surgically aspirated the bursa. The wound was medicated and bandaged and I was given instructions for the application of poultices. By the day prior to the test, the swelling had receded and I could again stand and bear weight on the leg.

The family car at the time was one of the newer Oldsmobiles featuring Hydromatic Drive, one of the first automatic transmissions, which enabled me to drive without using my left leg. I drove the hundred miles home by myself, stayed overnight, took the tests the next day and returned to the family that evening. In a few weeks I was informed that I had been admitted to the Sculpture Department.

On arrival to register in the Sculpture Department I was given an orientation by an upper class student who casually informed me how the department operated. "These cans (fifty gallon steel garbage cans) are what we mix the clay in. We grind up the used clay, pulverize it, add additional new clay powder and water and let it sit for several days. Then we strain it to remove any impurities and let the water evaporate until it's the correct consistency. Then we have to take it out and work it like dough until it develops body and is useable. It's a messy process. You'll need to have a separate set of shoes and clothes that you can use here in the studio and leave here, because they'll get totally impregnated with the clay. You'll find the lockers and the showers over there." I was suddenly alert. Shoes? Lockers? Showers? I hadn't anticipated this kind of situation. I couldn't do this. I couldn't handle undressing and showering in this kind of a situation. Unlike the boys to whom I had handed towels in the showers in junior high school, I had never had the experience of the male locker room and I wasn't prepared for it. I wasn't a prude and didn't care about being seen naked, but revealing my disabilities was another matter. In any event, without shoes I was unable to stand and would have to crawl in and out of the showers on my knees. It was a completely impossible situation. I would require a number of special arrangements, and it simply wasn't possible to have two pairs of shoes. My single pair, with the prostheses installed, was what I wore every day, no matter how I dressed or where I went. They were all I had.

I made a quick, pragmatic decision. I thanked the upper classman and sought out the department head. "I think I've made a mistake. I don't believe I'm going to be able to handle some of the physical aspects of the work in this department." It was the first time I had ever suggested that some accomplishment was beyond me, and I knew that in actuality the physical aspects weren't beyond me, but I wasn't prepared to deal with the circumstances that surrounded them and how they impacted on my disabilities and privacy. Even as I spoke to the department head, I was unable to bring myself to a frank and open discussion of the real reasons for my concern. Had I done so, I might have been a sculptor, but the pattern of lifetime secrecy about my disabilities prevailed. It was my problem; I had to solve it on my own, whatever that required, and if that meant that I would not be able to do what I wanted to do, then that's the way it was. The department head was sufficiently sensitive to my concern to not press the issue. "Would you like to change your program preference?"

"Yes. I think that's what I need to do."

"In that case you'd best take it up with the registrar. I don't think there'll be any problem." There wasn't. The registrar, in consideration of my long-time involvement in the Saturday morning classes, facilitated my transfer to the Department of Painting and Design.

College was in many ways a continuation of my high school experience. During the day I was consumed by the academic schedule of in-class activities which involved exposure to a new and wonderful world of social contact, intellectual discussion and aesthetic stimulation unlike anything I had ever experienced, in a world of middle to upper middle class behavior and expectation that was new to me, but when classes were finished for the day, I again returned, intellectually, aesthetically, socially and physically, to my working class milieu. My evenings were invariably spent in the company of those friends and associates from the neighborhood with whom I had grown up, whom I knew intimately, but with whom I did not find the stimulating experience of the college environment that was becoming increasingly and enjoyably familiar.

While my college classmates were spending their free evening hours attending campus concerts, plays, cocktail parties and fraternity beer parties on the weekends, I was attending small neighborhood dances—at which I didn't dance, and hopping from one local bar to another, searching for I knew not what, and in the process wasting time that could have been better spent on my studies. My growth at this point in my life, instead of surging ahead into that world of new sensitivities and values that enthralled and excited me, was instead a schizophrenic assemblage of conflicting values and emotions which hovered over me, like a stalled weather front, and retarded any movement to either withdraw from my historical milieu, or to enter the new one which enticed me. Mine was a separation that was both physical and intellectual.

On New Year's of my freshman year at college, my neighborhood friends were planning on going out together to a roadhouse to celebrate. Everyone had a date but me. I had been dating no one at college or at home and knew no girls I could invite with any chance that they might accept. Marty said, "I'll get somebody for you" and arranged for a friend of the girl he was dating to be my date. She was attractive, pleasant and made herself at home in a group of strangers and we enjoyed the evening. It was a week later that one of my friends asked me if I'd seen the latest newspaper. When I arrived home I picked up the newspaper and there, on the front page, under the heading "Gang Moll Arrested" was the picture of my New Year's Eve date.

Most Carnegie Tech students lived on campus. Its student body came from all over the country and from foreign countries, and there was an active Greek life with numerous fraternities and sororities. At the end of classes each day, the social life on campus blossomed. At the beginning of the term, the fraternities and sororities were consumed with rushing, the process whereby they each examined the lists of new students and made their selections for new members. Prospective members were invited to attend parties and dances so they could be closely examined by members to determine whether they would be invited to join. New students attended as many different Greek functions as possible, trying to sort out the differences between them in order to develop preferences in anticipation of being invited to join. The social frenzy continued for a few weeks until the memberships were proffered and accepted. Those without invitations to join a fraternity or sorority were then eliminated from direct involvement in that aspect of college life and had to pursue activities elsewhere. For some it would become the highlight of their college years; others were reduced to a sort of second-class citizenship unless they had the ability to develop their personas via sports, academic achievements, or individual interests. There were also those who, either mature for their years or already dedicated to a career plan, had no interest in Greek social life, content in the knowledge that they were pursuing their goals and not wishing to be encumbered with what they perceived as distractions. For commuting students like myself who departed the campus at the end of classes each day to work or travel home, there was less hope of being an integral part of the continuing social life on campus unless they possessed outstanding characteristics or personal accomplishment that distinguished them as individuals.

I had no specific career plans, indeed, I had no idea of what career possibilities might be open to me, and in addition I was both naïve and immature. I was in college because my parents had determined that an education was an advantage and I needed any advantage I could get. Moreover, in their deep concern for the type of employment that might be possible for their disabled child, they had focused on my artistic talent and although they had no idea how that talent translated into employment, they believed that developing my artistic skills would ultimately provide the best chances for a productive life. I, too, had no idea how, as an artist, I might earn a living, but I had confidence in my abilities and was eager to improve them.

As the first in my family to enter college, I was breaking new ground. No one in the family or among family friends had ever been to college or could offer advice. While my parents were deeply motivated and highly supportive, they had no experience or perspective of the process in which I was now involved. I was literally on my own.

The structure and organization of college life was a mystery to me as I followed the instructions given to freshmen, collecting books and supplies, locating classrooms and fulfilling the sequential freshman routine. Since I arrived in the morning, attended classes, and then went home each day, I was not privy to the informal discussions or activities that took place after class whereby freshmen learned about campus life and the social activities that were available. And there was little time for such discussions during class. During the second week I overheard two classmates talking about the fraternity/sorority rushing process, discussing the parties they had attended and those to which they were going. My naïve question, "How does the rushing happen?" was met with unbelieving stares and I was given a brief and condescending answer by two fellow students that nevertheless provided me with some information, enough to realize that there were a lot of things happening on campus about which I knew nothing. My assessment of my informers was that they were enormously more experienced and sophisticated than I was, and although their manner intimidated me, I continued to question until I had some sense of what was occurring. One of them, a tall, handsome, athletic blond, was a professional dancer just returned from being in the chorus of a Broadway show; the other had no such personal glitter, but did have a shrewd understanding of what it took to get where he wanted to go and he had no time for anyone who could not help him. The dancer was generating his own equity as an important addition to any fraternity, the importance of which the second fellow, by association, hoped to utilize for his own purposes. It was clear he perceived that befriending the dancer, whose professional performance skills and ad-lib performances had already been noticed by the fraternities, could help him.

During the next week I waited patiently and with hopeful anticipation that in the examination of the lists of new students by the fraternities, my name might be noticed and an invitation issued, before they found out about my disabilities; I knew I'd never make it with a personal appearance, but I was never contacted. My presence did not go unnoticed in class however. In my innocence I had, at the end of my high school year, in keeping with the dress modes of my friends, adopted a conservatively modified version of what at the time was glamorized by popular performers, a full drape "one button roll" double-breasted suit coat with padded shoulders and trousers minimally pegged at the bottom to affect a balloon type appearance. It was what, in extreme versions, was characterized as a "zoot suit." In my lack of sa'voir-faire' I didn't realize that in my new environment my costume, in association with the unusual nature of my physical disabilities, combined to focus attention on my appearance to the point of making it bizarre. In this new college environment most common college dress consisted of khaki slacks, white bucks and fatigue jackets of the returning war veterans, and Scottish tweed sport coats and conservative three button Brooks Brothers suits of the upper classes. One talented fellow art student saw fit to capture the combination of my suit and my disabilities in a deliberately caustic and discriminating cartoon that was posted anonymously on the Department bulletin board. Discovered early by another more empathetic student who ultimately became a dear friend, it was removed and destroyed. Without being aware of it, I was faced, not only with a disability which I could not hide and of which I was well aware and able within reason, to handle, but with the behavior and values of my working class origins that until now I had never had reason to question. In one way I was fortunate. Had I been immersed more directly into the social scene of campus life, there is little doubt that I would have suffered significant embarrassment regarding my behavior, my naïveté, and my dress as well as certain of my values. As it happened, my exposure to campus life, to the degree I experienced it, was fortunately peripheral, and largely confined to my classes albeit opening no doors into the broader college community. As I became acquainted with my classmates, I was able to glean from them a second-hand understanding of the life and activities in which they, living on campus, were engaged.

Slowly, as I became familiar with my new environs and more observant, I began to alter my behavior and language, as well as my values. My education had begun. I was not the only student who had come from the working class, but I was perhaps one who had the least experience in the give and take of adult social intercourse and the nature of polite society. On occasion I was afforded a glimpse of the world beyond the one in which I had grown up, sometimes with humorous overtones.

The first time I tasted lobster was such a time; I didn't care for it. The occasion was my first experience at a polite dinner party; I was only eighteen, a freshman. I had no knowledge of cuisines, culinary arts or gourmet dishes; even the terminology was foreign to me. I was a "which fork do I use" person and had never faced the task of eating a lobster tail, served in its shell. The dinner, an invitation from the parents of a new college friend, took place on a small patio at the rear of a house that, to my inexperienced eye, was most impressive. The flagstone patio was small and on two levels. It was a warm summer evening and the area was illuminated with candles in glass chimneys hung on black wrought iron hangers. It was essentially an "eat on your lap" type of arrangement. A few small tables held accessories, a perfect setting for a comedy featuring a one-handed, non-sophisticate, on a candlelit, flagstone patio in mixed company confronting, for the first time, a lobster tail in the shell on a plate on his lap. On the one hand, I was petrified. On the other, the inherent comedy of the situation did not escape me. I desperately wanted to appear nonchalant as my mind raced to deal with the micro-logistics of this complex situation. Taking a lobster tail out of its shell with one hand was a formidable task. I kept thinking what Harold Lloyd might have done. Now add some melted butter in a small sliding cup, a side dish or two, a passing relish tray and some breads. I fluctuated between panic and hysterics as I tried to cope. I was almost convulsed in laughter at the complete absurdity of the situation, my physical struggle and the struggle to contain the hilarity that was engulfing me and threatening to explode, plus my concern that my hostess could possibly be enormously embarrassed if perceived to be insensitive to my needs. With considerable shifting, balancing and rearranging, I managed to survive with minimal damage to the lobster, my clothes or the surroundings. I've always thought I didn't do too badly for I was invited back...much later. For many years I've enjoyed the memory of that occasion, and learned to love lobster.

My academic program was heavily weighted in studio work: drawing, design, color theory, painting, model making, industrial processes and materials. College life, although physically difficult and socially unrewarding, was nevertheless aesthetically and intellectually stimulating. With only a limited number of liberal arts courses included in my program of study: English, Psychology, and History of Arts and Civilization, the latter course attracted my attention. Discussion of the evolution of civilization and the arts raised questions about religion, its function, its use, and its empirical beginnings—or lack thereof—and I began to question the viability of the religious faith in which I had been raised.

My home sheltered persons of two different religions. My experience was that neither religion contained or required anything that precluded their practitioners from having a loving and understanding relationship and a happy and loving family, nor did either present any unique answers to the problems I dealt with in my life. I was also aware, from first hand relationships with God-loving Christians, of anti-Semitism. As I matured, I realized that love within my family and our relationships with one another superseded any possible benefits that either of my parent's religions offered. Neither of their religions, nor any others as far as I could determine, had anything to offer beyond the practical morality and respect I had learned pragmatically in my home. My studies of the beginnings of civilization and development of cultures made me question the spiritualistic concept of an omnipotent God which I had been taught, and I abandoned it in favor of a less emotional and more rational explanation, evolution, a decision I've never had cause to change or regret.

My lack of knowledge of the English language haunted me in my freshman English class with Gladys Schmitt, whose then newest novel "David the King" had just made the best seller lists. Knowledge of concepts of grammar and syntax to which I had never been introduced in my working-class high school English classes were assumed and discussed. Though I lacked knowledge of them, my saving grace was an ability to tell a story, and my written work generated sufficient credit to offset my inadequacies.

Most of my studio classes were three or four hours long; some lasted all day. Work was done either on easels or on a 20 by 30 inch wood drawing board to which we attached a small screen door handle to facilitate carrying. The drawing board was essential for work done at home. It never occurred to me to buy two drawing boards so that I could keep one at home. The $225 tuition fee for the first year plus an additional $75 for supplies had been a considerable expenditure. There were no funds to spare, so when homework assignments required, I carried the drawing board, together with a large artist's portfolio and a book or two, on the long walk across campus from the Art building to the streetcar line, struggled my load onto three streetcars, and finally up my steep street. Usually, I was able to manage the trip without trouble, but when the car was crowded with people returning home from the day's work and I was unable to find a seat, it became a torturous effort.

I noticed that informal gatherings: teas, cocktail parties, coffees, and the like were invariably affairs in which people stand and talk to each other, move from group to group, and seek out those with whom they can relate. As I learned later, at work and socially, standing and talking in large or small groups (networking) was a standard format for such gatherings, each person searching for the one they want to meet or proposition. Only those who have something others want can afford to find a comfortable seat and wait for their constituency to gather round. With a teacup or a glass in my hand I couldn't shake hands so I'd take a drink, drink it quickly and sit the glass down. I could stand for only a brief time and although I pushed myself to the point where the pain was unbearable, the time quickly arrived when I had to excuse myself from whatever group or conversation in which I was fortunate enough to be included, find a place to sit and rest, and plan how I would make it to my car, or to the trolley and home. I noticed that a person in a wheelchair could function more easily. Wheelchairs make a statement and the condition of their users is tangible and visible.

People show deference to it. People in them can move from group to group and people take notice. Although my disabilities were obvious, my discomfort was invisible and I was unable to find a graceful or non demeaning way to let anyone know about it.

The realization that it was unlikely that I would become involved in campus social life to any extent motivated my search for other ways to be a part of campus life and to perhaps meet students other than those with whom I took classes. I made three attempts.

I discovered that it was possible to earn a college athletic letter and the right to wear a team sweater by becoming a manager or even assistant manager of an athletic team. Investigating the matter, I opted to become an assistant manager of the college swimming team and with no difficulty, established myself in that capacity. The activity was less than exciting, but with my eye on the coveted big chenille "C" and a tartan sweater on which to wear it, I was happy to maintain the records of the swim team, pass out towels as I had done in junior high school, and generally serve as a "go for" for the coach during the off season practices that were currently under way. As the initial weeks went by, although I couldn't swim, I learned a lot about swimming by listening to the coach and watching the swimmers Then came the first inter-collegiate swim meet. The other manager was assigned the first meet and, since it was not a home meet, I did not accompany the team. At the next practice session he told me the story. We had won, and as tradition demanded, the team threw him in the pool. Alarms went off in my head. I could not be thrown in the pool. I could not swim, and in any event, the water would seriously diminish the shock absorbency, if not the condition, of my prostheses. If I were thrown in the pool I would be unable to walk, I would not be able to repair the damage, and I would have to explain, either before or after being thrown into the pool that my shoes were my only pair and could not be immersed in water. I made a reluctant, but quick decision. I sought out the coach and instead of simply explaining my situation, invented a reason why I could not continue as a manager, shattering my dream of attaining the coveted letter. My perception that it was my private problem and my responsibility to solve it resulted in denying myself something I desired. It never occurred to me that a simple explanation might have resulted in understanding and cooperation.

My interest in participating and gaining recognition did not stop, however. I made another attempt. The following spring the Beaux Arts Ball, temporarily discontinued during World War II, but long a traditional and major social event of the Art School, was to be resumed. The organization and management of the affair was to be handled by the Men's Honorary, Phi Beta Kappa. One of the first of the veterans returning to complete schooling interrupted by the war was a tall, handsome, sandy-haired Errol Flynn type known in his pre-war college days as a bon vivant and for his devil may care attitude. He had barely returned to campus when he was afforded the responsibility of decorating the first floor of the Art School for the Ball. Almost before realizing it, I was involved in his project, working endless hours after classes. The effort continued for several weeks during which massive wall hangings were painted and hung in the ovular main entrance to the building and a twenty-foot high paper Mache figure of Buddha was erected above the entrance.

The motivation for my labor was the potential reward of an invitation to become a member of the Men's Honorary, usually issued to those who worked on such projects. As preparations for the ball progressed, it attracted the attention of Life magazine which sent a photographer to cover the event and generated great excitement on campus and in the city newspapers. The ball was a success and I attended it in costume, sans date; I didn't want to miss this very high visibility event. In the weeks that followed I awaited the announcement of the new members of the Men's Honorary. When it came, my fellow student's name was on the list; mine was not. I was given an Honorary Key, to be worn on my key chain, a kind of Honorable Mention, but I wasn't invited to become a member. I hadn't made the social grade.

Sophomore year was a difficult one. The work was intense, the weather was cold and the end of the semester brought with it the usual charette, as students prepared their work for "judgement" the grading procedure at which the semester's work was evaluated by the entire faculty. All of the hundreds of pen, pencil, charcoal sketches, paintings, designs and three dimensional models and exercises had to be culled, selected and then mounted, framed and identified on what seemed to be endless 22" x 28" white poster board sheets and submitted by the deadline. It required almost two weeks of never ending work, and classes continued until the last week. It was also necessary to take time out from the work to take tests in academic subjects. During the week after deadline, all work was transported to the attic of the building where the studios of the faculty were located. In the wide hallway extending the length of the building, student work was mounted on the walls by the Massier, Russell Twiggs, in charge of all student work. Faculty, seated on chairs mounted on a large riser with wheels, would be pushed slowly along the exhibition, collectively discussing and judging the merits of each submission. Exceptional works were stamped with the word "placed" which indicated that they were above the general level of the class work. These placed works would be subsequently exhibited on the walls of the main corridor on the floor where classes were held.

During the last weeks of the term, there was frequent comment by several students in the class that as soon as judgment was over; we were "taking off," to celebrate. How this was to happen, or just who was to be included was unknown, but it was agreed by all that after the tedious and exhausting semester, it was a time for celebration, and it was decided that we should drive south to warmer weather. As the days passed a group of seven of us, two men and five women emerged who were ready to do something, anything.

In the course of the semester's work, I had developed friendships with several women in my classes. With one in particular I had developed a close friendship based on popular music and, what was exciting to me, a seeming man-woman relationship which included double entendre jokes and references to sexual behavior, all in a light manner. I had never before enjoyed what I now perceived as a friendly and intimate conversational relationship with a woman, and, based on my previously unsuccessful relationships with girls, I had no intention of risking what I had by attempting to push it further.

I was aware that I was infatuated with this woman, but rationalized that she, like some others I had approached, had better things to do with her time than spend it with me. Also, I sensed in her an experience and sophistication which daunted me and I was quite certain that I was neither sufficiently sophisticated nor experienced to live up to her expectations and so resigned myself somewhat reluctantly, to enjoying her company in the context of our class time camaraderie.

The group organized. The other fellow was able to borrow his family's car. The stage was set for everyone to leave as soon as we were able to turn in our work. One of the group, in the excitement of the moment, suggested that we should drive south to Hagerstown, Maryland, where, we stupidly assumed, the weather during the winter would be warmer. Amid much laughing and shouting, enjoying the relief from the long, exhausting semester, we left in the afternoon. The other fellow drove with two of the girls sharing the front seat. I was in the back with the other three, seated jammed in tightly to my would-be lady love, who immediately wriggled and twisted into a comfortable and intimate position which required, in the cramped space, placing my right arm around her shoulders. This prompted her to lay her head on my shoulder and turn toward me inviting a private sotto voce conversation from which we occasionally emerged to participate in the flow of conversation. The cramped quarters soon became uncomfortable for four seated abreast and at some point she suggested that she sit on my lap thereby easing the situation, a suggestion with which I readily agreed. On my lap, with her arm now around my shoulder, she lay back against me and as I raised my head she lowered hers and we kissed. I was astounded. I had kissed a number of girls, but always it was a goodnight kiss, given hastily and briefly or as a reward for having provided an evening auto ride, snack or favor; never, I thought, because it was what the girl wanted to do. Now, in this ridiculous situation, I was being kissed as never before, by someone who, it was clear, was giving me every indication that she meant it. I didn't understand what was happening to me, but I was certainly overwhelmed by the circumstances and could only continue to enjoy the moment. Like a thirsty desert traveler, I had reached an oasis.

For a number of months, I enjoyed a close relationship with my lady and for the first time felt the joy of being wanted by a mature, desirable young woman. I held no illusions that the relationship was anything but here and now and the more I learned about her the more I was intimidated by the gap in our respective life experiences and sophistication. Through the spring semester we enjoyed dating and, as commuting students, attended a few campus activities although I realized that my social and financial capabilities had little to offer her. At the end of the sophomore year, when the art faculty enacted a qualitative forty to fifty percent reduction of the size of the class that would be permitted to continue into the junior year, her name was not on the list of those who had survived. Without the class context and the daily contact, the relationship ended, although I wanted desperately for it to continue. I knew that chances of my finding another woman who would feel about me that way, someone who could see the person inside the disabled body and respond to it, was most unlikely.

I made a final attempt to belong. During the spring of my junior year, a classmate mentioned that the Spring Carnival Committee was searching for a person to take charge of decorating the gym that would be the venue for the major event, the Spring Carnival Dance, featuring a big name big band. I inquired and found myself in charge of decorating for the dance. My plan was a simple one, in keeping with the limited budget available, but the dance and organizing committee delivered a large number of volunteers to do the work. With great quantities of red and white crepe paper and numerous volunteers, we turned the gym into a massive circus tent surrounded by a train of cardboard circus wagons with the entire floor open for dancing. I didn't have a date for the dance, so I volunteered to take tickets at the door.

When graduation day arrived I was not motivated to attend. I didn't want my college days to end, had accomplished no particular achievements, would receive no awards, and had enjoyed no recognition. I was just one of the graduating group with no idea of what might be in store for me beyond college. Graduation was closing a door on what had been an enjoyable time of my life, but now it was over and I had no wish to celebrate. It was not a happy time. I would have avoided the commencement ceremony entirely had it not been for the great pride and satisfaction of my parents. I was the first in the family to receive a college degree and for my family it was an enormous occasion. Graduation itself was a blur. I didn't understand the logistics, was confused about the seating and the procession, and disoriented throughout the ceremony. When called, I made my way to the dais and was handed a diploma that was not mine (the diplomas were distributed without regard to whom they belonged); it remained for the graduates (in an anteroom following the ceremony) to trade back and forth until each person found and obtained his/her own diploma. I knew none of this beforehand. I was not in the loop. I found it a final indignity in a ceremony I had wanted to avoid in the first place.

Without college there was a vacuum in my life. For four years all of my waking hours had focused on school; college was my entire world. Days were busy with class work in company of people I had grown to know well and enjoy. Nights were either occupied with study or, with decreasing frequency, in the company of neighborhood friends, from whom I had drifted apart. I preferred the values and offerings that college had opened to me, and I had now left it having had no opportunity to establish links from it to the larger world of similar values beyond.

During the four college years, unlike most of my fellow students, I had had very limited social exposure, and no travel. The world of work awaited me. I had absolutely no experience in it, nor any clue as to where I might find employment. Unlike friends in the neighborhood and at college, I had never had the experience of being employed. My strength and endurance had been greatly challenged in meeting the requirements of being a full-time student. The complex factors of limited available time and special transportation needs had precluded consideration of even part-time employment while at school.

Suddenly, my life was empty. I had nothing to occupy my time, no idea of where I might fit into the commercial world or how to go about gaining entry. In retrospect, it is puzzling that I had no plans, no dreams, no ideas as to what I might be able to do or how to go about doing it. It was as if I had been living in a vacuum. I had no one to advise me, and no understanding of how to obtain help. I was supposedly a trained artist/designer, with no idea who might hire me, how to contact potential employers, or proceed with the rest of my life. My parents, knowing nothing of the type of work for which I had ostensibly been trained, and having no connections with the world of industry or art, were equally bewildered. It was as if all my connections to a world to which I had become accustomed had been severed. I was isolated; for eighteen months I vegetated. I was bewildered, unknowing, unhappy and unable to creatively plan a way out of my situation.

7

The World of Work

When I graduated college, my father's store window display, or as he called it, "window-trimming" business, was doing well, but as with most one-man businesses, was extremely demanding of his time. His clients, owner-operators of men's, women's' and children's clothing and shoe stores, were spread across more than two hundred miles in western Pennsylvania, West Virginia and Central Ohio. Each store was serviced at least monthly, some every two weeks and, when there were special sales, Dad would frequently be called upon to organize the sale, hand letter all the sales signs and price tags, and advise the owner regarding the types of sale merchandise that should be purchased. Two of his customers owned strings of stores and his visits were scheduled to accommodate the owner's schedule and convenience. He flew to stores in central Ohio on the popular DC-3's widely used at the time, and I chauffeured him to and from the airport. His very demanding travel and work schedule frequently required working evenings after the stores had closed, when the owner or an employee was available to assist in the selection of display items and to dress mannequins and display forms. As each season changed, backgrounds and fixtures in each display window were changed to reflect seasonal colors and fabrics, special jobs that took more time than the weekly or monthly "trim." For each seasonal trim, Dad would order new materials to be shipped to the store from Art Cohen's window display company in downtown Pittsburgh. Each storeowner had an approximate budget for a seasonal trim and Dad would use his own judgment in making the purchases.

In the course of being in the business for a number of years, having begun at the end of the Depression, he had developed other income sources in addition to the fees he earned trimming the windows. His relationship with materials and fixtures providers generated commissions from purchases he made for his customer and he also received salesman's commissions on materials his customers purchased directly. He had a similar arrangement with a mannequin manufacturer and refurbisher who also created paper maiche display forms for women's blouses and lingerie. From time to time, Dad would adroitly call a customer's attention to the need to update, repair or restyle his mannequins and then assume responsibility for facilitating the process. With the mannequins refurbished and restyled, Dad would return them to the customer. Each job earned Dad a commission.

As the result of a driving accident in the past, the mannequin refurbisher no longer drove. When he mentioned to my father that he needed a driver to help him deliver mannequins to Steubenville, Ohio, about an hour's drive from Pittsburgh, my father suggested that I could help. On Dad's assurance that I could handle the station wagon with its valuable load, he was willing to take a chance on a handicapped driver whom he did not know. When I was informed of the opportunity, I was happy to have a chance to earn a few dollars.

The trip was uneventful and I had no trouble driving the station wagon. In early evening, at the destination, I parked in front of the store and we began to unload the mannequins, a few pieces at a time. Suddenly, I became aware that I was attracting attention. The contrast of my misshapen legs and feet and the beautiful mannequin arms and legs I was carrying presented an incongruous picture to passersby and one or two people bumped into each other as they stared. Although I wasn't comfortable in the situation, I sensed a certain amount of humor in it. "What the hell", I thought, "let them look. It's not my problem." I received generous payment for the driving and when he later mentioned to Dad that he was looking for someone to work in his shop making display forms that were used variously for blouse, brassiere or jewelry display, once again Dad saw an opportunity for me and suggested that I might be willing to give it a try. Unfortunately, my first job proved to be more difficult than the driving.

The shop, in the basement of an old building on the North Side, was in many ways reminiscent of the sculpture studio at college. The blouse forms consisted of a truncated Venus De Milo type female torso without a back. The work-station was a waist high bench on which rested the concave plaster mold of the form. The materials were a stack of heavy rag paper, a pot of white paste, and a big brush. The process required spraying the mold with a separating agent and building layers of paper in the mold by coating each layer with paste, and squeegying excess paste out to prevent air holes in the form. When thick enough, the form was lifted from the mold and laid on a special rack to dry, then coated with fine plaster, sanded meticulously and spray painted.

Though the process was a simple artisan type of job, and required skills I had learned in model-making at school that were neither difficult nor strenuous, the work had to be done while standing in order to get the leverage and motion needed to press and rub the paper into the mold. By the end of the day, I was covered with plaster dust and in such pain from standing that I could barely make it to the streetcar stop to go home. I had no problem doing the work. I learned quickly to do it satisfactorily, but after a month, the pain of standing at the bench hour after hour proved to be unbearable. I had to quit. Except for this brief work experience, almost two years had passed since my graduation and I had still not found a viable entrée to the world of work.

Fortunately, my father knew another man. In fact he knew two men. They were brothers who owned a plastics manufacturing company. Both Ben and Joe Steiner had been salesmen who now owned a five story brick building just a block from the part of Fifth Avenue that was the wholesale dry goods area where Jewish-owned wholesale houses sold everything imaginable. Ben managed the company sales force and Joe ran the factory that manufactured draperies and curtains made of very thin plastic, and they needed someone to coordinate portions of their marketing activities. They agreed to try me out.

In the fifties, plastic drapes were one of the newest products of technology, enabling working-class housewives to inexpensively dress their homes with a broad variety of visually striking window curtains in all patterns, styles and colors. Joe would order thousands of yards of specific patterns printed on base material from a printing plant in New York City. The printed material arrived on rolls two feet in diameter and 36, 48 or 54 inches wide and would then travel through the factory's five production floors to be cut, stacked, cut again, sewed and packaged until the finished curtains ended up in the shipping department on the first floor. The curtains were retailed in all major chain stores across the country and the salesmen were kept busy traveling from one purchasing agent to another in their respective territories.

My title of Advertising Manager had neither meaning nor substance —the company did not advertise —but it gave me a feeling of importance. My actual duties were to create single page black and white flyers of each curtain or drape product manufactured, and to keep the salesmen and special accounts supplied with them. Each flyer comprised a picture of a curtain or drape on a window, information on available sizes, and swatches of the actual material, in every available color, neatly edged with pinking shears. A salesman might discover that a certain number was a fast seller and he would call for twenty or thirty flyers of that number express mailed to him so he could sell new customers the hot item. I designed a window curtain display unit, had it erected in my office, and hired a photographer to take pictures of each curtain, ten or twenty at a time. The pictures were sent to the printer together with the layout and specifications. The cutting room cut the swatches and arranged them in bundles and stapled them to the flyers, and I personally completed the packages of samples and mailed them. It was a continuous process with new materials and designs arriving every few weeks. In addition, I designed a company color scheme, a new corporate logo, and a packaging design plan for all shipping boxes, product labels, tags, invoices, and display logos for sales counters. I was pleased at having designed the entire process.

At a company party, singing with a group around the piano, I met an attractive young woman. She complimented my singing and asked if I had ever sung any serious music. I had to tell her that I hadn't and that I really didn't know anything other than what she'd heard. Although I'd been invited several times to sing in my church choir, it was at a time when I was experiencing an increasing disenchantment with religion and wasn't looking for closer ties to a church and so had declined. She asked me if I would be interested in joining a singing group of which she was a member? My reaction was immediate. A serious and friendly gesture by a girl didn't happen to me very often. I recognized it, I needed it, and I responded positively. She explained that the group was the Downtown Chorale, but being a musical illiterate, the name had no meaning for me. It took little time to discover, however, that in Pittsburgh, the Downtown Chorale was the prestigious chorus that sang, once each season, in a major performance with the Pittsburgh Symphony Orchestra. The Chorale at that time was conducted by Lorin Maazel, then a youthful musical boy wonder, later a famous conductor. I met my new friend at the group's next rehearsal and was introduced to Mr. Maazel for whom I sang a few bars of the "Donkey Serenade." Maazel's only comment was, "Second tenor, over there", and pointed to a tiered section of narrow portable stadium seats on which the choir stood as they sang. I was handed a musical score and shown my place in the second tenor section. The Chorale was rehearsing *Beethoven's Ninth Symphony* for a performance with the orchestra in a month's time. Mr. Maazel signaled for attention and the rehearsal began. I immediately knew I was out of my depth. Singing familiar pop songs was one thing; singing Beethoven, from the musical score, in German was something else. I couldn't read music, I was completely unfamiliar with the *Ninth Symphony*, and despite my maternal German heritage, neither spoke nor read German. I was chagrined that I had willingly inserted myself into a situation that was so obviously absurd, but it also struck me that my immediate situation was not without humor. Despite the strain of trying to maintain my balance as I stood on the narrow stadium seat with nothing to hold on to for support, while at the same time attempting to provide at least the appearance of singing the unfamiliar German words to music I'd never heard before, I couldn't help seeing the humor in my situation and remembered the time years before when I had tried to eat lobster. During the course of the rehearsal Conductor Maazel shouted and pointed at me twice. Both times he said, "Sing!"

My immediate goal was to get through the rehearsal without falling and without making a complete ass of myself. The rehearsal seemed to go on forever, and exciting as it was to be welcomed into such a group, and as delighted as I would be to be able to do it, I knew that singing second tenor with the Downtown Chorale was definitely not in my future. Even if I knew the music and could speak German, I couldn't attempt it, because the choir stood for a long time on the narrow choir stands, before, during and after performance. I was unable to stand for such a long time and had great difficulty balancing on the narrow stands. I tried in vain to figure out how it might be physically possible for me to continue, but no solution presented itself. I lacked the words, as well as the courage to explain my situation to my newfound friend, so I simply thanked her and talked casually about the next rehearsal, which I never attended. I couldn't even bring myself to call her afterwards. I could only think that, if I hadn't been so ignorant, I would never have even been there. Sometime later, with a dear friend, a lover of Beethoven with an extensive knowledge of music and familiar with my very limited musical awareness, I chose just the right moment to sing the phrase, "Zeid un schlungen Millionen," startling and surprising him. As I told him of my experience we both had a good laugh. Given time I might have memorized both the music and the language and would have enjoyed being a part of the performance, but it just wasn't possible. I considered making a try for a later performance, but the physical strain it would entail was simply too much.

******

During my tenure at Steiner's, my father dropped me off at work in the morning and frequently picked me up after work. When that wasn't possible I'd walk the short block to the streetcar stop and take the streetcar home. It was only with great difficulty that I was able to move around the city via public transportation, however, and I had to plan carefully so that I would not be caught without a place to rest. Whenever possible, my father would generously, frequently, and at an inconvenience to himself, arrange for me to use the car. On those occasions he took the bus, making his working day longer and more complicated. There was nothing that he and Mother would not do in their attempt to assist my physical needs, but it became increasingly obvious that if I were eventually to be able to functionally move about the city with some relative comfort and security and be able to work, I would have to have my own transportation. In 1949, post war automobile production was still far behind the orders for new automobiles and cars were

• •

difficult to obtain. Automobiles had not been produced since the beginning of the war, and used cars were old and well used.

My father never considered my getting a used car. He didn't want me to be encumbered by the lack of dependability and inevitable need for repairs on a used car. He had had that experience and didn't want it for me. He wanted me to have a new car and as usual, he knew a man. He always knew a man. No matter what was needed, he knew a man from whom he could buy wholesale. Dad's sister Sylvia's husband, Jack, owned a wholesale children's clothing store on the "Avenue," as the wholesale district was known. Dad helped out in the store on Sundays when storeowners from the area, some of them his window-trimming customers, would come to make purchases. As a result, he knew every wholesaler on the street. As he prospered with his business, and because he loved his wife and children dearly, he wanted to shower us with gifts, and was always looking for something he thought we needed or could use or would make us happy. It drove Mother to distraction. He would often appear with boxes or packages and present them to Mother. "They just got these in. They're the newest style." or "He only had this one left. Do you like it?" Except for a fox Kalinski and once even a mink coat, which she immediately told him to return, he never brought just one item, but several different styles or colors, knowing he could return them all. On rare occasions Mother would deign to accept a dress or a scarf or a blouse, or stockings, but more often than not she would say, "Sam, I don't need it. Take it back."

She lived in the fear that the more she accepted, the more he would bring home, and being neither a clothes horse nor a spendthrift, she was reluctant to accept his offerings even when the price was wholesale. "If I ask him to get one thing he'll come home with a dozen," she said. During the war if gasoline was needed, Dad could get it. If Mother needed silk stockings, Dad knew where to get them. Now, when he wanted to buy a car he had a Ford dealer friend who, although autos were difficult to obtain, promised him one in six weeks if he was willing to take any color. Six weeks later we took delivery of a maroon, 1950, two door Ford sedan with a manual transmission featuring a gearshift mounted on the steering column and a V-8 engine. The price was $1,585.

******

There's little question that my disabilities drove me to continuously demonstrate that I could do anything anyone else could do, that I was not handicapped.[4] I was very proud of my driver's license and constantly improved my driving skills. Now I began to wonder if someone with disabilities like mine could or would be permitted to learn to fly. Since childhood I'd built model airplanes and was fascinated with airplanes and flying. At twelve I'd had my first airplane ride with a friend of my uncle's, one of Pittsburgh's early pilots, in his Curtis Junior pusher type aircraft. I loved it.

Now that I had a means of transportation I decided to find out, so one day I stopped at a small marina that housed both boats and a flying service. There I was fortunate to meet Bill, a soft-spoken, friendly, middle-aged man who walked with a pronounced limp. As I later learned, he had suffered from both polio and osteomyelitis while still a child and had fortunately survived them both, albeit with some relatively moderate muscular and skeletal disability in his legs. Despite his disabilities, however, he had become an experienced pilot, held commercial and instructor licenses, and was an FAA flight inspector. Bill owned and operated two float mounted J-3 Piper Cub aircraft, the proven old tandem style (one seat in front of the other) warhorse of training planes.

On the basis of his personal experience, Bill assured me that all I need do was apply for a student pilot permit and then obtain a waiver for my physical condition until I was ready to take my license examination at which time my passing or failing would depend entirely on my capability. If I could prove I could do it, I could obtain a license. I was always conscious of my disabilities and their limitations, but I met the challenges as they presented themselves and tried to find solutions to them. When I realized that vehicles eased my life I became expert in operating them and flying presented a new challenge. There were many physical activities in which I was unable to participate. I wondered if I could handle this one. Subliminally and symbolically, it very probably represented a dimension of freedom otherwise unattainable.

---

4 "The stigmatized individual can also attempt to correct his condition indirectly by devoting much private effort to the mastery of areas of activity felt to be closed on incidental and physical grounds to one with his shortcoming. This is illustrated by the lame person who learns or re-learns to swim, play tennis, or fly an airplane, or the blind person who becomes expert at skiing and mountain climbing." (Goffman, p.10)

Following World War II, a pack of cigarettes was 12¢, a gallon of gas was 28¢, and flying instruction cost $12 an hour including both the instructor and aircraft. I filled out the application for a student pilot permit and Bill said he'd have the permit when next we met. He suggested that I come in the late afternoon or early evening when the air was quiet and the flying would be smooth. I made an appointment for my first flying lesson.

You really need two hands to safely fly an airplane. One hand must always be on the control stick and the other must be free to operate the throttle. It was obvious that in order to operate the control stick and the throttle with only one hand, some adjustment had to be made. My designer training took command and I conceived a control stick revision that I knew would be operational, but wasn't certain it would be approved. Today there are a variety of sophisticated electronic, hydraulic and mechanical devises that assist persons with disabilities to drive, but in the 50s I was a little ahead of the times.

The J-3 had a dual control system operated from both forward and rear seats, and when regularly used for passenger rides, one of the control sticks was easily removable by means of a spring clip. I located an unused control stick that could replace the one in the plane, and then I designed and fabricated a full size wooden model of an extension to be mounted at the top of the stick. I had no right hand, but I had full use of my elbow, arm and shoulder, so I built a cuff that attached to my right arm and had a quick action release latch. It fastened to the top of the stick with a universal joint that made it possible to manipulate the stick in any position. I took my wooden model to my neighbor, a foundry man at the Jones and Laughton Steel Works and asked if he could cast the two pieces in aluminum. A week later, with the two pieces in hand, I fabricated a universal joint from a small iron bar and finished up the castings and latch with a drill and two files. When I tried it in the plane it worked perfectly. With the stick clamped to my right arm, I could steer the plane and my left hand was free to operate the throttle.

At $12 per lesson, I tried to take a lesson every week and spent every spare moment at the seaplane base, learning about the aircraft and sitting in the cockpit whenever possible, analyzing and studying as I had done before obtaining my driver's license. The choice of a seaplane had an additional advantage. Most land-based aircraft of pre-WWII vintage had mechanical brakes known as toe brakes that are activated by extending the toes with an ankle motion. I had no ankles, but fortunately, floatplanes had no brakes.

I was filled with enthusiasm, practicing take-offs (full throttle, back the stick to get the floats up on the step, then forward to release the water suction and then back again and off); landings (throttle back, drop the nose, level off, nose up a bit and let it stall); flying S turns across a road, practicing degree of bank against the wind; learning stalls and recovery and doing all the required exercises.

At the end of a year at Steiner's, I received a ten-dollar bonus and a five dollar a week raise. I was disappointed. I had expected more, and in not receiving it I realized my job, though I had done it well, was perceived not as a function that directly related to sales, but simply as a manufacturing function. With that analysis came the instant realization that there was no other job to which I might advance. I still didn't know what I wanted to do, or what I might be able to do, but now that I had worked successfully for a year, I knew I could hold a job and wanted to be able to do something more closely related to my talents and training that might eventually lead to something better. I was almost ready to solo when I began to think about trying to get other work, hopefully as a designer. Without work there would be no more money for flying.

I discussed the situation with my father. The fact that for so many years I had lived on the largesse of my parents shamed me and, although my Dad's business was now going well, there had been times of great financial strain when he had provided for my needs. I was now a college graduate, and I was still a burden. In addition to their taking care of my general needs, he and Mother had given me a car and continued to support me with room and board. My father had found a job for me, that I now wanted to quit. Feelings of inadequacy and guilt were uppermost in my mind and yet I knew that continuing on my present course would not enable me to become independent. I was certain that my work at Steiner's, while keeping me afloat, was ultimately a dead end. Someone with less skill could do it. Surely somewhere, there was a job where my skills might lead to a more satisfying and rewarding situation. My father's reaction was typical. "You're young. If you don't try things while you're young, you'll never have the chance to try later on in life. One way or another, things will work out. If you think you can do it, do it."

I had recently renewed contact with a fellow Tech classmate, Jerry Bell, who had returned to Tech to complete his degree after serving as a bombardier in the Air Force. Jerry was freelancing and although he wanted to do industrial design, he had been successful only in doing two-dimensional layouts and designs for a couple of advertising agencies. After talking with him I began to wonder if perhaps I might be able to get some work as designer.

******

My car made it possible to travel around the city in search of employment. My first year of full employment was a period of enormous growth. I had finally experienced the world of work and begun to develop a sense of the kinds of jobs I might be capable of doing. I was ready to try to find them. I was to learn, however, that it would not be simple, or easy. Many potential employers were reluctant to hire me, because they misconstrued my appearance to be an indication of an inability to perform. They simply didn't understand that my capabilities, even physical ones, transcended what my physical appearance suggested was possible. In addition to misunderstandings about my capabilities, there were some real limitations. One came to light when I had an interview at the Westinghouse plant where there was an opening for a designer. When the quite pleasant interview was almost over, the employment officer told me that I couldn't be hired because the job would require me to walk through the shops and with my disabilities, the company's insurance policy would not cover me. It brought a new dimension to my difficulties. Being an industrial designer required working with machinists, foundry workers, model makers and engineers, more often than not at their work stations to discuss the details of a given job, to experiment with different materials and processes, and to stay abreast of new developments. This was what I had been trained to do. Was it now going to be impossible because of lack of insurance coverage? It was a devastating thought.

In the course of my search, I called on a large industrial display company whose business was creating and fabricating displays for industrial trade shows for clients that were major national corporations. Here I was surprised to encounter a senior designer whom I had known at Tech who had graduated from the same program a year ahead of me. On his recommendation, I was given a month's trial, provisional on my being able to learn the special rendering style that the company used for all their presentations. Gus gave me a number of his own drawings to study. The renderings were done in colored pencil on various shades of charcoal paper and they had a sparkle and professional gloss that was very effective. I was given a few design assignments that were found acceptable, but encountered difficulty in getting the knack of the presentational rendering style that the company preferred. My friend was generous in his support and frequently made recommendations on how to handle the rendering. I worked hard at it and my skills developed quickly, but never quite reached the perfection the company wanted to present to a client. At the end of the month I was told that regretfully, I hadn't made the grade.

At long last, I was learning, the hard way. I tried a smaller display company on the other side of town, one engaged in creating displays primarily for local companies. I was hired as a designer and my renderings, which hadn't been of sufficient quality at the first shop, were here considered more than adequate. This company was creating small displays intended for numerous glass enclosed display windows being installed at the new airport building. In this job I was responsible for creating preliminary sketches of displays that met the client's expressed criteria and then, if approved, developing the construction details in cooperation with the production foreman. Unfortunately, the company did not have steady stream of jobs and the work became uncertain.

I visited Carnegie Tech's campus employment service for alumni and learned that while they did solicit and post jobs, they did so only for engineering school graduates. Employment openings for engineers were well organized, industrial needs were specified, and the college employment service catered to those graduates. Moreover, the engineering curriculum, designed to serve industry in accordance with the precepts of the university's founder, Andrew Carnegie, prepared graduates for specific industrial jobs. The service did not include the Art School. I was astounded and disappointed. It appeared that while a degree in engineering actually qualified an individual for an entry position in industry, a fine arts degree was little more than a permit, and a very limited one, to search for a job as an artist.

I took the opportunity of being on campus to visit my favorite and most respected professor; the person who had most influenced my thinking and understanding, Robert Lepper. Lepper was an unusual man. Analytical, perceptive and enormously talented, Lepper, a professor of Industrial Design, was a distinguished painter, muralist, sculptor, writer, teacher and philosopher who, during a productive career, went quite unappreciated and unrewarded in his local academic environment. His major achievement was synthesizing how humans perceive and respond to their sensory environment into a single taxonomy that, stated simply, was, "The form evolves out of necessity of the content." This brief premise planted millions of seeds in thousands of minds—a process that continues to challenge and inspire those who would presume to instruct in the organization of ideas. Anyone can understand what the words mean, but their implementation may require a lifetime. Lepper's teaching included intensive study of "systems" decades before the word became popularized. His *Elements of Visual Perception* in 1938 was the genesis of hundreds of design curricula in art schools across the United States. Robert Lepper and his colleagues at Pittsburgh's Carnegie Institute of Technology inaugurated the very first college program in industrial design in 1934. His murals became critically regarded as on a par with those of Diego Rivera. [5] As a philosopher, his formidable intellect built whole structures with thoughts, and it is the strength and beauty of these structures that are his most enduring legacy. Among Lepper's many innovative endeavors are his pioneering uses of aluminum as an expressive material. In the words of Dale Stein, another of Lepper's former students, "Lepper, assisted by hand tools only, constructed, assembled, rent, carved, bent, and perforated this familiar substance, transforming it into brilliant structural metaphors of our age. At once architectonic, quirky, and sensual, the works exemplify the contradictions in our society's complex relationships with the machine. Lepper invested these relationships with consummate artistry and wry humor, based on a depth of understanding that

5 Richard Guy Wilson, Program, *The Machine Age In America* 1918-1941, Brooklyn Museum, 1987

reveals, indisputably, the touch of a modern master." It is perhaps a mark of Lepper's creative threat and potential that a number of years later he was informed, by the then head of his department, ironically a person who had been one of his former students, "We will have no stars in this department." His visibility and recognition were subsequently deliberately repressed.

Lepper very thoughtfully recommended me to Louis Blum, one of three brothers who operated the Hyman Blum Ornamental Iron Company. I was hired as a designer/draftsman responsible for translating architect's drawings of building facades into shop drawings from which the structures were fabricated in the shop, then dismantled and shipped to the sites where they were reconstructed and installed. I was delighted to be employed in a job that was interesting and required both imagination and an understanding of construction and production methods. Unfortunately, my workstation was a large drafting table at the edge of the company showroom, isolated from all other work areas, and I was the only draftsman in the organization. I quickly learned to duplicate the architects' designs with various stock configurations of extruded bronze and aluminum. The knowledge I had acquired in the industrial design courses at Tech served me well. I understood the work and the processes, and was conversant with the language and terminology.

Occasionally there were different jobs; designing a sandblasted glass fireplace screen, or a new promotional sales brochure for which I created a number of wash and ink drawings illustrating the kinds of work done by the Blum Company. My tour de force at Blum's was the detail design, specifications and model maker's drawings for a major fabrication of a set of intricate gold anodized, cast aluminum chandeliers to be hung from the highest reaches of the vaulted ceiling in Pittsburgh's St. Paul's cathedral. The project provided me a great sense of accomplishment and pride when I eventually saw the chandeliers hanging in the cathedral.

Hyman Blum, the company's founder, was a very special man. A highly skilled craftsman from Latvia, he had started the company by hiring only European master metal smiths as soon as they arrived in Pittsburgh and the hiring pattern had never changed. Each of the workers was capable, at the forge, of manually creating beautiful decorative works from a simple bar of iron. Hyman was semi-retired and did not come to the shop every day. When he did appear, with a large cigar in his mouth and a homburg on his balding head, his diminutive figure (he was little more than five feet tall) was impeccably turned out in a conservatively cut suit that never had a wrinkle. Always courteous and friendly, Hyman sometimes watched me work at the drafting board, questioning me about details, and when the opportunity arose, advising and gently teaching me how best to solve a particular problem, such as the complicated process of drawing the diminishing circular arc of an Acanthus leaf or a construction drawing of a rail for a descending spiral stairway. I always enjoyed Hyman's visits, and had even greater enjoyment on the few times I was able to accompany him into the shop.

On one such occasion, we stopped by a forge where an employee, a large hulking man, was forging an Acanthus leaf from a one-inch bar of iron. Not liking the way the man was doing the job, the diminutive Hyman asked for the bar and the hammer, and, in his immaculate suit, with cigar in mouth and homburg on his head, plunged the bar into the hot forge. When it had heated enough to satisfy him, he brought it to the anvil and with the skill of a master craftsman, proceeded to hammer out a flawless leaf, heating it once more and then trimming the edges of the red hot metal with a heavy snips. He laid down the hammer, took a puff on his cigar and then thrust the bar at the workman with the words, "Here! That's how to do it!" And the workman nodded, smiled, and said, "Thank you."

Jerry Bell and I both wanted to design products. In addition to our respective jobs, we had a need for a small shop in which to design and experiment with prototypes. Together, we decided to find an inexpensive industrial space and equip it with a few power tools with the idea that perhaps we could obtain some small non-design jobs that would pay for our expenses. We found space in the sub-basement of an old private mansion on Pittsburgh's North Side in what had originally been a storage and wine cellar, reachable only by a freight elevator installed by a previous light industrial company. In short order we were able to acquire a table saw and lathe, a belt sander, a spray gun and compressor and we built a spray booth. We added an electric welder and a manual rod bender to our equipment and taught ourselves to weld. Working evenings in addition to our daytime jobs, we began to look for ways to generate income. Before long, a plastic molder in the building asked us if we could fabricate a couple of wooden molds for his heat-molding process. We could, and did. Next, a crafts shop that sold fine individually produced art works needed a turned wooden bowl that, with a decorative fired enamel on copper plate (created by a local ceramicist), mounted in its center, would be used as a church collection plate. I turned the bowl from a choice piece of walnut. At the time, modern design wrought iron furniture was in vogue and the same store wished to sell custom built black iron units but needed a supplier. We took a chance on designing and building some and concentrated on one or two designs that could be mass-produced. The results were so well received that we produced several sets of bed frames, sofas, tables, bookshelves and cabinets finished with foam rubber, redwood and glass. After a number of tries and several prototypes, we designed a small stacking stool made of black iron and redwood that could be produced and sold in small volume. Seeking additional products, we designed lamps made from driftwood, found three hours north of Pittsburgh at my old fishing spot, a flood control impoundment that had acres of stumps flooded out many years previously. Although we sold some lamps with custom made shades to local department stores and found no difficulty developing and even manufacturing products, we had no knowledge of sales and marketing, and for a time we searched unsuccessfully for a person to act as our salesman. Making a living was critical however, and when Jerry was offered a better opportunity out of state, we sold our equipment, and our lives and careers went in different directions.

The solitary aspect of my work at the Hyman Blum Company, with only occasional contact with Hyman or his sons, and very limited trips to the shop to see works in progress, began to take its toll. I was isolated and had no contact with other employees from day to day. In addition, the long hours at the drawing board produced muscle cramps and spasms in my left hand and arm, so much so that it was difficult for me to raise a cup to my lips without shaking and spilling the contents. Again I sensed that this job, like the one at Steiner's, held no potential for progress. The fact that Jerry and I had created and manufactured several saleable products renewed confidence in my abilities and having gained some working experience and actually done some designing, I was impatient to reach out and find more challenging opportunities. I decided to try freelancing.

I scoured the yellow pages to find product-producing manufacturers, those who might have use for a design service. I assembled a portfolio of work that best represented my skills and began to make personal calls, asking to speak to whomever was in charge of design projects. There were many large heavy industry plants in Pittsburgh, and numerous fabricating plants, but few companies that produced consumer, or even industrial products. For the most part it was either basic metal production or job shops that worked to specifications. I covered an area of fifty miles around the city and although I kept at it for a couple of years, the results were minimal. I managed, with occasional small jobs, to make enough to cover expenses. Nevertheless, living at home and being subsidized by my parents for food, lodging and occasionally clothing, impacted heavily on my self-esteem and confidence. I wanted so badly to be independent; to participate in the kind of activities that others were enjoying and above all, to get on with my life. My childhood friends had returned from military service, a few had married, others were enjoying steady relationships and, with high school educations or less, they were all working and earning more than me. The whole idea of obtaining an education so that I could make a good living rang with a falseness I had trouble accepting. Things weren't the way they were supposed to be.

Making business calls was new to me; it meant shaking hands with many different people and that sometimes posed problems. Occasionally an alert person would extend his left hand to shake mine. Most people, however, would automatically extend their right hand and then, noticing that I had no right hand, would engage in a kind of full body stutter; embarrassed, they would tardily extend their left hand while muttering an apology. It had the aspects of two people meeting head-on and trying to pass each other on the on the sidewalk. It was not a good way to begin a sales presentation. It called attention, however indirectly, to my disabilities, so I developed the practice of quickly extending my left hand, turning it over, and grasping the other person's right hand in a smooth movement that permitted them to cover any unease or embarrassment they might experience. It worked for me, but it also irked me because I realized it was a case of a disabled person extending himself to prevent the able-bodied person from embarrassment. I resented that I had to assume responsibility for making others feel comfortable in my presence; pragmatically, however, it was good business behavior.[6]

A toy manufacturer hired me to redesign a stamped, sheet metal baby doll's high chair and a child's wheelbarrow. I located a custom kitchen fabricator for whom I made sales presentations, colored-pencil perspective drawings translated from floor plans, which earned me $25-$30 dollars per drawing. Considering that I could do a drawing in two hours, it was good pay, but there wasn't sufficient volume to make a living. I called on Palley Kitchens, a manufacturer of steel kitchen cabinets in competition with Youngstown Kitchens, a national manufacturer and distributor. Mr. Palley awarded me a small job creating a few presentation drawings. With that job successfully completed, he engaged me in a detailed discussion about a major problem he was facing. His kitchen cabinets occupied so much cubic space when being shipped, that only a relatively few units could be packed into a boxcar. This lack of volume in relation to the number of units in a boxcar load made shipping charges so high that Palley Kitchens was unable to compete with Youngstown Kitchens west of the Mississippi. Mr. Palley had a seemingly revolutionary and innovative idea to make his company competitive. If he could manufacture a knockdown kitchen capable of being assembled on site, he could fill boxcars with the component parts stacked flat, quadruple the number of units in a boxcar, and be able to compete. He asked me, "Can you design a knockdown kitchen for me that we can manufacture here?" It was the first comprehensive industrial design problem I had ever faced. Indeed, it was a major design project. I was exhilarated. I had no immediate idea as to how to do it, but it was a viable idea and a tremendous opportunity to design a new kitchen that would be nationally distributed and advertised. It would undoubtedly make my career as a designer. "Yes, I'm cer-

---

[6] That the stigmatized individual can be caught taking the tactful acceptance of himself too seriously indicates that this acceptance is conditional. It depends on normals not being pressed past the point at which they can easily extend acceptance—or, at worst uneasily extend it. (Goffmam, p-120-1)

tain it's possible, and I think I can do it." It was agreed that I would work on salary at the Palley plant on a regular basis for several months until the design was either completed or rejected. I was exuberant.

I was provided a drawing table and introduced to key plant personnel, specifically the young man in charge of creating and testing new products and who had an extensive knowledge of which specific materials should be used for strength or flexibility, the fabricating methods available in the plant, and where and how new tools and/or jigs and fixtures could be developed to perform specific functions. The new product components would have to be produced on an assembly line in the plant and would require new jigs and fixtures, and possibly new tools.

By the end of the first month I had created a basic styling and structural design with a modern look that utilized a mix of steel, plastic extrusions and laminates. The basic design pleased Mr. Palley. I began to draft working drawings so a prototype could be constructed and tested.

When my first shop drawings were completed, the products supervisor, although friendly and cooperative, expressed doubt that the cabinets, when assembled, would be able to support their own weight and withstand the normal use given to kitchen cabinets. I had faith in my designs. "Will you humor me and build it anyway so we can see what the problems are?" "Of course, but I think it will require some changes." When the prototype components were fabricated, assembled and hung on the wall, everything fit and lined up. The prototype was strong, firm and had a modern, stylish appearance. Some fine-tuning was necessary, but that was to be expected. Again Mr. Palley was pleased.

Several weeks later I had a meeting with Mr. Palley. "You did an excellent job on the kitchen design. It is everything I asked for. I'm afraid, however, that my original concept of manufacture, shipping and on-site assembly is unfortunately too large for my organization. We are not capable of producing the volume here in this plant necessary for such an enterprise; in addition, in order to implement it, I would need to find a national organization like Sears, Roebuck and Co., that would have the capability to custom install the units anywhere in the country. Right now that doesn't appear to be a possibility. I've already spoken to the CEO at Westinghouse about their taking it on, but he doesn't think they're in a position to do it either."

My design effort was a resounding success. My dream that it would be produced and nationally distributed, affording me bigger and better design opportunities collapsed. I couldn't even boast of my successful product design since the product didn't exist. It was time to get back on the street and attempt to find some new opportunities.

8

My Métier: The Battle Begins

With the Palley kitchen design job completed, and with it the evaporation of any hope to parlay my design into a viable career in product design, I reverted to my list of potential employers and again began to make calls. Announcements in the newspapers about the advent of a new television station in Pittsburgh, scheduled to go on the air in April of 1954, conjured up long forgotten dreams of being a performer. Was there a chance that maybe in this new enterprise I might be able to move into the world of show business and perhaps find a spot for myself? I located the station, a large old gray stone building originally built as a private residence in the heart of the City's cultural center, in close proximity to the University of Pittsburgh, Scheneley Park, two large hotels, and just one long block from the Carnegie Museum where I had spent so many Saturday mornings in art classes. It was an area of the city I knew well.

Non-commercial television, initially known as Educational Television, was a child of the 50's. In 1953 the City of Pittsburgh, on receiving a channel allocation, became the third Educational Television station in the country, but more importantly, the first community-sponsored non-commercial station thereby establishing a new organizational model for non-commercial, Educational Television stations. WQED's founding board of directors boasted some of the most powerful and prominent men of Pittsburgh's industry, education and journalism.

On entering the building, I was met by the coordinator of volunteers, Lenore Elkus, a middle-aged woman well known in the cultural life of the city. I introduced myself, "I'm an artist and designer and I'd like to tell you about what I do and show you my portfolio. I freelance, on either an hourly or job basis." Her response was warm and friendly, "Oh I'm certain we can use your skills here. We have a need for just about any kind of skill that's available, but you see, we're a volunteer organization. I'm afraid we haven't any funds to hire you, but we certainly could use you. This is an exciting venture. Can you take a moment to have a look around? I'm certain you'll find it interesting and maybe you'll decide that you might want to become involved with us, as a volunteer?" It was immediately clear there was no opportunity to generate income, but I was here, why not look around and see what it was all about? I'd never been in a television station.

Mrs. Elkus conducted me through the station. The building had beautiful woodwork and fireplaces still in place, but the interior had been sub-divided to form offices and work space. I was shown the studio and control room, filled with racks of lights and electronic equipment, the director's and announcer's booths, and the large basement being converted to a scene shop and art department.

Back on the main floor again, I was introduced to the new Director of Children's Programs, Fred Rogers, native of nearby Latrobe, PA with a degree in music, ties to Pittsburgh's social elite, and production experience on NBC's popular *Hit Parade*, *The Voice of Firestone*, and the *NBC TV Opera Theater*. On learning I was an artist, Fred asked, "Could you make us something we could use visually like the NBC chimes?" My response was politely evasive. I said I wasn't certain I could be of much help although I was privately intrigued with the challenge. Of course I knew I could do it, but they wanted it for free?

WQED was an interesting place; I couldn't help myself, I wanted to be involved. As my tour was ending, Mrs. Elkus suggested that if I had a few hours free, anytime, I might find it interesting to stop by and help them out, while at the same time learning something about television. I knew I was hooked. I had come to find paid work and left as a volunteer, having scheduled myself for a few hours one evening later in the week.

On my first evening as a volunteer, I met Rudy Bretz. In the brand new world of television, Rudy was already a veteran and had written a "how to" book about television production, one of the first to be published. There was a copy of it right there to examine. I was impressed. Rudy, it appeared, knew everything worth knowing about television production. He'd been hired by the station to organize its initial production operations and was happy to teach anyone who was interested. For the next couple of hours Rudy gave me my first indoctrination in the practice of creating art and programs for television. I learned that television had a gray scale of only six tones from black to white; that high contrast burned in, that is, left an after-image on the camera's image orthicon picture tube, that there were rigid parameters for title cards sizes and copy location; that the aspect ratio of the television screen was four units wide and three high; and that all colors translated on camera to their gray scale value, but with less sensitivity than black and white film. This was an entirely new set of dimensions to which I immediately related and understood. The more I heard and saw, the more interested I became. I pored over Rudy's book when he departed, fascinated with the challenge this new medium held for an artist and designer. I had no doubts about what I could do here. After struggling through six years of trying to find where I could fit in the scheme of things, I had found my métier. This was where I belonged. The next day I went to the library, found Rudy's book and devoured it from cover to cover. With my artistic training, Rudy's book, and the rendering skills learned working with displays, I was a natural. Everything fell into place. Overnight, my orientation switched from industrial design to television art and production design. By learning a few simple concepts and requirements I found it easy to immediately create usable television art.

The station was scheduled to begin broadcasting in April, but as yet there were no station identification graphics (I.D.'s) that the FCC required to be shown every hour. With black and white pencils on gray paper, I created three or four attractive ID's and offered them to the program manager. When the station went on the air they were all used repeatedly. I was delighted. It was my first experience seeing my work broadcast.

Every program opened with titles and closed with credits identifying all who had contributed to the program. Titles and credits consisted of graphics, printed copy, sometimes with drawings or photos, each individually created by the art department. Each piece was drawn or painted on a stiff poster board eleven by fourteen inches, mounted on a three ring notebook mounted horizontally at camera height on a wooden easel. Each card was punched with a three-ring punch. The first card was hung on the lower arc of the rings so the camera could focus on it. A production assistant held the rest of the cards on the upper arc of the rings and, on cue, permitted them to drop one at a time into the camera frame, creating an instantaneous change of picture, in television parlance a cut. Each program required three or four cards at the beginning of the show and two to four at the close.

On April 4, 1954, WQED, Channel 13, went on the air. At the outset, the station was on the air from mid-afternoon until 11:00 P.M., a seven-hour broadcast day with fourteen half hour programs, each requiring title cards. Despite the fact that some programs were broadcast more than once a week, there was a continuing need for new title cards, and most programs required additional artwork for use within the program: photos to be mounted and coated with a dulling spray to prevent reflection; signs; captions; graphs; illustrations; and even mechanical animations. The need for artwork was overwhelming. There were a few artists like myself who found it enjoyable to volunteer for a few hours each week, but most of them were spending most of their time making a living and did not appear to have the intense interest that I had so quickly developed. I spent more and more time at the station and less and less time looking for work. I explained to my parents how I felt about my new involvement, which I believed was something for which I was uniquely suited and with a little luck could become my lifetime pursuit. As always, my parents agreed that I should give it a try. "You have a place to live. You do what you have to do."

The atmosphere of the television station was similar to that which I had enjoyed at college. The station was the newest cultural, educational, aesthetic, and intellectual enterprise in the city and as such attracted people from all walks of life. The broad spectrum of volunteers included artists, technicians, laborers and professionals as well as numerous Junior League women from Pittsburgh's most influential families. The wide range of participants on the various interview, talk and entertainment shows included the most prominent members of the community. Most of the City's professional radio performers, newsmen, disk jockeys, and entertainers became volunteers. Josie Carey, an actress from the Pittsburgh Playhouse, joined the staff as an on camera spokesperson. One of her colleagues at the Playhouse, a then unknown young singer and actress, Shirley Jones, also made an occasional appearance at the station. For those who envisioned pursuing a future in broadcasting, it was the only venue available where it was possible to learn television production in an "on air" situation. In this exciting and creative ambiance of intelligent discussion and activity I felt as if I had come home. Little by little my skills became recognized and I was swamped with requests for artwork of one kind or another.

Josie Carey teamed up with Fred Rogers to produce WQED's first children's show, *The Children's Corner*. Loosely patterned after the popular network puppet show *Keukla, Fran and Ollie,* Josie played the front of the proscenium while Fred, like Burr Tillstrom, manipulated hand puppets from backstage and provided music on the organ. *The Children's Corner* had an extremely modest beginning. The set consisted of a plain three-fold flat painted gray with no decoration. Dorothy Daniels, wife of the publisher of Hearst's Pittsburgh Sun Telegraph and one of the station founders, gave Fred a hand puppet, a tiger with a very benevolent countenance and Fred immediately named him Daniel Striped (two syllables) Tiger in honor of Mrs. Daniels. In a whirlwind of planning activity Fred and Josie decided that Daniel would live in a clock. Fred requested a clock be drawn on the flat and a hole cut into it so Fred could play the puppet through the hole. A clock with a pitched roof and a door large enough for the puppet was painted on the flat. Roy Nelligan, the lone union stagehand whose presence the local union had agreed would satisfy their representation demands and also represent their support, cut the hole in the flat. The next day Daniel Striped Tiger made his appearance on the show. In the following weeks, in quick succession, as Fred acquired additional puppets, Granpere who spoke only French, and for whom I painted an Eiffel Tower with a small doorway on the balcony (courtesy of Roy), then King Friday, a very regal puppet arrived, and we created a castle. Sometime later, I made the castle three-dimensional. Slowly, organically, the set grew, Fred wrote music, and he and Josie created stories and songs, expanding the world of *The Children's Corner* and capturing the imagination of the small children in the area. Fred, working the puppets from backstage, and inventing unique voices for each one, was not seen in the early days of *The Children's Corner*. The puppets and their voices however, became well known to local children. Children all over town sang the delightful songs created collaboratively by Fred and Josie. I was pleased to be asked to create a cover design for their first publication, the words and music of *Good Night God* and to illustrate their first book *The Children's Corner.*

As summer approached, The University of Pittsburgh scheduled a new workshop in basic television production and direction. I enrolled immediately. With what I had already observed at WQED, it was a breeze. For four weeks, I had access to a small, improvised studio with two cameras and a control room. By the end of the workshop I'd had a chance to test my capabilities for quick decision-making, physical operation of cameras, audio board and lighting, and to try my hand at the rudimentary skills of directing. I returned to volunteering with great excitement; I was no longer content with just artwork and scenic design. I wanted to be involved in producing and directing. I wanted to be in charge. Creating programs was where the action was; that's what I wanted to do.

At the end of the summer of 1954, station management decided to tackle a Herculean job, the broadcast of the Allegheny County Fair from South Park, a job that no commercial local station had thus far dared attempt. The Fair encompassed many acres with exhibits housed in a number of large barnlike buildings as well as outdoors and events covered several afternoons of intense scheduling and television coverage. The heavy studio cameras, designed for use on a smooth, level floor posed endless problems in transporting them from venue to venue. Long, heavy camera cables had to be disconnected, carried and reconnected each time a camera was moved, almost entirely by volunteer technicians. An on-site director's booth was established at the Fair for the live coverage. Periodically directorial control was switched back to the studio for promotions and an occasional film to provide the field operation time to move to the next venue. Every volunteer available was pressed into service. Art work of all kinds was needed and I managed to produce them with other volunteers' assistance while at the same time working a daytime shift as a background color announcer at the Fair. My announce position was twenty feet up on a construction scaffold overlooking the fairgrounds where I had a chair, a monitor, a headset and a clipboard full of reference information to be used for ad lib fill when needed. The first day I parked my car at the base of the scaffold and as I opened the door and swung my flexed left leg out, my foot struck the door in such a position that it twisted my lower leg in a clockwise direction. I felt no pain, but as I proceeded to exit the car I found that I could not straighten my leg, and it did not feel normal. I tried several times to flex it and straighten it and although it would flex fully, it would only return to within 15 degrees of full extension. I was due to announce in fifteen minutes. I could stand on the leg in its bent position but it hurt. I limped over to the scaffold and climbed the ladder with difficulty. I was unable to determine what was wrong. It had never happened before and seemed that my knee was dislocated. I made it up the ladder, picked up the headset, reported for duty and for four hours did the color and background announcements seated on the chair, until the end of the day.

With difficulty I managed to climb down from the scaffold and drive my standard shift car home. The condition of my leg hadn't changed by the time I arrived, and I explained the situation to my mother as we both worriedly examined the knee. The leg appeared normal, but it still wouldn't straighten out. I had a clear remembrance of just how it had happened, that the leg had been twisted and I suggested to Mother that perhaps we could reverse the action and twist it back. At my instruction she grasped my lower leg very tightly and as she held it firmly I pulled and twisted my body in the direction opposite to that which had caused the dislocation. We tried it several times and quite suddenly the leg straightened out fully. I tried flexing it and straightening it and it appeared to be again functioning as usual, but we noticed that the knee was now slightly swollen and tender to the touch. I rested that evening and the next day I was back on the scaffold, taking great care entering and leaving my car. In a few days the leg had returned to normal. No medical assessment was pursued, and over the course of the next several years dislocation would on occasion reoccur. I learned that if I relaxed the leg completely, it would in a matter of hours return to its natural position. Many years later, I was advised that indeed, I had dislocated my knee, due to the fact that my left lower leg contained only one of the two usual bones, the tibia. The absence of the second bone, the fibula, was a congenital anomaly hitherto unknown, and therefore the lower leg lacked the musculature and rotational stability that would permit it to resist torque.

At the Fair, Fred acquired a beautiful owl puppet for which he and Josie immediately invented a provenance. The owl appeared on the show when asked his name responded "X." When Josie asked: "What is your full name?" the owl said, " X-cape. I x-caped from the Fair." So X it was, and of course there was an immediate need for a home for X. After introducing him on the show Josie, having prepared in advance, fastened an acorn to the flat next to the clock with a piece of scotch tape saying, "Maybe it'll grow into an oak tree and then X will have a place to live?" After the show, I painted a tiny sprout above the acorn. Next day Josie made a great show of discovering the new sprout, and every day for the rest of the week I "grew" the tree with a paintbrush until by the beginning of the following week it was fully-grown with branches and foliage and had a knothole with a hinged door that Roy fabricated over the weekend.

As I was busy creating art for the cameras, other volunteers were learning various aspects of production, serving on either engineering or production crews. The former worked under the direction of the chief engineer and his assistant, operating cameras, audio boards and control room equipment; the latter, under supervision of the production manager, served as stage crews, production assistants, floor managers, lighting technicians, assistant directors, announcers and when they had attained the necessary skills, directors and producers. At the beginning, only the production manager and program manager possessed the skills necessary to direct live shows.

My continued and regular presence resulted in my being asked, as a volunteer, to coordinate the art department that consisted of myself and a few other volunteer artists. I scheduled the work, did as much of it as was possible, and assigned the rest to others, directing and teaching them my newly learned skills. As a volunteer, I hadn't authority to realistically guarantee that requested art work would be completed in time, or at all, and there were occasional mishaps, but most of the time I was able to deliver and people began to depend on me. In the process I familiarized myself with the limited number of set pieces that were on hand, which Roy Nelligan was trying to augment by constantly building new flats as quickly as his time would allow. Roy was an experienced stagehand, expert at building, lighting, setting, painting and dressing sets. In the beginning he was a one-man stage crew who quickly taught volunteers, to set, dress and light every program.

His temper was long suffering, but when he erupted, which was not often, it was an event.

Roy and I developed a liking for each other, worked well together and were soon planning settings for various new programs. I would design the set, with Roy's advice and consultation, he would build it, and I would paint it. I immersed myself in the detail of set construction and staging and was able to see the results of my labors aired daily. It was always possible to place a piece of art before a camera to see how it looked. If it needed revision, it was obvious and I was able to fine tune. Within a few months I found that I had become a consultant. Both staff and volunteers sought me out for solutions to production problems and I was soon in the thick of planning productions with various producers and directors. Creating productions tantalized me much more than art work.

I volunteered for the production crew. The volunteer coordinator wasn't eager to see her art director disappear into the production crew, but I was, after all, a volunteer, and determined to learn production. I was by now spending my entire day at the station so I agreed to continue to do artwork if I could also work production. Other volunteers were already ahead of me in the learning process, but I started in the studio setting up flats, lashing them together and sandbagging them for stability. I worked lighting, carrying the 500 and 1000 watt spotlights and scoops up the fourteen foot ladder, plugging them into the pigtails hanging from the grids, and into the control panel. Others watched me with concern and then awe as I performed these actions and ultimately concluded that I didn't need any assistance. I was very much aware that although station staff were aware that my physical activity at times caused concern, there was never any suggestion that my involvement might not be covered by the station's insurance. This permissive atmosphere, similar to my having been "mainstreamed" in school, allowed me to participate, to learn, and to climb the lower steps of this new career ladder on the basis of my capabilities rather than being eliminated on the basis of my appearance. On a personal level, the physical strain was severe, but I drove myself in spite of the pain. Working in the studio required constant standing, walking, climbing ladders and carrying heavy spotlights.

By the end of an evening shift I could barely stand, but never did I allude to my discomfort.

My days of hauling lights up a ladder ended when I became a floor manager, in charge of the show in the studio, responsible only to the director, but floor managing also required standing and walking during set up and performance. Responsibility for making a show ready to air was the floor manager's who supervised the setting, lighting, and dressing of the set and summoned performers to position. He received the director's commands via telephone headset, relayed the instructions to the performers during rehearsals, and cued all actions during the performance.

It was strenuous, exhausting, but a totally exhilarating activity. Never before had I felt such a surge of confidence and satisfaction, it was as if I were a part of a magnificent instrument. There was a rhythm and a beat and a harmony of actions that thrilled me. I was in the midst of the most exciting experience of my life. And it wasn't enough; I wanted to direct.

The first step to directing was directing station breaks. Between the end of one program and the beginning of the next there was a program break, during which it was necessary for the station to identify itself by presenting, via audio and video, its call letters. Also at the break, promotions for upcoming programs would be aired. The procedure, which took two minutes and thirty seconds, was a complex sequence of slides, live camera I.D.'s, announcer cues and physical manipulation of the director's console to activate the aural and visual changes, each action readied and then cued by the station break director.

As each program ended, its director would rise from the director's chair, hand the head set to the station break director who immediately began cueing as he sat down. Two and a half minutes later, as he finished, he would rise, handing the head set to the next live program director who would begin the next program. To enable an entire evening's programming in the single studio, all of the evening's shows were set up before the first one began and from then on, each live show followed the preceding one, with only the station break in between.

After being a floor manager, I began training as a station break director, sitting with the person on duty and memorizing every movement and command. Eventually, I had an opportunity to try it myself and although I did occasionally make a mistake, I took to it as I had taken to driving and flying and had soon mastered the procedure.

At the same time, I was also taking a turn in the announce booth, doing regular three hour stints as the off-camera station announcer, reading copy from double-spaced typewritten pages. I had a good voice, but there were others whose vocal instruments had greater tone or timber and were used more often. That was not important. I delighted in the fact that I had done it and was doing it, I was busy, I was learning, I was involved, but I still wasn't directing.

The move from station break director to show director depended on how many new shows were being added and how many directors were available. Beginning with only a few shows a day and two directors, as the station began to fine tune its operation it also increased the number of shows and the first of the newly trained volunteers began to direct. When a new batch of shows was being readied for airing, volunteer directors as well as station break directors lobbied for the opportunity to have a show of their own. Once assigned, the same person directed a regular weekly or daily show series.

As a qualified director of station breaks, I eagerly awaited an assignment to direct a regular show. When word circulated that a few new shows would be added, I was confident I would get one, but when the assignments were made I was not given a show and instead was asked to be the trainer for the next batch of station director trainees.

I was furious, I was also hurt, and I was frightened. Had I reached another dead end? Being aware that my disabilities resulted in people perceiving me differently was, by now, old hat, but this was the first situation in which I felt that the perceptions of my disabilities, resulting from either misguided or illogical thinking, had led directly to my being discriminated against. Although trained and able, I was not being given the opportunity to assume responsibility and authority as an on-air director, but I was perceived as being sufficiently skilled to be trusted teaching others to do it. On learning that it had been the decision of the program manager, I approached the production manager to whom I reported and complained. If I was not competent to direct, I argued, how could I be competent to instruct? Confronted with the logic of the situation, and recognizing that he was about to lose a potential director as well as a productive art director, the program manager relented and decided to take a chance on my directing. I was assigned, not to one of the new shows, which would require designing new camera blocking and shot sequencing (which I sometimes designed or implemented with art as a consultant art director), but to an ongoing show, a so-called easy, daily instructional program in which the patterns had been already established. I accepted the compromise; it was a move forward and the professional risks were minimal.

The director of extension education for the Pittsburgh Public Schools, Dr. Harry Snyder had taken advantage of the new television station to establish an instructional program, "High School of the Air," that offered the first opportunity in the nation for persons who had not completed high school to earn their high school diplomas by watching instructional programs and then taking qualifying examinations. If passed successfully, students earned credits toward a High School diploma. Dr. Snyder made a special effort to enroll inmates at the local penitentiary and as a result received significant favorable publicity when several inmates earned high school diplomas, a first time event.

WQED broadcast direct instruction in high school English, Math, Spanish, Science and History from Monday through Friday from 7 to 7:30 P.M.. My new assignment was as director of three of these programs. Each show was a two-camera show with one camera used for wide shots and the other for close-ups. The director played a kind of leapfrog with the cameras; while one shot was on the air the other camera would be readied for the next shot and the director had to stay ahead of the action and anticipate it. If the stage movement changed from left to right or vice versa, the camera shots would be reversed. The cameras were well-used hand-me-down RCA field cameras with turrets that held four lenses. One of the cameras usually had only three lenses, a 35 mm., a 50mm., and a 75mm. The other had the same complement plus a telephoto lens, an 8½ inch lens used for extreme close-ups. The 8½ inch lens was capable of filling the screen with a view of a postage stamp at a distance of 12 to 15 feet.

Both in front and behind the cameras, almost everyone on almost every show was a volunteer, including the engineering crew comprised of an audio man, and the cameramen. We were all learning and trying very hard to do everything right. The director's job was to make it all look professional on the air, but that wasn't always easy. The equipment was old and well used, and sometimes a camera suddenly blacked out necessitating the director's finishing the show with only one camera as the engineering crew swarmed around the dead camera trying to resuscitate it. Everyone had to have a first time at a job and mistakes were frequent, and could rarely be anticipated, but "liveness" was an enervating factor.

On one occasion a brand new cameraman, a volunteer unfamiliar with the camera lenses and how to use them, was assigned to my program to operate camera 1 which happened to be the camera with the 8½ inch lens which was needed early in the show for a close-up of a book illustration. I started the show with Camera 2 on a wide shot. The next shot was to be an extreme close up on a book located on a stand far across the set. As I put camera 2 on the air I said, "Camera 1, give me an 8½ on the book." An uncertain voice came back on my headset, "What's an 8½?" Without a pause I said, "Cameramen, change cameras." Fortunately, the cameraman on Camera 2 was experienced. The experienced cameraman locked his camera on the wide shot, ran to the other camera and turned the turret to the 8½ inch lens and set up the close-up as the floor manager waved the new man to the vacated camera and cued the television teacher to begin to speak.

For a half hour each weekday evening I basked in the power of being in total control of a small group of people and equipment, and responsible for making their combined effort a professional presentation. Directing required an extremely high level of alertness, decisiveness, and judgment. It required total involvement and after a show ended, even a simple show, my pulse was racing and I was exhilarated. This was what I could do, and do well. This was what I wanted to spend the rest of my life doing.

******

It had taken a year of volunteer work to learn what I had learned and to develop the skills I now had. During that year, when several times the station had received grants for specific shows that required a new set design or art work, the program or production manager would tell me how much money they had to spend and ask if I wanted to do the job as a freelance. I always accepted and was happy to have the extra money. At the first year's volunteer awards ceremony I was awarded an enameled pin that specified that I had served 1,500 hours. As summer neared I approached the program manager with an idea for a series of programs I wanted to write, produce and direct. The series, a survey of private aviation in western Pennsylvania, would be titled *Folks Who Fly*. While taking flying lessons I had developed many contacts among private pilots with whom I kept in touch. I planned several shows of my proposed series and outlined content and participants. The idea was approved with the very specific understanding that the programs would incur no financial outlay by the station. I would be given the airtime and studio use, but any other costs would have to be from my own pocket. At the same time I was informed that if I was going to produce and write the show, I might not have time to direct it and, while I found this disappointing, I perceived it as a trade off in which I had the best of the bargain, particularly since Colin Stern, the station's new Music Director who, like myself, was a fledgling program director, would direct. I knew Colin well and had worked with him.

The first show featured as host a prominent Pittsburgh eye surgeon who was a licensed pilot and glider pilot. The guests were a man who had flown the first mail from Pittsburgh to Cleveland and a woman who had been the first pilot to land at the Allegheny County Airport when it had been constructed many years previously. In addition, the setting I designed featured a collection of suspended airplane models that were both decorative and objects of discussion. The show as aired was perfect. It was highly visual, had a professional flair, the performers were top notch and Colin's direction was masterful. When the show ended, Bill Wood, the general manager, who had been watching the show in his office on the second floor, came running down the steps in great excitement. "That was terrific. That's the kind of show we should be doing all the time." and seeing Ed Horseman, the chief engineer, who had come out of the control room to see what the excitement was all about, said: "Ed, did we make a kinescope of that?" Ed gave Bill a look of disbelief that revealed his true feelings about being at WQED instead of CBS in Chicago, where his socializing had shortened his tenure, and said: "Hell no, how would I know it was gonna be any good?"

For the second program, which dealt with the structure and operation of an aircraft, I arranged for a J-3 Piper Cub aircraft, the kind on which I had taken lessons, to be brought into the studio. In exchange for on air credit, I persuaded the owner/operator of the flying school at a nearby airport, to lend me the plane and I also persuaded the owner of the Pittsburgh Aviation Institute, a school for aviation mechanics at the Allegheny County Airport, to fly the plane to their shop, disassemble the wings, trailer it to the studio, and re-attach the right wing inside the studio. I used a large rear screen projection of clouds behind the plane and the show opened with the host sitting in the plane, ostensibly flying it before the cameras pulled back to show that it was in the studio. It worked so well that several weeks later I brought in a sailplane, set it up the same way, and was able to find aerial footage of soaring which I integrated into the shot sequence to further the illusion of flying. Several days before the show, the program manager informed me that Colin Stern had taken on additional responsibilities at the University of Pittsburgh and would no longer be directing so I would have to direct my own shows. The news shook me. As artist and producer I had been creating illusions. Free from the responsibilities of physically directing, I had increased the complexity of the production values in an effort to enhance the illusions. This manifested itself in increased numbers and kinds of shots, more complicated camera movements, and integration of visuals and film. Colin had risen to each new challenge and the upcoming show, which I would now personally direct, was, as planned, a complex one. I had some real fears that, as my first attempt directing a complex show, I might not be up to it. The shows I had previously directed were simple ones. This show was different. I knew all the motions, and given enough rehearsal, I was certain I could do it, but with only a brief walk through, which was the way the live shows were done, I was fearful I'd blow it and more than embarrassing, it might end my short directing career. With the thought that discretion was the better part of valor, I took my script, on which I had already listed every shot and movement and began to methodically rework the show. I stripped it until I had reduced it to the very basic program and then I added only those extras that I felt comfortable in handling. It wouldn't be as glamorous as I had originally planned, but it would still be a good show.

As I took the director's chair for what everyone knew was my first big attempt at directing, my director friends gathered in the control room to wish me well and to watch. I brought up theme and announcer and was into the show, cueing the host and moving rapidly ahead, oblivious to everything except the upcoming action and camera shot. With only one or two minor discrepancies, which I managed to gloss over, I completed the show and it had looked good. My co-directors offered their congratulations and compliments. I heaved a sigh of relief and was reminded of the saying I had heard frequently at the flying school, "Any landing you can walk away from is a good one." *Folks Who Fly* was a successful series and I gained confidence and skill, so much so that when the local Air National Guard suggested that the station might want to do another series, this time on military aviation, I was assigned to be its producer.

At about the same time, in summer of 1955, the station was awarded a large Ford Foundation grant to establish an elementary level team-teaching project in which in-school teachers would team up with television teachers to teach English, math and French to students within WQED's broadcast reception area. An educator was hired as project director, and, since her project would require large numbers of title and easel cards on a daily basis, the station administrators made a decision to use the budget amount allocated for the project art work to hire a station art director who would be responsible for satisfying both the project's and the station's art needs. I was offered the job at $65 per week. I felt that I was back at square one. I had made $55 at Steiner's, and $75 at Blum's and gambled a year's volunteer work on getting a worthwhile job in television and now I was being offered $65 per week. When I got home that evening the enormity of the situation hit me. I was so disappointed I wept. What would I do now? If this was what television had to offer, was there any future in it for me?

The next day, I discussed the offer with my supervisor. "You know I appreciate the offer and I'd like to accept it, and we both know I would do a good job at it, but I was making more than that before I started freelancing and if that's all I can expect here then maybe I'd be better off going back to doing art work and design wherever I can find it." Carl's response was, "I understand. Let me see what I can do." And later that day, in a second discussion he said, "We can offer you $80, but unfortunately that's the best we can do." I wasn't happy, but I also wanted desperately to be a part of this new industry. "OK Carl, I'll give it a try." At least I was now employed in the television industry and I hoped that the doors would finally open on a new career, one for which I felt I was uniquely qualified.

The project director was not satisfied that "her" money had been used to hire a station art director. She had wanted a full-time artist and she told me frankly what her expectations and my obligations were. Carl had assured me however, that they needed me for station work and I'd be able to use volunteers for much of the project's needs since they were simple and virtually unchanging. I assured the project director that her needs would be met and that if there were problems she should contact me at anytime and I'd resolve the problem immediately. On a personal basis we had respect for one another, but we each had our own agenda. My job began on Aug. 1 and I was immediately overwhelmed on two fronts, both the new broadcast schedule and the teaching project would begin in early September. I was given specifications for the type of work the project needed, mostly simple printed sheets with pull-off or add-on tabs which a volunteer could easily do, and as the orders came in I assigned them to volunteers who were able to produce them quickly. The work was satisfactory and a pattern of production quickly evolved with deadlines and criteria. The stations new programs in the fall broadcast schedule, however, required more time and imagination. I met formally and informally with the producers and directors, of whom there were only a few, each responsible for several shows. Every show needed a new setting which had to be designed using available set pieces and dressings. Opening and closing artwork had to be prepared, set dressings allocated or acquired, and each show's visual opening sequences designed. Most of the volunteer directors were competent in physically coordinating a show. They, like me, had learned how to manipulate the audio and video-switching console to direct cameras, to cue action and coordinate the physical effort, but none had training in the arts. They were caught up in the excitement of manipulating the physical aspects of television production, but lacked aesthetic sense for making their shows good theater. Moreover, since their interest concentrated itself on the actual act of directing on the air, they had little interest in developing the necessary production components if a short cut could be found. As my design and staging capabilities became known, I became the shortcut. By the time the last new show was aired, in mid-September, I had designed, staged and mounted thirty-five new shows for the fall season and had the elementary teaching shows' art needs well under control.

My first opportunity to design and stage any type of dramatic presentation came with a proposal from Duquesne University. Boris Goldofsky, then a young man becoming known for his direction of opera was a resident Consultant and Director of the Duquesne University Opera Workshop which was currently scheduled to perform Puccini's Sister Angelica. WQED had been invited to stage and broadcast the performance. My boss, the production manager and I visited a rehearsal at Duquesne, studied the stage blocking, and decided that we could recreate it for broadcast so we made arrangements to borrow a few pieces of their stage set (a large statue, a doorway, and a well), and I set about adapting them to our studio. With the gray drape drawn taught, faux doorways and cardboard cutout windows placed against it, rag paper fastened with masking tape to the dark linoleum floor, and some special lighting, we managed to create the scene of a courtyard outside the church, all of which fit the stage blocking, and with only a single studio rehearsal, the ambitious presentation was an unqualified success.

With non-commercial television stations springing up like mushrooms all over the nation, a number of universities had added television career programs to their curricula at the same time that they were applying for channel assignment. The University of Michigan was one of the earliest in establishing its program with the result that when the Ford Foundation was searching for a location at which to establish a new organization charged with creating a national programming distribution center for this fast growing enterprise, it granted a large amount of money to the University to establish the National Educational Television and Radio Center in

East Lansing, Michigan. WQED was early on the scene, receiving a grant from NETRC to produce a pilot television program of the well respected, long running *Town Hall of the Air* radio show which had originated and aired on radio from Philadelphia for several years.

NETRC dispatched an executive producer, Richard Goggin, to produce the program at WQED. Prior to coming to NETRC Goggin had been a writer, producer and director for ABC and CBS and technical advisor for Twentieth Century Fox Films and Universal Pictures. Having a visiting professional producer in house was a new experience for everyone and the staff was anxious to provide professional level skills. Goggin asked me, as station art director, if a new set could be designed and built with input from him and Carl Freeborn, who would direct. I made some sketches for the set of "Town Hall of The Air" and designed an opening sequence that included a three-dimensional model of the exterior of the town hall on which were mounted the opening titles for the show. As the camera traveled along the outside of the model of the hall it revealed three bulletin boards that held the sequential title information. The camera then arced around to the front of the model, up to the great double wooden doors that opened, and then through them into the main set of the show. Alvin Urey, the prominent chemist was the guest and the show was kinescoped for national distribution.

Production of the Town Hall show was followed by a series of several special programs kinescoped for other uses. The first were three programs honoring poet Robert Frost, who met for discussion in simple living room settings, first with community leaders, then with college students and finally with children, in each instance quoting his poetry. Pennsylvania State University, which for several years had produced filmed instruction for the United States Armed Forces Institute, a correspondence school that offered additional degrees and rank for service men and women stationed all over the world, decided to experiment with producing instructional programs on television (kinescope) rather than directly on film. Academics from Penn State arrived at WQED to produce two series of high school level Math and English programs. I was assigned as one of two directors to work on Saturdays and Sundays to direct two courses. I was also charged with providing visuals for both programs. The project moved along to completion quickly as we each did two programs each weekend.

The major project of the year began in mid-fall with a large grant for a series of fourteen art programs. No significant art series had yet been attempted by an educational station and WQED, as the third station in the country and the first community sponsored one, had the advantage of a year's experience producing educational and instructional programs. Unfortunately, state-of-the-art educational broadcasting still lacked color, so its first art series, *Looking At Modern Art*, was to be produced on kinescope, which not only lacked color, but also high quality resolution. As the first such series to be produced for national distribution to the growing number of educational stations, however, it was both important and ambitious. Imported as executive producer and director for the series was Robert Snyder. Snyder, a documentary filmmaker and editor, had won an Oscar for best documentary feature in 1950 as producer and editor of *The Titan: Story of Michelangelo,* a production sponsored by Robert Flaherty. The Titan was re-cut and edited from footage of Curt Oertel's original 1938 Swiss/German film, *Michelangelo: Life of a Titan.* By the time of his death in 2004, Snyder's ouevre included documentaries of Pablo Casals, William DeKooning, Henry Miller, Anais Nin, Claudio Arrau, Ruth Asawa and Buckminster Fuller.

Snyder set up shop in the attic of the building with a rented moviola and his presence was much in demand at gatherings of arts patrons in Pittsburgh's cultural community. Pittsburgh had been selected for the series because the host was to be Gordon Washburn, Director of the Carnegie Museum of Art, known and respected among artists and art patrons around the world as director of the Pittsburgh International Art Show and as consultant/ buyer for well known local art collector G. David Thompson and members of other prominent Pittsburgh families. He was a delightful gentleman whose knowledge of art, artists and patrons was worldwide. In the studio, he was cordial and cooperative, always appreciative of suggestions offered to ease or improve his performance.

Snyder had firm and imaginative concepts as to how the show should look and outlined basic requirements for the set design that would facilitate that look. Meeting someone as renown and skilled as Snyder was a unique experience and I was pleased, when after several discussions, instead of importing a known production designer, he invited me to work on the series in that capacity. Given his specifications and suggestions, I created a set patterned after Mondrian's painting *42nd Street* that comprised a number of set pieces which, viewed head-on by the camera, appeared as a single plane, but as the camera drew closer or traveled to either side, opened up new perspectives and facets. Snyder's production approach was filmic. Each scene was a separate take, slated and kinescoped on 16 mm film; and although he filmed Washburn's narrative in chronological sequence, many art works, set pieces and lighting were filmed separately and inserted into the film in the editing process. Crated sculpture and paintings, many of enormous value, were delivered to the studio from all over the country at the behest of Gordon Washburn. All had to be unpacked, staged, filmed and then repacked and returned. Gordon was always fearful that some damage would result from the handling of valuable paintings while in his custody and his anxiety together with his gentle nature made him easy victim to teasing and practical jokes.

In those days of image orthicon television tubes, particularly with the used tubes donated by several commercial stations, it was not unusual for the camera to retain an after image, a "burn-in" it was called, from any unusually bright or highly reflective spot. Accordingly, when lighting could not remove the glare from a hot spot, it was necessary to utilize a dulling spray, sometimes on an expensive, intricately carved and gold leafed frame. In less critical circumstances, a small piece of paper or masking tape could be placed on the hot spot and the camera would not notice it, but with gold leaf frames, there was a danger that masking tape could adhere tightly enough to pull the gold leaf from the frame on removal creating damage which was expensive to repair. I teased Gordon by picking up a roll of tape and acting as if I were going to apply it to the hot spot on a gold leaf frame. "Oh my God, don't do that." Gordon would exclaim and then laugh as he realized he'd been had.

As the winter wore on, film footage accumulated. At Christmas I was invited to Snyder's home for a holiday drink and there had the pleasure of meeting Bob's father-in-law, Buckminster Fuller, whose Dymaxian car had been a subject of great interest during my days studying industrial design at Carnegie Tech. Although we were still shooting scenes with Gordon and inserts without him, Snyder had begun the editing process and hired an assistant to catalog and organize the film footage. His assistant, George Lorey, had no background in film or television, but was friendly and gregarious, a natural hustler and manipulator. George was one of those people who was always around, but who had no specific career interest. He had no pretensions concerning his own capabilities, made no claims about his status or skills, and had no particular interest in television or filmmaking. His job was just another in a series of short-lived jobs which enabled him to meet his obligations. It appeared that he never worried about anything. Somewhere in his past were a wife and children to whom he rarely referred and then only obliquely. Content to follow Bob's orders, in that pursuit he became an ubiquitous presence around the station although never intruding in any aspect of the operational process. As friendly colleagues we developed a relationship and understanding that was extremely candid and direct.

As the months rolled by WQED administrators, unfamiliar with the post-production aspects of the filmmaking process and accustomed to having a finished kinescope in hand at the instant the program was completed, began to worry that with all the funds expended, they had no completed programs. Fearing their own culpability they pressured Snyder to complete his work, but Snyder, a perfectionist as an editor, refused to hurry. Relationships began to break down and there was less contact between Snyder and WQED executives. By the summer of 1956 however, Snyder announced that his work was completed and delivered fourteen half-hour programs within the time schedule promised.

At the station, I found myself drawn to a particular young woman who was a fellow volunteer with whom I had risen through the ranks and was now a volunteer director. In the ensuing months of working together we had found in each other a certain kindred spirit that manifested itself in how we perceived the phenomenon of WQED and the various interrelationships of those who worked there. Our conversations focused on activities at the station and we compared opinions of many of the personalities who were continually coming and going, our impressions of the staff and administrators, and our likes and dislikes among our co-workers. Each of us was interested in the other's perceptions and since we spent large amounts of time at the station, we had ample opportunity to get to know and appreciate each other.

As much as we had in common, we nevertheless came from two worlds that could not be further apart, I from a working class, middle European ethnic community on Pittsburgh's North Side and she, from the highest level of Pittsburgh's social elite listed in the society Blue Book. Like many of her Junior League friends, Abby was motivated to volunteer at WQED for a variety of reasons not the least of which was a certain *noblesse oblige*. She was pretty, intelligent, had an irreverent sense of humor and unlike her friends, her interest in the station was not a casual one. We were both college graduates, but she was educated at Vassar while I had attended a technical school.

Our points of view on many things, however, were strikingly similar and as we were both sensitive and aware of the nature of events at the station, we were somewhat critical of our surroundings. Mine was an emerging awareness; her's a mature and experienced one. I was struggling to find a way to develop a meaningful career and hopefully earn a living; she was observing the scene from a position of affluence and social status, marking time until marriage. We found agreement on many things and developed a meaningful friendship.

She was interested in every aspect of the new enterprise and had the ear of important people who had leverage to make changes if they were deemed necessary. As our friendship became more personal, we occasionally would take a break for a gin and tonic at the Webster Hall Hotel across the street to hash over the day's events, many times with other volunteers and occasionally by ourselves. It required only limited conversation for Abby to understand my station in life, and where I fit into the broad socio-economic spectrum; I on the other hand was virtually ignorant of her status other than that she was apparently well positioned and seemingly affluent.

When she made a passing reference to the world of which she was a part, I was curious. Sensing my interest and naïveté, she began to explain how her social status facilitated visits to other cities and countries, how she could expect to be treated and by whom, and how her social position and security at home in Pittsburgh was automatically transferred to any city she chose to visit.

I began to develop an initial, if somewhat superficial, understanding of the structure and complexity of the powerful world to which she belonged that existed, side by side with my own, barely touching, but affecting it with great force. Her answers to my questions were direct and detailed. I was fascinated that our two worlds could co-exist in such close proximity, yet separately, except in certain official, utilitarian and philanthropic ways. It occurred to me that a great majority of the country's and world's populations lived, like myself, in almost total ignorance of what lay beyond the reach of their immediate families and jobs. I was amazed, enthralled, shocked and outraged. I was twenty-nine years old. How could I have lived so long, graduated college, and yet remained so unknowing? How uninformed and inexperienced I was, a child of the working class who had spent four years in a technical school and knew little of history or society or most importantly, the power structure.

My only glimpse of her world, and a private one at that, was an invitation to her home for lunch, where a man-servant, a new experience for me, served us. As our conversations turned eventually to her life and status, she provided me a behind the scenes orientation of the values and activities of Pittsburgh's upper class which included the preferential order of residential locations, professions, organizations, country clubs and activities not only in Pittsburgh, but also across the country. As she explained, her world was totally secure; she never had to worry about her safety or her needs. I was stunned by her revelations; it was the type of life I had read about in "America's Sixty Families" and which I was unable to comprehend. I was face to face with a member of the elite. My $80 per week job and my home on the North Side existed in a different world. And despite the ridiculous nature of our incomparable positions, I was stupidly, impossibly, falling in love with her.

She came to me one day to ask a favor. I would have refused her nothing. She had a friend she said, "A fellow with whom I grew up, attended dance classes, parties and golf tournaments, a member of an affluent family, and in serious trouble; he's developed a drinking habit." He was presently, at her urging, volunteering at WQED and as she mentioned his name I realized I had met him. What was the favor? "Would you please help him to learn to direct so perhaps he might be able eventually to get a job in television and make his life worthwhile?" The irony was overwhelming. Was she, in her concern for her friend, unaware of it? I was working at a low paying job, hoping to make a life for myself out of nothing, overcoming severe disabilities to do it, and was being asked to help an overindulgent, healthy, wealthy, spoiled young man my age to make something of himself. I couldn't believe she would make such a request. Had she no idea how difficult a time I was having and what it was costing me to try to make something of my life? Her apparent insensitivity belied what I perceived to be her character, and then I concluded, from my infatuated point of view, that perhaps she really didn't understand what a difficult time I was actually having and had had? Certainly, in a sense, I was "passing." My visual appearance did not go unnoticed, but I had so well hidden my discomforts and difficulties, that she, who had come to know me better than most, still had no more understanding of my real condition than I had of her social status. In a strange way, I reasoned, her asking for my help could be construed as a compliment in that she perceived me as somebody who, despite obvious difficulties, had his life in some reasonable order.

Together we found a volunteer production assignment for Andrew and in a short time he was directing station breaks and spending many evenings at the station helping out, and working crew instead of sitting in bars. Abby was hopeful. It is ironic that Andrew later found a job as a director at one of the local commercial stations that declined to hire me.

A few months later Andrew invited me to his home for a drink one evening after we had completed our respective directorial chores. Beside myself, there would be Abby, Andrew, and another volunteer, a woman whom both Andrew and I had dated occasionally and who worked as a legal secretary in an office adjacent to Andrew's father's office. She knew his father and playfully called him "Uncle Jack." After I received the invitation, Abby drew me aside. "You're about to have your first encounter with my milieu. I have to tell you what is going to happen so that you can appreciate it when it does. Otherwise you'll never know it." I was obtuse. "It's simply an invitation to have a drink. What is the big deal?"

"The big deal is that because you'll be in Andrew's house you're going to be presented to his mother and you'll be rejected

by her." That got my attention. "You're putting me on. How do
you know she'll even be there much less reject me?"

"I know she'll be there because its her place to be there, to
know who is in her house, and she will reject you because she will
examine you and you won't pass the examination." What was she
telling me? Suddenly a simple invitation for a drink had assumed
alarming proportions. I was now aware that we were discussing
something about which I had no knowledge, something that had
to do with the fact that I didn't belong. She had my undivided attention. "This is what is going to happen. When we get there Andrew
will take us into the family parlor and we will have a drink. Then
his father will come in and you'll be introduced. You'll like him,
he's a great guy and he will be very man-to-man, very cordial, and
will chat with you for a moment or two. Then he will excuse himself at which point Andrew's mother will enter and you'll be presented to her. Don't shake her hand unless she offers first. She will
be gracious and say "Hello" to everyone, with deference to me,
and then she will chat a bit with you. It will be a very innocent conversation but within it, very tactfully, she will ask you three questions: "Where do you live? Where did you go to school? and What
does your father do? If you answer honestly, and there's no reason
not to, your responses will tell her that you didn't attend a socially
acceptable school, like Princeton, Yale, Dartmouth, or Harvard,
and you don't live in one of the socially acceptable areas that I've
told you about; and your father is not in a business that is socially
acceptable like a banker, broker, lawyer or doctor. That tells her
that you are a person with whom she does not have to bother and
to whom she has no obligation, so she will excuse herself, come
and spend a few minutes with me since my status obligates her to
do that, and then she'll excuse herself." I was in shock. Even with
the information she had previously given me, I never had imagined that such a calculating, demeaning ceremony existed. That it
was a standard ritual was disturbing. How precise. How surgical.
With three questions she would establish my pedigree and eliminate an intruder from her world. I couldn't help asking again,
"You're putting me on?"

"No, I'm telling you about the milieu in which I live. It's a
damnable practice, but that's the way it's done and if a person does-
n't belong, there are not many possibilities for them to get through

the screening. It's a protective wall that permits people who belong to avoid interference and possible exploitation from those who do not. I think it stinks, but I've lived in it all my life and it makes life very simple and secure." My amazement was evident. "Don't worry about it. I just thought you'd want to know."

I'd no idea of the relative social standings of many of the people with whom I had casual, friendly contact at the station, all of whom were educated, well dressed, well mannered, friendly, and seemingly very sophisticated, but ignorance is bliss and I had forged right ahead, unknowingly. Now I began to wonder how many times I had made a fool of myself in their eyes. It wasn't a happy thought.

I realized I wasn't unique in my ignorance. There were many volunteers like me, working class people who saw the advent of this new television station as a potential stepping stone to an interesting career, who had no idea as to the complex mix of people of disparate status that met at WQED and formed a seeming esprit de corps. It was a healthy mix, on the one hand, a group of young people, and some not so young and of independent means who were earnestly dedicated to making the enterprise succeed while satisfying their need to do something they could call real work. On the other hand, there were those of the working class who, for a variety of reasons, wanted to be a part of something new and exciting, launch a new career, or fill a void. I belatedly realized that there was probably a significant amount of social activity among the upper levels that surrounded the daily activities at the station in which people like me were not included. Apart from the occasional gin and tonic at the hotel, my social group consisted of staff members and volunteer staff that lunched together or had a beer and a sandwich after signoff each evening and as far as I knew there was no one of social status in that group.

We arrived at Andrew's home, a large, expensive, stone house in a very desirable part of the city, similar to the old mansion that housed the television station. Wood paneling was exquisite and everywhere. In the spacious entryway a large main staircase boasting an intricately carved rail rose gracefully to the second floor; large fireplaces were in every room, expensive appointments, drapes, furniture, crystal and silver were in abundant display. We were shown into the family parlor: a large room with comfortable, well-used furniture and several shelves holding silver pieces and expensively bound books. Andrew served drinks, and it wasn't long before his father entered and was introduced. I was producing my first television shows, about private aviation. His father had seen one of them and, having flown in the army in World War I, was interested. We talked about flying, man to man. Abby had positioned herself directly across the room from me easily within my line of vision. I caught her eye. Andrew's father shook hands and excused himself, spending a moment with Abby and then leaving the room. Andrew's mother entered and said hello to both women. Andrew introduced me. She sat on a chair next to me and was charming. I could feel Abby's eyes on me. Andrew's mother chatted about how wonderful it was to have an educational television station in the city and asked what I did there, and then, quite casually, "Where did you go to school?" First question. It boomed through the room, echoed in my head. I flashed a quick glance at Abby. She looked back, her eyes twinkling. "I studied art at Carnegie Tech" and as I said it all of the "glorious history" of Tech came back to me in a torrent. Andrew Carnegie had founded Carnegie Institute of Technology with the express purpose of providing his developing steel industry with the number and varieties of technically trained engineers needed to make the industry grow, a school to train his workers, an investment with a phenomenal payoff. And now, in 1955 I was sitting in a family parlor, talking to the very socially conscious wife of a man whose fortunes were directly tied to the Mellon steel, oil, railroad, coal and other interests and I had just told her that I was one of the workers. Strike one! We chatted some more. Was I a Pittsburgher? Yes I was. "Oh really. Where do you live?" Second Question. I glanced at Abby. She had a mischievous grin, and as she met my glance she engaged Andrew in conversation and looked away. It was well she did. As I began to realize how accurately Abby had called the play, the reality of my situation appalled me. The process to which I was being subjected was at the same time both humiliating and hilarious. I bit my tongue to repress a smile. "North Side" and I continued the thought in my head "...where all the workers live" as she prepared her last question. It came without preamble. She was sure of her ground now. There was no more need to prolong matters. All that her position required was that she be gracious. "What does your father do?" There it was. My father was a store window display decorator. "Oh really, that must be very interesting." Strike Three! "Please excuse me; I must go chat with Abby. It was so nice to meet you." I saw the humor in the situation and could read "Was I right?" in Abby's eyes, but I was angry as hell. I had been insulted and there wasn't a thing I could think of that I could do about it. However adroitly applied, this was the first demonstration of actual naked power I had ever witnessed and I couldn't imagine what might happen to me if I decided to tell her what I thought of it. All I knew was that I had been invited for a drink, in all probability as a means of being thanked for being kind to her son, and in return had been demeaned and humiliated. It seemed senseless for her to have even initiated the routine. Andrew, via Abby, could have given his mother all the information she needed, if indeed she needed it and I doubted that she did, since the closest my life could ever possibly come to hers were my lip prints on one of her gin and tonic glasses and the temporary depression in her well worn parlor chair caused by my working class derriére. I had been led into a situation that could have been avoided, except that Abby had thought that, as an objective observer I would be interested in the procedure, and so she had explained it to me. But it had happened; therefore apparently there was some need for it to happen. What was that need? Was it actually out of insecurity and protection, or was it simply an exercise of power? Was it enjoyable? Did the examinee's feelings never even enter into the equation? It was an educational and frightening glimpse into an America of which I was not a citizen and the more impressive because it was my first encounter and brought home how really inconsequential, how unimportant I was to people of means and social position. I was devastated. It would stay with me the rest of my life. I understood how, for the majority of Americans, the upper class remains as invisible as the fourth dimension.

******

As the summer of 1956 flew by it was apparent that my days at WQED were numbered. The project director had grown in stature with the success of her project and she used her newly gained leverage to exert pressure on station management to ensure that come fall, she would have her own, full-time dedicated artist. I was approached with the suggestion that I assume that position. She liked what I had done for her and told me so, but she wanted all of me, or all of whomever replaced me. I viewed my recently learned skills and experience in this new industry as my ticket to a new and bright future. With new television stations opening all over the country, I assumed I could break free from graphic hackwork that held no future potential and minimal rewards. I wanted to produce, design and direct, if not at WQED, then elsewhere. My understanding was that if I did not remain as artist within the funded instructional project, there was no other staff job into which I might fit. Unbeknownst to me, my lack of sophistication and discretion in political matters, and my tendency to be outspoken and direct, placed me at a disadvantage. Candid I was; politic I was not. When the program manager invited me to a meeting to discuss future employment at WQED, I was surprised to hear him say, "It appears that every time I turn around I hear your voice commenting." It was an oblique reprimand. Indeed I had been outspoken. As a volunteer that could be tolerated; as a staff member it could not. At a time when a politic reply might have been, "Have I offended someone? If I have, I am sorry. It was not my intention," I foolishly, and stupidly placed my need to express what I perceived as my rights above my need to have a job and responded, "I suppose I was merely expressing my opinion," thereby closing the door to any discussion of jobs which might be available. Of one thing I was certain. I was a good director, I could feel it deep inside me. With more experience I could be even better. Somewhere, somehow, I was going to make directing a career.

Snyder's film project had drawn to a close as my final days as Art Director approached. He was headed back to New York City. George approached me one day, "Are you staying here?"

"No."

"Where are you going?"

"I'm thinking of going to New York and trying to get a job there. What are you going to do?" George had a knowing grin on his face as he answered, "I've got a job in St. Louis."

"What are you going to do in St. Louis?"

"Well, Bob got me the job with a friend of his, Alfred Stern, who is producing a big celebration called the Mid America Jubilee."

"And what are you gonna do at the Jubilee?"

"I'm Director of special events shows."

"What's that mean?"

"There will be a large exhibition, a small World's Fair type of event. It will have an afternoon pageant every afternoon that will utilize every potential performer in the area, the idea being that the greater the number of people that take part in the pageants, the greater will be the number of their friends and relatives who will buy admission to the fair in order to see them perform. I'll produce the pageants."

George grinned. In the open and frank manner we had adopted between us I said, "George, how the hell are you going to do that? You don't know a damn thing about producing shows." George grinned again, "I'm going to hire you to do it." My response was explosive, "In a pig's ass you are." George headed for the door, "Well, give it some thought. It's only for August and September at $150 a week plus a place to live and a big expense account. And you can go to New York in October."

The final days slipped by and every once in a while George would reiterate the invitation. The last thing I wanted was to be placed in the position of having to do the job that George had been hired to do and, knowing George, being paid half of what he would be paid. Nevertheless, it was almost double what I was making at WQED and the more I thought about it the more I felt that it might be a good project to have on my resume and I'd be able to save a few bucks at the same time. In addition, my brother had just graduated in June and taken a job with McDonnell Aircraft. He was living with his wife and baby in St. Louis. It might be fun. I anguished about it, my pride hurt at the thought of working for George, but with nothing else on the horizon and two months' salary tantalizing me I decided to accept George's offer and arranged to meet him in St. Louis on August 1.

Saying my goodbyes at the station was difficult. It had been my whole life for two years. In saying goodbye to Abby I couldn't resist making an oblique reference to the possibility that our relationship might possibly develop further. Her quick response was, "Oh no, that's impossible." The window through which I had had a peek at a different world slammed shut. It was a delightful friend-

ship, but it stretched across an unbridgeable chasm. I was heart-
broken.

******

The Mid America Jubilee of 1956 was the first time that the
city of St. Louis had made a bid for national visibility since the
1904 World's Fair. After fifty-two years, the City fathers had finally
decided to create a major industrial fair as a precursor to a World's
Fair they excitedly planned for 1960. Mid America Jubilee was to
be, in effect, a practice run. Forty acres along the waterfront, immediately south of the Eades Bridge, on the site occupied subsequently by the Saarinen Arch (Gateway Arch), was the location of
the fair grounds and work had begun months before, anticipating
opening for a thirty-day period, on September 1. At the main
entrance of the Old Cathedral, the oldest religious edifice west of
the Mississippi, a multi-level stage had been built and a five thousand seat grandstand erected. A full, Broadway style historical pageant featuring singing and dancing would be presented each
evening with lights, sound, scene changes and special effects
manned by Hollywood technical crews. On the same stage every
afternoon there would be a pageant that showcased the talents of
local performers. On each of the four Sundays in September one of
the local religious groups would present a program. These afternoon programs, one for each of the thirty days of September, constituted the Special Events Shows.

As of Aug. 1 our goal was to audition every possible performing act in the area, and, using as many as possible, write, produce,
and direct thirty pageants. With the assumption that it might rain at
least twice during the month, we arbitrarily set two rain dates and
began immediately to lay out and prepare twenty-eight pageants.

In response to newspaper ads and articles about the Jubilee,
individual and group performers came forward by the dozens from
all over the St. Louis area. For the first two weeks, George and I
were constantly occupied auditioning performers and collecting
contact information. Our "auditions" had little to do with quality;
our purpose was to identify individuals and groups interested in
performing in one of our loosely produced pageants. Among the

variety of individual acts were singers, dancers, whistlers, one-man bands, jugglers, contortionists, instrumentalists, magicians and aerialists, plus a variety of professional entertainers from the surrounding area. Group performers included gymnasts, acrobats, choruses, choirs, bands, dance troupes, marching and drill teams, motorcycle and horse troops, and dog acts. As the lists of performers grew, each was assigned a slot in a specific pageant and when the shows started to fill up, George continued to travel around auditioning while I began to write loose narrative scripts which served to draw together a variety of disparate performing acts in viable relationships by inclusion of local historical events and personages. As the scripting progressed it was frequently necessary to switch performers from one show to another, requiring follow up contacts and negotiations.

The process was a hectic, but enjoyable one and most evenings, since we worked late each night auditioning, we sampled a broad variety of St. Louis restaurant fare on the expense account. By the third week of August, I had booked performers and completed scripts for the first ten shows. A number of others were well along in development that was to continue through September as performers dropped out or new ones appeared. The respective religious groups were planning Sunday religious programs that necessitated periodic meetings to plan technical considerations. Invariably, I would be asked by some church official, "What happens if it rains on our Sunday?" to which my standard reply became, "Gentlemen, you are much closer to the source than I. I leave that in your hands." By mid-August we had a need for a typist familiar with typing two-column television scripts. After two tries with a temp service we located and hired a very talented woman who was a great addition to our two man staff.

My brother had just begun his first job and as yet did not have a car. I was surprised one day when George asked me where my brother lived and whether he had a car. "Ask him if he'd like to use mine for a couple of weeks. I have access to a rental car." My brother was delighted and came to pick up the car. A few days later while George was out, I answered a call asking for him. "Could you tell me where he is or how he may be reached? This is the collection agency." I gave them an evasive answer as I thought, wily George, always one step ahead. I called my brother immediately.

"Listen, George loaned you the car because the collection agency is trying to find it to repossess it. If it's not where you left it, don't worry. Just let me know." I didn't mention the matter to George.

The audio technicians who manned the Special Events Shows were the same Hollywood crews who worked the evening extravaganza and their pre-set mikes, which were strung along the proscenium of the multilevel stage, were more than adequate for the afternoon shows' needs. For special circumstances they could add whatever was needed. The director's booth, which enclosed the audio controls, was set in the middle of the grandstand with a full view of the stage so the audio man could easily see which mike the performer would be using. To operate the cueing for entrances and exits, four experienced stagehands from the local theater (each wearing a headset), served as stage managers at the various stage entrances. I directed the programs like television shows, assigning each performer to a specific stage entrance and exit to add variety to the programs. On my cue, by headset, the stage manager would push the performer on stage after telling him where to exit.

The musical element for the shows was a fourteen-piece band under the direction of Carl Hohengarten, music director for KMOX. Carl had formerly been music director for CBS Radio in New York City and had returned home to St. Louis to enjoy a less hectic life. Each show had a pre-show walk-through rehearsal during which Carl established the music and key required for each performer. With his skill Carl was able to make many of the amateur performers sound more professional.

In addition to the Special Events Shows, George was responsible for organizing the opening parade that consisted predominately of high school bands from around the area and several military marching units and bands including the American Legion, and the Veterans of Foreign Wars. A week before the parade, while George was out of the office, the phone rang. "This is the United Federation of Musicians. We understand that you are having a parade?"

" Yes we are."

"Do you have a union band in your parade?"

"All of the bands are high school marching bands. We didn't know there was a union band in the city."

"There isn't."

"I don't understand."

"Well don't you think there should be a union band in your parade, a paid union band?"

"If there's no union band, where will the musicians come from?"

"Well, there are a lot of union musicians in the city, in the Symphony, and the Municipal Opera Orchestra and in several bands."

"And they want to march?"

"Sure"

"And they are uniformed?"

"They will be." It was clear that if there were no union band in the parade there would be no parade. "Well, if there's a union band, and it has uniforms, and it marches...they have to march the whole parade and play... then we'd be delighted to have them participate." I chuckled as I envisioned all those symphony musicians in uniform, marching in a parade. I wondered how many of them would be able to do it, but if the union wanted to exert its power there was no sense arguing. As it happened, by the time the parade was in the final few blocks, most of the union musicians were having a hard time just walking, much less playing. They earned their union wages that day.

On Sept. 1, the sun was bright and hot for the first show and it proceeded without a hitch. There was a good crowd at the fair and in the stands. I was in my element. It was a new kind of directing situation, but it was essentially the television form. The crew was professional and cooperative, a friendly group, respecting my directorial authority and doing everything they could to help me. With George things were a bit different because the stagehands recognized immediately that he had no knowledge of theatrical production. George had been watching television and saw a singer enveloped in a swirling fog, a studio production effect that utilizes special equipment to mix dry ice, hot water or steam and fans to create fog in a closed studio environment. George made the mistake of seeking out the special effects crew chief for the night-time show and asked him how he could get the fog effect for a number in one of the daytime shows. The crew chief knew a rookie when he saw one and the next day, under a bright sun, George was in the middle of the stage with a wheelbarrow, in which he had a cake of dry ice and a teakettle with hot water. He was pouring the water on the ice and of course, under the bright sun, there was not even a wisp of vapor. I came on the scene about that time and, not noticing the crew, who were hiding behind the set pieces and laughing tears, asked, "George, what the hell are you doing?" As I did so I caught sight of the crew and in a flash knew what had happened. George began to explain that he was trying to make fog for a particular number so I nodded to the crew, left George to his own devices and ran to hide my own merriment.

Once in a while the stagehands played games with me, too, although good-naturedly. One day the British bagpipers, The Black Watch were scheduled to appear and my stagehand at the pre-assembly area called me on the headset to tell me that they were upstairs in the rear of the church, raving drunk. He wasn't kidding. I told him to just let them be and I removed them from the show. In the midst of the confusion, he called me again and said, "Norb, what do you want me to do with the elephants?" "Elephants? For Chrisakes, what elephants?" I screamed, at which all the stagehands roared over the headsets.

For the following two weeks things went smoothly and hundreds of performers each had their time in the sun. The shows were pulling an audience and the more people in the show, the more people in the audience. The second Sunday was the Lutheran program. They had prepared a spectacular. It was a ninety-minute program with two hundred speaking and singing parts and dramatic action all over the multi-level stage. Julie, a drama teacher at the Lutheran High School had written the lengthy script and directed the show, rehearsing it in acts at the Lutheran school. There was barely enough time for a full rehearsal, but with Julie seated next to me in the control booth following the script and serving as assistant director, we managed to complete a run through.

A highlight of the performance was a thirty-voice choir, hidden in the Old Cathedral, which served as the stage backdrop. At a specific point, the cathedral doors would open, the choir would emerge singing, do a processional around the stage, and re-enter the cathedral. A stage manager was inside the church ready to cue the choir and open the doors. As the time for the choir approached, the lead actor, on stage, blew two pages out of the script, pages that contained entry cue lines for the choir. Realizing his mistake, he paused. Going back would have thrown the entire show into turmoil. To the stage manager near the actor I said, "Tell him to go on. Do not go back." And to the stage manager in the church, I said, "Lock the door and get the hell out of there." Julie was almost apoplectic, but she was familiar with stage work. She questioned me. "Julie, if we try to go back we'll lose the whole show. We'll never get it started again. We can't do it. Tell them I'm sorry as hell, but we have to go forward. Blame it on me. I won't be here." Without further incident, the pageant concluded and I made a hasty departure.

Lack of rain required producing two extra shows, but by that time it was old hat. The Jubilee ended at the end of the month. Although judged a success, the St. Louis sponsors, after examining the books at the end the Festival, decided that the better part of valor was to forget about having a world's fair in 1960. I headed east, first to Pittsburgh and then on to New York.

9

In, Out and Back Again

I arrived in New York City in October with no immediate prospects. Mother's widowed sister, Marge, offered me a cot in her small single bedroom apartment in Flushing. Marge, like Louise, had married a Jewish man, Joe Levin, who was also a Pittsburgher. Joe worked as an engineer employed by the New York City Department of Public Works. As a young man during the Depression, he had worked in the freight yards in Pittsburgh unloading freight cars while he took engineering classes at Carnegie Tech in the evenings. As the economy improved he had stopped his studies to work full-time in order to assist his younger sister, Rose, acquire a college education; she ultimately completed her doctorate and became an influential member of the Pittsburgh School System's administrative staff. Joe never completed his degree.

As a Jew, Joe found job advancement difficult in Pittsburgh and eventually found work as a metallurgist for the Roebling Cable Company in Trenton, New Jersey at the time the company was fabricating cables for the San Francisco Golden Gate Bridge. Marge, visiting him one weekend, phoned Mother to announce that she and Joe had married. Joe's work subsequently took them to New York City where they lived quietly until Joe succumbed to a massive heart attack leaving Marge alone and far removed from family. Having worked as a secretary, Marge found a job through a friend in a small, privately owned varityping service where she soon became expert in the then new typesetting machines that were replacing linotype machines in the newspaper industry. At the time I came to stay with her she had advanced to the position of head of the varitype department at the New York Times. After taking my car into Manhattan a few times, I discovered that it was not only trouble, but expensive, and opted to use the subway. Marge's apartment was several blocks from the end of the Flushing IRT subway line, too far for me to walk, so I located a place closer to the subway to park my car. The daily commuting situation was much like the experience I'd had going to and from junior and senior high schools. In addition to the discomfort it caused me, it brought back the unpleasant memories of those strenuous years. Using the subway, and, when in the city, buses, required much walking and standing during each day's ad hoc schedule which I pieced together as the day progressed. I'd make calls from the apartment in the morning trying to set up appointments and then, in Manhattan, as my schedule changed from hour to hour with appointments invariably being delayed, changed or cancelled, I'd rearrange my day using pay phones. It was necessary to be immediately at the beck and call of anyone who would agree to see me and consequently, I never had the opportunity to plan the much needed rest stops or pace myself through the day. I would frequently have to walk to and from bus stops and subways, then stand while waiting and sometimes while riding. Invariably, there would be that last extra block between the bus stop or the subway and my destination.

For anyone living in a large metropolitan area, the use of public transportation is both a necessity and convenience, a regular routine that over time becomes not only least demanding and time consuming, but also contains predictable periodic breaks for eating and opportunities to use restrooms. I had no such routine; every day, every hour was unpredictable as I searched for employment. I was constantly on the move and frequently, when I needed to rest, there was no convenient place available. I tenaciously continued, soaked with perspiration, as I had done in school.

My contacts in the City were very few: Bill Wood, the first general manager of WQED was now teaching at Columbia; Bob Snyder was in and out of the city as he continued his film productions; and Seymore Siegel, general manager of the city's non-commercial television station to whom the friendly Lenore Elkus had written me an introduction. Both Bob and Bill were empathetic and each offered a few names to contact. I read Variety and the daily newspapers, but soon learned that it was rare to be able to obtain a television job from newspaper ads. By the time the ads appeared, the jobs were filled. In my search for employment, I did all the usual things. I networked with the few people I met and attempted, wherever possible, to move through them and up the ladder to people who were in charge of hiring. I answered ads, signed up with placement agencies, production companies, stations, networks, ad agencies, using every trick in my not-so-sophisticated-bag to get to that one person who had an opening and the authority to fill it. I made lists of key people at the networks and local stations and made cold calls repeatedly trying to obtain interviews. I was convinced that if I could meet and talk with the right person, I would have a chance to be hired. Although I was not directly refused, I was met with the evasive, finessed responses for which every worthwhile New York secretary had infinite skill, and more often than not, no appointment resulted from my efforts. I visited employment offices, filled out applications and left my resume and while there fished for names and any information which might facilitate further calls. I talked to a lot of people, and actually met a few important ones, usually those who were doing someone a favor by meeting with me, and who knew they were not expected to hire me. All of these people were nice to me. I was not streetwise and above all, I was not New York City wise, but it didn't require a lot of experience to know that I was unable to penetrate the outermost defenses of the industry that held so much promise and allure. Slowly, ever so slowly, I began to develop a feel for how the system worked, what the questions would be and which responses permitted my phone calls to be extended if only to gather additional information.

I examined every possible approach. I contacted Alfred Stern who had produced the Mid America Jubilee in St. Louis. Alfred was under contract to the United States government to produce certain aspects of the government's exhibits at the world's fair in Zagreb, Yugoslavia. Alfred's first question was, "Can you speak German?" Without the language, Alfred couldn't use me. I'd had considerable experience at WQED doing scenic design; perhaps I could gain entry as a scenic designer.

John McMahon, then head of scenic design at ABC had written a book on scene design, which I had read and from which I'd learned a lot. Surprisingly I was able to obtain an appointment. It had been my experience that if an important person agreed to an interview, it meant that there were no jobs available and the person had some time on his hands, but I was nevertheless always thankful for the opportunity. Who could tell, perhaps something might come of it?

Mr. McMahon gave me a lot of time. He examined my portfolio carefully and asked questions: "How did you do this? This is good." Or "How did you light this?" and then proceeded to describe similar things he had done in his days of live television in Philadelphia. It was a pleasant conversation. "So you're thinking about becoming a scenic designer? Are you familiar with what it entails? No? Well, first you'll have to find a designer in the union who will take you on as an apprentice. That's not really a problem, but you'll have to pay him about $1,200 to $1,500 for that. He'll coach you and teach you for about six months and you'll be guaranteed to pass the union exam. And when you do you'll be one of several hundred designers, nationwide, about four percent of whom are making a living in the industry." A possible career, even an entry, as a scenic designer seemed to blow up in my face. Another dead end. Considering the fact that scene painting was hard physical work requiring much standing, and I didn't have $1,500, it wasn't difficult persuading myself that scenic design might not be my yellow brick road.

My cousin Walter, back in Pittsburgh, gave me an introduction to a neighbor who was the BBD&O Advertising Agency's Pittsburgh liaison for the United States Steel Hour drama series and commuted to New York from Pittsburgh weekly. He met me in the plush BBD&O offices and was quite friendly, but quick to inform me that there were no openings at that time in the agency. He referred me to the Creative Vice President in charge of all television activities who arranged an appointment for me that very day with an executive at WNEW-TV. The executive, an amiable Jewish man, greeted me pleasantly and suggested I see one of two executives at WOR-TV and their counterparts at WABC, WNBC and WCBS. I thought about what was happening. I had actually walked on the golden carpet at BBD&O and spoken to their creative vice-president who introduced me to the general manager of a large metropolitan television station who had, in turn, identified persons elsewhere in the industry with whom I should talk. In a devastating way it was amusing, but it was also terrifying, for it gave me an insight into the enormity of the task at hand. I imagined myself as a ball in a four bank carom shot on a billiard table, from my cousin to BBD&O to WNEW-TV to WOR-TV to back on the street. Each man had fulfilled his obligation to the other, been civil and friendly and even empathetic, but nowhere had I had a job interview or any suggestion that one might be possible. I had simply been passed on from one man to the next. With all of my cousin's friend's influence and leverage at BBD&0, he couldn't, or wouldn't arrange for me to be interviewed by anyone there, so he arranged for me to meet a man who was the head of one of the local New York television stations, and who happened to be a Jew. I remembered my father telling me how impossible it was for a Jewish man to find employment in Pittsburgh in any of the industries that were in any way a part of the Mellon interests and I remembered, looking back at my own meager and naive days of freelancing as a designer, that every one of the people who had hired me had been a Jew. Now here I had talked to a BBD&O advertising man who managed an account for United States Steel, and I was referred to a couple of Jews. I had never thought of myself as disabled and I never thought of myself as a Jew. I had to admit however, that as far as the wider world was concerned, I fit into two of Goffman's three categories of stigma.

It was arranged for me to watch a rehearsal of that week's *United States Steel Hour*, a live-broadcast drama, and I enjoyed watching the complex production. It was fascinating to observe the skill with which the disparate parts of the live production were brought together. This was television drama in its finest hour and for a few minutes I had a ringside seat. I was impressed at the speed with which the cameras were able to move to catch an actor going through a doorway and coming out the other side, how the settings were positioned to permit such travel, how a microphone on a long bamboo pole could be held over a flat just long enough to pick up a single line of dialogue, and how the lights were hung and focused. I knew enough about the process to appreciate the details and nuances. It was an education.

Bob Snyder introduced me to Biff Liff who at the time was stage manager for the hit Broadway show *My Fair Lady* and Biff invited me to come watch the show from the wings. I stood in the wings at stage right adjacent to the lighting man who, it developed, knew Roy Nelligan, the stage hand at WQED. The only place to stand afforded no possibility for me to lean for support and as the show progressed I became increasingly uncomfortable. Julie Andrews had several entrances and exits near me and I was thrilled at my proximity to the star. Seeing the show from such a unique perspective was yet another learning experience, but I was in such pain when it was over that I could hardly make it out the stage door and once on the sidewalk I had to find a place to sit and recover.

I learned that appointments with upper-level executives were almost impossible to get and that many of the lower level "would be executives," engaged, in their free time, in an ego building game of interviewing applicants that apparently enhanced their own sense of importance. I experienced the usual number of: "Call me later in the day. Call me later in the week, Call me next week," situations. When I did obtain an interview the would-be employer would look at my resume, usually with interest, and then, with surprise or bafflement, give me a more intense examining look. I could see his confusion between what my resume stated I had done and what his assessment of my appearance suggested I could do. I was never asked about my disabilities. I was simply not someone they could envision as being useful.

I noticed an article in the paper about closed-circuit television being used at NYU and called to ask if I might visit and see what they were doing. I was connected to the office of Dr. Harvey Zorbaugh who headed the Communication Arts Group and invited to visit. I had an enjoyable, but brief meeting with Zorbaugh who referred me to another office in the next building. When I entered the second office I was surprised to see Richard Goggin who had been the producer of the "Town Hall" program for which I had designed the sets at WQED. Dick was now chair of the Television, Motion Pictures and Radio Department and greeted me with a pleasant show of friendship. "Tell me what you're doing in New York?" I outlined what I had been doing since we last met and Dick gave me a tour of the tiny, low ceiling studio that they were using and introduced me to Mike Volpe, the engineer. Back in his office Dick asked if I might be interested in designing a grouping of set pieces that could be used for their closed circuit broadcasts. We talked about how the pieces would be used and Dick apologetically told me the small amount he had to spend. It was OK. It was something to do, and a few extra dollars. I did the designs and drew the construction drawings and the maintenance men at NYU built the set pieces in the next few weeks. After seeing the completed units installed, Dick questioned me about my directing experience and then asked if I'd like to direct a special program they were planning for entering students. "They'll see it in the large assembly room in the next building, but you'll do it here in the studio." The straightforward script had already been written; essentially a talking head. I asked if they might wish to make it a bit more interesting and proposed a number of ideas and visuals that Dick accepted with great interest and the show was well received. As the result of that directorial assignment, having demonstrated that I was quite familiar with all aspects of television production, Dick had another offer. "Do you think you could handle a beginning class in television studio production and direction? Right now I'm teaching it, but I could use the time for other things." Dick briefed me on the syllabus and the routine exercises of the course and I taught the course, which met weekly in a four-hour session. Dick and Haig Manoogian, who taught the advanced production course, visited my class several times and were highly supportive.

The extra dollars and the acceptance at NYU heightened my hopes, but it was just a part-time arrangement. My days were spent on buses, subways and in phone booths, trying and hoping to find someone who might hire me. On one occasion I thought I had a real "in" since I had obtained an interview with the Director of Public Affairs at NBC through his secretary who had been a volunteer with me at WQED. She was attractive, very bright, extremely well connected socially and had been working in various secretarial jobs at NBC for several months searching for the right position. I hoped that, since I had an inside connection, there might be a chance of a job. I was wrong. I was in and out of the Director's office in less than five minutes without a chance to even engage him in conversation, the shortest interview I ever had. I was humiliated, embarrassed and angry, but all I could do was thank Sally and leave as fast as possible.

I tried in every way I could imagine to find a job in New York, any job in the television industry, with never a doubt that I could perform. Confidence in myself, however, proved to be of no consequence in my finding a job. Deep inside me I knew that when an interviewer looked at me they were unable to reconcile what they saw with what my resume proclaimed I had done. Then one day, I had an unusual interview with the program manager at a local television station. The man was very kind and forthright. He studied my resume and looked at my portfolio with great care and interest, taking his time, and then, easing back in his chair he looked directly at me. "You have good experience and I believe that you can do everything you say you can do." This was an obvious reference to the difference between my physical appearance and my resume. I waited. "I'm sure that if I put you in the director's booth you could do the news with only a couple of hours practice. Unfortunately, that's not the way it happens in New York. If you want to produce or direct here, it would require some experience at a commercial station outside of the City and then you could come in and I could hire you for that kind of a job. Otherwise, the road to the director's chair begins as a gopher, and in all candor, I can't personally justify putting you in that kind of an arms and legs job where you'll be required to get coffee for people who may not know as much as you do." It was a disappointing moment, but an enlightening one. I was wasting my time trying to get a job in New York City. This man was sufficiently empathetic to tell me what I was up against. He knew I could not take on a job as a gopher, and so did I. The interview proved to me, not only how people who were interviewing me and seeing me for the first time perceived me, but also revealed something about the system. I either had to begin at the bottom again or I had to come to New York with sufficient commercial experience to permit an employer to overlook my disabilities. Wouldn't this same criterion prevent my developing a track record outside New York? "Thank you for your candor. "I said, "I want you to know how much I appreciate it. It's not what I want to hear, but it's what I need to know." I'd been in New York for eight months. I'd had a try at fulfilling a dream and it hadn't worked. It was time to go home.

******

Back in Pittsburgh I was at a loss as to how to proceed. As I contemplated my experience in New York, I tried to conceive a job-hunting approach that might assist me in leaping the barrier posed by my disabilities. I was beginning to understand that in the world of work there existed a general hierarchy in which the physical, laborious jobs were at the bottom and the creative and intellectual ones were higher up the ladder. It appeared that unless one was able to persevere at the bottom there was very little chance to gain the middle ground. For someone like me who was unable to perform the menial physical tasks, the possibilities for anything higher were extremely limited. I believed that I had put in my time, paid my dues so to speak, on the lower rungs as a volunteer at WQED and had indeed been rewarded with more challenging responsibilities and assignments, but my accomplishments there held little weight in the competitive world of New York City, or elsewhere. WQED, as a new and innovative organization, had a more pliable atmosphere and I had taken advantage of it to the fullest and done well, but it was also misleading regarding the type of jobs and activities I might expect to be able to obtain in the industry elsewhere.

I also had the feeling that there was an additional factor at work in the mix, that a disabled person who could perform a task competitively with a normal person could sometimes be perceived, subjectively, as a unique threat. I knew that there were countless would-be, able-bodied directors and actors who were having just as difficult a time as I was, pursuing their dream while they worked at menial jobs as waiters, janitors, messengers, or taxi drivers. Unfortunately, I couldn't pursue my dream that way because I couldn't perform those jobs, not even driving a taxi. Although I was an expert and safe driver, no company would hire me because their insurance policy wouldn't cover me.

If I wasn't going to be able to find work in the television industry, what was I capable of doing? I was now beginning to perceive my job search as an adversarial situation. What would "they" permit me to do, I wondered? And then I asked myself, where did the "they" come from? Who are "they"? This was a thought I hadn't had before. Was there actually some kind of conspiracy in play? Certainly, I knew that my disabilities made it more difficult to find the kind of employment I sought. I realized that a blind man couldn't be an airline pilot, but was I in that category? Was I actually attempting to do the impossible? I couldn't believe it was impossible. Obviously there was a difference between what a stranger believed I could do and what it was actually possible for me to do. Putting television programs together was a process I had no difficulty performing. Why did it pose such problems for others? I remembered though, that John Ziegler had assigned me to teach directing rather than to direct, and when I produced the aviation shows, he had not designated me as director, and John was someone who had seen me in action for a number of months. In addition, directing jobs were highly paid and highly competitive and there were thousands of able bodied young men and women who wanted them. So where should I go? What should I do? If I wasn't going to be able to direct, could I write? I'd already written a number of shows.

I still had little understanding of how commercial television and advertising worked, but I began to explore. I gained an appointment with Roger Wolfe, Program Manager at KDKA-TV. Roger was a warm and sensitive man who just happened to be looking for a writer for a monthly public service medical program called *House Call* that was cooperatively produced by KDKA and the University of Pittsburgh Medical School. Each month House Call spotlighted a particular disease and featured prominent physicians from the University of Pittsburgh Medical School. Carl Ide, the KDKA news anchor-man, was the show's host and Roger was interested in making the no-budget show as theatrical as possible. I was invited to try my hand at writing the show and was introduced to Janet Farrell, Pitt's public relations liaison for the show. I met the studio director for the news department and the station cinematographer and began to work on the first program. For the next nine months I wrote, and as it turned out, produced as well as staged—one thing led to another—a monthly show on geriatrics, diabetes, anatomy, allergies, arteriosclerosis and other medical topics for the magnificent fee of $75 per show. Each month I would meet with that month's designated expert, a physician from the University of Pittsburgh Medical School. After interviewing the physician, I designed the sequences, selected the visuals and exhibits, wrote the script, planned the staging, directed the few bits of location filming that were permitted, and personally and manually edited the film. Then I scripted a series of questions for the interviewer, and turned the package over to the studio director at show time. In my insecurity, as I researched and wrote about each month's disease, I experienced symptoms of that disease.

No other opportunities appeared on the horizon even though I applied for jobs all over the country in the rapidly expanding growth of newly organized educational stations. I had only one interview, in Fort Lauderdale, Florida, for a job that was a combination director, audio man and telecine operator, requiring more physical activity than I believed I could satisfactorily handle and I was forced to bow out. It was a great disappointment.

I troubled over how to present myself in an application letter. Should I frankly state my disabilities and skills at overcoming them or just infer that I had some disabilities? If I did the latter and then appeared, what would be the reaction? I experimented with all options, and when it seemed to make no difference, I decided to be honest and succinct. I enclosed a carefully drafted statement with my letter of application that suggested "...although I do possess a physical disability it is not one which hinders the scope or quality of my work..." It didn't appear to make any difference; I just wasn't generating any interest.

The father of my good friend, Dale Stein, was a partner in a small company that manufactured scientific instruments. One of three partners, he was the only one who believed that the external appearance of their products was an important consideration in their sales and marketing; his partners had no interest in industrial design. Accordingly, Mr. Stein had hired Richard Felver, the head of the Industrial Design Department at Carnegie Tech, to execute the company's designs. As Mr. Stein expressed it, if one of his partner's had a criticism of what was being done or why, he would refer them to the chairman of the Carnegie Tech Design Department, saying "Do you know more than he does?" and that would end the discussion. Nevertheless, Mr. Stein generously and thoughtfully called me and offered me a small job designing the casing for an instrument that measured the airflow through furnace filters. I had taken courses with Richard Felver and had not been impressed with either his designs or his teaching and the idea of being in competition with him, even on a tiny job, was an ego boost. My designs were well received and adopted with the result that Mr. Stein gave me a second job, but with a high priced, highly touted designer such as Felver already on retainer, the two jobs were all that would be available. As Dale told me, "My father would offer you a regular job, but he's afraid that if you accepted it and then you had a chance to get a job in television, you would take the TV job." It was a trial balloon Dale was flying for his dad and we both knew the answer. "I appreciate your dad's interest and I'd enjoy working for him as a designer, but he's right. One way or another, I'm going to work in television."

A new program manager replaced Roger Wolfe at KDKA in the spring of 1959. He was a young, ambitious television executive with primary interest in audience ratings and little interest in public affairs programming. *House Call* was taken off the air. A one time public relations program sponsored by ALCOA, featuring a tour of a newly built house in which all of the electrical circuitry, wall framing, doorways and doors were aluminum, was in planning. The new PM offered me the option to write the show that was to star John Cameron Swayze, the national television spokesman for Timex wristwatches who was being imported from New York City to do the show as a live remote. "It's a one hour show. I'll give you $65," he told me. It was a take it or leave it offer with no room for negotiation. I took it. John Cameron Swayze flew into Pittsburgh from New York and did the show live, from the Aluminum House. There were very few changes made in my script.

1959 was the year of Pittsburgh's bicentennial and a wide variety of activities and events were planned, among them a massed band festival to be held in the University of Pittsburgh's football stadium. With the sensational success of Meredith Willson's musical, *The Music Man* on Broadway, massed band festivals had become a big attraction across the country, particularly in the Midwest. The new NBC television affiliate, WIIC, which had been on the air a little more than a year, planned to produce some television specials. When WIIC had first organized, their staff resided at WQED the year I had been art director. I'd had the opportunity to meet the people who would be in charge at the station and attempted to convince them to hire me, but hadn't been successful. Now, with nine health shows behind me, I proposed an idea to their program manager for a documentary drama on the history of the development of medicine in Pittsburgh that I hoped to write, produce and direct. My short synopsis of the show, entitled *A Point In Time* was as follows:

*"Who is the old man who, when accosted by a young
boy, reveals that he possesses a supernatural ability to
manipulate time, and while he learns of the boy's interest
in medicine, uses his strange power as the means to
answer the boy's questions? In answer to these questions, the history of the development of the science and
art of medicine unfolds in a series of dramatic, musical
and dance sequences that bring to light the names and
happenings of the past world of medicine. The manipulation of time proves to be a critical task and the old man's
miscalculations cause Dr. Meeks, circa 1785, to be
transplanted into modern time. The ensuing conversations between Meeks and well-known Pittsburgh doctors
of the present day provide a first person comparison
between the methods of yesterday and today. With Meeks
transcending the barriers of time almost at will, few of
the problems of modern medicine go untouched. The
dance sequences provide the visual story of the development and growth from a triangle of wilderness to a modern city. In* A Point In Time *this proves to be a continuing
sequence of health problems."*

WIIC bought the idea for a fee that was laughable. With my
imagination running far afield I contacted Genevieve Jones, predominant Pittsburgh dancer whose dance studio was the best
known and respected in the City, and asked if she would be interested in creating a dance sequence which portrayed the founding
of the City at the juncture of the three rivers. She was, and the result
was a successful, if overly ambitious, one-hour docudrama.

Once again the Stein family came to my rescue. Dale confided
in me that a friend of the family, Stanley Levin, then Director of
Music for the Pittsburgh Public Schools, was to produce a massed
band festival for the bicentennial. The Steins had told Stanley about
my producing and directing pageants in St. Louis and Stanley
wanted to meet me. Stanley had great experience with marching
bands and school orchestras, but a massed band festival was something new to him. He viewed the assignment that he had been given
as a monstrous joke. "You know, this could be a phenomenal flop,
it's a complicated piece of work and I'm not sure where to start.

I have to get fifty different bandleaders together to work out how all their bands are going to march at one time, with one brief rehearsal, under the direction of one famous conductor. In addition we have to arrange parking for their buses, box lunches for everyone, police supervision and traffic control and God knows what else." We discussed possible organizational approaches and Stanley hired me to write and direct the festival. Together, we developed a reasonable schedule for the project. The following week Stanley announced that he had contracted with Meredith Willson to make a personal appearance to lead the massed band, with seven hundred and fifty trombones, playing his hit tune "76 Trombones." I wrote the narrator's script, patterned after the loose narrations I had written to serve as continuity for the diverse acts in the pageants in St. Louis. It was a sprawling assemblage of historical sentimentality that traced the city's development from a frontier town to a steel-making metropolis. When Stanley read it he laughed, "My God, it's such schlock. But its O. K., it will work fine." I agreed.

The day for the festival dawned bright and clear. From my director's booth high up on the rim of the Pitt stadium, I was in contact by headset with the announcer and a single assistant, Vitold Sporney, down on the field. Vitold, a high school band leader and friend of Sidney's relayed my directorial commands to assistants on the field who in turn would direct the various bands to position and signal when to begin marching and playing.

The mayor of Pittsburgh came to the director's booth to make a formal welcoming statement on the public address system and on arrival slipped and gashed his shinbone. With blood flowing freely from his leg and a police medical team trying to treat the injury, the mayor made his welcoming address over the loud speaker system and the massed band festival began. For the next hour and a half, the individual bands performed, and guided by Vitold and his assistants, entered the field from their seats in the stands, formed at one end of the field, performed, and then exited smartly back to their seats. For the finale, all of the bands formed on the field, each in the respective positions they had practiced on their home fields and marched while playing a number of marching tunes as a massed band, conducted from a specially constructed podium on the fifty yard line, by Meredith Willson. All of the participants enjoyed the day; but the audience in attendance in the massive stadium, because of conflicting bicentennial events in the same section of town, numbered only a few thousand.

My various small jobs were time consuming, enjoyable and individually successful, but each was a peripheral kind of activity, work that those regularly employed by the sponsoring institutions did not have time to do. I still wasn't earning enough to live anywhere but home, which was a constant source of embarrassment and shame, and between projects I had a lot of time on my hands. To keep busy, I enrolled in a basic playwriting course in the Drama Department at Tech. As an alumnus, I had no trouble being accepted and found it enjoyable and worthwhile, so much so that as the end of summer approached and there was no job in sight I decided that, since theater directing did not require the physical, equipment centered, instantaneous control that was the nature of television, perhaps I should take a closer look at it. I decided I'd get a Master's Degree in Directing at Tech. I talked to the department head, outlining my interest and despite my lack of undergraduate training in drama, I was accepted in the graduate program for the fall semester on the basis of my television directing experience. With only a few days remaining until registration I received a phone call from Dick Goggin at NYU. "We've just gotten a grant from RCA to establish a Center for Educational Television. How would you like to come here and be our Production Supervisor and do some directing on our closed circuit?" Goggin could have hired any number of qualified persons in New York, but had gone out of his way to give me a chance. He knew what a difficult time I was having and wanted to help.

10

Prelude

I returned to New York immediately and again stayed temporarily with Aunt Marge. Now a resident, I was eligible to receive a special handicapped parking permit available from the Traffic Division of the New York City Police Department. I submitted the application and obtained a permit enabling me to park in no-parking areas excluding bus stops and fire lanes. Having a car in New York City put a totally different light on my living there. Places that had been logistically impossible for me a year ago were now accessible. Living in Flushing, I could drive into Manhattan each day. Getting to work at NYU's South Building at the southeastern corner of Washington Square was no longer a transportation problem; it became a comfortable and convenient daily routine.

NYU's new Center for Instructional Television, cooperatively founded by NYU with a grant from the Radio Corporation of America had, as its Director, Lawrence Costello, hired from the State Education Department in Albany where he was involved in closed-circuit television development in the public schools. Larry was a large, overweight bear of a young man with the attitude of a jocular and somewhat obsequious used car salesman. He was essentially a technician with considerable knowledge of the engineering aspects of television, he knew what made it work, but had little interest in or sensitivity to the academic or aesthetic aspects of the medium. Charged with administrating and growing a new organization which included developing new funding sources, he perceived the Center's primary function as teaching teachers how to use television, something he was accustomed to doing in the secondary schools. For Larry this was little more than teaching manipulation of the equipment. My own approach was quite different. I was convinced that the real potential of teaching with television lay in the unlimited and as yet unexplored possibilities for providing visual references, relationships, and examples that could create discovery and enhance, in the mind of the learner, the content being presented. I took great joy in creating ways to do it. Larry never thought about it.

As Production Supervisor my job was to assist Larry in instruction, and prepare the studio for the classes. In addition, and separate from these duties, I would direct an introductory credit course, "Man's Cultural Heritage" being offered to freshman on closed-circuit television by the Sociology Department. I learned on arrival that Goggin was not expected to return from vacation until the week following the one I began work, but he had scheduled a luncheon meeting for me at the faculty club on the north side of Washington Square with the three professors who would teach the course: Dr. Muntz, an elderly gentleman then in the autumn days of his teaching career and Drs. Bressler and Westoff, two brilliant, young and extremely confident professors at the beginning of what would be illustrious careers. I took quick stock of these gentlemen whose tenured professor confidence and superiority seemed to overflow, and wondered why Dick had thrown me, like a Christian to the lions I thought, into this initial meeting, alone and without reinforcement. I had some feelings of uncertainty. We introduced ourselves and had hardly been seated when Bressler looked me square in the eye and in a flat voice laid down a challenge. "And just what is it you're going to do for us?" Returning the look and smiling gently, I riposted, "I'm going to teach you what you don't know about teaching on television, that is, as much as you want to learn."

"And just what might that be?"

"How to act, how to stand, what to do with your hands, how to handle things; how to move, how to organize your presentations so they have a sequential logic to make them understandable and above all how to take advantage of the visual aspects of the medium to emphasize your intent. We won't just point the camera at what you do in the classroom."

My immediate and knowledgeable response surprised them and as we relaxed into a friendlier and less adversarial mood the luncheon progressed and they more or less accepted the idea that we were going to be working together and began to ask more technical questions. I explained my approach. "I would like to meet regularly with each of you prior to your lectures in order to know what you will be discussing, in what sequence and where and how we might be able to develop visual presentations, words, graphs, illustrations, which will punctuate, enhance and clarify your discussion. I'll show you how to use graphics and other props, but we'll use your ideas taking care not to dilute or detour the content. After a show or two it will become second nature to you."

The next week when we met, Dick, with a mischievous glint in his eye, asked me how the meeting had gone. "I thought you had thrown me to the lions," I said. "They were ready to eat me alive, but I think it ended up all right." Dick chuckled, "Bressler and Westoff are two young Turks, but they're nice guys and Muntz is a fine old gentleman. I'm sure you'll do well with them."

The three teachers fell into the pattern with little difficulty. Professor Mundt, a much older man was the least flexible and experimental. I aided him as much as possible by limiting the staging and movement. Bressler was by far the most adaptable and halfway through the semester, in the midst of a planning discussion of his next lecture, he broke off the discussion to say, "You don't come to me with the humility of a student and I'm not used to that. After I've explained my lesson, you ask me what my three main points are, and I realize that although I do have three main points they are not clearly articulated, which is why you're asking me about them, and then I go away and restructure the lesson. I'm ending up with a course which is much better than the one I usually teach, thanks to your probing and organizing." At the end of the semester, Bressler asked if he could have all the visuals I'd made for the course. He wanted to use them in class.

The spring semester featured two other Professors, Dr. Hope Klapper and Dr. Esther Alpenfels, the latter of whom was a widely known, much published anthropologist given to dramatic presentations. She enjoyed exploring television's options. Professor Klapper was less dramatic, but most adaptable, willing to experiment and quick to learn. The two women did not have a close personal relationship; they were not friends. They were two professionals who respected one another, but did not frequently agree. Nevertheless, they had divided the content of the course according to individual perceptions of their respective areas of expertise, and, as had the three men, they each concentrated on these areas. It worked well. The highlight of the course, for me, occurred when Alpenfels brought Pearl Primus, a doctoral candidate in anthropology at NYU and her husband Percival Borde into the studio for two sessions to demonstrate symbolic meanings of African dance. Pearl Primus, a nationally recognized ethnic dancer, had taken New York City by storm a number of years previously and generated national press notice with her presentation of African Dance, featuring prodigious leaps into the air, at Barney Josephson's famous Greenwich Village night club, Café Society. A seminal influence in American dance, her repertoire of choreographed works was numerous and included: an interpretation of Langston Hughes' *The Negro Speaks of Rivers*; *Strange Fruit* based on a Lewis Allen poem about a lynching; *Hard Time Blues* based on a Josh White song about sharecroppers; *The Wedding*, performed by the Alvin Ailey dance Troupe; *Fanga* an interpretation of a traditional Liberian invocation to the earth and sky; and *Michael Row Your Boat Ashore* about the 1963 Birmingham, Alabama, church bombing. Pearl's appearance in the Sociology course offered dramatic staging opportunities not inherent in the rest of the course and together Pearl and I were able to block out movement and positions that even in the tiny, low-ceilinged studio presented her in a complimentary and professional manner. She enjoyed my direction and we became friends. She was interested in producing a film about African Dance and we talked about doing it cooperatively. Within the next few months however, Pearl received a commission to travel to Liberia to teach dance and study tribal dance and we lost track of each other for several years. It was nevertheless the beginning of a long friendship with Pearl and Percy that involved future plans for exciting projects, but was plagued with long interruptions and ultimately went unfulfilled.

The Communication Arts Group in the School of Education (CAG), chaired by Dr. Harvey Zorbaugh, included the Departments of Drama, Journalism, Communications in Education and the TMR (Television, Motion Pictures and Radio) Department. The CAG was located in a large central bullpen filled with desks of faculty members and secretaries surrounded by small private offices occupied by chairmen of the respective departments. Dick Goggin occupied the corner office that, although no larger than the others, boasted windows on two walls. Faculty members used two open alcoves between offices for student conferences and advisement on a first come, first served basis. Though I was unaware of it, I was living in august literary company. Vance Packard, professor of journalism with whom I exchanged little more than morning greetings, occupied the desk adjacent to my own. His special field of interest was human behavior that had led him to analyze new psychological techniques then being developed to persuade and manipulate modern Americans. His research resulted in his national best-selling books: *The Hidden Persuaders* (1957), *The Status Seekers* (1959), and *The Waste Makers*(1963).

The faculty members with whom I had most contact impressed me. All were highly experienced professionals who had, and in some instances, continued careers in broadcasting and filmmaking. Irving Falk, a former radio writer, and Bob Emerson, a former CBS radio writer and network administrator, taught radio and television writing and operations. George Gordon, one of the original radio Whiz Kids, taught courses in educational communications in association with Charles Siepmann, Chair of the Department of Educational Communications. Siepmann had been involved in the creation of the British second network and was the primary consultant to the Ford Foundation on matters pertaining to educational television in America. Haig Manoogian, Professor of Film Production, was a dynamic and explosive Yale Drama School graduate whose film production classes had earned the NYU film program a national reputation. His students adored him. The brilliant Martin Scorcese, then an NYU student, shared that view, dedicating his film *Raging Bull* to Haig.

I sent a constant stream of job applications and resumes around the country with no success and was forced to realize that there was almost no possibility of my ever working in commercial television, or even again in educational television. I began to wonder if perhaps my future could lie in higher education. If so, it would be advantageous to possess an advanced degree. As an NYU employee, I was entitled to tuition remission for coursework at NYU so I enrolled in the Master's Program in the department in which I worked and began taking courses, several of which, according to my instructors, I was qualified to teach.

In late fall I saw an ad for an apartment in Greenwich Village and took a look at it. The occupant wanted $300 for the furnishings

which included a bed, several inexpensive painted drawer and cab-
inet units, a small desk and an assortment of pots and pans, cutlery
and glassware and even some linens. It was a one room efficiency
one floor up from the street, in a well kept five story elevator building in the West Village with a bath, a tiny kitchen, four large windows facing the street, a hardwood floor and a working fireplace.
The rent was $109 per month. I took the apartment and bought the
furniture. On the day I was to move in I packed all my clothing
and assorted gear in my car and driving to Washington Square,
parked it, as usual, in front of the NYU South Building, intending
to unload at my new apartment after work. I worked all morning
and had lunch at the grill around the corner. On my return, I saw
the door of my car open and realized, as I approached, that
whomever had opened the door was now inside the car. I didn't
hesitate for a minute. With never a thought of danger or consequence, or my own ability to handle the situation, I acted. I arrived
at the open door. Inside, a black man was on his knees on the front
seat and reaching over to look through the belongings in the back.
I reached in and tapped the man on the shoulder and said, "Hey,
you lose something in there?" The thief turned slowly and looked
up at me standing there in the open doorway. I grabbed the thief by
the shirt just below his neck and pulled him out of the car and into
an upright position with his back against the car, all the while
yelling at the top of my lungs for the police and yelling at the thief
for breaking into the car. I kept pushing him and banging him
against the car and the thief was docile the entire time. In the heat
of my anger and frustration I realized that my hold on the thief's
shirtfront at the neckline was, when the thief stood erect, at the
level of my face as the thief towered a full head over me. The university guard at the South Building, hearing my shouting, came
out and quickly took custody of the man. In due course the police
came to pick him up and at that time they found a screwdriver lying
under the car. I was required to make an appearance at the precinct
station and to report the details to the detective in charge and to
file charges. The detective listened politely and asked a few questions and thanked me for my cooperation. Then he took a long look
at me and I was aware that he was taking stock of my physical condition and was pondering what to say to me. Finally, he said, "Do
you know that this man has a string of nine counts for breaking

and entering? He's a sneak thief and you're fortunate that he is not a violent person. He used a screwdriver to break into your car and he had it in his possession when you grabbed him. He dropped it in the gutter because if he were caught with it on his person it would be considered as an entry tool. But, if he were anything other than a sneak thief you could have had that screwdriver in your belly, and you didn't know what he was when you grabbed him. What you did wasn't at all wise. Think about it and next time don't think about losing a few possessions. Think about losing your life." I thanked the detective and left, but I got the message. There was a circular steel stairway leading down from the detective's office and I was shaking so badly at the realization of my actions that I had a difficult time making it to the ground floor. Back in my car, I had to just sit for a while before attempting to drive.

While working in the South Building I ate many meals at the Chock Full o' Nuts restaurant on 8th Street. Sometimes, when I felt the need for a change and could afford it, I'd go to a restaurant a bit further up the block that was a cut, but no more, above Chock Full o' Nuts in selection and quality. On one occasion I had an amusing experience at dinner there.

I'm always interested in just how long it takes a tradesman, salesperson, doorman, or waiter to notice the absence of my right hand at the wrist and I watch closely as they decide how to deal with it. On this day the sun was bright, Washington Square held its usual afternoon crowd, I'd taught my last class of the week at NYU, and I strolled slowly across the park, enjoying the September air. With no plans for the evening, and not relishing cooking in my one room efficiency, I decided to treat myself to dinner. I considered the Blue Mill, where I knew the fare, but then decided instead to be adventurous. A menu posted outside a plain, home-style restaurant on Christopher Street featured a special on T-bone steak. I went inside.

It took about six seconds for the waiter to notice my right arm. With an exaggerated flourish he showed me to a table, held my chair, unfolded the napkin, handed me the menu, and then stood, smiling, hovering for a few seconds, before leaving. People who want to be helpful can frequently be clumsy and awkward in trying to help. I take it as it comes, recognizing that each person experiences with me a situation they had rarely if ever encountered and they honestly attempt to cope, however ineptly. I had a feeling that I was about to experience one of those times.

Before I could open the menu the waiter was back, this time to pointedly move my water glass from my right side to the left, and rearrange the silverware and artificial flowers on the table. He then stood back, pleased with himself, gave me a big smile, and once again departed.

I opened the menu. A T-bone steak special was on a flyer clipped to the menu and I decided to give it a try. As I closed the menu and laid it on the table, the waiter was back at my side. I ordered the steak, medium rare, baked potato and salad. He again hovered for a moment, studying my table and, satisfied that everything was in order, smiled at me and disappeared into the kitchen.

Repeated, and unneeded attention given to my disability frustrates me and I'm known to respond in ways that surprise, confuse, or sometimes displease others. I'm quite skillful at dealing with my disability and I'm even known to strike back, on rare occasions, at helpful intent that I consider invasive annoyance. That day, in that restaurant I reacted, perhaps unfairly, to the waiter's obvious and excessive attention.

In a short time he appeared with my salad, a basket with a short length of Italian bread partially cut into three sections, and a plate with three pads of butter on tiny paper servers. When he again disappeared into the kitchen I moved the breadbasket to my right, held the bread down with my arm, tore off one piece, and replaced the basket. With my knife I tested the butter. It was hard. Butter is always my adversary in a restaurant; using it requires two hands, and hard or soft, it invariably lies in wait for me, testing both my temper and skill. Inserting the tip of the knife between butter and paper I attempted to separate them, but as I raised the knife, both butter and paper adhered to it. I put the knife down, and grasping the paper, scraped the butter off against the side of the plate. Hard butter doesn't spread, so I cut it into thin strips, but when I tried to apply it to the bread with the knife, the bread, unanchored, slid off the plate. Separating the thin strips of butter on the plate, I cut the bread in half by pressing down hard on the knife, then, picking up a piece of bread I used it to scrape the first strip of butter off the plate and took a bite.

As I sat chewing the bread, the waiter appeared with my steak.

With a flourish, he placed it in front of me and, bending over me with arms poised, ready to reach forward to pick up my knife and fork, and assuming that the offer would be readily accepted, very politely asked, "Would you like for me to cut your steak, sir?" It was a thoughtful gesture and not the first time I had experienced it, but his effusive manner made me uncomfortable, or perhaps just contrary. I thanked him politely and said, "No, I think we'll be O. K." My response was not what he expected. He paused, off balance in mid-motion, and executed a full, physical, whole body "take," recovering his balance. "Are you sure?" he said, "It will only take a moment." Now that hit a nerve. Am I sure? Does he think I'm not sure? Again I refused, politely. "No thank you, I'll be just fine." He hesitated. He didn't want to leave. I could envision his brain grappling with the situation. I could almost hear him thinking, "This guy has only one hand and he ordered a steak. How is he going to eat it? Will he pick it up and take a bite?" Professional that he was, however, he quickly resumed control of himself and once again, gave me a big smile. "Well, enjoy your dinner. If I can be of service, just call."

I looked around. It was early and the restaurant was almost empty. My seat at the table faced the swinging doors of the kitchen, each of which had a small glass pane at eye level to prevent collisions between waiters and busboys. The waiter slowly worked his way to the doors, stopping to arrange a cup on one table, a napkin on another, every few seconds glancing back to see what was going to happen to the steak. I was amused by his actions, but by now I was also irritated and decided that come hell or high water I wasn't going to let him see how I was going to cut my steak. Actually, it wasn't an Olympic feat because I had long ago learned to steady a fork with end of my right arm. Placing the fork in the meat with my left hand and then transferring the fork to my arm, I could hold the meat in place as I used the knife to cut with my left hand. With the fork again in my hand, I would transfer the food to my mouth.

As previously mentioned such actions sometimes disturb others. Accordingly, although I resent being saddled with the responsibility for protecting other people from being upset by actions made necessary by my disabilities, in my own interest I try to minimize actions that might draw notice. Even when dining out with friends, unless they are very close ones, I invariably order a meal that does not require the use of my arm: meat that can be separated with a fork like meatloaf, or fish, stews, certain pastas or even finger foods. Now, with the waiter watching, I didn't touch the steak, but instead picked up my fork and began to eat my salad.

The waiter finally went into the kitchen, pausing only for a quick glance back through the tiny window. As soon as he was out of sight I scraped two more butters off their paper servers against the edge of the opening cut in the baked potato, quickly cut a few pieces of steak, and laid the knife down. When the waiter came by carrying his next order I was placidly chewing on a piece of steak. It brought a look of mystification to his face. On his way back to the kitchen he stopped to ask if the steak was satisfactory. "Its fine thank you, just fine."

My meal progressed and I enjoyed my steak, cutting it each time the waiter was out of sight and calmly eating when he was hovering about. Never once did he see me cut the steak, but I left the t-bone stripped clean and the waiter no wiser than he had been when he had taken my order. I chuckled fiendishly to myself, uncertain as to what, if anything, I had accomplished, but I felt good as I thought of comedian Flip Wilson's famous line, "The devil made me do it." I did leave a generous tip.

I recognized that the waiter had only been trying to help, and my actions were clearly a response to the seemingly unrelenting pressure I experienced daily as the result of casual curiosity and intrusive behavior. I sometimes felt compelled to respond, but few opportunities presented themselves. It felt good to be able to occasionally confront it adroitly, without making a scene.

There is little question that the pressures that impinge on each of us affect our behavior. If experienced on a regular basis they may motivate us to seek relief in ways that can be perceived as antisocial. Over long periods of time such stress induced reactions may become formative factors of our personalities, characters and behaviors. For people with disabilities, the pressures society imposes can result in development of character and behavioral traits that can be more disabling than the original disability.

It is unclear, when one hears statements such as: "Blind people are this…" "Blind people are that…" or "Handicapped people tend to be…", whether the person about whom the statement is being made is that way because their behavior is an inherent part

• •

of their disability or because society's stigmatizing as the result of their disability has made them that way. In this context, Goffman suggests that the normal's—that is the broader society's sense—of "good adjustment" of the stigmatized can differ widely from the stigmatized's own sense of good adjustment.[7]

I was 31 years old and just becoming familiar with living in my own apartment for the first time. It was a good feeling. I was finally completely on my own. I was surprisingly paying my bills. I wasn't very secure, but I seemed to be finally independent. I knew I was far behind my contemporaries. Back home, those with whom I had grown up were married with children and had had steady jobs for years.

By mid-year the continued existence of the Center for Educational Television was unpredictable. It was unclear if RCA would renew the grant. I continued to search for a steady job. By this time there were two educational television stations operating in New York City. One was the municipal station, owned and operated by the City of New York, directed by Seymour Seigel. My letter of introduction from Lenore Elkus produced an interview, but there were no openings available then or in the near future. The second station was owned and operated by the New York City Public School System and directed by Jim MacAndrew. A young personable science teacher by the name of Barbara Yanowski had become the most popular and visible television teacher in the City and, due to her gregarious activity in several newly formed educational television organizations, was well on her way to becoming a nationally known television teacher. In Indiana, at Purdue University, a startling new kind of educational television organization, aided by a massive grant from the Ford Foundation, was underway. Television broadcasting had not yet developed the technical means—

---

[7] "...the stigmatized individual cheerfully and unselfconsciously accepts himself as essentially the same as normals, while at the same time he voluntarily withholds himself from those situations in which normals would find it difficult to give lip service to their similar acceptance of him. Since the good-adjustment line is presented by those who take the standpoint of the wider society, one should ask what the following of it by the stigmatized means to the normals. It means that the unfairness and pain of having to carry a stigma will never be presented to them; it means that normals will never have to admit to themselves how limited their tactfulness and tolerance is; and it means that normals can remain relatively uncontaminated by intimate contact with the stigmatized, relatively unthreatened in their identity beliefs. It is from just these meanings, in fact, that the specification of a good adjustment derive." (Goffman, p.121)

coaxial cable, microwave and telephone lines—to send programs intra-regionally from city to city or locally to school districts interested in participating in this new found teaching method. Educational television and television teaching was in its initial growth and development stages. The Ford Foundation, having successfully demonstrated television teaching via broadcast signal in Pittsburgh, and closed circuit in Hagerstown, MD, was now seeking a viable means to distribute instructional television to a larger audience. The newest, and most unusual project, was the Midwest Program of Airborne Television Instruction (MPATI) at Purdue University. This experiment used a DC-6 four engine aircraft, equipped with new two-inch videotape machines, to broadcast instructional television programs. The aircraft was equipped with a retractable broadcast antenna mounted under the fuselage which, when airborne, was lowered inverted, to a vertical position. It flew in sixty-mile circles across several counties, broadcasting instructional programs to midwestern schools. Making two trips per day, morning and afternoon, the plane would stop mid-day for refueling and videotape reloading.

At about the same time, a third educational television organization was formed in New York City, the Metropolitan Educational Television Association, (META) under the leadership of Art Hungerford. The creation of educational television stations by cities and universities had blossomed during the five years following the creation of the first community sponsored station in Pittsburgh in 1953. New York City, however, despite having both a municipal and a school station, had not been allocated a useable broadcast channel by the FCC and had thus been slow to organize its community resources. Now, following the model of WQED in Pittsburgh, META, as yet without a broadcast capability, was established as a production facility on 63rd Street between 1st and 2nd Ave. Serendipity resulted. META had a facility and was in need of production work and the income it would bring; MPATI was in need of an elementary science course and had tapped Barbara Yanowski to teach it. The result was a contract between Barbara and MPATI to produce a science series at META, beginning in the fall. I had met Art Hungerford and knew he would be hiring a few people so I arranged for an interview and applied for the job as director for the series. I learned from other sources that Barbara would have a strong influence over who was hired and that she could be a difficult and demanding person for whom to work. I assumed I was up to the challenge.

I continued with my own studies that required completion of a television production and a production report, the equivalent of a master's thesis. I was not content to simply do a production. I had done a number of those for broadcast and knew I could do it. In casting about for a suitable project, I developed an idea that television, which was essentially a dynamic visual medium, could be used for people whose primary informational input was visual, namely the deaf. I decided on an experiment to teach deaf youngsters via television. John Harrington, principal of the New York City School for the Deaf, PS 47, in midtown was intrigued with the idea and was working on a doctorate in deaf education. John agreed to create four language lessons and to organize two matched groups of students. He would teach each lesson in class in the traditional way to one group; the other group he would teach as a television teacher in the NYU studio and the deaf youngsters would watch the lesson in another room on TV. He would then test the children and we would write up the results of the control group study. It became evident that such an experiment in teaching the deaf had never been done; it was a first. I created a mass of special visuals, some of which were mechanical animations, filmed special sequences for inclusion in the shows, even one that included permission to use a New York City Police helicopter. Since my effort was a first, I wanted to document it, but NYU had no capability for kinescope and did not possess a videotape machine. I made a desperate attempt to obtain funding, about $3,000 dollars, just enough to record the four half hours on kinescope so that others could see them and I hoped I might possibly parlay the study into a full-time job. I contacted every organization I could identify that had an interest in the deaf, including hospitals and state and federal government agencies, among them, the Deafness Research Foundation, the Rusk Institute for Physical Medicine and Rehabilitation, and the newly established federal office of Captioned Films For The Deaf in the Bureau for the Education of the Handicapped, United States Office of Education, all with no success. The new Director of the Office of Captioned Films, John Gough, however, returned my call, and was sufficiently interested to make the effort to meet with me personally while on a business trip to New York City and to spend time discussing the project. Funding was generally unavailable, however, and where it was available, the lead time was too short, so of necessity, I was compelled to do the programs without any means of recording them. John Gough came to see three of the programs and was impressed. A feature story about the project in the NYU student newspaper was picked up and expanded in the New York Times documenting the first use of television to teach the deaf and I was surprised and overjoyed to learn it had also been featured in the London Times.

Larry Costello, who had been expected to generate additional funding for the Center, had sold a research project to a sponsor and had proven unable to execute it. Dick Goggin had had to take it on personally and complete it. By late spring the continuation of the Center for another year was in question. As summer approached, it became known that RCA had declined to provide a second year's funding and efforts to obtain funding from other sponsors were unsuccessful.

Dick asked me if I'd like to teach a four-week summer educational television workshop in the TMR Department. This course was under the aegis of Charles Siepmann, Chair of the Communications in Education Program and provided me an opportunity to have a closer relationship with this nationally known figure whose academic stature had made him one of the most important advisors to the Ford Foundation on the matter of educational television.

Siepmann's background was notable.[8] Born and raised in England and educated at Cambridge, he had been Director of Program Planning for the British Broadcasting System and had come to the United States in 1937 under the auspices of the Rockefeller Foundation to study educational broadcasting. In 1939 he served on the British Government committee that determined radio's role in wartime and was university lecturer at Harvard University until 1942. During World War II he wrote *Radio in Wartime* and later served as Assistant Director of the Office of War Information.

In July 1945, following several decades of controversy surrounding the Federal Communications Commission's policies on

---

[8] Richard J. Meyer, "International Review of Education/Vol.10, No.2 (1964) pp.211-220

rule making and standards for broadcasting, the then progressive commissioner, Clifford Durr, succeeded in having the FCC authorize a study of American broadcasting. Charles Siepmann was retained as consultant to the FCC and charged with conducting the study that resulted in *The Blue Book*, (so named because of the color of its cover), which compared broadcast licensees' performance with the promises made to obtain or renew a license. Examination revealed that the promises were blatantly ignored. The result was a two-year campaign by the broadcast industry to kill *The Blue Book* and, since it would be difficult to attack a study for merely proposing that broadcasters be held to their promises, the focus centered on Siepmann. In scurrilous attacks, the National Association of Broadcasters heaped all manner of accusation and innuendo upon him, much of it focused on his British roots and association with the BBC. In 1946 Siepmann assumed the Chairmanship of the Department of Communications in Education at New York University and settled into academe where he authored *The Radio Listener's Bill of Rights*; *Radio, Television and Society*; and *Television and Education in the United States*; the latter written for UNESCO. His book *TV and Our School Crisis*, published in 1958, received the Frank Stanton Award for Meritorious Research on the Media of Mass Communication. The advent of educational television in the United States brought Charles back into the educational and broadcasting limelight as the primary consultant to the Ford Foundation Fund for the Advancement of Education. His thinking had been most influential in the nature and scope of the initial grants made by the Foundation that were crucial in directing the development of this new phenomenon, including the one which had provided for my job as art director at WQED. Siepmann's national visibility in this new field soared; he was called upon to speak at educational colloquia across the nation, but he remained unrecognized and unrewarded at NYU.

Charles was first and last, a scholar. He allowed nothing to interrupt his work, which was continuous and intense. His days were filled with teaching classes at NYU, writing speeches and making personal appearances across the country. He could not be bothered by trifles, a fact which was illustrated by an unusual incident one day in the office. Charles smoked a pipe and was given to emptying it into his wastebasket when it was time to refill. One day, while his nervous secretary was rushing about attempting to organize her work and his schedule, the glass paned door to Charles' office opened and Charles emerged holding a fiber wastebasket from which flames leaped upward. Placing the flaming basket on the floor outside the door, Charles, in his cultivated British voice, without a trace of alarm, said, "Mary, the basket is on fire." then turned back into his office and shut the door.

Dick suggested that I confer with Charles to solicit advice and comments. Charles was most interested and accommodating. He asked what I intended to include in the workshop and I described the course syllabus which he found acceptable. He was then interested in discussing NYU's closed circuit teachers. Fixing me with his eagle eye and a hard smile, Charles asked, "Are any of them any good?" My answer was candid and just as direct. "Yes and No. One is very good, one is quite bad and one is mediocre." The real problem was the limited time available for an instructor to prepare. Charles agreed, "Television has the ability to do exceedingly well, many things which should not be done at all." Charles requested that at a point midway in the course he be given two sessions to lecture about his perceptions of the nature and value of using television in education and it was arranged that he would do that.

The spring semester ended and during the summer I assisted Larry Costello in teaching the Television Workshop for Teachers and also taught the four-week course for Siepmann. My job terminated at the end of August, but my life was about to change dramatically and miraculously.

Top: (Left) Nathan Nathanson;
(Right) Sophie Nathanson
Bottom: (Left) Gottlieb
Haisch; *(Right) Caterina
Haisch*

Clockwise from top:
Sam Nathanson and
Louisa Haisch, 1924;
Sam Nathanson, 1962;
Louise Nathanson,
1962

Clockwise from top left: Sam and Louise,1966; Norbert Nathanson, age 8 mos.; Norbert, age 2 ½.

Top: Louise and Norbert, age 4 ½.;

Bottom (Left): Norbert, age 5 ½.;

(Right): Norbert, age 12.

Clockwise from top left: WQED, In the coal bin art department; One of WQED's first IDs.; In the Director's chair, WQED; *(left to right)* Gordon Washburn, Robert Snyder, on the set of "Looking at Modern Art."

Clockwise from top left:
On stage at the Mid-America Jubilee, 1956; TV Production Class, NYU; Directing closed circuit television, NYU; Sociology 101, in studio, NYU.

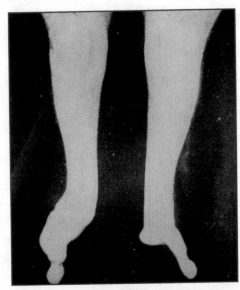

Clockwise from top left: Barbara as I first saw her, ICMR, 1961; Lower limbs pre-surgery, age 34; First set of prostheses, 1961.

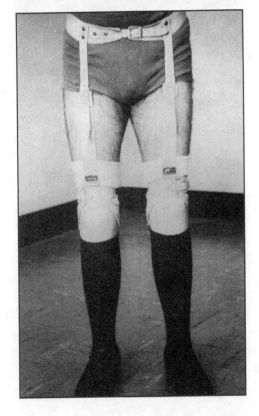

Clockwise from top left: Post-op, Institute for Physical Medicine and Rehabilitation, with Wayne, New York, 1961; At home in Pittsburgh with Dad, 1961; Wedding day, April 11, 1964.

Clockwise from top left: Barb, New Paltz, 1965; First time father, with Jessica, 1968; All dressed up for Mary Lou's Whitney's party

Clockwise from top left: Jessica, ready for college; Jared, valedictorian at Darrow School; We four.

11

Metamorphosis

I could have taught the fall semester at NYU as an Adjunct Professor, but uncertain of my anticipated surgical date, I opted out of teaching. Dr. Russek called to inform me that OVR, establishing a new precedent, had approved my total rehabilitation project. One major problem remained, identifying a surgeon, and Russek was determined to find the most qualified surgeon in New York. A few weeks later he selected Dr. Ernst Bergmann, a specialist in surgical amputation and preparation of limbs for prosthetic devices. Bergmann was willing to undertake the surgery for the modest fee OVR offered, but he had an extremely busy schedule that resulted in postponing my surgery from early fall to winter.

Dr. Russek escorted me to my first meeting with Dr. Bergmann in mid-fall. Bergmann's appearance and behavior was reminiscent of a no-nonsense Prussian (short, stocky, formal and official). He conducted a general examination, and then used a device to measure the blood flow in my thighs and lower legs. The results of that procedure did not please him. He mentioned to Russek that there was insufficient blood flow for the amputations and both doctors adjourned to another room while I dressed, and I overheard the murmur of mild argument. As we departed Russek said only that Dr. Bergmann had some concerns, but that they would work them out. Fortunately, I was unaware of the critical nature of this discussion at the time. I was enjoying an euphoric state of mind imagining the future. As I learned much later, Bergmann was convinced that there was insufficient blood flow in the upper legs to insure necessary blood flow in the post-surgical stumps. He had not agreed to do the surgery. What concerned him was his assumption that without sufficient blood flow, the legs would not heal following the surgery and would be unable to absorb the stress of physical contact with prostheses, possibly resulting in vascular disease or gangrene from the pressures of standing and walking. Russek, as a rehabilitation specialist, would not accept the idea that less than normal blood flow constituted sufficient grounds for not amputating. He reasoned that since the lower legs in their natural state had so much less bone and muscle mass than normal legs, and the available blood supply had facilitated the overloaded extremities for thirty-four years; it would continue to provide what was needed post-surgically. Russek's position was of course a speculative one wherein he used his experience and practical knowledge as factors that mitigated standard scientific standards. In short, he made a calculated guess, and in a sense, laid his reputation, and perhaps my future, on the line. That decision was later to cause him significant concern when my left stump took a longer time to heal than was anticipated. However, Bergmann finally accepted Russek's point of view and agreed to do the surgery. With the OVR approval in hand and the surgeon committed, Russek was ready to proceed.

Russek's interest did not end with surgical rehabilitation. He was also concerned about completing my physical image by providing an artificial hand for my right arm. "Wouldn't you like to be able to have the appearance of having two hands?" I had never given that idea any thought. I was accustomed to using my arm functionally. I was dependant on it. I had always assumed that people stared at me primarily because of the appearance of my feet and legs and my gait, not because of my arm, and certainly it did not cause me any pain.

Russek's question, however, brought to mind a conversation I had had with Lenore Elkus several years previously at WQED. "Had you ever thought," she had asked me, "of having an artificial hand? Wouldn't it be helpful?" My answer, perhaps a bit too quickly had been, "No, I use my arm all the time." My skills at using my arm were considerable, and at the time I had responded truthfully to the functionality of her question, but there was a cultural gap between Mrs. Elkus, who was an affluent and cultured person circulating at the upper levels of Pittsburgh's society, and me. Now it suddenly struck me that she had been trying, in a kindly way, to tell me something, and perhaps that was what Dr. Russek was doing now? Was I, at long last, beginning to listen?

We discussed at length the pros and cons of my having an artificial hand. I tried to be objective about just how much I actually used my arm functionally and for what kinds of things. The options, explained Dr. Russek, were twofold, a cosmetic hand, realistic in appearance, but non-functional, which would be slipped over my arm like a glove; or a hook-type prehensile functioning hand which had been developed during the war and which Harold Russell, the bi-lateral hand amputee, had made both visible and acceptable in the motion picture, *The Best Years of Our Lives*. I had thirty-four years of instinctive, practiced training in the use of my arm for anything I did, including opening the button of my left shirt sleeve and rolling up the cuff, and I didn't want to be encumbered. If the problem of my legs could be resolved, I really had little interest in concerning myself further with my arm, for either functional or cosmetic purposes.

Then bureaucracy raised its head, ever so tentatively, and fortunately I had sufficient sensitivity to recognize it. Underlying all of the preparations, arrangements, and promised support there was a logical question for a normal person or a funding agency, Why would a person who is undergoing major rehabilitation that will functionally and cosmetically transform his physical appearance from one of abnormality to one of normality, not wish to make his new image complete and whole? If I were getting two legs that would make me appear normal, why would I want to continue to be seen with only one hand? It would be unfair to suggest that OVR would not have funded my rehabilitation if I decided to not accept an artificial hand, but, as Russek put it, "What have you got to lose? Perhaps you'll find either the hook or the cosmetic hand useful." I acquiesced. "I'll try the cosmetic hand." It was my assumption that functionally I could best serve my needs without the hook. Neither prosthesis required surgical preparation. They were simply fitted to the body.

One of the aspects of the forthcoming surgery that caused me great anxiety had no direct bearing on rehabilitation. It was the possibility that, after release from the hospital, I might chance to meet someone who had known me previously and my new appearance would startle them or even cause them to not recognize me. Having been the object of unwanted and personal questions for so many years, I did not want to enter a new phase of life that required continuous explanations of my new normal appearance. I had visions of meeting an old acquaintances and having them look me up and down and ask, "What the hell happened to you?" and then I'd have to explain. A lifetime of avoidance of such personal explanations made it the problem larger in my mind than in reality. I wasn't sure I could take that in stride. And I also feared the kind of answer I might be tempted to provide.

How prophetic I was. A number of years after I had married and was living in Washington, D.C., I found myself at a cocktail party for Carnegie Tech Alumni, face to face with a former classmate with whom I'd had only a casual relationship. A big bear of a man not known for either intellect or tact, but quite friendly, he literally looked me up and down, scanning my new (five and one half inches taller than before) height, said, "What the hell happened to you? You used to be a little shrimp!" I couldn't believe it, but it happened.

******

Knowing I would soon enter the hospital, I mentally projected the kinds of situations in which I might later find myself and it prompted me to find a way to offset, to the degree possible, any awkwardness that might ensue from post-rehabilitation surprises. I wanted everything to proceed smoothly. Accordingly, I organized a plan.

The scope of my social and professional contacts was not extensive. There were only a few groups of people: family, old friends and acquaintances primarily in Pittsburgh, former professional colleagues associated with WQED, and professional colleagues plus a few friends in New York. As a matter of course I informed my colleagues at New York University, among them Dick Goggin and George Gordon, of my pending plans. They were anxious, but delighted for me. My mother and Aunt Marge would inform relatives and former neighbors while I was in the hospital, and my friend Dale Stein would inform friends in New York and in Pittsburgh. I needed only to find someone to spread the word to my former associates at WQED in Pittsburgh. Fred Rogers, with whom I had been casually exploring a collaborative project on what turned out to be an abortive attempt to write a musical based on Antoine Du Saint Exupery's "The Little Prince" was scheduled to be in New York during the fall and we set a luncheon date. Over lunch I told Fred of my plans and asked him if he would spread the word among my former associates at the proper time. Fred was immediately concerned at the seriousness of my undertaking, but was happy for me and offered to do anything possible to spread, as he put it, "the wonderful news."

Bergmann's commitments left very little choice; he would be available only during the Christmas holidays so the date for surgery was set for Dec. 22 at the old New York University Hospital on Second Avenue at Twentieth Street. Rather than possibly experiencing a rejection on my application to META, which I couldn't accept if chosen, I decided to withdraw my name from further consideration, so I called Art Hungerford, thanked him for considering me, and informed him that I was withdrawing. One of OVR's criteria for providing support was that the recipient be indigent, so I was counseled to spend the $500 I had available, not a difficult thing to accomplish since I would have no income beyond the end of August and the monthly rent, electric, phone and food costs would continue. I informed Fred and Dale that my announcement "release date" would be December 22, the day of the surgery.

Fall passed slowly and I had time on my hands, too much time to think about the experience I was about to undertake. It was perhaps inevitable that I begin to have second thoughts, not as to whether or not I would go through with the surgery, but about how things would work out afterwards. I was beset with worry about exactly what, in practical terms, my post-surgery physical capabilities would actually be. I knew exactly what my current capabilities were and was secure in my own being, but what would they be post-surgery? Would my physical activities be more limited? Dr. Russek was sympathetic and somewhat amused by my concerns and reiterated that I would be able to do everything I was now able to do. "In addition, your height will be increased four or five inches and anyone looking at you casually will probably not be able to tell that you are wearing prostheses."

As December approached, I made plans to get my affairs, simple as they were, in order. I had an apartment and numerous belongings from which I would be absent for three months. The rent and service charges would continue and I would have no resources as of the time I entered the hospital. A solution appeared in the person of Statton (Buzz) Rice, who together with Fred Kelley was studying television on Ford Foundation Fellowship Grants. Both Fred and Buzz , students in one of my television production classes, had approached me outside of class and we had spent time over coffee discussing the future of educational television. We had even begun to plan a cooperative project.

By a fortunate coincidence, Buzz was to be married on New Year's Day and was searching for an apartment in the City. It was arranged that Buzz and his new bride would take over my apartment for the time of my incarceration and assume the rental costs. By letter and phone, I also arranged for an old friend in Pittsburgh, a master mechanic, to do some repair work on my car while I was hospitalized.

******

On the weekend prior to my hospital entry, I drove to Pittsburgh to spend a few days with my parents. It was a tense time. My brother and family were expected from St. Louis for the Christmas holiday but would not arrive until after I had departed. Christmas Day was my mother's birthday, always celebrated on Christmas Eve with champagne toasts at midnight. Mother and Dad wanted to be in New York when I underwent surgery, but couldn't be there without upsetting the family's plans. The impending events hung over us those few days, and on the evening of the 19th Mother and Dad drove me to the airport for the return flight to New York. The following day I was admitted for pre-surgical tests, and on the 22nd of December, Dr. Ernst Bergmann amputated both my legs six inches below the knees. True to their promises, Fred and Dale spread the word as per plan and within a few days, aided by Mother and Aunt Marge, most of the people with whom I had had more than casual acquaintance knew what was happening. As time passed the word quickly spread and I was content that my public information campaign had been successful.

The first several days following the surgery were difficult. Entries in my journal indicate the following:

Dec. 22: Came to in my room in the Intensive Care Unit at 3:30 P.M. Aunt Marge was with me.

Dec. 23: Feeling much better under sedation for pain. Slept a lot.

Dec. 24: Drs. Yaslow and Bergmann in to change dressings at 11:30 P.M. No bedside phones in Unit so asked about calling home for Mother's birthday. Dr. Georgi (resident) gave approval and I was loaded on a stretcher and taken down the hall to a pay phone. Mother answered and all were relieved to hear from me.

For me, as for my mother and father it was an enormously emotional moment. They had been advised by my aunt that I was well and that the surgery had gone as well as expected, but waiting for two days to hear my voice had only increased their tension and unease. We all cried over the phone. Hearing my voice and knowing I was well released my mother's and father's anxieties and fears and as I wished Mother happy birthday I knew that she and Dad were experiencing the fulfillment of an impossible dream and I had finally rid myself of those two lower extremities which had been the cause for so long of so much pain and anguish.

Dec. 25 Christmas Day: Mostly sleep, pain pills and milk of magnesia.

Dec. 26. Uneasy night. Legs felt as if they were tightly bound.

Dec. 27. Another uneasy night. Fred Rogers called today to wish me well but was not able to speak with me due to lack of phone in ICU ward.

Dec. 28. Medication changed today to injection only. Resulted in horrible night of pain and discomfort ending almost hysterically in the early morning. Little doubt that the change of medication did not suit my needs. Tried holding legs in air to ease pain.

Dec. 29. Dr. Bergmann in in the morning and changed medication. Ate no breakfast, little lunch, and went without drugs until 2:45 P.M. when I got a shot. My newest position is on my stomach to prevent muscle flexing of upper legs. Told Dr. Friedman, who had assisted in surgery what

I thought of last night's experience and left little room for doubt. I was angry as hell. Met Peg McDuff, a Scottish nurse, beautiful, skilled and intelligent. She washed me, gave me a rub down, shamed me out of my anger, and had me eating out of her hand by noon. Took most of the day to recover from the night.

Dec. 30. Feeling better today. Mother and Dad arrive. It's good to see them and they're much relieved to see me. Drs. Bergmann and his assistant Dr. Yaslow in to see me and removed some sutures. Peg around all day. Splendid company. Want to know her better.

Dec. 31. Nine days since surgery. Yaslow and Bergmann removed rest of the sutures and re- bandaged my legs. Peg visited in evening with her date and smuggled in a New Year's drink of Scotch for me, and some ginger ale for Mr. Milinger, my roommate, an elderly gentleman who had undergone hernia repair.

Jan. 1. To the bathroom in a wheelchair. I can get in and out of it by myself. Bergmann changed dressings. Said my legs looked good. Team of three male residents and one female visited and asked lots of questions. I'm beginning to wonder about moving to the Rusk Institute. Peg in several times and promised to visit me there.

Mother stayed on for several days; Dad had to return to Pittsburgh for post holiday window trimming.

Jan. 4. Dick Goggin called in late afternoon.

Jan. 5. Feeling good. Had some visitors, relatives. ICU is full and staff is short. Mr. Millinger going home today. Nice gentleman, 72 years old, very happy to be on his way, promising to visit.

Jan. 6. Bergmann in, dressed "stumps." His comment, "Everything is good. As good as anyone's stumps." "Stump" is a new and seemingly crude, harsh word to me. Doctors and prosthetists generally use it to denote that part of the arm or leg that remains following any loss.

When I first heard the word "stumps" used in reference to my legs, I was startled. I thought it a coarse reference, but I acclimated quickly. I noticed a tingling in my stumps when I listened to the radio. When stringed instruments were prominent in the music, my stumps seemed to pick up the vibration and transmit it directly into my groin. I also experienced electric-like charges shooting to my stumps that would make my legs twitch noticeably. As I healed, the intensity of this activity lessened and disappeared, but when first experienced, it was quite uncomfortable. I mentioned it to one of the doctors and for the first time learned about phantom pains and sympathetic vibrations. Dr. Friedman explained that when a part of an arm or leg is lost, the nerves that had previously transmitted the signals to the part now gone do not recognize that it is gone, nor does that part of the brain that had previously controlled it. A neural memory of that part remains. Depending on the individual, it is possible for a person who has lost a member, a hand for instance, to have the sensation of actually "moving" every part of that hand even though it no longer exists. Although many years after my surgery, I could still feel my legs and "feet" as they were originally; they were so much less complex in muscular and neurological structure than normal that the neurological remains and memory were also infinitely less complex. Therefore, I experienced an extremely small measure of phantom pain. For some amputees, phantom pains are a continuing source of great discomfort.

Jan. 7 Getting around in a wheelchair quite easily, to and from the bathroom, in and out of bed. Able to "stand" up on my knees (with my legs flexed of course) although I wasn't pushing it.

Contrary to how I had always perceived myself, I was now obviously a triple amputee. As I thought about it I realized that I always had been, but now it was quite apparent. Having always resisted medication unless absolutely necessary, I tried to get to sleep without a sleeping pill. It didn't work. I had a sleepless night and was exhausted the next day. Another nurse came into the room and in the course of conversation let it drop that she was angered with "my girl friend." I wasn't certain how to respond to the remark, so I ignored it.

Jan. 8. Have a sinus problem and asked to take one of my antihistamines. Felt like sobbing, was not sad, but a bit nauseous. Had no Equinol today and despite head nurse's suggestion that I take it I demurred, feeling that the sooner I was off the drugs the better I'd be. Took only aspirin and sleeping pills despite some nausea.

Peg came in, angered at the other nurse. She had been accused of carrying on an unprofessional relationship with me. I was ecstatic. My thoughts flew back to those days as a young teenager when everyone was saying things like "Joe loves Ethel" and "Rosie likes Harry" and I had never been the topic of such comments or teasing. Now I was. My nurse, for whom I was already developing an attachment, was being accused of being attracted to me! How had that happened?

Jan 9. Up and washed early. Felt reasonably fine. Pat Daly called and came to visit as did Mother and Aunt Marge. It was bad day, nausea, and lightheadedness, diarrhea started in mid-morning and continued all day. Resident came to see me three times. Wanted to be left alone. Mother and Aunt Marge wanted to comfort me. I didn't want comfort. We finally had words and I hurt their feelings and felt worse for it. Mother and I both finally reduced to tears.

******

Other than my colleagues at NYU, I had only one other friend in the city. She was Pat Daly, who had been a casual friend during college. A talented artist, she was one of a number of attractive girls in my classes whom I had perceived as mature, sophisticated and intellectually aware and informed far beyond my ken. The daughter of a Pittsburgh dentist, she had traveled and studied ballet and music while still in high school and was prone to the use of polysyllabic words and French phrases, none of which I understood. I could never decide whether or not she was sincere or just "putting it on." When I arrived in New York City to search for employment, on impulse I had called her at her home in Port Wash-

....

ington where she lived with her husband Sean and two small children. She was delighted to hear from me and insisted I visit for the weekend. I met Sean, who had a well paying job in an advertising agency in the City, and was deeply involved in mail order marketing. I was impressed with their old, but spacious home, two cars and small sailboat. It startled me to realize that it was possible for someone my age to be able to afford such luxuries, in contrast to my own unsuccessful efforts to find employment. At the time, I existed on just enough money for gasoline and an occasional hamburger; I was awed at what I perceived as considerable affluence. I enjoyed the weekend however, and as I was leaving I was invited to return anytime. "Even if we're not here, come use the house and relax. It will give you a change of pace." With Sean's encouragement, I began to visit from time to time, and then two things happened, about a year apart.

I had been invited one weekend to sail on their 16-foot open cockpit boat and was delighted at being shown how to operate the boat. Enjoying my enthusiasm, Sean, a neophyte sailor himself, after demonstrating how to manage the sails, had allowed me to take the tiller and, with my affinity for operating vehicles, I had quickly risen to the challenge and absorbed the basics of steering and tacking and jibing, learning very quickly to command the boat's movement. When not in use, the boat was kept in the midst of a moorage of more than a hundred boats, arranged in several parallel lines. To get to the mooring it was necessary to sail down one lane between boats to a given point, then make a 90 degree turn to the mooring and round up into the wind and grab the mooring buoy. I was completely involved with the experience of sailing the boat and having noted the wind direction, I asked, "Would you mind if I sail it into the harbor?" Sailing into the harbor meant that we would sail into the edge of the moorage and then start the British Sea Gull outboard motor and motor up to the mooring. "Sure, go ahead," Sean agreed, and smiling, handed over the tiller and relaxed. I sailed the boat into the harbor on a port beam reach and, abreast of the third line of anchored boats, close hauled the sail and turned to port into the open lane, intent on sailing right up to the mooring in the middle of the anchorage. Sean started to ready the motor and Pat, realizing my intent, said, "Wait honey, let's see how far he can get." We were now approaching the cross lane which would lead to the mooring. When we reached it, I swung hard to starboard and eased the sail out and reaching the mooring, swung again to port, rounded up into the slight breeze and luffed the sails, right at the mooring. Pat was excited, "Oh that was great. Wasn't it, Honey? We've never done that!" Sean had a forced smile on his face and he nodded without comment. For the moment the feeling of my mastery over the vehicle, the feeling I had when flying, overwhelmed me, and then I became aware of Sean's silence as he went about the tasks of dropping the sails and closing up the boat. Uh oh, I thought, I just made a terrible mistake. I, a disabled person, had just out performed an able bodied person, and had done it with his own boat. I begged off staying for supper, excused myself as soon as possible, noticed that indeed, Sean's attitude toward me had undergone a change.

It became evident a year later, after I'd had my surgery. Pat visited me in the hospital; Sean did not. Later, when I was working at the United Nations I indulged myself in a longing for a lamb shearling coat. I wore the coat on a visit to Pat's one day and as I was taking my leave Sean noticed my coat and opined that those shearling coat imitations were certainly very realistic. I puzzled at the remark. It was such a direct and snobbish put down that I wondered what had motivated it. When I had unintentionally outdone him a year ago on the boat, it hadn't generated any hurtful comments and I had then still been visibly disabled. Now I was no longer the crippled, unemployed and seemingly unemployable person with whom Sean had had a relationship. Now I was employed, my appearance was as normal as anyone's, I was five and one half inches taller, and I had a new and expensive coat. I suddenly realized that Sean's former warm and friendly treatment of me had been addressed to that other person, the disabled one, and it had come, not out of friendliness and compassion, but out of pity and a sense of the most patronizing noblesse oblige. It was a startling revelation.

******

Jan. 10. Slept well last night and feel fine. Ate breakfast and then found out I would be transferred to the Institute at 11:00 A.M.. that day. Things were a whirl from then on.

The fresh air smelled wonderful as an attendant loaded me into a Volkswagen bus for the trip a dozen blocks up First Avenue to the Institute. As I later realized, and the head nurse confirmed, the nausea and diarrhea I had experienced a few days before had actually been withdrawal symptoms caused by my abrupt discontinuance of the pain relieving drugs I had been taking around the clock for 16 days. With my body again functioning normally, I was happy that I had rid myself of them so easily.

In the Intensive Care Unit I had become aware for the first time of a feeling I had never before experienced. I had always known that my lower legs and feet were what set me apart from everyone else. It wasn't a simple matter; it was complex and at the very center of my psycho/physical being. One had only to look at my legs and feet to know that they were very unusual, and had there been any doubt in the neighborhood as to the precise nature of my deformities, I had removed it along with my shoe that day long ago in kindergarten. People in my neighborhood knew, from the stories my kindergarten classmates had taken home, that my feet were not simply misshapen, but were actually incomplete. To those who asked too many questions or wanted to see more, my response, sometimes politely, and sometimes less so, was simply "It's none of your business." It always amazed me, and in many instances angered me, at how direct and insensitive a very large segment of the public was or could be. When they wanted to know something, they simply asked, and they had no awareness of how their inquiries impacted the feelings of those asked. As I grew, that problem lessened since with maturation my contacts and activities changed from the working class environment of my childhood to a middle class one where people were more sophisticated and acclimated to more polite behavior. I had to fend off those who "wanted to see" on fewer occasions. My situation didn't change, but my milieu had. The basic problem however, remained.

My early defenses resulted in my being very protective with regard to revealing the precise nature of my disabilities and ultimately resulted in my refraining from participating in a variety of activities that would require the removal of my shoes. In most cases a simple "No thanks," or "I'd rather not" were sufficient deterrents to those who, in complete innocence and desire to be friendly or helpful would invite me to go wading, swimming, or sleep overnight. Despite my appearance, I was so physically able, I "passed" so well, that they projected their own activities and abilities on to me. Everyone assumed that I could do anything I wished to do; I could never bring myself to tell anyone that if I took my shoes off I could not stand, much less walk. I had had a few experiences at the beach while still a youngster when mother had fabricated a pair of high top sneakers filled with cotton so that I could get into the water, but the combination of the difficulty encountered in attempting to walk on sand with the makeshift shoes, and the relentless stares that were directed at me made it clear to me that that type of experience wasn't worth the discomfort and humiliation it engendered. Although Mother wanted me to have the experience, she never pushed it after the early tries. When I was old enough to wear long pants, I was much relieved since they offered a modicum of privacy. Now at least I didn't have people staring at my legs. It helped, but didn't completely eliminate my being noticed and yet there was some comfort in knowing that even though they stared, they couldn't really see. I held on to that tiny shred of my dignity. Years later, reading about the Nazis forcing people to strip, and later, of unnecessary strip searches conducted by American police officers, it struck me forcibly. A great feeling of empathy welled up in me for all those whose dignity is eroded and whose privacy is invaded by such actions.

In the hospital, in the Intensive Care Unit, I was relieved that those feet and lower legs that had been the source of life-long pain and humiliation, and a magnet for mindless stares of legions of strangers, were gone. Nobody would ever stare at my feet again. Never again would I experience that three part sequence which I had grown to detest: first the stare at my feet, then the penetrating look directly in the eye which conveyed, mirth, derision, shock, embarrassment, pity or compassion, which I returned directly and in kind, and finally back again to my feet, to confirm they had actually seen what they thought they saw, and to record a clear mental image so that they could recall it later. The congenital deformities that had for so many years affected my life and behavior were gone and in their places were two clean, surgically sculptured antiseptic stumps of natural, normal flesh and bone. What had also disappeared was the need to cover, conceal, mask or camouflage any part of my body.

The impact was significant. As I recovered from surgery, tension flowed out of me and relaxation set in. For the first time in my life I was completely at ease. All guardedness disappeared; I opened up. My physical body had nothing to hide. I became almost an exhibitionist. I did not care who saw me in any stage of undress. I almost begged to be seen. I had never known such freedom.

Jan. 10, 1961, First day at The Institute for Physical Medicine and Rehabilitation. Relatively uneventful. Underwent entry process and assigned to Room 131 on the first floor, one floor above ground level.

At the Institute, in an environment of progressive disease and post-trauma, every patient was fighting to regain or maintain some vestige of physical and/or mental control of his/her body that had been recently lost, and hoping against hope that some small increment of improvement would result in the next day, or week, or month; that nerves would mend, paralysis lessen, movement improve, and miracles happen. I alone possessed a body that was infinitely better than it had ever been. As I became acquainted with my fellow patients and heard their stories, that reality grew in me daily. Others were learning to live with the results of disaster; I was experiencing a miracle. Even as a triple amputee (I was the only one), I had more going for myself than anyone else. And as for the world outside, I'd think about that when I got to it.

I was assigned a room and provided a wheelchair that permitted both wheels to be controlled on the left side. My sense of freedom continued apace as I ranged up and down the halls in my chair. Room 131 was a four-person room. Andy Caparossi, in the bed beside me was a high school math teacher until he dove into the surf in Atlantic City on the fourth day of his honeymoon and hit an old unused pipe that a previous hotel had neglected to remove. He had broken his neck at the third and fourth vertebrae, and was now a quadriplegic who lay in bed, his head in a wire device that held head and neck in position while the vertebrae healed. Psychologically, Andy's rehabilitation was at an extremely difficult stage and his spirits fluctuated between despair and near hilarity. During the few months immediately following his injury surgeons had done everything possible for him and it was now clear that, short of a miracle, there would be no further return of either muscle or nerve function. Andy's Catholic family prayed that with the continued healing would come return of at least some muscular control. Unfortunately, those prayers were not to be answered. With limited remaining functional movement of his arms it was not possible for him to move his chair down the hall to the dining room, so an attendant pushed him. Lacking prehension in his fingers, a utensil strapped to a supportive brace on his hand enabled him to laboriously go through the motions of lifting food to his mouth, and he was learning to develop some control in his remaining arm muscles. His devoted wife, Terry, visited after work each day at suppertime to feed him and so they could have dinner together. Given the tension of becoming accustomed to his greatly reduced capabilities, he could sometimes vent a sizeable temper, but his sense of humor was wonderful to behold. When a nurse was painting a bedsore on Andy's behind with a bright red medication, he suggested she make it a non-representational design so it could be photographed and framed. We spent many hours talking and developed a close friendship.

In the Intensive Care Unit at New York University Hospital for twenty-two days, I had had no contact with other patients, not unusual since patients in ICU were all in need of critical attention. The Institute, however, was a completely different environment. It was not a hospital per se'. The Institute's focus was physical and educational rehabilitation; entertainment and social activities were encouraged as a means to assist restoration of patient independence. Those in need of hospital services were temporarily transferred to a hospital, usually for a only a day or two to meet their needs.

Entry into the Institute brought with it the realization that, despite the improvements in my personal physical condition, I was nevertheless a severely disabled individual and thus one of a group who were labeled handicapped. That had never been my orientation. I never perceived myself as belonging to any such group, but now I was at the Institute with other handicapped people. Without question, I was one of them, and there was no escaping the fact that in this particular zoo, I was not one of the keepers.

My doctor at the Institute was Donald Dowie, an Australian, former military doctor and pilot, now doing a residency in rehabilitation medicine. Dowie was informal, laid back, intelligent, easy to talk to and friendly. Just what I needed. We were friends right away. He had not seen my pre-surgery x-rays so I drew pictures for him of my former legs and feet. He suggested that I stop taking the sleeping pills that were readily available, so I took two aspirins at bedtime and two more during the night. It worked. The next morning Dr. Dowie, Dr. Levine and the chief prosthetist, Mr. Tosberg, a gentle elderly man with a gruff exterior and a twinkle in his eye, visited me to observe while a nurse removed the dressings on my stumps and washed them. I was impatient to be again in control of my body. Having to be attended by a nurse gave me a feeling of inadequacy. A note in my journal indicates my feelings.

"There is much to be said about the pride and dignity of man and its relation to his being able to stand on his own two feet."

Where the hell was Dr. Russek? I hadn't seen him since well before the surgery. Now I had been at the Institute for a week and he still hadn't shown up. My irritation at Russek's absence disappeared for the moment when I learned that there was a shower room just down the hall. I hadn't had a bath or a shower for almost a month. I longed to feel the water running over my body. I wanted to soak and soak, but because my stumps still had open wounds I wasn't permitted to do so. However, with the help of a nurse, I was able to secure two surgical rubber gloves and by pulling one over each stump and up over the knee I was able to waterproof my stumps. The shower room was just perfect. All I had to do was transfer from my wheelchair to the shower wheelchair and then, after the attendant had adjusted the shower, I wheeled into the shower and enjoyed myself. What a relief. What luxury. I got up on my knees on the seat and "stood" under the water. I felt like a new person. I also astonished the attendant who, when I emerged from the shower and was asked if I wanted my back dried, said, "No, just hand me the towel." Then, on my knees, I draped the towel over my right arm, gave it a special twist that locked it to my arm and grabbing the other end in my left hand, flipped the whole towel over my head and sawed it back and forth across my back just the way anyone with two hands does. I took such a thing for granted and had been doing it since I was a kid, but to the attendant it was some sort of magic trick. "How'd you do that?" And so I had to do it again and teach him to do it using one of his hands tightened into a fist. When he succeeded, he was all smiles. I was amused that it had occasioned such interest; to me it was simply a normal occurrence.

The following morning I met three young men in wheelchairs at breakfast in the dining room down the hall. I was my usual independent self, in all probability more than usual after having spent almost four weeks in bed and now being able to enjoy what I perceived to be the freedom of a wheelchair. Getting to the dining room, selecting my food and feeding myself was a pleasure. One young man, a patient being rehabilitated after suffering head trauma, suggested to me that I shouldn't do so much myself and should ask for more help. According to him "they" didn't like it when you did that. My response, immediate and direct was typical, "if 'they' don't like it that's their problem." I subsequently learned that the patient who had advised me was a brilliant fellow who had suffered brain damage in an accident. My future responses to him were softened by that knowledge.

On returning to my room I was given a schedule of activities that were to begin the next day, but that afternoon I was to report to room 234 for muscle evaluation and testing. Being fitted with lower leg prosthesis is a bit like learning to walk on stilts. The point of contact with the ground is beyond the extremity of the limb and one must learn to manage the dead weight of the artificial extension (prosthesis) that is attached to the natural limb. As long as it's hanging down it can be swung more easily than if it is lifted up and forward, as in a high kick position. When lifted, the full weight of the prosthesis is extended from the end of the leg as a cantilever and strength and athletic ability is required to manage that dead weight and make it go where it is supposed to go. Accordingly, before being fitted for a leg, the leg muscle strength and tone necessary for the job must be developed. The first step in that development is to determine one's existing physical condition so a base point can be established from which to measure future progress. The physical therapist that tested me wore an artificial leg of the same type that I was to have and I studied her carefully.

I was concerned that there could be a big difference between having just one rather than two artificial legs, but as I watched her very closely and saw how easily she moved about I was reassured. I just hoped that I would be able to move as well as she did. As she performed the tests, it became evident that I was in pretty good general shape. There were no problems with my hips, both my stumps were the same length, my upper legs were the same lengths and my knees were both strong and functional despite the fact, as I had learned from the x-rays, I had no fibula in the left leg, and the fibula and the tibia were fused at the top in the right leg. The range of motion exercises to which I was subjected were of great interest to me. Their purpose was to determine if the joint moves freely in all directions, and if each of the several muscle groups which facilitate its motion have normal strength and function. In the upper leg different muscle groupings power the leg to move forward, backward and laterally in and out. The same muscles, used differently, facilitate rotation of the leg. The therapist checked each movement separately for function and then exerted resistant force preventing movement that I had to try to overcome. The tests showed me to be functioning normally and my legs to be strong.

Dr. Russek did not visit that day either and even Dr. Dowie seemed put out at his absence. Mr. Weissfield, my caseworker from the Office of Vocational Rehabilitation dropped by in the afternoon and we chatted. He reaffirmed that the circulation of the right leg prior to the surgery had been approaching the point of developing vascular disease and had not the amputation been performed, there would have been a fair chance of losing that leg at the knee at some later time, possibly as soon as a year or two. It was reassuring to know that I had elected to undergo the rehabilitation when I did, but at that point I no longer had any doubts as to its success.

That first evening, Hernando Munoz, a Colombian soldier who had lost both his legs above the knee in an explosion while on military maneuvers, came into the room with his guitar to introduce himself, and despite the language barrier, we had a good time singing. Another patient, Nicky, who had lost his right hand and part of the forearm in an accident joined us, playing guitar with his hook, and having trouble holding the pick tight enough. After the singing I watched TV in the room across the hall for an hour and the second day ended at 10:30 P.M.

Jan. 13, Friday. Today began my exercise program. The schedule is 9:00 –10:00, Progressive Resistance Exercises; 10:00 –11:00, Whirlpool Bath; 11:00 –1:00, Free time & lunch; 1:00 –2:00, Progressive resistance Exercises; 2:00 –3:00 Mat Exercises.

The first day of exercise worked out very well. I surprised everyone with what I could do; I was not surprised. I knew then that I was going to be very successful at whatever was necessary to do in order to stand up and walk. I started weightlifting with fifteen pounds resistance on my knees, flexing and straightening. My arm, chest and shoulder exercises were done with a fifteen pound dumbbell in my left hand and an eight pound dumbbell fastened to my arm with an ace bandage. At last, Dr. Russek stopped in to see me in the early evening and advised me that he had ordered a concentrated exercise schedule to build up my arms and shoulders for crutches. Dr. Dowie was in and we discussed the matter of a prosthesis for my arm. Dowie thought it would be a good idea. Apparently Weissfield wanted me to have it, as did Tosberg. I still had ambivalent feelings about it. I knew what I could do with my arm; I had no idea what I would be able to do with a hook or a cosmetic hand. I was still certain that either a hook or a hand would just get in my way and with my legs looking normal I didn't see my arm as an important concern.

After a few days of exercise my legs began to react to the exercise. When I relaxed in the evening I would get hyper and the nerves in my legs twitched and jumped. I reverted to the sleeping pill and it knocked me out.

One morning, one of the nurses, Miss Wilmer, came in to talk to me. She was probing, not too adroitly, about what she thought was my "affected behavior." When I eventually realized that she thought that I was going to exaggerate lengths to let everyone know that I was independent, I tried to convince her that what she was observing was not an affectation, but simply who I was. As she departed, I experienced a moment of concern. Did I really have a problem? Then I chuckled to myself and put it out of my mind.

Soon after my arrival at the Institute my father and mother visited. I needed a wheelchair, but I was free to leave the premises on completion of my daily routine, and we had a delightful afternoon driving out to Long Island and visiting the then new Idlewild Airport where we encountered a problem. Needing the use of a restroom, Dad and I sought the men's room only to find that the doors on the stalls in the men's room of the "brand new" 1961 airport were too narrow to permit the passage of a wheelchair. Fortunately, my chair was a collapsible one and with a considerable amount of struggling, me on my knees on the seat of the chair and Dad pulling on the chair, we managed to collapse the chair sufficiently to pass into the stall. Physical access for the handicapped was not to be taken for granted in the early 60s. After a long search we also finally found a restaurant that was wheelchair accessible and had an enjoyable dinner before they delivered me back to the Institute.

Roaming about the hallway in my wheelchair I had met a stroke victim in the next room, a Dr. Miller, a neurosurgeon from Pittsburgh. Although Dr. Miller's reasoning hadn't been affected, he suffered from aphasia and was unable to speak. Using a blackboard, we discussed the need for more Rehabilitation Centers and Dr. Miller bemoaned the fact that Pittsburgh had a dire need; although a new Rehab Center was opening, it had only one MD who had been trained at IPMR. When I mentioned Dr. Miller to my father, Dad became excited. "I think he's the guy who played basketball at Pitt years ago and was a big star. Where is he? I'd like to meet him." I explained the circumstances of the doctor's affliction and my father hurried off to find him, returning an hour later. "I was right. He's the same guy."

Jan. 20, after beginning exercises a week ago with 15-pound weights, I'm now lifting 25 pounds with my knees and can do 50 times without stopping. Peg visited. We chatted a bit. Buzz Rice and Fred Kelly visited. Discussed the project to create original design for a rear screen projector that would play a cassette type 8 mm sound film.

Across the hall, in Room 130, was Lenny, not yet twenty, who had dived into a swimming pool, struck his head on the bottom and was now a quadriplegic, and Mark di Suvero, a beatnik artist in his late twenties with a beautiful red beard and sharp intellect who, many years later achieved international recognition as a sculptor.

Mark had been in a freight elevator accident in a studio loft in lower New York and was now a paraplegic, quite active and able to move about with leg braces and crutches. Mark kept his schedule of classes at the Institute, but was out every night with his friends visiting his old haunts, and returning late. He took a special interest in Lenny and was encouraging him to develop an interest in painting and drawing. They had a TV and I invited myself to watch.

It didn't require more than a day or two to become aware of the in-group humor among patients. Invariably shocking to the outsider, it was candid and matter-of-fact to the afflicted. Each knew his respective condition and joking about it relieved some of the anger, sorrow and despair they all shared. I was the lone exception. One evening, as I was watching TV in Mark's room, I shifted myself around in my wheelchair and casually threw one leg over the arm of the chair to be more comfortable. Mark, watching me from the bed, gave me a hard look and said, "Quit moving your legs around, you God damned showoff!" It was a funny remark and we laughed, one man who could move his legs and two who couldn't, but it was rough humor, too sharp and biting for outsiders. Mark and I were friendly, but never close friends, and our paths never again crossed outside the Institute, although I followed the progress of his enviable burgeoning reputation as reported in the media.

Tuesday, Jan. 24. Saturday evening I played John Rose's harmonica. That was a mistake. John had strep throat and by Sunday I had it too. Penicillin cleared it up, but it took a few days.

Charlie LaSister was assigned the bed diagonally opposite from mine. A handsome black man, Charlie was in his sixties, had suffered a stroke which paralyzed his left side, but was already experiencing return of some muscle control. Charlie had a wife, an ex-wife, and a mistress and they all came to visit, but their paths never crossed. How it was managed was a mystery, but the timing was exemplary. Charlie was what is known in the underworld as a banker, he loaned money at usurious rates, and he was into everything. Each day, late in the afternoon just before dinner was served, his bag man (he actually carried a brown paper bag), would come in, stand beside Charlie's bed and give Charlie the bag. Very nonchalantly—he wasn't a bit concerned who saw him—Charlie removed a five inch wad of bills, and lying in bed, counted it, returned it to the bag and the man took the bag and departed.

Charlie and I had a couple of exercise classes together and as we exercised we talked. Our roles as patients gave us something in common and our personalities seemed compatible. Charlie had a friend he called "Bro", whom I met one day. Charlie explained that he had set Bro up in a junkyard on Staten Island and as the conversation continued it was clear that the junkyard was really a chop shop in which stolen cars were dismantled and sold for parts. Charlie had cautioned Bro to maintain a low visibility concerning his personal spending so as not to draw attention to the wealth he was drawing from a small junkyard, but, as Charlie explained, Bro wasn't getting the message and he might just have to take the junkyard away from him. "There are some people who just don't listen when you talk." Charlie said.

The day came when Charlie's recovery was no longer being helped by the treatments at the Institute and he was being discharged. It was obvious that he was known as a powerful figure in Harlem, and was perceived as an important personage among the attendants and aides at the Institute, most of whom were either black or Hispanic. Each of them had, during his stay, used every possible artifice to stop by and say hello almost every day. As he left there was a line of people coming to wish him well and he passed out a beautiful silk tie or scarf to each of them. Finally, before taking his leave from the room, Charlie came over to my bed, shook hands, looked me square in the eye very seriously, and said, "If there's ever anything I can do for you, anything," he said, emphasizing the last word, "you just let me know. And give me a call sometime."

At the time I had decided to opt for the surgery I had an overdue, uncompleted course paper for which I had secured an extension. I tried to make some progress, but with the many distractions in this new environment, I was unable to concentrate. Instead, I obtained some colored paper, glue and a razor blade from the arts and crafts room. I conned a nurse to filch some 1/8 inch diameter wooden swab sticks ten or twelve inches long. Then, with razor and glue, I scarfed them together to make longer sticks, and using the colored paper, began to construct mobiles. The first ones were simple affairs of one or two pieces that I hung by threads from the acoustic ceiling. Soon, the nurses and the doctors were commenting about the mobiles and patients and staff were coming in to see them. A couple of nurses wanted them, so I gave them away and made replacements.

A regular procedure in the Institute was that doctors made rounds visiting each of their respective patients every morning at about the same time. I was Dr. Russek's patient and he did not visit on regular rounds, preferring to come at the end of the day and then only when there was a need. The chief physician on my floor, Dr. Covalt, however, served a very large number of patients and the joke was that every time he bid a patient good morning he was earning a visitation fee. Of the four patients in my room, I was the only one not in his charge, and it became noticeable, even to members of Dr. Covalt's entourage each morning as he entered with them, that he would say good morning to each of his patients, but not to me. The nurses and therapists in the entourage, on the other hand, said good morning to everyone. Andy was the first to notice it and we laughed about how the other staff members would engage me in conversation about my mobiles, but the doctor studiously ignored me. I took it as a challenge. I told Andy, "I'm going to make him say hello." I kept building larger mobiles and finally, one day when I had a four foot wide multicolored mobile with several balanced parts hanging over my bed and twisting slowly in the slight draft from the air conditioner, the doctor walked in and there were so many comments from his associates that he was forced to recognize it. He walked over to my bed and said, "Good morning, that's a lovely mobile." Andy was beside himself and laughed uproariously.

Peg would visit occasionally and I looked forward to her visits. If we could find an unused corner, we would briefly hug or exchange a kiss. I was infatuated with her and in my newfound openness more gregarious than I had previously been. With nothing to hide, and free from the stigma that had been occasioned by my legs, my attitude toward the opposite sex had become more direct and flirtatious. I was invited by a nurse, Barbara DeSandis, to attend a party that she and her sister were having at their apartment a few blocks from the Institute. I was free to come and go from the Institute when not scheduled for classes or treatments so I accepted the invitation, but the Institute frowned at relationships between patients and staff so the event took on a clandestine air. I was to proceed, in my wheelchair, to the corner outside the Institute and wait, and someone would meet me there and push the chair the couple blocks to Barbara's apartment house. The conspiracy proceeded without hitch. Barbara, and her neighbor, Freddie, appeared on schedule and I went to the party. As I was pushed into her apartment, it struck me suddenly that this was really my maiden voyage into a mixed social gathering since my surgery. I felt a bit strange sitting without legs in the midst of a group of men and women I didn't know, but I was more at ease than I had been in similar situations prior to the surgery. I just didn't give a damn.

The exercise schedule continued and I became more agile and stronger than I had ever been. My right stump had healed and following Dr. Russek's instructions, I massaged both stumps daily to loosen up the outer skin. At other times I kept them wrapped tightly with ace bandages to reduce the swelling from their enlarged post-surgery size. My left leg was healing slower than the right one, causing Dr. Russek some consternation in view of his previous confidence that there was sufficient blood flow to support the amputations. As Mr. Tosberg told me confidentially some time later, "You had the old man worried."

In anticipation of wearing prostheses, and because I would be at least five inches taller, I needed both new pants and shoes. My father sent a pair of eight and a half size shoes; the size I'd been advised would work with the prostheses and be correct for my height. The black wool pants I had worn to the hospital had folded and sewn cuffs, so I asked my aunt to remove the stitches in the cuffs and press them out, lengthening the pant legs to serve temporarily until I obtained some new clothing.

When my legs finally healed, the prosthetist, John Eschen Jr., of Eschen Prosthetics Company in Harlem, came to the Institute to pick up the my shoes and made plaster casts of my stumps for use in the fabrication of my new legs. A few weeks later I was transported to the company's shop and confronted for the first time by what appeared to be a pair of short stilts with my new shoes at the bottom and cups at the tops. The tops and bottoms were connected by what appeared to be a piece of pipe. The cups, or sockets, had been molded from the plaster casts and represented the concave negative shapes into which my stumps would fit. With cotton, and a woolen sock on each stump the prosthetist eased my legs into the sockets and instructed me to press some weight into the sockets. It was not a comfortable feeling. The prosthetist adjusted a couple of leather straps just above my knees, and then, supporting me under the arms, lifted me to an upright position.

For the first time in almost three months I was standing erect, and it hurt. I was reminded of the pain I used to have. The present situation was painful, but it wasn't as penetrating. He let me stand for a moment or two, holding on to a balance rail on the wall. "Would you like to try to walk?" Holding my breath, I replied, "Sure." "Go very slowly. Just swing one foot forward and then the other." Holding tightly to the rail, I swung the awkward appendage forward with my right leg and then slowly leaned forward and transferred my weight from the left leg to the right and then repeated the motion until I had taken six steps and was at the other end of the small room. Carefully, I turned around and the pros-thetist now offered his arm in place of the rail that was now on my right side, and I made the return trip and sat down. My stumps hurt. "Right now your stumps are tender, but you did very well. As they shrink you'll be more comfortable and we'll have to make numer-ous adjustments in the next few months." After a couple more trips to the prosthetist I was told, " Take these back with you and keep them on as much as you can tolerate. Stand up in them every chance you get. What's important now is to get used to them and condition your stumps to tolerate them."

I now awakened each morning, unwrapped the ace bandages from my stumps, pulled on the heavy wool socks, donned my new legs and with crutches and wheelchair, began my day in the dining room and then in classes. At lunch break and after classes I would shed the prostheses, massage my stumps, have a shower and relax until supper and at night re-wrap the ace bandages.

My parents were scheduled to visit again in a few days, on Good Friday. When it was time for them to arrive, I sat on the end of my bed, my lengthened black pants covering the stilt like legs with only my shoes showing, and as my parents entered the room I stood up to my now increased height, with my natural appearing legs presenting an image that was totally normal. The impact on my parents was profound. In that moment they witnessed what they had never in their lives expected to see.

My journal read:

> *"They were completely overcome. Mother came and held me close, crying, and Dad was close behind, clasping my hand with tears streaming down his face. I cried as well. This experience for them, even more so than for me, is a culmination of years of hopes and prayers. What it means for them is much more than I could ever understand, to have that which was never expected to be, come to life in actuality. Just to see them so happy at this miracle is worth whatever risks were involved."*

A few more trips to the prosthetist, as I developed a greater tolerance for standing and taking tentative steps with crutches, resulted in the cosmetic aspects of the legs being completed and once that had been accomplished, I felt I was ready to go anywhere. I asked Barbara DeSandis if she would accompany me to the Village some evening and was delighted when she agreed. Sporting my new legs and crutches, we took a cab to Greenwich Village, had a drink and listened to music in a small bistro. I had a difficult time getting my legs in and out of the cab. It seemed that they were a mile long and I couldn't manage them well at all in such circumstances.

The next morning I related my difficulty to Mr. Tosberg and he informed me that the length of the prostheses had been calculated on the basis of measurements taken of my upper legs, "But frequently that doesn't work well, because you have no ankle motion so you're unable to twist your foot around the way everyone else does when they're getting in or out of a car. I think we'll shorten them two or three inches. You'll be slightly shorter, but that isn't really important. What's important is functional use."

Eschen picked up the legs and a few days later returned them, shortened. The new length was more manageable, but I was still taking only a few tentative steps with the crutches. I wasn't yet able to walk without them, but I was already worrying about whether I would be able to drive with my prostheses. I teased another nurse, about taking me out in her car until she invited me to go for a drive one Saturday afternoon. I was impatient to find out if I would be able to drive with the new legs. Her car was a standard shift and just before dark, we found a park in New Jersey that appeared deserted. She stopped the car and we switched places.

When using prostheses, either arm or leg, one develops a kinesthetic sense as to where the prosthesis terminates in space, and what and when it touches something. It is a sense that develops with experience. If one has an artificial hand and, in the dark, touches something, the impact, however slight, travels along the prosthesis to the stump and it is immediately apparent that something has been touched, but it is not possible to know, from only touch, just what has been touched. Vision plays an important part in providing ancillary information that permits a person with prostheses to know what is touched and where it is. Similarly, the average person, when driving a car, feels the location of the pedals with their feet without looking to see where they are.

A person with two lower leg prostheses, attempting to drive a standard shift for the first time, has neither time nor opportunity to look at his feet to see their location. Given these circumstances, Rose was taking a big chance allowing me to drive her car. I sat in the driver's seat and looked down at my feet. I placed the right foot on the gas pedal and then lifted my leg and moved it to the brake. Then I put my left foot on the clutch I decided that I'd keep it there just in case I needed it. With parking brake set and the gear in neutral, I pushed the clutch in and out a few times to get the feel of it and did the same with the brake and gas pedals. When I was satisfied, I released the brake, pushed in the clutch and put the car in gear pressing lightly on the gas pedal. We were moving. I shifted into second, then high gear and rolled along the park road. I was exultant. I couldn't even walk yet, but I could drive. I would have no problems. I moved my foot to the brake, slowed the car, pushed in the clutch, stopped, put the car in neutral and set the brake. It was enough. I had eliminated my concern.

It was only two months since I'd had both legs amputated and I had become infatuated with one nurse, been taken driving by another, been invited to a party and then dated a third. It seemed to prove my old theory that while there was a very dim possibility of my having a relationship with just any woman, the odds were more in my favor with someone who had some connection to the medical establishment such as a nurse. At least there was a better chance that they would look beyond my disabilities and not be immediately turned off. At the same time, I knew that I was undergoing emotional and psychological changes as my physical rehabilitation progressed. I didn't understand it, and couldn't articulate it, but I could feel it. With my legs cut off I had the feeling of being more whole than ever before.

Goffman explains that a stigmatized person can expect some support from a set of people who share his stigma and are therefore defined and define themselves as his own kind.[9] Of particular interest to me is Goffman's more precise definition of the wise. Apparently I was living in a paradise composed of the "wise" and enjoying every minute of it.[10]

Taking several steps slowly while leaning on crutches was one thing; walking free and establishing a gait was quite another. Learning to walk with prostheses was not easy. The problems were twofold: overcoming the discomfort in my stumps which were not yet conditioned to the task; and the physical manipulation of the two inanimate extensions attached to them. Slowly the stumps were adapting; they were shrinking and my tolerance was increasing. A variety of different kinds of artificial feet were available, but basically they were of two types: the articulated ankle, and the non-articulated ankle.

The former has two moving parts, an upper part approximating the lower portion of the leg just above the ankle and the lower that approximates the toe and heel. A metal pin set laterally at the ankle rotation point permits the lower part to flex in a toe-up and toe-down motion. Fore and aft of the pivotal point, rubber bumpers, available in differing densities, are inserted to limit the extent of ankle motion under prescribed pressure.

---

[9] "...The second set are—to borrow a term once used by homosexuals—the 'wise,' namely, persons who are normal, but whose special situation has made them intimately privy to the secret life of the stigmatized individual and sympathetic with it, and who find themselves accorded a measure of acceptance, a measure of courtesy membership in the clan. Wise persons are the marginal men before whom the individual with a fault need feel no shame nor exert self control, knowing that in spite of his failing he will be seen as an ordinary other." (Goffman, p. 28)

[10] "One type of wise person is he whose wiseness comes from working in an establishment which caters either to the wants of those with a particular stigma or to actions that society takes in regard to those persons. For example, nurses and physical therapists can be wise." (Goffman, p.28-9)

The non-articulated ankle consists of a one-piece wooden keel encapsulated in resilient plastic and permanently fixed in its relationship to the leg. The keel ends just at the metatarsal arch and the toes and heel are made of dense, but pliable rubber, the heel serving as a shock absorber as it strikes the pavement and the toe providing an ability to roll over easily as the body moves beyond the point of pavement contact. It is known as a Satch foot.

The articulated ankle is frequently used for a person with only one prosthesis since, although it facilitates walking, it is not stabile and when just standing the natural leg must be used to enable the wearer to maintain balance. With two lower leg prostheses, it is usually necessary to use the Satch foot to maintain balance.

My two Satch feet enabled me to easily stand motionless without losing balance, even with my eyes shut which was one of the tests required by the therapists. In order to walk, the leg would be swung forward and just as the heel touched the ground and the forward momentum carried the body over the foot and leg, the knee had to be slightly flexed pulling the body forward. A split second later, as forward motion carried the body beyond the weight bearing foot, the knee was extended thereby putting pressure on the foot that in turn provided push-off pressure for the next step. It was not difficult to take several continuous steps, but it was extremely difficult to develop the sequence of moves and the rhythm necessary to establish a comfortable gait that could be sustained until it began to feel natural and instinctive. My early attempts were reminiscent of a person who had had too much to drink trying to walk a straight line. Each day I would practice walking for the doctors, therapists and prosthetists as minor adjustments continued to be made. I increased the amount of time I wore the legs. With Dr. Dowie's assistance, and holding the banister, I attacked the stairs to the second floor going up and then down again, a process that required placing the foot on the upper step and then using the knee muscles to lift the weight of the body. This action generated a moderate amount of posterior and anterior pressure on the stump as the knee was extended. Walking down the steps reversed the action and I had to gradually flex the weight-bearing knee as I slowly lowered the other foot to the lower step. Without ankle motion the rigid foot on the weight bearing leg assumed a tiptoe position, with weight on the toe only, as the other foot landed flat on the lower step. Whereas the relationship of my stump to the prosthesis provided a stable and secure support in a standing upright position, as the knee was flexed, the degree of support lessened and the strain on the stump increased. As the days passed however, and as I gained both confidence and expertise and was able to walk further and further, my walking acquired an increased smoothness of gait and balance. My days were now spent walking, from morning until evening, occasionally resting and massaging my stumps, which were slowly becoming toughened to the constant pressures of the prostheses. I had ample strength to manipulate the prostheses. The Institute staff had done their jobs well; there was no more they could do.

The final step in the rehabilitation process was re-entry into the world outside the insular environment of the Institute to learn how the miracle I had just experienced would affect the rest of my life. I was discharged on the 21st of April, 1961.

12

Vicissitudes of the Real World?

My return to the real world was almost indescribable. I experienced the equivalent of a drug induced high. As I looked around from my new height, five inches taller than I had previously been, all my surroundings took on a new perspective. Everything was bright and shiny and positive. I had no doubts or fears about anything. I recalled the line from Orwell's *1984*, "Ford's in his Flivver, all's right with the world." Certainly all was right in my world. With high spirits, I visualized a future quite different from the past and anticipated opportunities previously unobtainable. I would go back to NYU, complete the Master's Degree, teach, and look for a permanent job. My excitement and confidence were boundless.

I returned to my Aunt's apartment, quietly enjoyed being back in the real world for a few days and then flew home to Pittsburgh. For the rest of the month, until my friends moved out of my apartment in New York, there was time to relax with my parents. We recalled our many memories of the past, including the bad times I had experienced, and I basked in my parents' joyous reactions to my new appearance and capabilities. The events of the past three months were difficult to absorb, the changes were so profound and so far beyond anything anyone had imagined. It was virtually impossible to accept what was apparent. By our standards, we had experienced a miracle. Mother would look at me and we would both cry. All of the years of my parent's concerns and sacrifices and my years of pain and struggle seemed as if a dream. Our lives were so full of love and joy and visions of the future that the worries and concerns of the past now seemed to have happened in another lifetime, in another world. My mother's and father's dream of many years was now a reality.

My car had been repaired and delivered to my parent's home. I spent time practicing driving which, with an automatic transmission, required the use of only my right leg. I visited relatives and friends, had lunch with Abby and saw Fred. Everyone was delighted for me. By the end of the month I was ready to chance driving my car to New York. Although my parents were anxious for my well being, I was confidant of my capabilities and assured them that I would be able to manage without assistance, and true to my expectations, the trip was without incident. I had now gained confidence in my driving although when driving at night I still had not fully absorbed the kinetic senses in my stumps and had to concentrate as to where my feet were placed. It was interesting that, when driving during the day my peripheral sight informed me as to the position of my feet, but at night, with my feet in darkness, it was entirely feel and I had to function without the benefit of sight. Nevertheless, my kinesthetic sense amazed me. I became accustomed, when I put my foot on a pedal, to being able to discern if it was in the right place. I learned to differentiate between pressure being exerted on the toe or heel, or either side of my shoe. Each position minutely affected the position of the prosthesis in relation to my stump and each position generated a unique feeling. I was building a new sensory reference system.

Buzz and his new bride found another apartment in the Village and moved out of my apartment at the end of April. I had told Mrs. Murphy, the superintendent of my building, only that I was going to be in the hospital for a couple of months and my friends would stay in the apartment and pay the rent until I came back. She had no idea what was happening to me during my absence and when she saw me for the first time as I was exiting the building she was severely shaken. As I walked to my car I saw her shaking her head in wonder and repeatedly crossing herself.

A relatively new non-profit agency, J. O. B., an acronym for Just One Break, which had a close relationship with the Institute for Physical Medicine and Rehabilitation (IPMR), was dedicated to finding employment for persons with disabilities. I was advised by a social worker at the Institute that J.O.B. would be of great assistance in helping me to find suitable permanent employment. I looked forward to their assistance and made an appointment at my earliest opportunity. When I visited the JOB office and was interviewed by one of the placement counselors, it became readily apparent that my credentials and experience placed me far beyond the realm of JOB's market. The population JOB normally serviced and the kinds of jobs they regularly filled were low level, simple task jobs usually found in sheltered workshops. The J.O.B. personnel had no familiarity, nor could they be expected to have, with the placement of professional personnel at any level.

I found it difficult to believe that I was the only unemployed, disabled person in New York City who had professional capabilities. Was I that much of an exception? Was there any agency dedicated to MY needs? It wasn't surprising, but it was somewhat frightening. There appeared to be a mindset that the disabled were mentally deficient. How else could one explain the general practice of assigning people with functioning brains and disabled bodies to such menial physical jobs as sorting envelopes or wiring electronic circuits, making brooms or placemats, instead of utilizing their intellect, which was undamaged. I had some opinions as to why this was happening. Jobs that required intellect had already been taken by able-bodied persons who had climbed the job ladder, and they were not about to be threatened by those who had not or could not. In his book, *My Eyes Have A Cold Nose*, Hector Chevigny comments on the fact that disability appears to preclude employment that utilizes skills not subject to the disability.[11] He also suggests that New York charities job placement centers are little more than referral posts to sheltered workshops.[12]

I remembered the empathetic television executive who had told me frankly that he couldn't hire me to be a gofer for others who had less experience. I began to re-assess the hierarchy of employable skills that existed in the world of work, and realized it comprised a job ladder wherein the jobs at the bottom of the ladder were essentially physical and those at the top were predominantly intellectual. I had entertained the thought for a long time, but now it seemed crystal clear. Unless one could begin at the bottom and perform the physical jobs, there was no opportunity for advancement. Although I had always accepted my disabilities, I

[11] "... a man who had lost his sight, who was previously a publicity agent, was advised that he should become accustomed to working with his hands because most of the work the blind can get call for manual skills." (Chevigny, p. 113)
[12] Chevigny, p. 115

recognized that through sheer indomitable perseverance I had managed to break through several lower layers of the job ladder and reach a level where, on the one hand, I was beyond the capabilities of an agency like J.O.B., but on the other, at a decided disadvantage in competing with those non disabled persons who had similar capabilities, and who had progressed much farther up the ladder. It startled me that perhaps, despite my new facade and phenomenally increased physical capabilities, I might still be faced with the fact that given my age my lack of advancement could still compromise my future.

I visited NYU to say hello and to see if there might be any work. I met with Dick Goggin and George Gorden and Charles Siepmann, all of whom were delighted with the success of my rehabilitation and pleased to see me so happy. The spring semester was well under way and I learned that the Television Workshop for Teachers, which I had previously taught had been scheduled to be taught by Barbara Yanowski in the fall. Charles was most apologetic. "I am so sorry. We had no idea as to what your period of convalescence might be, when you might return if at all, and it was necessary to schedule the class, so I asked Barbara Yanowski to teach it. Do you know her?" I thought to myself, how ironic. I had applied for a job as her director and now she has my job. I hadn't met Barbara, but of course I knew who she was. And as much as I was disappointed, there was no doubt in my mind that had Charles known of my availability, the job would have been mine. For Barbara, who was fully employed, it was just an extra job, an added perk; for me it could be survival income. A week or two later Charles called to tell me that Barbara Yanowski was uncomfortable about having seemingly co-opted my teaching assignment. She wanted to meet me and, if I were willing, share the teaching assignment with me, working together as a team. Given the circumstances, I felt that Barbara had no obligation to me and her offer was exceedingly gracious. At the same time, I needed employment and was delighted for the opportunity to earn even half of the fee. I met with her and accepted her generous and thoughtful gesture.

During the time I had been hospitalized, I had given much thought to how I might be able to regenerate my career, wondering if perhaps my future might lay in higher education. If so, I'd need not only a Master's degree, but a Ph.D. I talked with Charles about it and sought his advice. 'It's a painful process," he said, "and I would encourage you to go that route only for the joy of scholarship, and not as a license for a job." What I needed immediately was work. Without it I couldn't afford to pursue further study, so I shelved the idea for the moment.

At the same time, Fred and Buzz had continued to work on our cooperative idea, namely, the design of an instructional system that would permit a student to independently study with specially prepared films utilizing the then new branching programmed instruction technique. The means to accomplish this system, which we termed *Indivision*, referring to individualized instruction, was a piece of equipment not then existent, but for which we had developed a design concept and specifications. It consisted of a small, portable viewer featuring a rear screen projected image on a viewing screen approximately one foot square that utilized an endless loop film in a plastic cassette. We hoped to obtain a grant from the Ford Foundation to underwrite the costs for developing both the equipment and some pilot films and to this end Buzz and Fred had obtained an interview with a highly placed foundation official. On the day of the appointment, soon after I had been released from the Institute, New York City was inundated with an unexpected late season four to six inch snowfall that posed a considerable problem for someone still relatively inexperienced at walking on two artificial legs. "Not to worry. We'll get you there," promised Fred and Buzz and they showed up with a large child's sled and proceeded to pull me through the streets of New York City to the Ford Foundation headquarters. The ensuing interview, although polite and courteous, unfortunately produced no support.

Back in my own apartment and once again mobile, I was anxious to see both Peg and Barbara DeSandis. Although I was infatuated with Peg, I liked Barbara, and in my new found emotional and psychological freedom, with what I perceived as my new "acceptability" to women I was ready to flirt with any female who looked my way, nurse or not. My new vision of myself was as a whole person. I no longer had anything to hide and it was a good feeling. It had been a couple of weeks since Peg had visited and when I talked to her, I had a sense that something had changed in what I thought was our developing relationship. She did agree to see me and one evening I picked her up in my car and we went for a drive up the West Side Highway. On the return I stopped at the small park at Ninety-seventh Street that overlooked the river, a spot that in those days was frequented by young lovers and a safe place to park. I parked in a line of cars facing the river anticipating a long awaited session of cuddling but as we talked I realized that something was amiss in our relationship. She told me then about Don, who was either an intern or technician at the hospital. I couldn't care less about who Don was. I was angry and upset at the turn of events and felt she had led me on. The evening, as well as the relationship, was over as far as I was concerned and I decided that the sooner I drove her home, the better I would feel. I started the car engine and backed up in order to drive out of the parking lot. In the emotion of the moment, I was not aware that while we had been talking, a car had pulled in and parked directly behind me, at right angles to my car, blocking my exit with its passenger side facing the rear of my car. I backed up and struck the parked car at its right front door. Quickly realizing what had happened I pulled forward, shut off the motor, stepped out of the car and walked back to the dented car. By that time the two young black men who had been in the car with their dates, had gotten out and were walking toward me, the driver extremely excited and yelling about how it was a brand new car. I looked at the man, and then turned to examine the damage as the man approached me. The next thing I knew I was lying on the ground not knowing how I had gotten there. My glasses were up on my forehead and my right arm was bleeding from having been scraped on the pavement. I shook my head and suddenly realized that I had been sucker punched and knocked out, for how long I didn't know, but I thought it was only momentarily. As I was struggling, with my new legs, to get up off the ground, a difficult task which I had not yet mastered, the second man noticed that I had only one hand and that I was having difficulty gaining my feet and he called to the car's owner. "Jesus Christ, he's a cripple." Frightening scenarios flashed through my head as I managed to get to my feet. I was still inexperienced at driving with prostheses and had been out of the hospital for only several days. If I had a chargeable accident now I could have restrictions placed on my license and there was a good probability that my insurance premium would be significantly increased. As my head cleared, these thoughts flew through my mind. How to avoid reporting the situation? I was about to offer to have the fellow's car fixed without resorting to insurance claims and avoiding any increased premiums, but he was still enraged and yelling about calling the cops. In a split second I envisioned a way out of the situation. It wasn't nice, but it was survival. The young man's car had been damaged. I had caused the damage. But the man had physically attacked me. My tactical position changed abruptly from defense and apology, to outrage and attack. Anger welled up inside me and, like so many times in my life, I couldn't hit back physically, but I could use what I had to fight and the odds were now on my side. A black man had physically assaulted a disabled white man. It was a loaded situation and I knew instinctively that although I had suffered discrimination of various kinds during my entire life, this enraged black man was, at least in this instance, lower in the pecking order than I was. In fear that my auto insurance might be cancelled, I used the advantage, unfairly, but decisively. "That's a good idea. Go call the cops and we'll report the accident. And then I'm going to swear out a warrant for assault." It brought the ranting and hostility to an abrupt halt. The car owner realized for the first time that a wild punch had eliminated the possibility of claiming damage. It was a moment of decision. I held my breath. The second man said, "C'mon, let's get the hell outta here or we're gonna have trouble. You shouldn't have hit him." Still upset, but now subdued, the owner got back into the car, the doors slammed and the car sped off with squealing tires. I stood at the rear of the car, still a bit rocky from the punch, and took long deep breaths. I was relieved that I had scared them off. Shakily I got back into the car where Peg was waiting, uncertain as to what had actually happened and fearful of getting out to see. "I just got sucker punched. I can't believe it. Its the first time in my life I ever got hit."

I took Peg home, but I was so shaken I had the need to talk to someone about the events of the evening. I drove down to the village and stopped to see Buzz and his wife and related the story to them. I found it difficult to comprehend that it had even happened. During my life I had been in numerous situations wherein I had challenged or been challenged, but I had never been struck. Being disabled my entire life, I had subliminally, no doubt instinctively, learned the kinds of behavior which would be tolerated by others without generating damage to myself and although I often had ventured close to the danger point, I had always been able to steer clear of physical contact. Each time I had stepped between my friend Marty and his would-be opponent, I knew instinctively that because of my highly visible disabilities, the other fellow would not hit me or rough me up, and I had used that knowledge to my advantage, probably unfairly at times. When I committed such acts, I did so knowingly and without fear, on the basis of lifetime experience. I knew what I could get away with. But now I no longer had a highly visible disability; that particular and unique cachet no longer existed. My facade had changed; my appearance was truly normal. People no longer stared, they did not even notice; I was now cloaked in anonymity. I was so intent on how I appeared, however, that I had never contemplated how my appearance might be perceived by others or what expectations they might have of one whose appearance was normal. I was still the same person, but I was now living in a different body and my new facade demanded behavior significantly different than before. The experience was traumatic. My head hurt and my arm was scraped and sore, but I couldn't help feeling that there was something wonderful about it. It proved just how critically successful my rehabilitation had actually been. A few days later, I called Barbara DeSandis and made a date.

******

With each succeeding day my walking skills improved and my range extended, but my rehabilitation was not yet completed. There was still the artificial arm. Once released from the Institute, it was necessary to visit the shop that would fabricate my cosmetic arm and hand. The procedures I'd experienced at Eschen's were duplicated at a one-man operation, not too unlike the mannequin shop where I had learned to make the women's blouse forms. Fascinated with the process, I had a lot of questions. The outer, cosmetic shell of the hand and arm was a realistic casting of a soft plastic material. The fingernails, wrinkles and veins were all visible in high detail. The prosthetist, like the mannequin maker, was an artist with both brush and airbrush and the final product was most realistic, including the hair on the wrist. Fitting was a simple problem, no more complicated than donning a glove. There was no discomfort and the prosthesis was easily put on and taken off. With it on however, I felt as if my arm had become a useless and bothersome appendage, no longer of any functional use to me. I couldn't use it to hold my tie as I tied it; to pull up my pants; to hold the fork as I cut my meat at dinner; and a hundred other actions I could do with my arm before I donned the cosmetic arm, actions that after thirty-five years of habitual use were now instinctive and automatic, but to which I had never given conscious thought.

Leaving the prosthetist for the last time, I carried the arm, (wrapped in tissue paper and safely lodged in a box), home with me. I felt I had cooperated with the doctors and the bureaucracy, and agreed with the recommendations that resulted in my having the arm. I had done my part in resolving a situation that I had felt at the outset was more bureaucratic than functional. Now that I had an artificial arm I puzzled as to whether it would ever be of any use to me. The prosthesis lengthened my arm by almost a foot. The right sleeves of my suit coats and sport coats and many of my dress shirts had been had shortened and tailored to fit the length of my natural arm. Clearly, I'd have to buy some new clothing. I pondered the problem. If I dressed up and used the arm my clothing would have to fit the situation, but I would lose function; when not wearing the arm, the clothing appropriate for use with it could not be used because the right sleeve would be full length, obstructing any functional use of my natural arm. It was readily apparent that if used at all, the prosthesis would be worn only on special occasions and I would need two sets of clothing. In my financial situation the purchase of new clothing was impossible. I wondered if perhaps the hook might have been a better option? I had studied the hook closely, and as impressive as its function was, I was convinced that I would never be able to develop the degree and variety of skills with the hook that I enjoyed with my arm. During the next few days, whenever I had a few moments, I put the arm on and tried to evaluate just what I could and couldn't do with it. I finally concluded that since wearing artificial legs had dramatically solved my major physical and cosmetic problem, and since I had pressing need for the functions I could perform with my arm, the concealment of my arm with another prosthesis was not a priority. Despite the knowledge that the prosthesis would unequivocally complete my physical appearance, I decided to settle for what I now had and returned the arm to its box and put it away in the closet.

My legs were toughening up, but as the amount of my walking or standing increased, the combination of my weight, the heavy wool socks and the thin layer of rubberized material lining the socket created pressure on the hair follicles on my legs resulting in abrasions, ingrown hairs and sometimes boils or sebaceous cysts that made walking and standing painful. My treatment of these eruptions was to pierce them in somewhat less than surgically acceptable aseptic conditions with a flamed needle. It took many months, but eventually the hair disappeared from the high pressure points on my stumps and I no longer had the problem.

13

Renewed Struggle, Marriage, Job Security

During the year I had been Art Director at WQED in Pittsburgh, the station's first general manager, with whom I had become friendly, had returned to New York City to a teaching position at Columbia University. He greeted me warmly, but there were no job openings at Columbia. He did, however, refer me to the Director of the Summer School in the Continuing Education Department at NYU, and was instrumental in arranging for me to teach a summer television workshop there. A week or two later Charles Siepmann advised me that Barbara Yanowski was uncomfortable about having seemingly co-opted my teaching assignment. She wanted to meet me and, if I were willing, share the teaching assignment with me, working together as a team. Given the circumstances, I felt that Barbara had no obligation to me and her offer was exceedingly gracious. At the same time, I needed employment and was delighted for the opportunity to earn even half of the fee. I met with her and accepted her generous and thoughtful offer.

Production of Barbara's elementary science instructional series "Scienceland" began at META that fall when we began to teach the workshop together. Barbara and I worked well together. My knowledge of television production by this time, and her skills as both a performer and television teacher made for an effective team. When I led the students through the rotational positions of television studio operation like an army drill Sergeant, Barbara was amused; when she demonstrated the tricks of handling props and the nuances of presentation in front of the camera I was impressed. As the workshop progressed we became friends. I also taught a second course at NYU, Designing for Television, a combination of the freshman design course I had taken at Carnegie Tech and the practical aspects of scenic design and lighting that I had learned

231

through experience. Both were evening courses and enabled me to resume taking courses for my Master's Degree.

In mid-fall Barbara asked me if I might be interested in working with her on "Scienceland." The production company consisted of three persons plus an executive producer located at Purdue University who had nothing to do with actual production. Barbara was the on camera teacher, Muriel Green, Elementary Science Supervisor for New York City Schools, was the science authority for the series. The job of producer/director for the series, for which I had applied and then withdrawn, had been given to a highly experienced commercial television director, Lee Polk. Lee, however, was beginning a new job at WNYT, New York City's new community television station, and had to be relieved of producing functions while retaining directorial responsibility, so they were in need of an associate producer. The irony of the situation didn't escape me. I didn't get the job for which I had initially applied, but was being offered the second in command post. I jumped at the chance. I would coordinate all aspects of the show, facilitate participation of any agencies or persons involved in the production, secure props, dress the set, and create visuals as needed. My capabilities for the latter were unknown to the others and came as a surprise when I created a number of visual props including mechanical animations.

During the time Science Corner was being produced, WNYT, later WNET, had become a full-blown television station utilizing an FCC channel authorized in Newark, NJ. In the process the new station absorbed the META studio. I assumed responsibility for tabulating and computing the hours and services our production used at META, now a WNET facility, and confirming the charges billed to the Science Corner production company. The series began to wind down to completion soon after the end of the year and I worked hard at exploring every possible avenue of networking to obtain a full-time job at the new station, including pressuring Lee Polk without success. Through Barbara, I met Frank Jacoby, a director of television commercials, many of which featured his wife as the on camera spokesman. Frank was also a producer/director at the United Nations Visual Services, across 1st Ave. from the META studio, where his primary assignment was the production of a monthly program, "International Zone," narrated by Alastair Cooke that focused on United Nations services around the world.

As the Scienceland series completed, word came from Purdue that ten to fifteen programs in a series previously done by Barbara were in need of updating and before the company disbanded, re-makes had to be done. With Lee no longer available, I was offered the job of directing the several remakes. The Executive Producer at Purdue, Leon Hibbs, wanted to meet me and discuss the re-makes with Barbara and Muriel, so we flew to Purdue where I met with Hibbs and negotiated an agreement to do the shows in six weeks.

******

When it was time to direct the first of the re-makes, and after I had set the stage and everyone was ready, I experienced an attack of stage fright. It was 1961. Other than the closed circuit shows I had directed at NYU, this would be the first live "professional" television show I had directed in six years and it was being videotaped for distribution. Most of my directing at WQED had been live shows and although live shows were always critical, particularly if anything untoward happened, when the show was over it was never seen again. The USAFI films I had directed at WQED had been filmed and as such were more critical, but the shows themselves were quite simple in format and action. This current situation offered greater challenges than I had previously experienced as a director. I was nervous and anxious. I excused myself, ran to the men's room and threw up. I felt a lot better when I returned and suggested we get going. Barbara gave me a long knowing look, walked into the studio and put on her mike. The show proceeded without incident and in a few weeks the re-makes were finished, the project was completed, and the company disbanded.

Frank Jacoby, in the meantime, introduced me to Michael Hayward, the Director of United Nations Visual Services who hired me as a writer/director. It was another peripheral, limited-time job. I continued searching for a full-time permanent job that had some security, but invariably ended up with temporary, or part-time jobs, invariably special projects that didn't fit into an agency's regular budget or staffing structure. My jobs always seemed to be part of an extracurricular activities category beyond the respective organization's primary functions. The job at the United Nations was no different. At the time, the United States had more than its allowed quota of US nationals as employees. In the earliest days of the United Nations, a number of the member nations, fearing political disadvantages, had been reluctant to permit their nationals to be employed at the UN. Accordingly, with the UN being situated in New York City, the job openings were easily and quickly filled with United States citizens. When the foreign countries realized that by not permitting their nationals to be employed at the UN, they were limiting the potential of their informal communications networks, a new regulation was enacted whereby Americans were temporarily (for many years) frozen out of any full-time jobs. The new regulation did not completely solve the problem; there were jobs that still needed to be filled by English speaking people that foreign nations could not supply. New York City remained a natural resource for fulfilling such a need. The loophole in the regulation was that anyone from any nation could be hired on a three-month contract, and the contract could be extended indefinitely, so I was hired for three months as a writer/director in the United Nations Visual Service.

Working at the United Nations gave me a feeling of traveling on a magic carpet. The many people, costumes, languages and behaviors were diverse and it was exciting to watch and mingle with other peoples of the world. Except for certain offices and the highest executive suites, the entire complex was open to staff, assuming there was purpose in one's presence there. The assembly halls were open for observation when one had time to observe, and the several different restaurants admitted all staff. Even the delegates' dining room was open on a space available basis. Language laboratories were available for studying any of the world's languages, and the library of national histories was world class. There was even a place to park my car within the building.

The United Nations was a separate country; when one entered the gates, one was no longer in the United States. American holidays and customs went unnoticed in the day-to-day activities. Television services were located in the lower levels of the Secretariat building and were far from luxurious, consisting simply of several offices and a bullpen that housed eight or ten desks for the majority of the department's personnel. There were essentially four functions performed by the staff: ordering, receiving, and cataloging film footage shot daily all over the world as either specific assignment or reportage; management and operation of a film library; writing, directing, producing and distributing films and audio tapes; and filming of selected speeches and actions in the General Assembly. This latter required the on-duty presence of one alert and quick-witted person, well informed on United Nations business. Armed with the daily schedule of subjects and speakers, this person watched the General Assembly proceedings on television, determined which portions were to be filmed for posterity on one of the several kinescope recorders and tape machines, and ordered the starting and stopping of the recordings at appropriate times. This job was held by a tall, slightly balding, and quite delightful gentleman then in his forties, who had a reputation for being an amiable, and trust-worthy escort for famous singers and actresses who were stopping over in New York briefly on business and who were without an escort for the evening. One afternoon when he was not present, I answered the phone and heard a woman's voice say, "Hello, may I speak to Cliff?"

"I'm sorry, he's not available. May I take a message?"

"Yes, please. Would you tell him Peggy Lee called and if he's available this evening, he can get back to me. Thank you." The message was delivered, with a certain amount of awe.

My boss was a South African national who presided over the television production unit. After only a few exposures to him, I concluded that his authoritarian manner was in inverse proportion to his creativity and imagination. That opinion, justifiable or not, was an indication of both my political ineptness and inflated ego. My first assignment was to write a script for an Alastair Cooke program that dealt with the world's food problems. With only minor alterations and corrections, the script was approved, produced and distributed worldwide in ninety-two languages, as were all of the Cooke programs. My second program, in a more poetic vein, dealt with how man's hands had created many wonders through the ages. It too was accepted, but rescheduled for production at a later date. I assumed that as a writer, I was expected to be imaginative and creative and that my imaginative and creative approach would be welcomed. Unfortunately, this was not the case. I had not realized my boss considered himself to be the creative force and my responsibility was to merely translate his ideas into workable program scripts. The inevitable happened.

For my third assignment, I developed a treatment rather different from what my boss had in mind. When he criticized my first draft, I made a vigorous and sincere attempt to re-write in a manner that I thought better fitted his point of view, but which did not entirely eliminate what I believed to be my own, more creative concept. I tried to make my point of view express his creative idea. Once again, he rejected my script this time telling me rather forcefully how he wanted it to be written. I found myself quite unable to write to what I perceived as the boss' flawed point of view. I was blind to the fact that my inability to serve his interests was being perceived as a recalcitrant attitude. My limited experience in the world of work had not prepared me for the realities of creative control. I attempted once more to write the boss' concept of the show without completely eliminating what I believed to be a more viable concept. Then I made a fatal mistake. I attempted to explain to him why his concept did not work. He didn't argue, but concluded that I was uncooperative and washed his hands of me. I had no further communication from him and at the end of three months I was transferred to the radio department to write continuity on a one-month contract at the end of which my relationship with the United Nations ended. Most people of my age would probably have had a more enlightened perception as to how to finesse the situation. I simply lacked the experience and interpersonal skills basic to survival and success in both profit and non-profit organizations. My inability to compromise was perhaps rooted in my need to constantly prove that I was not disabled. In the past, my single-mindedness had helped me to survive, but it could also be a road block

My biggest thrill while working at the UN occurred one day when the door to my tiny office in the radio section opened and U Thant, Secretary General of the United Nations walked in. Extending his hand, he said, "Good Morning, I'm U Thant. How are you? Are they keeping you busy?" I said, "Good Morning, yes they are," and smiling, he turned on his heel and left.

Fortunately, as my short tenure at the United Nations ended, I was still teaching two evening courses at NYU and my cash flow, though meager, covered rent, food and auto expenses, but it was always a case of extremely sparse living. When the gas tank showed empty and I had three dollars in my pocket, I would put one dollar's worth of gas in the car and hold the other two for emergency. I cooked and ate all my meals in my apartment.

The search for more permanent employment continued. Buzz Rice and Fred Kelley, who had been students in my Television Production/ Direction class, both found jobs at the State Education Department in Albany, then under the direction of Edward Almstead. Buzz thought there might be a good possibility of my getting a job there as well, so I obtained an interview and Buzz arranged to have me make a presentation, as a paid consultant, on the use of visual elements in televised instruction. Employment at the State Education Department was not forthcoming, but I had the opportunity to meet a number of people then engaged in developing television for educational purposes in the New York schools.

Bill Wood's replacement at WQED had been Jack White, a former vice president of Western Reserve University. White was an aggressive administrator and excellent politician and under his leadership WQED consolidated and grew. Within a few years White moved from Pittsburgh to become President of the National Educational Television and Radio Center, initially established at Michigan State University. White was instrumental in having NETRC moved to New York City. I had ambivalent feelings about Jack White, and did not enjoy the warm relationship I had had with Wood. On one return trip to Pittsburgh I had attended a cocktail party at which several of my old colleagues were present, including the young woman who had been one of my volunteers and had replaced me as art director. At the party Jack introduced me to someone with the statement, "He was our art director until we could get a girl." I was surprised at the hostility reflected by the statement and wasn't aware of a reason for Jack's actions.

In his new role, however, White enjoyed the top national leadership position in Educational Television and I was acquainted with him professionally and looking for employment. Despite an uneasy feeling about how he had treated me, I felt that, if he so desired, he could be of assistance in my finding a job. Believing I could not afford to overlook any opportunities, even questionable ones, I called White and was surprised to be able to gain an appointment. At our meeting, I explained that I had just undergone a miraculous rehabilitation and was now beginning to rebuild my career. His reception was amiable, even friendly, and he suggested I write to a man in Georgia who had just assumed new responsibilities for an educational television station and was building a staff. I was advised to say that Jack White had recommended me. I was delighted to have such a recommendation and posted the letter with my resume. Weeks passed without a response and then one day, in a casual conversation with an acquaintance who was working in the field, I learned that the person to whom I had written at Jack White's suggestion had been a member of Jack's staff whom he had fired. I never discovered the reason for Jack's actions, but I was now acutely aware that I had to maintain a distance from him.

******

The months flew by. I sent applications and resumes to every job opening I could find. I continued to teach two classes each semester at NYU and a special workshop session during the summer. I continued taking courses toward a Master's Degree in Communications. As a member of the National Association of Educational Broadcasters for a number of years, I had attended national conferences whenever I could afford them, primarily for the purpose of looking for a job. In the process I had met some of the national officers and that ultimately led to my being included on a list of consultants. As a consultant, I was occasionally assigned to assist schools in setting up and operating new closed circuit television systems and in training their staffs to use television. These activities were sometimes reminiscent of my experience at WQED when I had been asked to train others for the same job I was not considered capable of performing. From these various activities I earned enough to pay my rent and living expenses. I found it increasingly easier to get around, to walk, drive, go up and down steps, and except for a seemingly stagnant professional life, I was thankful for my current condition, buoyed by the possibility of potential career opportunities, and despite my lack of success, hopeful.

My relationship with Barbara DeSandis developed into an increasingly warm and close one and we found ourselves spending more and more time together. Taking advantage of the tuition remission benefit available to her as an employee of NYU, the same program that was underwriting my graduate degree studies, Barbara was taking courses towards a Master's Degree in Sociology at NYU, and finally had an opportunity to change careers to work as a consultant sociologist for the Neighborhood Conservation Program of the City of New York. Another year passed as I continued to teach at NYU and work on my master's degree. The pile of job rejections grew. I recognized that the longer I was not working full-time in my field, the less likely I was to find a decent job. I no longer advised potential employers of my disabilities. Since I felt that I was functionally normal, my thinking was that if I were able to "pass" and perform successfully at a job, I would be able at a later time to reveal myself, if necessary, and in doing so generate respect rather than negative reactions. I also began to protect the privacy of my new facade, studying the reactions of new acquaintances to determine if they had penetrated my secret. Could they detect that I had artificial legs? In the process I began to once again to build up walls around my "passing" that only served to complicate my life.

For three more years I struggled to parlay my skills into a regular, dependable living without success, barely managing to pay my living expenses by teaching at NYU and the New York Technical Institute. Barbara had become an integral part of my new life, and despite my inability to find steady employment, I still believed in the promise of my life becoming bountiful and rewarding, but had little confidence that my continued efforts to have a career would, or could, result in solvency and security in the near future. How long I could continue in my present circumstances was questionable.

As a risk taker, I had always been willing to rise to almost any kind of physical challenge and had succeeded at whatever I had attempted, but my professional track record, although replete with numerous assignments well done, seemed always to result, on their completion, in my being placed back at square one. I was unable to parlay any of my successful achievements into better, more rewarding situations. Despite my remarkable metamorphosis and my good feelings about myself, I knew that professionally I hadn't advanced.

My lack of professional success and continued search for employment consumed me and filled my horizon. I entertained fleeting thoughts of marriage, but they were easily dispelled by the more immediate problems at hand, and totally overwhelmed by my struggle. I recognized that Barbara was, in essence, everything I had ever hoped for during those many lonely and desolate years when I had reluctantly, but, I thought, realistically decided that there was no possibility that I would ever meet anyone with whom I could have a lasting relationship. Barbara had taken the initiative and hinted that we marry, but I found myself on the horns of a dilemma. I could envision no possibility for my being able to assume the obligations of a married man. Barbara didn't push me, but she let me know that she believed in me and my potential. Almost, as if in slow motion, I came to the realization that whatever my present situation, or however dim my prospects for the future appeared to be, I wanted to make my relationship with Barbara a permanent one. I had found in her the possibility for fulfilling what I had dreamed all of my life. I wanted her to be with me, I needed her, and weighing the risk of losing her against the risk of not being able to provide for her, I decided to ask her to marry me. We made plans to be married in the spring of 1964.

The circumstances surrounding our marriage were in some ways reminiscent of that of my parents. Both marriages exhibited aspects of ethnic and religious differences. Barbara had drifted away from her Italian family's Catholic faith several years previously. Her mother, Amelia Barbano, was both a devout Catholic and demonstrably proud of her Italian heritage. She had come to the United States in 1911 as a seven year-old-child with a sister, five brothers and a widowed mother who, so the story was told, had been manipulated out of her husband's estate by her step-son who had urged her to take her children to America, the land of opportunity. Barbara's American born father, Vincenzo DeSandis (Jimmy), whose surname name was a bastardization of DeSantis perpetrated by school officials upon his entry into school, was also proud of his Italian/American heritage. Unlike his wife, he did not attend church regularly except for weddings, funerals and other social occasions. As the Barbano children grew and married, raised families and made their way in the new country, a variety of sibling rivalries ensued, but on balance the families kept in close touch and celebrated and mourned together at weddings, births and funerals. With exception of her parents who left Brooklyn to live in New Jersey at the time Barbara entered nurse's training, most of the relatives remained in Italian neighborhoods in Brooklyn. Barbara's only sibling, an older sister Ann who was the first born grandchild of the DeSandis and Barbano families, was the pride and joy of the household. As the second born, Barbara frequently had to be satisfied with a second place role as attention continued to be focused on her sister, who became accustomed to the attention and grew to expect it.

My entry into this close-knit family situation generated alarm and resistance. Even at the age of twenty-eight, Barbara's announcement that she had decided to marry flew in the face of ethnic tradition that historically expected the first-born daughter to be the first to marry. Even without my presence, her intentions caused a certain degree of unhappiness, even disappointment within the family. Her mother was not so bound by her own ethnicity as to be particularly upset at her daughter not marrying an Italian. As far as religion was concerned, while she prayed that her daughter would remain a Catholic and hopefully marry a Catholic, she realized in her wisdom that it might not happen. However, the thought that her daughter was planning to marry a non-Catholic, triple amputee, "a cripple," who as she imagined it, would have to be physically cared for in later years by her daughter, the nurse, was frightening. It gave her cause for a near hysterical reaction resulting in discussions with other family members, bemoaning her fate and seeking support for her situation. Barbara's sister, who viewed her parent's concerns as ridiculous, regularly reported her mother's reactions. Barbara's parent's reaction, spoken directly in their alarm was, "Do you have any idea what you are getting into?" Their concerns focused squarely on my physical condition, a reaction with which I was completely familiar having encountered it so frequently, but about which, in fairness to them, they had almost no understanding. When it became apparent to them that Barbara's intentions could not be moved, despite their unhappiness and to their credit, they made all the motions of welcoming me into the family and treated me with respect, although throughout our marriage and the rest of her parent's lives, there was an undercurrent which set me apart as a "stranger", a word my father-in-law had used with Barbara's sister in referring to me. Also through the years, despite experiencing great joy in their grandchildren they were unable to completely reconcile their feelings with the result that, from time to time, I was the recipient of occasional acts of behavioral smallness. When Barbara's father died, his estate transferred, as expected, to his wife except for a sizeable certificate of deposit that he had held with his elder daughter as beneficiary. At the death of Barbara's mother, that preferential treatment was again evident when Barbara was denied an equal share of her mother's estate in preference to her sister, a situation ironically reminiscent of what her grandmother had suffered at the hands of her step-son in Italy many years previously. Following an acrimonious discussion with her sister in the office of her mother's and sister's lawyer, the lawyer surprised Barbara by suggesting that her sister was mean spirited.

For my family, Barbara represented the continuation of my incredible good fortune. My father, in his usual optimistic manner, enthusiastically accepted Barbara as one of our family. Mother, living for many years in a Catholic neighborhood strictly dominated by an extremely authoritative parish priest whose dictates were, in her mind, adversarial and dismissive towards other religions, had some moments of concern at the thought of her daughter-in-law's Catholic heritage. When she realized that Barbara was not, in fact, a practicing Catholic, nor indeed, any more religious than me, she adopted my father's attitude although, true to her nature, with a "wait and see" point of view. They were both in accord that the intended union, as far as their son was concerned, was yet another blessing they had hoped for, but had not expected to witness.

Barbara and I obtained a six-month sublet on 63rd Street off 1st Ave. and I moved in at the beginning of the month. I had less than $300 dollars and Barbara had about $1200 dollars in the bank. She had a full-time job and I was an insecure part-time adjunct professor. We bought a gold woolen rug and a sofa bed and together with my meager furniture, set up housekeeping. We lacked a dining table and decided that while on our honeymoon we'd look for one in antique shops, so we removed the back seat from my 1958 Desoto, a big gray four-door sedan with fins on the rear fenders, to make room for it.

Without religious interests of our own, but wishing to provide some kind of a religious setting as a palliative for Barbara's family, we arranged to be married in the Unitarian Church in New York City. Our wedding on April 11, 1964 was a small affair followed by a dinner at a local restaurant hosted by Barbara's father who limited the size of the party to a very modest number. Barbara's dearest friend, and her husband, as a result of directions from their priest, did not attend because the ceremony was held in a non-Catholic church, but joined us for dinner. Immediately following the dinner we drove to Wilmington, Delaware, where we stayed overnight and the next day drove to Luray Virginia and the Skyline Drive. For three days, we enjoyed the beginning of our new life together in the primitive isolation of one of the rustic trail workers' cabins of the Potomac Appalachian Trail Club. We had discovered it by accident in our search for a way to enjoy an inexpensive honeymoon for the few days we could afford to be absent from our jobs. Spring was just beginning in the Blue Ridge Mountains, the crocuses were just starting to bloom and the trees to bud, and the half mile trek down the trail from the parking lot just off the Skyline Drive to the cabin was a scenic wonder of woods and mountains. We spent a few days exploring the mountains and the antique shops and located a great buy and a rare find, a very old heavy hand-made black walnut, drop leaf, gate leg table. We bought it for $65, and loaded it into the back of the car.

Back in New York, as the spring semester began to draw to a close, I again applied for a job at the State Education Department in Albany in the Division of Educational Communications. Lee Campion had replaced Ed Almstead as Head of the Division that had two Bureaus, the Bureau of Mass Communications, headed by Dr. Bernarr Cooper and the Bureau of Classroom Communications, headed by Dr. Larry Twyford. The job opening was for an Associate in Educational Communications at a salary of $9,800 per annum in Cooper's bureau. The job description stated that the Associate would be responsible for developing broadcast educational television resources across the state, that is, assisting New York State educational television stations to develop and grow and to further assist them in the production of television programming which the Education Department would distribute state wide. It sounded like a great opportunity. Muriel Green with whom I had worked on *The Science Corner* was acquainted with Lee Campion and I asked her to speak on my behalf. As a result, I obtained an interview with Campion and in July learned that he had chosen me for the job. Finally, at long last, I had obtained a permanent job, one that was designated in the annual budget as a permanent line item in State government and which would be funded year after year. It was a full-time permanent appointment, conditional only in that it required my passing a Civil Service examination. I couldn't believe my good fortune.

14

All That Glitters

We had been referred by a friend to a Mr. Appleton, a realtor in Albany, who conducted his business from an historic house on Swan Street, just across the street from the State Education Department where I would be working. In our conversation with him we touched on art, and on learning of our interest he invited us to tour his house. We were astonished to discover that every wall in every room on all three floors as well as the stairways was totally covered with art of every possible type and size. We were doubly surprised to see, among this myriad of fine works, a number of pieces of great value and importance: an original Talouse LaTrec poster, a Rembrandt etching, several Picassos and Dalis and others. Mr. Appleton opened a clothes closet revealing a number of expensive suits and pointed to six or eight small paintings leaning against the side of the closet at the bottom. "They're Picassos," he stated very matter of factly. We spent a long time going from room to room, looking not only at the art, but also at the famous signatures. We were stunned.

Unfortunately, we found Mr. Appleton's aesthetic sense did not extend to his rental properties and decided to continue our search elsewhere. He graciously referred us to a lawyer friend in Schenectady who owned rental properties, and we found an apartment in Schenectady's Stockade section, the site of the stockade wilderness settlement that was burned and its settlers massacred by a French and Indian war party in 1690. We were captivated by the general ambiance of the "Stockade," an historic district featuring narrow tree lined streets and old picturesque houses with bronze date plates.

I learned belatedly that Lee Campion had hired me despite the resistance of Bernarr Cooper, the Bureau Chief, who was my new immediate superior. In any situation, that might have posed problems, but with Bernarr I was confronted with the epitome of a

Machiavellian, Byzantine man. His appearance and dress, although somewhat dated due perhaps to his penuriousness, were fastidious; his manners were impeccable, even diplomatic. He was well educated and a lover of art. He had been a radio actor during the heyday of radio drama and during World War II had become fluent in Japanese, spending considerable time in the Army in Japan and developing an interest and considerable knowledge of Japanese Art.

For Bernarr, every statement or action he encountered in the day's work was suspect, concealing a plot or hidden agenda that he would analyze and project to its ultimate and varied possibilities. In a similar vein, his every move or statement camouflaged a variety of actions he was prepared to take depending on the response or reaction, and he delighted in suggesting, by inference or body language, that there were aspects of the situation that were not readily apparent and of which only he had knowledge. In short, he was an eternal, multi-faceted, living chess game, always with a smile that reminded one of a Vincent Price portrayal of the Grand Vizier.

It would have been normal to begin the new job on the first of the month, thus permitting a timely transition of such things as rental leases, moving, etc. Bernarr, however, insisted that I report in the middle of August, citing a variety of personnel department regulations and procedures all of which later proved to be false or inconsequential. It was simply Bernarr's way of initiating control and intimidation. Reporting in mid-August incurred the added expense of my traveling to Albany and living in a motel for two weeks while at the same time arranging my affairs in New York. Once on the job, Bernarr set his clandestine intrigues in motion to see with what manner of man Lee Campion had burdened him.

I was given one of two desks in an otherwise empty office adjacent to Bernarr's, and a large pile of reports and correspondence that, as Barnarr explained, "...will help you to orient yourself to what we're doing here." At the same time, he piled a stack of audiotapes on my desk. "These tapes explain our program here and have been made for distribution across the state, but they have to be evaluated so we know they are without flaws. Please listen to them and O.K. the good ones so they can be sent out." I reread my job description that clearly defined a professional level of activity developing television across the state, and seemingly precluded such low-level operational tasks as evaluating multiple copies of an audiotape. I realized I was being tested. I'd been impolitic at the United Nations, but I'd learned a lesson. I was going to have to avoid doing some things which my new boss assigned, but without confrontation.

I plunged into the pile of documents and although there was much extraneous material, they were indeed informative. I listened to one of the audiotapes and then set the pile aside for a couple of days. When the opportunity arose, I took them to the department secretary and in a very polite manner said, "Look, whenever you can get a few minutes free, would you please listen to these tapes and see if any of them are defective?" The next day Bernarr glided silently into the room and asked if I had finished the tapes. I was well aware that this was my first test with Bernarr. "You know Bernarr, I listened to a couple and then I thought, that with all this other more important material to absorb, you wouldn't want me to waste my time listening to the same tape over and over so I gave them to…." Bernarr looked at me thoughtfully for a moment, then smiled his Vincent Price smile. "Of course, that was wise." And he left the room. An hour or two later Ray Graf, whom I had just recently met, and whose job was at my level, but in closed-circuit in-school television operations, walked in the door wearing a big grin. "I hear you didn't like listening to audio tapes?"

"Well, it really didn't seem to be in the job description."

"It sure as hell isn't." Ray responded, "He was surprised at what you did. He thought you were going to be a pushover. You did exactly the right thing. I'm glad you're going to be around." It marked the beginning of an enjoyable friendship.

With Bernarr however, the first gambit had been played in what would become a two-year chess game which would find me at times sent to meetings in various cities in the state only to find that an hour before my arrival, Bernarr would have called the person I was to meet and conducted the business I had been sent to conduct. On other occasions I might be given an assignment that had no purpose and then asked in an open meeting why I had done it. I was often undercut by statement and innuendo in group meetings with television representatives from across the state, or given chapter and verse of state law to refute my position or opinion in office meetings. I became aware that the knife was constantly at my back, ready to be thrust at the first opportunity. It was not a happy situation, but it became the best training I had ever had. It took me the better part of my first year and what I thought at the time was an ulcer, but which fortunately proved not to be, to fully understand Bernarr's techniques and how to cope with them. A month after my arrival another new Associate, a pleasant young man with a doctorate, joined the staff and was assigned the second desk in my office. Almost immediately the stack of audiotapes appeared on his desk and for several weeks I watched him listen to one tape after another as he fumed and complained at the demeaning task. Ray Graf threw meaningful glances at me and shook his head as he strolled by the office.

******

Living in New York's Capital District exposed Barbara and me to new activities and experiences. We discovered beautiful Lake George and the Adirondacks, bought a tent and sleeping bags and spent weekends exploring the lakes and mountains. Barbara had never been camping before and she adapted to it with great enthusiasm. I was unable to hike or swim and, although it was possible to have "swimming legs," (prostheses made for use in the water), they were extremely expensive and in any event I was not disposed to go swimming in any public place. I was liberated with my new legs, but not ready to exhibit them. Rather, I was disposed to hide them and to "pass." I was so relieved at no longer being the subject of stares that I actively maintained my anonymity so as to not engender the unusual interest that had plagued me for so many years. I could not bring myself to wear shorts although on a few occasions when I saw a one-leg amputee wearing them I was impressed by the courage and apparent nonchalance that was displayed. I wished I were able to do that, but couldn't make myself try it. As for swimming, I dreamed of immersing myself in the water on a hot day. I desperately wanted to be able, not only to go bathing, but also to be able to actually swim. I had never learned because I had never been able to get into the water. Without shoes I could not walk and in my teens had spent countless afternoons watching, while my friends, both boys and girls, went swimming in one or another of the favorite swimming holes in local creeks.

As we familiarized ourselves with the lakes in the Adirondacks, occasionally renting a small boat with an outboard motor, we realized that if we had a boat of our own and could get away from people, it might be possible for me to get into the water, so we began our search for a small boat.

One Sunday morning in a small marina south of Albany, we looked at a 16 ft. outboard runabout that was priced at $700. We thought it an exorbitant amount of money for anyone in our income bracket. We were amused by the conversation of two men working nearby on a small 20 ft. inboard cruiser. "Did you see the boat that George bought?" the first man said. "No, but I heard it's 24 ft," said the second. "You'd have to be making at least $10,000 a year to be able to buy something like that." We were astounded at the thought. My salary was almost that amount, and we thought $700 was more than we could afford.

We purchased the boat and trailer for less than the asking price and enjoyed spending weekends camping on the islands at Lake George. We found little nooks and crannies along the lake that were virtually ignored by other boaters, where we could anchor in shallow water over a sand bed, and I could get in the water. My legs had by then changed shape and my stumps had shrunken sufficiently to warrant being refitted with new prostheses which my new state health insurance covered, enabling me to use the old pair as swimming legs. What a thrill it was to be able to move around in the water and to experience the buoyancy. I learned to float on my back cautiously while holding onto the side of the boat and enjoyed the soothing effect of the crystal clear water. My prostheses had a core of balsa wood under a fiberglass exterior and were extremely buoyant. If I leaned beyond my center of balance, they would rise up and dump my head and shoulders under, but with a life vest and a snorkel I floated along in the shallow water, searching the lakebed and enjoying what had been denied me for so many years. In the privacy of our small hideaways we enjoyed an idyll I had never expected to experience.

******

The responsibility and power to administer capital and program funds that originated in the state budget and were intended for development of the state's educational television stations were included in my job description. Capital funds supported construction and physical plant improvement for a state educational television station and program funds provided the wherewithal to create new programming that was then distributed free to all stations. Each year board members of the stations, among whom were some of the most powerful and influential men and women in the state, would lobby the Commissioner of Education and the state legislature for funds and each year. Under the guise of adhering to the law, Bernarr would devise new regulations and formulae to be used to determine the amount of money each station could receive and in what installments, conceiving new hurdles for the stations to jump in order to obtain their respective shares of the funds. With each round of funds he found ways to underwrite special bureau projects beyond the intent of the subject funds, and extremely difficult to fund from other sources. As I acclimated to the bureaucracy of the Education Department and talked with State lawyers who assisted me in drawing up contracts, the legal instruments facilitating the transfer of funds to the stations, I familiarized myself with state law and soon realized that the success of Bernarr's power, and his actions, was dependent on others' ignorance of the law. He was not implementing the law, but rather using it as a weapon to control. I realized that his quotes of the law were frequently partial or out of context, full disclosure of which could be used to counter many of his assertions.

In the course of working with the respective station managers in Schenectady, Rochester, Buffalo, and later Binghamton, I at times acted as an unofficial, and frequently clandestine, ombudsman for the stations to selectively circumvent Bernarr's formulas and regulations. One particularly odious sequence of events began with the arrival in Syracuse of Thomas Petry, who the newly formed Syracuse Educational Television Council had hired as General Manager to plan, construct and operate their new television station. Petry had been highly regarded at WQED in Pittsburgh and there were ties between the businessmen of Pittsburgh and those on the Board of Directors of the new station in Syracuse.

State funding was available in the amount of two to four hundred thousand dollars for capital expenditures for new educational television stations. Receipt of funds required completion of a grant application certifying the nature and structure of the planned physical plant, and description of the need and use for which the funds were intended. The funding was in fact an example of state government assisting a local community to develop a facility that the state wanted to see developed. Despite political pressure, however, Syracuse's funding award dragged on for months as Bernarr examined their application with inexhaustible and relentless energy, using every minor flaw to delay the state's legal approval, necessary to release the funds to Syracuse. Finally, Petry called me to ask why the application was being held up, so I took a copy of the application to the state lawyer with whom I now worked on production contracts and asked him if the application was in order. He recognized the problem immediately. "He's playing tricks again, is he? I'll push it through." Syracuse received their funds.

During my first year I took the mandatory multiple choice civil service test for permanent placement. I'd never taken that type of test and I failed by three points to get a satisfactory grade. I was enormously embarrassed. Under Civil Service regulations, the job could be awarded to any of the three top scoring applicants, but it was general practice to award it to the incumbent unless there were other reasons to deny the appointment, and anyone not passing the test could request a re-test, which I did. Sample tests for my position were available at the state library and I obtained them and took them home. Barbara and I both took the sample test and she scored higher than me, in content areas with which I was familiar and she uninformed. "It's the test." Barb said. "It's similar to the type of test that every student seeking a New York State Regent's High School Diploma takes in most subject areas. I'm used to taking them. I don't think you are." It was true. I knew the content, but my lack of familiarity with the nature of the test was a problem. I studied the test and the second time I took it scored well above the required grade and received my coveted permanent appointment. Now nobody could fire me for anything less than an immoral act. For the first time in my life I felt professionally secure.

By the middle of my second year, having taken the time to familiarize myself with the law, I was ready to do battle with Bernarr. In concert with the station managers, I rearranged

Bernarr's complex funding formula into a simple, new, non-punitive formula that facilitated the early distribution of the annual funds to the stations. Just prior to the open meeting, having previously informed the station managers, I presented the new formula to Bernarr together with the legal justification for it. Bernarr was visibly shaken and unable to respond quickly enough to regain control and the new plan was implemented. Ray Graf visited me the next day. "What the hell did you do to the guy? He came to me last night in tears." I told Ray, "I showed him how to do what the law intended for us to do, to give the money to the stations." Ray chuckled, "You better watch your back."

******

Before we married, Barbara and I had discussed the possibility of having children. I wanted them, but the idea frightened me. Despite the fact that doctors had always taken the position that my congenital anomalies were in some way the result of a mechanical, physical or chemical interruption of the prenatal growth process and probably not hereditary, I nevertheless knew what my mother and I had lived through, and I feared that, should a child of mine have serious birth defects, I might not be able to handle the situation in the competent manner that my mother had managed both her own feelings and my well being. I had lived through it once and it had been difficult; I didn't believe I could do it again. Before we had moved to Schenectady, however, Barbara had convinced me that, rather than dealing with speculation, I should be tested in order to learn as much as possible about the likelihood of such a situation occurring.

The resultant chromosome tests, although in the 60s not considered to be ultimately exact or fully predictable, gave no indication of anything amiss. I was relieved, but not wholly convinced. During the following year, as we frequently discussed the subject, my resistance was slowly eroded by Barbara's positive attitude and medical knowledge and I eventually agreed that we should try to have a child. In the months that followed however, no pregnancy occurred. I assumed that, given my visible, physical disabilities, perhaps I had unknown internal anomalies which were at the heart of the problem, so we decided that it would be wise for us both to undergo fertility testing. The resultant tests revealed no abnormalities other than the fact that my sperm count was low, not critically, but sufficient to affect conception. The advice: keep trying.

Unfortunately, job security did not bring professional fulfillment. I was now professionally set for life and like many of the bureaucrats with whom I worked every day, I had the option of now relaxing in my job and earning the standard annual Civil Service pay increases and promotions for the rest of my working life. However, I found the work with which I was increasingly becoming involved was bureaucratic, uncreative, and frequently non productive. I observed that with few exceptions, the performance level at the State Education Department was rather low and employees, even professionals, were jaded and unmotivated. The daily tension between Bernarr and the station managers created a crisis-oriented atmosphere that hampered development, and I was spending large amounts of time protecting my flanks in skirmishes induced by my boss. At national meetings of educational broadcasters I was not surprised to learn that the activities and personnel of the Division of Educational Communications of the New York State Education Department, colored by the behavior of its leaders, was viewed in many quarters of the educational broadcasting fraternity as non-professional and by some with frank contempt. On a couple of occasions I was advised by well meaning and respected professional acquaintances from other states to leave my job at the earliest opportunity so as not to permanently damage my career.

I began to look for other opportunities. Gordon Washburn, with whom I had a good professional relationship back in Pittsburgh, had taken on the Directorship of The Asian Society in New York City. I talked to Gordon and learned that he was a good friend of Hugh Flick, the Associate Commissioner for Cultural Affairs of the State Education Department who had oversight over the Communications Department. With Gordon's intro, I had a private audience with Flick and told him of my frustration in my job and how things were being made so complicated for the station managers, but knowing of Flick's reputation at SED as one who would listen carefully and commiserate, but make no decisions, I was not surprised when nothing came of the matter.

I had met Prof. Edward Stasheff of Michigan State University, one of Educational Television's pioneers and a friend of Barbara Yanowski. He had just returned from Israel where he had been a consultant to the Israeli government on the development of Instructional Television. The Israeli's were ready to hire a person to direct their efforts and Stasheff had included my name on a short list of persons he had recommended be considered. This situation was well above any I had thus far encountered and I asked Gordon Washburn, a world traveler, for advice. Gordon arranged for me to talk with Edward Warburg, an influential member of one of America's first Jewish families who had strong ties to Israel, was a member of the committee that advised the State Education Department on cultural matters, and also well known to Hugh Flick. All three men traveled in the same cultural circles. Warburg's advice was most helpful in my subsequent interview with the two Israelis responsible for making the selection, one of whom bore the legendary name of Rothschild. I was not hopeful; I felt I had not come up to their expectations and I was correct. The job went to my friend, Tom Petry.

The inability of the Department of Communications to aggressively and successfully pursue the development of the connecting network which would permit the State's educational television stations to distribute programs electronically had not gone unnoticed close to home. Governor Rockefeller had withheld funds for pursuit of these goals from the State Education Department. With the appointment of Dr. Samuel Gould, (one of the founders and first president of New York City's new educational television station WNYT), to the position of Chancellor of the State University, the Governor removed responsibility for the construction and operation of a New York State Microwave Network from the State Education Department and assigned it to the State University. The network would connect the new stations in Buffalo, Rochester, Syracuse, Schenectady, Binghamton and New York.

The Governor's action significantly diminished my area of development. The network development had been specifically included in my job description, although I had not been able to address it because my superiors had been unable to convince either the Governor or the state legislature that the State Education Department had the capability for constructing and operating such a network, which was why the Legislature had never approved funds for it. Gould appointed Robert Thomas, his right hand man at WNYT, as Vice Chancellor for Communications and assigned him the task of building the network. On learning of these new changes I immediately sought out Thomas in hopes of having a continued involvement with educational television development in the state, but Thomas had his own agenda and had no wish to have anyone in his operation who had close relations with the State Education Department. I was surprised and both pleased and disappointed to learn in the forthcoming weeks that my former student and now good friend, Buzz Rice, had been hired by Thomas for the job I sought.

I continued my search for other opportunities. Donald Schein, who had created the public broadcasting station in Schenectady, then operating in the basement of what had been an elementary school, offered me a vaguely defined position which was part management and part production, but I had learned a lot since the United Nations and was aware, from having worked with him, that he ran what was essentially a one-man shop in which he made all the decisions and where there was little leeway for anyone working for him to exercise creativity. I demurred, and then an opportunity presented itself from an unexpected source.

In 1958 President Eisenhower had established a new program, Captioned Films for the Deaf in the Bureau of Education for the Handicapped, United States Office of Education. John Gough, an experienced teacher of the deaf, had been appointed the first director of the program. It was he who had shown interest in my experiment to teach deaf children using television at NYU, making a special trip to NYU to talk with me and to see what I was doing. The result of that discussion was that he had called on me from time to time to serve as a consultant for projects which utilized media in the teaching of the deaf, a relationship which led to a contract to write and produce fourteen short films to teach vocabulary to deaf children using animated letters and numbers, a technique later successfully refined in "Sesame Street" programs. As the scripts were nearing completion, and I had begun to seriously search for a job opportunity outside the State Education Department, I received an unexpected call from Gilbert Delgado, Assistant Bureau Chief at Captioned Films, who asked if I'd be interested in joining the Captioned Films' staff in Washington, DC.

Captioned Films, in fulfilling its primary purpose, had for several years been purchasing rights to caption popular commercial films for subsequent free distribution to deaf clubs for viewing. A lending film library for the deaf had been established and had been most appreciatively accepted by deaf organizations. In an effort to expand its services, some experimental television programs had also been produced, funded by the Bureau, and numerous projects to develop special media materials for teaching deaf children had been initiated. Now John Gough wanted to expand Captioned Films by developing a national television service for the deaf and I was being offered the chance to create and administer it. I found it a fascinating idea and an interesting opportunity. From my experience as a consultant I had met many people who were engaged in the education of the deaf. The new job would only pay essentially the same as the one I now held, which had by now increased to $12,500, but it was another steady, permanent position with a major consideration being that I had been sought out for my knowledge and capability, and my new workplace situation would be benevolent, unlike my current one fraught with stress and infighting. It was of course another government bureau, but they appeared to be doing useful and creative things. Neither Barbara nor I were particularly interested in returning to a major metropolitan area, having become accustomed to and enamored of the quasi rural atmosphere of upstate New York, but we agreed that if I could spend even a few years in Washington while I created this new network, my credentials would place me in a good position for advancing my career. I accepted the job, with some private conditions: we must live where a long daily commute would not be necessary; our apartment must be air conditioned; and there must be off-street parking. In the midst of this positive turn of events, as we looked forward to having a family, excited at the new career potential that had presented itself, I received the news that my father had suffered a heart attack and had been confined to bed for two weeks. For an active man in his late sixties, who loved to play golf and whose business kept him flying and driving from place to place on a daily basis, it was a heavy blow, but with his customary optimism he continued to believe that "things would work out."

My last formal meeting with Bernarr was a delight for both of us. I walked unannounced into his office and sat down. "Bernarr,

I bring you tidings of great joy." He drew himself up and a doubtful expression spread across his face. He waited. "I'm leaving," I said. He visibly relaxed, but did not allow himself to smile. "Oh?" That was as much of an inquiry as he would permit himself to make. "I'm going to work for the Education Department in Washington where as you know I've been a consultant for some time." Now Bernarr was relaxed and smiling. "Well that's wonderful for you. I know it's an area in which you have a great interest. When do you plan to leave? Of course we'll have to get all your projects in order."

15

Political Pawn

We were delighted to find an affordable one-bedroom apartment in a new eight-story building in Washington's then new Southwest that included a lovely view of the Potomac River. Our sixth-floor corner apartment featured a spacious living room with floor to ceiling windows the length of the two outside walls. It was only a few blocks from the Captioned Films' offices where I secured a handicapped-parking permit that permitted parking next to the building. There would be no long commute.

Getting to know my new colleagues, orienting myself to the maze of corridors and office suites in the massive, windowless building, and becoming familiar with the varied activities of Captioned Films programs as well as other programs of the Bureau for the Education of the Handicapped occupied my time for the first few weeks. I quickly realized that although there were a number of people with disabilities in professional staff positions, there were none at the highest managerial levels. Power of decision and policy making in the Bureau rested with able-bodied persons who had trained in organizations which provided services to the handicapped. These were teachers, social workers, physicians, psychiatrists, and PhD's whose various specialties were psychology, sociology, education, and medicine; professionals who had worked their way up a job ladder that a handicapped person could not climb and who now occupied positions of authority, making policy decisions for and about the disabled. I didn't question the skills or motivations of the decision makers, but I studied closely how those with disabilities, even professionals, were treated and I could not avoid recognizing, albeit with a touch of cynicism, that once again, as I had felt in the Institute for Physical Medicine and Rehabilitation, in this particular zoo, I was one of the animals, not one of the keepers. My enthusiasm for the job at hand nevertheless overrode my cynicism as I found my own activities of great interest.

With barely time to settle into the job, it was announced that President Lyndon Johnson had decided to balance the national budget and major cuts were being made in all agencies. Included in the cuts to the Bureau for Education of the Handicapped were the funds, requested and approved, for the creation of the national television service for the deaf that I had been hired to create. My project, the reason for our moving to Washington, was dead in the water. It would never see the light of day. It was another of those vulnerable, fringe activities. Everyone shared my disappointment. I felt that I had jumped out of the frying pan into the fire.

I was assured that my position was untouched by the cuts, but the question remained as to how my skills and experience could be utilized on a day-to-day basis, hopefully for a year, until funding could be forthcoming in the next budget. The dream of possibly parlaying this job and project back into television broadcasting where I wanted to be and where I believed I had the most to offer seemed to fade away. As the weeks passed, I was given a variety of assignments. I served as consultant on a project developing media materials for teaching of language, was sent to two educational television stations to evaluate and administer existing contracts for production of experimental programs for the deaf, and supervised and coordinated artwork for filmstrips for elementary grade usage. These activities, occasioned meeting with film and filmstrip producers, traveling nationally, and visiting schools for the deaf in several states. All of the these activities were interesting, utilizing some of my skills and creativity, but there was a dead feeling inside me as I felt I was drifting further and further away from where I had hoped my career would go. I was a capable director and producer. That's what I wanted to do.

As I traveled and met experts in the field, I learned about the nature of deafness and the needs of the deaf. I developed respect for the close knit national deaf community that had lobbied their collective voting power to overcome discriminatory regulations which had precluded obtaining auto insurance, driver's licenses and other rights that hearing persons enjoyed. I was surprised that although the deaf had been able to exercise such independence and maintain some control over their own destiny, the blind did not function as a cohesive group; sighted persons were numerous among those who guided their affairs.

Within the deaf community were numerous talented and educated men and women holding influential professional positions in the educational, social, and political lives of the deaf community. A striking example was a new colleague, Malcom Norwood, one of three deaf men on staff, whose duties included liaisons with deaf social groups and schools for the deaf. Mac was a delightful, warm and sensitive man who was adventitiously deaf, having lost his hearing at a very early age due to illness, but whose speech was quite normal. Barbara and I both began attending sign language classes.

I called Mac's attention to Erving Goffman's book, *Stigma,* and we had long conversations about how accurately Goffman had described the kinds of discriminating experiences to which we had each been subjected at various times in our lives. Mac's lip reading capability was astounding. I learned to communicate with Mac via signing, even though my signing was elementary and unskilled, but with Mac's lip reading we had no difficulty. When we traveled together it was sometimes necessary for me to translate for Mac, particularly when a person spoke while not facing Mac or spoke with minimal lip movement. In a restaurant one day Mac called my attention to a situation that he experienced frequently. "Watch what the waitress does when she realizes I can't hear her." As Mac ordered, the waitress jotted his order on her pad and then, unknowingly turning her head to a position where her lips were not visible to Mac, she asked about his choice of vegetables. Mac looked to me for clarification and as I answered using a few signs, the waitress immediately realized Mac could not hear and proceeded to ignore Mac and adopted a "What will he have?" attitude. I pointed to Mac and said, "Face him and ask him. He will read your lips." She followed the directions willingly and was pleased to have learned something.

During the ensuing year, which was the 100th anniversary of deaf education in the United States, Captioned Films was to produce a documentary film to celebrate the occasion. A non-filmic, factual, draft of a script had been written and I was asked for my reaction. I considered the draft not producible as a film so I offered to write an alternative approach, an offer that was immediately accepted. My version, when completed, was received with enthusiasm and I was assigned to produce the film. The advent of sound in motion pictures, in the Al Jolson movie, *The Jazz Singer,* constituted a crucial change for the deaf. From then on, the purely visual nature of films changed and became increasingly dependent on sound and the spoken word. Sound films of course posed a hardship for the deaf and their lobbying eventually led to legislation under President Eisenhower, which established the Captioned Films Program. I contacted the Jolson estate and secured permission to include a clip of the first minute of sound on film in our documentary. The production contract was given to a New York City production company, and for a few days I served in New York as a line coach for segments in which the narrator was on camera.

Barbara, completing coursework her master's degree in sociology at NYU, also became interested in the deaf. The Deafness Research Foundation of New York, one of the organizations to which I had unsuccessfully appealed for funding when conducting my television teaching experiment with deaf children at NYU, was engaged in cochlear bone research in an attempt to find a way to restore hearing in persons who were profoundly deaf. The foundation had produced a documentary film to elicit after-death donations of cochlear bones from deaf persons for research.[13]

Barbara's Master's thesis focused on questioning the members of one Deaf social group before and after viewing the film to determine their willingness to donate their cochlear bones after death. It was apparent that the documentary was ineffective for imparting a clear understanding of either the need, or for obtaining donation pledges. Barbara's conclusion was that the film was seemingly unable to communicate with deaf populations; its design was perhaps more appropriate for hearing audiences.

As the need for filmstrips for teaching deaf children continued to grow and could not be satisfied by using existing materials produced for hearing children, Captioned Films produced hundreds of filmstrips annually, a process in which, during my first year,

---

[13] Author's note: In the late 1900's cochlear implants comprising an electrode array evolved out of the efforts of the House Ear Institute of Los Angeles, and the Cochlear Corporation of Australia, began to be used to create a measure of hearing in some profoundly deaf persons thereby raising a new area of concern among the deaf population. Many deaf parents of deaf children did not want their children to be included in such experimental treatment, preferring to keep them within the deaf community.

I became deeply involved. Increasing production became a necessity. A filmstrip workshop was planned for summer to teach educators of the deaf the process of producing filmstrips, from concept to completion and teaching the summer workshop became my assignment. Thirty handpicked educators of the deaf arrived, at Captioned Films expense, from all parts of the country to learn the process.

******

In my spare time, I worked on refinishing the small outboard runabout we had brought with us and stored at a nearby marina. I did a comprehensive overhaul, installing a new deck, wooding down the hull and repainting it, and even disassembled the trailer and refinished it. By the end of the summer, with the overhaul finished, we set off for vacation at Lake George, NY, where we had spent many days in previous years. When weather turned cold and wet, we stored our little boat and decided to see Expo 67 in Montreal. There, faced with the complexities of gaining access to exhibits crowded with people waiting in long lines, I gambled and called the United States exhibit, making a pitch to the public relations officer who answered the phone; "I'm in town for only a couple of days. I work for the U.S. Office of Education. Can you be of any assistance in helping me see some of the exhibits?" The answer came back, "Of course, when will you be here? Just call when you're on the grounds, tell me what you want to see, and I'll arrange it for you." Once on the fairgrounds I made the call and we were greeted warmly at the first exhibit, taken past the long queue, seated in a waiting room, served coffee, and when the show was about to begin, ushered into front row seats. For the rest of the day, we enjoyed VIP treatment, seeing in one day what would have taken several days if we had had to wait in line. It was a demonstration of privilege to which we were unaccustomed.

******

During my tenure, Captioned Films supported two major projects that eventually were to have long reaching impact. The first was sponsorship of development of a black box which, by initially utilizing discarded teletypewriters, made it possible for deaf persons to communicate via telephone, a service (TTD) which in later years was improved and made available by telephone companies, and ultimately superseded by the texting capabilities of increasingly sophisticated cell phones. The second research project funded was initial development of equipment that facilitates instantaneous captioning of broadcast television programs.

During the winter of my second year at Captioned Films, we were delighted when Barbara became pregnant, and after being again revisited by the doubts and uncertainty that had plagued me at the thought of having children, I was able to harness my doubts, share Barbara's delight and optimism and realize that I was indeed a fortunate man.

At about the same time, my boss called me into his office. "I know you are unhappy that you were brought to Washington to do a job that funding cuts made impossible. I share your disappointment. You have been an asset to our work and I appreciate your willingness to contribute your skills wherever they could be of use. Unfortunately, it appears that our television plans will not be funded next year either and the question now is how to use your skills in a manner that will make you happy here. Your job is secure, but I'm uncertain how to use you. I could keep you busy, but not with things that would utilize your skills." He continued, "One possibility, if it's of interest to you, is a temporary transfer to another agency. There is a project that is just beginning at the Graduate School of the Department of Agriculture that might utilize your skills and experience. If you're interested, and decide to have a go at it, we can arrange a transfer for you and then later you can return and we'll reassess the situation. I have spoken with them and they'd like to meet you."

My initial discussions with the administrators of the Graduate School of the Department of Agriculture were cordial and positive and I was retained as executive producer for a series of television training films that were to be produced jointly by the Graduate School (GSDA), the Department of Civil Service (DCS), and the Washington, DC, public television station WETA. The project would begin in the spring and last for six months. In subsequent meetings I was introduced to the respective project directors at the CSD and WETA, the latter including the station's program manager and executive producer. It was a comfortable feeling being back in the realm of television production.

******

The training program of the United States Government is massive and worldwide, and training is available to government employees in almost every discipline area and every level. Each government agency has its own training staff that focuses on specific needs of the respective agency. In addition, the Civil Service Department operates a comprehensive training program accessible to all agencies. Finally, the Graduate School of the Department of Agriculture operates a training program similar to that of the Civil Service Department, but which also includes a Correspondence School that serves government employees stationed all over the world.

In the 1960's a government wide human resources problem had been identified regarding the behavioral aspects of government secretaries. Historically, the majority of government secretaries had been female high school graduates from white working class homes whose office behavior reflected the dress, manners and comportment of their social environment. In the years following WWII these young women more often became college students than secretaries and their numbers in Washington dwindled. At the same time, Washington experienced a voluminous influx of black Americans from the south which brought with it numbers of young, intelligent, and capable black American women who sought government employment in secretarial positions. Although these women quickly became expert at secretarial skills like shorthand, typing, filing and letter writing, their office behavior was significantly different from their predecessors in matters of dress, make-up, telephone manners and procedures, office conversation, and eating at the work station, in short, the social aspects of office behavior. Their behavior had become a widely recognized problem in government offices and was overwhelming government training officers.

Neither the Department of Civil Services nor the Graduate School had the staffing or knowledge to address this large scale problem within their regular training programs and it was decided that to achieve economies of scale the problem might be best addressed using televised instruction. Television had the capability to demonstrate correct behavior; programs could be distributed by broadcast and closed circuit; and secretaries would be able to take the course in their own departments with the aid of a mentor in the pattern of previous successful experiments in television teaching in Pittsburgh (for which I had served as both a studio director and art director), and Hagerstown, MD. Teaching by television in this instance would also save countless hours of travel time and lost work. For it to be successful however, the training directors of sixteen different government agencies had to sign on to the project to ensure that once completed, the course would be used by their respective agencies.

My workplace was in the National Press Building on 16th Street where the USDA offices were located. Similar to the United Nations, it was a place where one could expect to see important personages. On leaving the building for lunch one day I approached the revolving door only to step back hurriedly as Vice President Hubert Humphrey came through smiling, leading his secret service team and nodding to everyone.

First priority in my new assignment was identification of content areas that the course would address and creation of a working draft of a course syllabus. Civil Service assigned their most experienced and skillful secretarial trainer, a beautiful intelligent young woman, to be the content expert and television teacher. I hired a former teacher to write individual lesson plans and research and select ancillary learning materials, readings and references. Our three-person team drafted a proposed course syllabus and obtained approval from both DCS and GSDA. The next step was gain approval from the training directors of the various government agencies.

Normal work in Washington, D.C. was interrupted on that fateful day in April when Martin Luther King was assassinated. The next few days, my colleagues and I watched from windows in the National Press Building as flames were visible and police cars and fire trucks screamed back and forth and smoke curled up into the clear sky from dozens of flaming buildings as far as the eye could see. Along 14th Street, enraged African Americans ran back and forth in the street shouting, looting, crying, and being chased by police. By the end of the second day, stores on portions of F Street, which bordered the Press building, had been looted and police had blocked off the street. Slowly, the City settled down: fires were extinguished, streets were blocked off and the cleanup began. At the end of the week, Barbara and I decided to drive to Maryland. It was an extremely unnerving experience being stopped for identification by National Guardsmen at sandbagged gun emplacements on the streets of the nation's capitol.

Within weeks of the King assassination, having had only minimal time to overcome the initial inertia of the project, I found myself in the middle of a political dispute. I was summoned to a meeting with the project directors of CSD and WETA at the Civil Service Department. The GSDA representative was not present and I was informed that leadership and sponsorship of the project had been changed. USDA had been eliminated from further participation in the project. The organization that had hired me, and to which I had reported, was no longer a member of the producing team. Was I also now out of the project; and out of a job? Was I to return to Captioned Films? No, they explained, I was to continue as executive producer, but would now coordinate my efforts with the two remaining agencies, and continue to be on the government payroll. Although never fully explained, the action apparently hinged on a conflict of personalities, and I was in this instance wise enough to avoid pursuing the details. Clearly there had been a coup. I phoned my contact at USDA to find out if they were aware of the new situation and was informed that they had only at that moment been advised of the change.

I was in the unenviable position of having been hired by one agency and possibly appearing to have been co-opted by another, in which case I could be easily suspect for having facilitated the change of events in some way. I headed for USDA to have a frank discussion and to inform them that I had not been a party to their ouster from the project. The USDA administrators were angry and disappointed because they had seen in the project something which they thought was a good idea and to which they had dedicated their good auspices and resources. They were unable to explain the turn of events and had no cogent idea as to the reason for it, but fortunately they understood that I had simply been caught in the middle and did not suspect me of having been a party to it. They advised me to continue with the project, offered their assistance should I require it, and hoped I would stay in touch.

My workplace was changed to offices in the WETA-TV building and at my request, Civil Service's training director invited training directors of sixteen major government agencies to a meeting to inform them of the intended project. After the initial welcoming remarks the meeting was turned over to me. I faced the group with some trepidation. Although I already possessed a rough outline of the syllabus that I and my colleagues believed would amply address the problems, I needed to obtain endorsement and support for it from each of the sixteen attending agencies. I knew that if I presented them with a syllabus that had already been prepared without their input, I would never obtain agreement. They must have a hand in its creation. I had therefore instructed my associates to not mention the existence of our syllabus. I wanted the representatives of the respective agencies to believe they had created the syllabus, so I led them through a two-hour discussion, about the nature of the problem we were trying to solve, and the kinds of actions necessary to solve it, which included the use of televised instruction. I answered many questions about logistics and management of televised instruction, taking pains to elicit consent at each step in the discussion. With agreement on the problem and the potential solution established, I systematically elicited from them the primary and secondary concepts that they believed should be taught in the programs as well as the general sequence of their presentation. When the agency representatives finally reached consensus on what was essentially the same content as that contained in the syllabus my colleagues and I had previously created, I adjourned the meeting promising to send each of the training directors a copy of the syllabus they had collectively designed for their inspection, correction and approval. My colleagues were ecstatic. In a single meeting we had obtained endorsement of the project as well as acceptance of the syllabus for the course from sixteen agencies, all of them promising to use the televised instruction when it became available. It was a major step forward. Now it was time to produce the programs.

I secured permission from the owners of the syndicated office cartoon *From 9 to 5* to use the title for the series, and reprint permission to use the cartoons in the instructional materials. I created a set design of abstract pieces that could be set in a variety of ways. We identified specific concepts that needed to be demonstrated: correct and incorrect behavior; phone procedures; applying makeup at the workstation; and dress. I located a writer capable of turning these subjects into humorous understandable skits, and then wrote the fourteen scripts, dovetailing the special dramatic material into the lesson and designing the opening and closing artwork and titles. The station assigned their most experienced director to direct the shows and with a few rehearsals, the talented Civil Services trainer adapted to the television medium. With the director's assistance, auditions for skit roles were held, actors cast, and production began. Once begun, two programs were taped each week and in seven weeks, with only the usual fine tuning and editing, the production phase was completed.

******

We found a place to store our boat at Broom Island on the Pautauxet River and enjoyed using it frequently, even during Barb's advancing pregnancy, but the summer sun was frequently so fierce that there were days when it was too hot to be out on the water. Our apartment building installed a large swimming pool just in time for the warm weather and Barb was able to swim almost every day, her buoyancy in the water providing a welcome, if short, relief from the weight of the baby she was carrying. We enjoyed the summer, taking daylong sightseeing trips to explore the Chesapeake area, looking at boats, dreaming of having a larger one and eating Maryland crabs. I would often buy a bucket of oysters from the nearby fish wharf in the Southwest, and after scrubbing them in the sink, place them in a large pot in the refrigerator. We enjoyed them as appetizers for several days. Sometimes we would buy blue crabs, boil them and sit for long dinners, cracking and picking.

Barb had decided that she would have the baby by natural childbirth and so enrolled us in a class of about a dozen couples. My assumption that I was well informed on such matters was soon disproven; I was chagrined to realize how much I didn't know. Barb's parents came to visit and on August 21st Barb called me at work to say that her labor had begun, three weeks early. I rushed home and drove her to George Washington Hospital where, since she was having natural childbirth, a somewhat unusual occurrence at the time, she was the center of interest among hospital staff. After several hours Barbara gave birth to a beautiful, perfectly formed, healthy, normal, baby girl whom we named Jessica. I remained with her for the entire time and was fascinated and over-whelmed to be able to witness the birth of my own child. The doubts and fearful concerns that had continued to remain in the back of my mind during the past nine months were washed away in the wonder of the awesome experience I shared with my beloved wife. My joy was boundless. Once more I had experienced an event that I had long ago considered to be beyond my wildest dreams. Grandma and Grandpa DeSandis were of course delighted to be present for the arrival of their first grandchild and assumed their new roles with alacrity. As soon as the DeSandis' had returned home the Nathanson grandparents visited to see the new grand-child. My father's heart condition had deteriorated, but he persisted in driving and even tried to play golf despite his need to take nitro-glycerin pills.

In the last weeks of summer, the student and teacher's manu-als for *From 9 to 5* were completed, edited and printed, and toward the end of August the project was nearing completion. WETA and the Civil Service Department were laying out plans for the first broadcast schedule in September. Following a brief training period for the in-class mentors, which was conducted by the same trainer who was the television instructor, the programs were broadcast, used by most of the agencies in the first go round and achieved notable success. They were then repeated several times and used by all of the original participating agencies with repeated success. With the job completed, I once again began to cast about for the next way stop on my frequently sidetracked career. I was now 42 years old and had yet to work anywhere longer than two years.

WETA was impressed by my work, but there were no staff openings and no sizeable projects scheduled for the near future. My job at Captioned Films was at the G-12 grade level, but on the basis of education and professional experience I qualified as a G-15, which paid significantly more and carried more responsible administrative duties. However, one had to find an opening classi-fied at that level and gain an appointment to it, and with President Johnson's balanced budget there were no new jobs and unfilled openings were almost non-existent. The Civil Service administrators with whom I had worked on the project were interested in adding me to their staff, but no openings existed. USDA was also interested in having me join the staff of the Graduate School. I had several conferences with them with the result that I was offered directorship of their correspondence school program. I perceived the future of correspondence school instruction to be dependent on the utilization of media materials and the possibility of developing that future held considerable appeal. I recalled the United States Armed Forces Institute films I had directed at WQED several years before, which were sent to military participants all over the world. I studied the Correspondence School and found it to be print oriented, print bound, and stagnated by a number of procedures that made it inflexible and difficult to manage. I presented my ideas for both improving the management and developing mediated correspondence instruction that would include development of television programs, audiotapes and filmstrips. The administrators understood and generally agreed that media was the future, but given the budgetary situation, they foresaw no means to acquire capital funding to make it possible. In its present state, I viewed the existing correspondence program as essentially a bookkeeping exercise which held no allure or hope for creative development, and although I liked the people there, with reluctance I did not accept the offer, and prepared to return to Captioned Films until some better opportunity presented itself. My efforts in Washington, although eminently successful, were nevertheless a disappointment in that they had not led to more substantial career growth, or a meaningful position in broadcast television. In retrospect, I wonder why, given past experiences, I valued job creative potential over job security. I could have remained, as many do, in my secure federal position, working my way up the rewards and responsibilities ladder, concentrating primarily on opportunity regardless of direction. It appeared there was no parlay possible that would offer a step up the broadcasting career ladder either in Washington or elsewhere, even on the heels of a project as successful as *From 9 to 5*. Once again fate intervened unexpectedly, and at an appropriate time.

16

Academic Pawn

The State University of New York consisted of seventy-two separate units: four-year arts and science schools, graduate centers, medical schools, agriculture and technical schools, specialty schools and community colleges. Although each of the units had both a president and administrative staff, a large Central Administration staff, located in Albany, NY, administered the entire University.

In the two years I had been in Washington, the University had been engaged in an enormous expansion and construction program. Robert Thomas, Vice Chancellor of Communications, was charged with constructing and operating a new television network which would link various locations of the State University with New York State Public Television stations in Albany, Syracuse, Rochester, Buffalo, Binghamton and Plattsburgh. With completion of the network, Thomas established a new instructional service, the University of the Air, which produced college-level instructional programs that were broadcast by the respective stations and could be taken for credit at various state campuses.

On the various campuses of the University, multi-media lecture halls were included in the construction plans, a decision based in part on the success of an architectural design experiment in media-use instructional spaces by Morton Gassman, an architect at Rensselaer Polytechnic Institute. Gassman had created an experimental multi-media classroom, equipped with a variety of front and rear screen projection capabilities, sophisticated sound systems and electronic equipment control. The experimentation had led to Gassman's moving to the State University Construction Fund to lead the planning and design of innovative instructional spaces in the many new buildings that were being constructed on the campuses of the State University.

With numerous multi-media lecture halls under construction, problems inherent in outfitting them with state of the art equipment was unlike anything ever before encountered in New York State's higher education system. Several major problems had to be resolved: the lecture halls must be equipped with sound, projection, lighting and control systems adaptable to each of the many varied locations; all equipment and services must be purchased in large lots under state bid contracts; staff must be hired to operate the new facilities, and faculty must be oriented and encouraged to use the new facilities to develop new patterns of instruction which would make productive use of the new media capabilities.

In the twelve four-year schools and the four graduate centers, new positions of Communication Center Directors were created with staffs and facilities capable of producing a wide assortment of filmic, photographic, television and graphic materials to support anticipated improvements in the instructional program and specific needs of instructors. The Office of Instructional Resources, headed by Buzz Rice, coordinated these efforts from Albany, although the activity required frequent travel to New York for meetings with Thomas at his office on 42nd Street just across the street from Grand Central Station in the same building that housed the office of the new Chancellor, Samuel Gould.

Each new campus communications center had, among its newly hired staff, an engineer/electronics technician. These talented engineers were assigned the task of collectively designing a generic electronic control system capable of being used on every campus. This system must control operation of every type of electronic equipment being used, and be simple enough for the average faculty member to operate. The resultant design specifications were put out to state bid.

In order to motivate faculty to explore the use of media in instruction, a grant program was established with discretionary funds to underwrite the costs of faculty directed development of new patterns of instruction that would innovatively utilize visual and intellectual materials. The multi-skilled communication centers' staffs of artists, filmmakers, and producers would transform instructors' intent into finished materials. The increasing burden of coordination and development justified additional positions in Buzz Rice's office.

I was delighted to hear Buzz on the phone one morning explaining the situation and inviting me to come to Albany as the Director of Instructional Development in the Central Administration of the State University of New York. My responsibilities would be to direct and administer the development of new media materials, new patterns of instruction and to coordinate a variety of experiments that used media in instruction. For those who were familiar with the use of media in instruction it was evident that the new media, particularly television and film, offered numerous opportunities for improving teaching effectiveness and improving learning. My experience with producing, directing, and designing materials for instructional television in Pittsburgh, Washington and New York coupled with teaching large numbers of teacher's how to use the medium at NYU convinced me that increased use of media in instruction promised a new age of teaching and learning.

Almost every major university in the country echoed the State University's move into this new age. Educational communications experts were becoming increasingly visible in educational planning and curriculum development. The success of experimental courses utilizing media at Berkeley, Purdue, Michigan State, Ohio State, Pennsylvania State and numerous other colleges and universities had been documented in educational journals, and the Ford Foundation television experiment in Hagerstown, MD had proven the efficacy of televised instruction for an entire school district.

The offer to return to upstate New York to work creatively in an atmosphere of respect would free me from the disappointing budget-stifled Caption Films status quo, and so it was as welcome as had been John Gough's invitation to come to Washington two years previously. Given the heat and the humidity of Washington, the furor and unrest resulting from the assassinations of Martin Luther King and Robert Kennedy during our two short years there, Barbara and I both welcomed an opportunity to return to the relative quiet of upstate New York where we could boat and camp on beautiful Lake George, removed from the excitement of the nation's Capitol. I looked forward to a relationship with Buzz that would be wholly collegial; we complimented each other and perceived the educational establishment and its flaws from similar points of view. I considered it a bit ironic that I would be hired by one of my former students, but was anxious to be involved in what

I perceived as a meaningful effort. Barb and I planned our move upstate for early November.

During our two years in Washington, DC, Barbara's father had retired and her parents built a house on acreage they had acquired years before in New Paltz, NY, a quiet former Hugenot village in the Mid-Hudson area. By the summer of 1968 construction was completed and her parents moved in. It was a convenient stopover, as we made our way north again to Schenectady with baby Jessica. The news from Pittsburgh was not good. My father's heart condition had worsened and although Mother, in our phone conversations, never told me the worst, I knew it was serious.

Returning to New York State's Capital District was like coming home. We quickly resettled in the familiar surroundings of the Stockade section of Schenectady in a basement apartment that faced out on a small yard on a quiet street. The commute to the office in Albany was twenty minutes and I soon was deep into a whole new area of media development. Barbara, who until then did not drive, obtained her license, and I occasionally rode the bus from a stop two blocks away, freeing the car for her use.

******

We were pleased to again be in upstate New York where the opportunities for camping and fishing were unlimited and I indulged myself whenever possible. Barb and I fished from the boat. In early spring I netted smelt in the small streams that flowed into Lake George, but my favorite fishing was for trout in the many Adirondack streams and rivers. Trout fishing in streams is not the easiest kind of fishing. It requires hip boots or waders and wading in cold, rocky, uneven streams where even anglers with two good legs use a wading stick for support. I used a wading stick too, and with my rod and landing net and only one hand it was a veritable balancing act. The force of the current pressing against the bottom of the leg, at the end of the prostheses, poses a difficult problem as it tends to sweep the leg downstream and requires concentration and balance to prevent being tipped over. I very carefully selected the places I waded and never waded on rough bottom or where the stream was particularly fast or deep. I knew my limitations. On one beautiful April day fishing with Buzz in a small stream, I noticed, as we worked our way along the stream, that he wasn't wading much at all. He was jumping from rock to rock, and missing many tantalizing spots. I waded out into the stream about 10 feet, found a big boulder to lean against and in a matter of a few minutes caught two 10 inch rainbow trout. Buzz came by about then and I suggested he wade out to his left and try another spot where I'd seen a trout feeding. Buzz looked over at me and said, "I can't." "What do you mean you can't?" I replied, "Just cross over here behind me." Buzz shook his head, "What I mean is, you don't feel it, but the water is too cold for me and my feet can't take it!" I hadn't thought about that problem because I had never experienced it and the ironic humor of it struck me. We looked at each other and laughed and I said, "Seems you have a disability."

Two years after my first fitting my stumps had shrunken sufficiently to require new prostheses. I'd made several trips from Schenectady to New York for the necessary fittings. In the course of moving from New York City to Schenectady and to Washington, DC, it had been necessary, whenever I experienced a problem with my prostheses, usually a matter of adjustment and refitting due to the continuing shrinkage of my stumps, to continue to visit the prosthetist in New York City. Back again in Schenectady two years later, I located a prosthetist at the small rehabilitation center who constructed my third set of legs, almost identical to the first set, fitted with leather straps above the knees and connected to a waist belt under my clothing to provide additional security. The nature of the arrangement created pressure at the rear of my waist that induced some forward pelvic tilt and caused me to lean forward slightly when standing or walking. The weight-bearing sockets into which my stumps fit tended, when I was standing or walking for a considerable time to cause chaffing and sometimes blisters at the weight bearing locations. A couple years later, when I was ready for another new set of prostheses, I identified a different prosthetist in the area who recommended a new prosthesis design that utilized a rigid outer plastic shell molded to fit tightly to the configuration of the natural leg just above the knee and a gel sock that replaced the woolen one which distributed the weight and eliminated pressure spots. It held the leg securely. The new legs eliminated need for straps and waist belt and permitted me to stand more erect and walk with a more natural gait. Moreover, they were extremely comfortable.

Having moved from Washington in November, we were still settling in our new apartment and were unable to make the trip to Pittsburgh for Christmas. Knowing of my father's deteriorating health, we made a special trip to see him in February. A few weeks later he was hospitalized, and on a business trip I was able to visit him in the hospital.

In anticipation of the next summer's activities we looked for a boat somewhat larger than our runabout in which we could safely take our baby, and found a nineteen foot outboard cruiser with a deep cockpit, small cabin, and a dinette that transformed easily into a bunk. It needed a lot of work, but we bought it for delivery in the spring when we planned to sell our runabout.

During my visit I told Dad about the new boat and how we would both enjoy it the coming summer. He was over-whelmed that I had had such a successful rehabilitation, found a lovely wife and now had a steady job and a healthy, normal daughter. That I was able to have a boat was a bonus and he was elated for me. His dreams for me had been fulfilled, and now he was critically ill.

Several weeks later, on March 18, as Barbara and I were entertaining a visiting Japanese educator at dinner, I received word by telephone that my father was dying. Within the hour I was on a plane headed for Pittsburgh, my anxiety heightened when my luggage was mislaid. By the time I boarded the limo I was frantic, fearing that I would not arrive in time. Mother, and Dad's sisters were waiting in the hospital when I arrived. I asked to see my father, but was not permitted to enter his room due to his critical situation, and was only able to catch a glimpse of his face amid the tangle of intravenous tubes and oxygen mask. Sometime after midnight the doctor came to inform us that he had expired.

My father had been, for me, the one person who was always present when I was in need; he had the solution when I had a problem, never questioning or criticizing, and always offering a helping hand. Now he was gone and with him a part of me. I had never lost anyone that close to me; I was devastated. Soon after Barbara arrived the next day with the baby, I fell ill and was unable to be present at the funeral home until the time of the internment. Mother, asked her sisters-in-law to identify a reform rabbi to conduct the burial services. They were surprised at her request, assuming that Mother's pastor would bury their brother, but she was true to the arrangement that she and Dad had made at their betrothal, and wanted him to be buried with the rites of his religion.

Although I was already envisioning returning Mother's house to its previous two-apartment status thereby providing an income for her, I was greatly relieved when her sister Marge decided to move from New York City to Pittsburgh. Mother would not be living alone. I found solace in the comfort of my wife and new baby, but was a long time recovering from my grief. As the warm weather came I kept myself busy scraping and painting the new boat. Working alone at the marina on weekends I would be suddenly overcome with the thoughts of how Dad would have enjoyed boating with us and I'd cry as I lay under the boat, until I was able to begin working again. My mind was filled with memories of the goodness, dedication, generosity, and the total selflessness of my father, that kind and stalwart man who had been my supporter and protector and for whom there had been only one concern, his family.

******

There were many academics in all fields and at all levels who were convinced that traditional instructional methodology was effective and needed no revisions. For them the old idea that teaching and learning required only "two men on a log," a teacher and a learner, was sacrosanct. They flatly resisted the challenge to attempt to make what they were doing more interesting, more effective or more productive by incorporating media. They could not be induced to participate in the experiment. There were, however, large numbers of imaginative faculty, ranging from newly hired assistant professors to tenured professors on campuses across the state, who rose to the challenge and in a relatively short time were developing exciting new and innovative patterns of instruction that included all types of media, and in a number of instances student achievement soared.

In my first year we broadened the scope and fine-tuned the organization and administration of what had been previously been a modest informal grant program. When the new fiscal year brought the requested amount of $400,000 in discretionary development funds, we expanded the number of experimental projects. In the next fiscal cycle we requested and received permission to hire four Instructional Developers to consult with and direct campus grantees in their developmental activities. At the same time we created and conducted studies that assessed the impact and productivity of each faculty experiment. These studies quickly developed into cost-benefit analysis studies which revealed that many of these nontraditional instructional models could generate more learning at less cost than many traditional courses. Numerous prototypes of new, nontraditional patterns of instruction emerged, well before the popularity of the personal computer.

One of the simplest prototypes was as follows: In University Centers (graduate schools) a faculty member who taught a lecture course would normally present fourteen lectures during the semester and graduate students would conduct small weekly group discussions between lectures. If the instructor audio taped or videotaped one third of the lectures, copies would be made in the communications center and the tapes installed in the campus library on reserve for that class. Every third week the class would not meet, but students were charged with listening to those lectures on tape at their leisure and the faculty member would have that time free. Independent evaluation revealed that student test scores were as good or better with this instructional model as with the traditional one.

The real potential was that if there were three lecture courses in the same department and each followed this example, there would be three faculty members, each available to respectively teach one-third of a new course in that department. If that were done the department would generate an increased number of student credit hours with the same staffing, and the increased student credit hours were a critical part of the formula for increasing departmental staff. Cost analysis revealed that when ancillary costs for materials development and production, instructor development time, and additional costs were all input to the equation, it was still less expensive to teach the course the new way rather than the old. The major problem was that although almost every new pattern of instruction was shown to produce a cost savings, no way existed within the traditional University accounting system, for the University to tangibly extract the savings and share it with the instructor. The University would have to find a way to accomplish this before it could take broad scale advantage of such innovative practices.

In the course of our work involving the outfitting of lecture halls and instructional development projects I frequently visited various campuses across the state. On one of these trips, to the SUNY College at Binghamton, I was surprised, at a meeting to be seated across the table from Percival Borde, Pearl Primus' husband, with whom I had worked at NYU years before. We were both delighted to renew our acquaintance and at lunch I learned that Percy was an adjunct instructor at the College teaching African Dance. He and Pearl still had an interest in creating a series of television dance programs and our conversation took on the nature of a planning session that excited us both. My renewed contact with Percy put me back in touch with Pearl and we began to explore how we might recreate her most recognized choreographed works.

The instructional development projects across the University continued for a couple of years and as positive data documenting the successful use of media in instruction began to accumulate, we became more confident in the worth of our experiments. Instructional Development was gaining higher visibility at national conferences, but as we made several presentations of our cost/benefit analysis approach we had only limited response, usually from those who were developing similar theories. We found the mind-set of the traditional educational organization and structure an impenetrable barrier. Thomas Petry, who had accepted the post in Israel, invited us to present our views at an instructional television conference he had organized in Jerusalem and Buzz deferred to me to take the all-expense paid trip. My presentation in Israel did not garner great notice; most of the participants were involved with northeastern television stations and were more interested in broadcasting than educating. They assumed the problems of education could be solved with more money and more teachers; few were interested or experienced in studying the basic structure of the educational system and no one dared to confront the collective eminence of academe, the faculty.

Apart from the conference the trip to Israel, my first outside the United States except for brief visits to Canada, was an exposure to a different and fascinating world. We toured Jerusalem, Haifa, visited the Dead Sea, the Galilee and Nazareth. I stood at the Wailing Wall at sundown on Friday; walked through the old section of Jerusalem and across the plaza to the Dome of the Rock;

watched a procession of Christians carrying crosses on the Via Del a Rosa; stooped low to enter the small medieval door to the Church of the Immaculate Conception in Bethlehem where I observed Russian Orthodox priests conducting services; and studied the hole in the floor where the cross of Christ was supposed to have stood and the small rock pile which was presented as the cave in which the body of Christ lay after the crucifixion. In a basement of an old monastery I listened while a British Anglican Nun rapturously called attention to supposed wheel ruts from the original Via Del a Rosa worn into base rock and pointed out deep water filled cisterns carved in the rock as she spun tales of the happenings that surrounded that momentous crisis in Christianity. What touched me most deeply however, was the fact that when people heard my name they welcomed me warmly and I was overcome with the feeling that I was totally accepted as belonging in this land. For the first time in my life I was a member of an in-group. Never before, as the son of a Jew, had I had that experience, not even among my father's family, because I had a Christian mother. Here in Israel, in what was essentially the birthplace of Christianity, I was being welcomed as a Jew and even though I wasn't one, I felt warm and secure. On a visit to the Knesset, the guard at the entry, looking at my passport, exclaimed, "That's a very famous name in Israel. Are you related to the rabbi?" I knew nothing of the famous Rabbi Nathanson, but was pleased to even be asked the question.

On my return I was greeted with the news that Barbara was again pregnant. In the previous year we had decided to purchase a house and had looked for some land and an old farmhouse we could fix up. The market was driven, however, by a surge of affluent downstate buyers looking for upstate property to serve as vacation homes. Realtors told us of buyers purchasing property on impulse for cash. The prices rose as we looked and after losing a few houses to higher bidders who were willing to pay more than the asking price, we found ourselves priced out of the market. With a second baby on the way we needed a house and I told Barbara, "If we can find something that you would consider renting, let's buy it." We found a small house in good condition in a quiet tree lined neighborhood in Schenectady and moved in June. I did not worry about our second child as I had about the first, but was nevertheless relieved to learn that our new baby boy, Jared, born at the end of October, was normal.

My children were for me, the ultimate proof of my capability and potential. When my children were born healthy and whole, my joy was unlimited and as I watched them attend school and play and do all the things that children did, I would compare their young lives with my own. For me, they and my wife were the second miracle in my life. Being a husband and father of two beautiful, intelligent, normal children was a gift beyond my most extravagant dreams. However skilled I was in various ways, I could never deny that by whatever definition, my disabilities unalterably categorized me as being less than top grade, but as a man who had created two healthy children, I knew I was second to none, and, as the children grew, better than many.

Barbara bore the brunt of child raising and her devoted nurturing was to a degree balanced by my disciplining, although with the Spartan attitude that had enabled me to survive I tended at times to be overly demanding. Through the years, as the children grew, I enjoyed their adventures, took enormous pride in their appearance, a matter of importance to me, and their ability to reason with sensitivity and concern. From an early age, both children learned that there were certain aspects of family life, particularly my disabilities that were not to be discussed outside the family. There were occasions, when I had an abrasion on my stump and had to rest without the encumbrance of the prosthesis, when the children would be requested to not bring their friends into the house. They both became adept at managing such situations and in protecting my privacy, and in so doing became unknowing enablers for my "remaining in the closet." Schneider and Conrad cite instances of persons who protect their disability out of fear of being demeaned.[14]

At SUNY, faculty members who became involved in instructional development almost invariably became dedicated and continued the process, several building national reputations and careers

---

[14] "...with potentially stigmatized conditions identify their condition as undesirable and discreditable and, hence, grounds for being 'in the closet' and ...attempt to manage this discreditable information in such a way as to protect their reputations and rights as normal members of society." (Deviant Behavior: A Text-Reader in the Sociology of Deviance, Delos H. Kelly, pp. 228-238)

on their achievements. Of those who did not, some perceived it as activity that lowered the status of teaching, some were fearful that such new developments could threaten the security of both tenured and non-tenured faculty, and some simply feared that it might perhaps raise the standard of endeavor. There were many traditionalists among the faculty however, who viewed the entirety of the University's massive expenditure on new multi-media lecture complexes and the creation and staffing of communication centers as a waste of funds that could have been more wisely spent on increasing academic staffing, facilities and rewards.

With the University's communications centers construction completed and fully staffed, the development of new instructional patterns began to blossom aided by the new instructional developers. They were barely on board when politically motivated unrest on the state campus in Buffalo posed a crisis for Chancellor Samuel Gould that ultimately resulted in his resignation. Dr. Ernest Boyer, who had served as Executive Vice Chancellor under Gould, was appointed his successor.

Dr. Boyer, an audiologist, had been with the University prior to Gould's accession to Chancellor. Robert Thomas, Gould's right-hand man in Gould's previous position as President of the new Public Television Station WNET-TV in New York City, had been brought to the University as Vice Chancellor for Communications and in that capacity maintained a close relationship with Gould who, valuing his previous service, continued to use him in areas beyond the assigned scope of his position. For Executive Vice Chancellor Boyer, Thomas posed a continuing threat. It was not surprising therefore, that when Boyer was appointed to his new position, Thomas resigned. In his first meeting with the faculty senate, Boyer was asked, by one of the faculty who considered the recent expenditures for communications centers and staffs as unproductive, "Are you going to continue to throw good money after bad?" Boyer's response was a simple "No." It was an answer that resounded across the University.

The new Chancellor, anxious to establish his authority and creativity, sent a team of trusted staff members to London to study the successful Open University that had gained high visibility in educational circles as the new way to develop easy access to educational services. While his team was still overseas and before he had received a report from them, Boyer announced the formation of the Empire State College that was to become New York State University's "Open University," based in Saratoga Springs. At about the same time Boyer imported a young academic administrator from Washington, D.C., to cut the dead wood from his administration and sweep his new court clean.

The hatchet man met with Buzz Rice privately, and without ceremony informed him that the Office of Instructional Resources was to be dissolved. He did not extend the courtesy of a private meeting to me. I was called to a meeting with my entire instructional development unit (four newly hired developers, plus three other staffers), and in their presence was treated to the humiliating announcement that my grant program was terminated, my office dissolved, and my staff transferred to the new Empire State College. The status of both and me was as yet unresolved.

Within the next few months, communications centers' budgets across the University were examined with an eye toward downsizing activities and staffing. The new age to which we had looked forward was over. The irony was that, had the kinds of activity we initiated and engaged in for the past few years been integrated into its program and structure, the new Empire State College could have benefited. Unfortunately, our knowledge and capabilities were ignored.

Ironically, and unknown to us, Buzz and I were both offered to the State Education Department where Bernarr Cooper had the pleasure of declining the offer. Ultimately, we were transferred to the Office of Dr. Bruce Dearing, former President of the State University College at Binghamton, poet, and currently Vice Chancellor for Academic Programs. We were asked to tie up the loose ends of our former programs and assigned make-work projects.

Before the year was out, Boyer issued a public announcement of a new Chancellor's awards program that recognized exemplary expertise in teaching. There were to be two levels of awards. The first was a Distinguished Teaching Professorship in which the recipient would receive a salary increase and recognition as a Distinguished Teaching Professor. The second was an Excellence in Teaching Award. In addition, the Chancellor announced a new and "precedent setting" instructional development grant program that would award selected faculty with development funds for improving instruction. Summoned to Dr. Dearing's office, I was invited to design these new programs, an invitation I was in no position to refuse. The new precedent setting grant program was identical to the one I had developed and administered and which had been eliminated. It had now been re-invented by the new Chancellor, but with far less funding. It was déjà vu. The teaching awards were, on the surface, the Chancellor's pledge that teaching was to be given more importance in the University. In reality however, these newly announced programs, which I was now called upon to re-create, were essentially public relations motivated and as such, even though they would be implemented and have high visibility, would in no material way either improve productivity of the University or necessarily raise the level and quality of instruction. Buzz and I had made an attempt, perhaps presumptuously, to improve the quality of teaching. Although our efforts had not been within the mainstream of University programs, we had hoped that, with documentation of success, which we had, they would eventually become an integral part of the University's policy and program. I was convinced, however, that the Chancellor's new programs were only peripheral to the main business of the University. Although not presented as such, they were simply faculty perks.

As I designed the new programs I assumed it was likely that I would be assigned to administer them since such peripheral programs would not normally be assigned to regular staff members who were involved with academic planning and administration. In the new design therefore, in order to protect myself from any question on matters related to future award recipients, I structured the process of each award program so it operated under the aegis of a committee of respected university scholars, chosen by the faculty senate, who would review the applications and proposals, evaluate their merit and decide on the award recipients. My cynical attitude produced a good design. When, as I had expected, I was subsequently assigned to administer the programs I had only to concern myself with the process (operation, administration and payments). By design, I was insulated from the awards determination process. The effectiveness of my design was proven one day, after I had set the process in motion for the first round of awards, when I had an unexpected visitor to my office in the person of my dearest friend,

Dale Stein, a tenured professor of Art at the SUNY College at New Paltz. "What brings you to Albany?" I asked him.

"I had a meeting with the Chancellor."

"You did? For what?"

Dale looked at me with puzzlement because he was aware of my involvement with the design and administration of the new programs. "Don't you know?" "Know what?" I responded, puzzled. Dale smiled, "I'm one of the first nine to receive the Distinguished Teaching Professorship." It was news to me.

******

For the moment I possessed a steady job in the central administration of a major university. I had no other obvious options. All around me were men and women who possessed doctorates. Buzz departed the University to pursue doctoral study at Harvard. Should I pursue a doctorate myself? I was forty-four years old. I had waited twelve years after receiving my baccalaureate degree before obtaining a masters degree. Should I make the effort? It was clear that I wasn't going to be a television director and circumstances had thrown me into higher education. If I had a doctorate I might be able to consolidate my position. I now had a wife and two children. Could I do it?

I talked with a professor in the School of Education at SUNY Albany explaining my background and experience. "You shouldn't have any problems. You could probably teach some of the courses. Fill out the entry forms and we'll talk about your course work. I'll be happy to be your advisor." In the following two years, working full time, I took all of the courses necessary, and passed the comprehensive test. All that remained was the dissertation. My final degree would be an Ed.D. The Ph.D required a comparative statistical study; the Ed.D required only an exploratory statistical study. I elected to do an exploratory study. My subject was one that I had uncovered in my newly assigned position. While reviewing SUNY's application and enrollment statistics, I discovered that more than fifty percent of applicants with disabilities who were accepted for enrollment did not enroll anywhere within SUNY system. I was able, at work, to conduct a preliminary study as to the reasons for this rejection and was not surprised to learn that the

SUNY campuses, even the newly constructed facilities, were in large measure inaccessible to persons with mobility problems. It was a natural. I could do portions of the statistical study at work and write the dissertation for my doctorate. I would need some funding to complete all of the research however. I sought an appointment with the Commissioner of the New York State Office of Vocational Rehabilitation. "I am the result of one of your more successful projects," I told him, "You funded my rehabilitation and as a result I have had a reasonably successful, if somewhat uneven professional development. Now I want to do a study that I think may be important to both the University and your office and I need to find funding for it. Will you give it some consideration?"

After a number of weeks I received word that OVR had agreed to award me $5,000 to do the work necessary to complete my dissertation. On investigating the situation at the college I learned that as far as those on staff were aware, I was the first graduate student to ever obtain a grant to complete a dissertation. I wrote the first two chapters of my dissertation, the description of the problem, and the review of the literature. And then the bottom fell out.

In early fall I was summoned to the Vice Chancellor's office and Dr. Dearing, as gently as he could, informed me that Governor Carey had cut ten percent from the University's budget, and my position, not a regular line-item position, was being eliminated. I would be terminated at the end of the year. I could hardly believe this was happening again. On the 200th anniversary of the founding of the nation, just as I was turning fifty years old, I was back again on the outside. If only I had stayed at USOE. If only I had stayed at the Education Department. If only, if only, I had stayed in Washington. If only I had been content to just stay put. Barbara was a great comfort. She assured me that given the situations I had made the right decisions in the past and whatever happened we would survive.

In the last months of my tenure with the University, a newly appointed Vice Chancellor, a former English professor at the University College in Buffalo, wrote a plan for the development of the University in the next five years. It was circulated to central staff members for their comments and suggestions. On reading it I was surprised that it made no mention of the treatment of handicapped students or of improving physical access to campuses.

As a continuing consultant to the Captioned Films Branch of USOE I knew that the Rehabilitation Act of 1973, PL 93-112 required that "... any building constructed in whole or in part with federal funds must be accessible to and usable by the physically handicapped. Among the architectural changes to be considered for colleges and universities under the requirements of this new law were: ramping of buildings, slanting curbs, sidewalks and street crossings, placing Braille markers on buildings, classroom doors and elevators, providing space for wheelchairs in theater auditoriums and other such places, installing automatic outside doors on major buildings, placing wide doors on toilet stalls and attaching rails inside stalls, providing visual fire alarms for the deaf, lowering public telephones and lowering water fountains..."

As the State University of New York neared the completion of its massive building construction and expansion program, it was generally not accessible to the handicapped. Unlike Hofstra, Kent State, Southwest Minnesota State, San Jose State, Wayne State, Southern Illinois University at Carbondale, the University of Hawaii at Manoa and the University of California Berkeley, each of which had for a number of years been adapting both their campuses and academic programs to provide greater access to the handicapped, the State University of New York had expended almost no effort to alleviate what, according to its own data, was a crucial problem. Moreover, neither its publicity seeking new Chancellor nor his newly appointed Vice Chancellor appeared to be knowledgeable about this major new concern that loomed on the horizon of higher education.

The key sentence in the new (1973) legislation, Section 504, was far reaching: "No otherwise qualified handicapped individual in the United States, shall solely by reason of his handicap, be excluded from the participation in, be denied the benefits of, or be subjected to discrimination under any program or activity receiving Federal financial assistance." By 1976, when my position at SUNY was terminated, President Nixon had twice vetoed the legislation. The third, cut version, finally passed Congress, but the Office of Civil Rights of the Department of Health, Education and Welfare did not implement Section 504 Regulations, and subsequently, under the Carter administration, HEW Secretary Joseph Califano delayed signing the implementing regulations for Section

504 until 1977. The delay created a nationwide movement among disabled groups that led to the formation, subsequent to the 1974 meeting of the President's Committee on Employment of the Handicapped, of The American Coalition of Citizens with Disabilities which included The American Council for the Blind, The National Association of the Deaf, The National Paraplegic Foundation, Paralyzed Veterans of America, The Center for Independence at Berkeley, and a variety of disabled student programs at colleges and universities.

Resultant demonstrations, in ten cities across the nation, were generally failures except for the one in San Francisco that was organized and directed at the Berkeley Center for Independence and which ultimately became the nucleus of a national social movement and an independent living philosophy that ultimately resulted in the Section 504 regulations being signed.

I was not a part of this broad social movement that began in the 70s. I had spent my life fighting the same battles, but on a personal level. I was familiar with all of the inequities that were now beginning to be addressed on a national level. I was so concentrated, however, on perceiving myself, although I knew better, as a non-handicapped person, that although I had a peripheral awareness of the new movement that was taking place, I had no contact with it, knew none of its participants, and had no experience, or motivation at the age of 50, for becoming an activist. Nevertheless, I was aware that the legislation in the pipeline would pose serious problems for a large university that, in the closing days of its multi-year, multi-campus, multi-million dollar construction and expansion project, had never seriously considered handicapped access. My doctoral dissertation would address that problem.

With nothing further to lose at the University and my termination almost upon me, I wrote a stinging response memorandum to the Vice Chancellor's plan noting with unchecked sarcasm the oversight of new federal legislation that, to any higher education official should be a predominant consideration of any future planning. I was summoned to the office of one of the Chancellor's close advisors who happened to be a friendly colleague. "That's quite a memo you wrote. Are your facts correct?"

"Yes they are and there's a lot I left out."

A wide grin spread across the face of the advisor, he chuckled and shook his head. " You know it's raising a lot of fuss? It's wonderful." I took the occasion to respond, not without a bit of unrepressed sarcasm, "Well you can add to that the fact that the University is firing the only person on its Central staff who is severely disabled, and the only staff member who is working on or knows anything about this problem." A couple of months following my departure from the University, the same colleague called me to invite me to serve as a resource person at a University conference on disabilities and higher education at the Rensselaerville Conference Center.

17

My Dream Job

Since completion of my dissertation was so near, Barbara and I decided the wisest action might be to concentrate on finishing it while I searched for work. I pursued my studies with renewed energy. A month after leaving the University I had a call from Donald Schein, the general manager of WMHT-TV in Schenectady. "Would you be interested in writing a funding proposal?"

"Of course." A proposal for a film entitled "Molders of Troy" about the historical significance of how competing ethnic and class interests had shaped the 19th century industrial city of Troy, NY had been brought to WMHT by a social historian and a recognized filmmaker with the request that WMHT endorse the project and become the fiscal administrator should it be funded. WMHT, in exchange for a fifteen percent administrative fee, a usual arrangement in such instances, agreed and the proposal had been submitted to the National Endowment for the Humanities. Reviews of the proposal were mixed, but it was thought that if rewritten it might have a good chance to be funded. The assignment: rewrite the proposal. The fee; $500.

I spent a couple afternoons with the original proposal writer, and spent a few days on the rewrite. The proposal was resubmitted and several months later a $300,000 grant was awarded to WMHT. The money earned so soon after my dismissal was welcome, but the "Gods of Ill Will" had not yet finished their work, and I was caught in the crossfire as they dispensed their wrath.

In anticipation of some difficult days ahead, we placed our boat up for sale and were fortunate to find a buyer. The sale provided a boost to our deficit financing situation. On the academic front however, dark clouds gathered. My academic advisor, a delightful, elderly man, expert in counseling his advisees how to clear doctoral hurdles, was diagnosed with a particularly aggressive form of cancer. He was immediately hospitalized and in two months was gone. Arranging for a new advisor was not easy and I considered myself fortunate in being accepted by another faculty member who, in addition to his full-time academic responsibilities, operated an extremely busy and profitable consulting business that concentrated on exploratory and evaluative studies. With my new advisor's assistance, I set to work developing my statistical plan. I found it a particularly difficult task. Statistics was my Achilles heel. I wished for my father's or brother's acuity in matters mathematical, but with concentrated and repeated studying, together with my advisor's coaching and direction, I was ready for the important meeting with faculty in early spring that would result in formal approval of my statistical study. Once my statistical plan was approved, I could proceed with the study and complete the dissertation. It was the practice of the faculty to conduct these meetings in both the spring and fall semesters to facilitate the needs of doctoral candidates, but changes were afoot in the department and the spring meeting was abruptly canceled.

The death of my advisor and the retirement of two other faculty members had resulted in the hiring of three new faculty members who, once aboard, had initiated a coup d'etat that changed the department's power structure and rules of procedure. Young Turks were now in charge and my advisor was not one of them. They were examining the department's entire structure and had declared a moratorium on doctoral procedures. They would plan the faculty meeting for the fall. Without faculty approval, I could not conduct my study and must now wait until the fall meeting to be approved. As I was now unemployed and receiving unemployment compensation, shelving the dissertation until the fall constituted an unexpected hardship. I sought out the department head and pleaded that my statistical design be evaluated during the spring so I could get on with my study and my life, unfortunately to no avail. And that was not the end of a difficult turn of events.

During the summer, my new advisor received the devastating news that his nineteen-year-old son had lost his life in a motorcycle accident somewhere in the West. Caught between his grief at the loss of his son, the burden of his contracted, extra curricula consultant services, and the new pressures on his academic life brought about by departmental procedural changes, his academic activities were severely affected. He was frequently unavailable, and when available, had difficulty concentrating on the matters at hand.

The summer passed and the pile of job rejection letters grew and it was finally time for the faculty meeting for approval of my statistical design. The meeting was a disaster. I was attacked from all sides. I was harshly informed that my exploratory study design was unacceptable and that it must be a comparative study. I couldn't believe what was happening. I had worked on the design with the counsel and approval of my advisor. I had spent months fine-tuning what I had been advised was a good design and now it was not only being torn apart but also dismissed. I felt betrayed. I argued to no avail that I was applying for an Ed.D, not a Ph.D. My advisor, who had counseled me in the design of the exploratory study, had lost his leverage in the changed power structure of the department. He sat quietly and did not come to my defense. I was distraught at the outcome and furious with my advisor. There was no way I could revise my plan and regenerate the study. I had already been unemployed for nine months and the grant was already gone, used for living expenses. I discussed the matter with Barbara, who had been able to do some occasional substitute nursing and teaching in the Schenectady Schools, and as usual she told me that whatever I decided, we would work it out.

My decision was that it was time to cut my losses, forget the doctorate, and concentrate on finding employment. It was only much later that the thought occurred to me that perhaps I had been only a pawn and the real person who had been under attack was my advisor. Although I had given some thought to suing the University for my job in the context of the new federal legislation for the handicapped; it never occurred to me to attempt to utilize my connections in the Central Administration to apply leverage on the young Turks.

The loss of what I had thought was a reasonably secure job, following the new Chancellor's reorganization that had preceded it, gave me great concern. I had not been terminated because I had failed to meet the obligations and responsibilities of the job. Indeed, just five months previously I had been given a pay raise and told by the Vice Chancellor that my raise was one of only a few in the office and had been awarded on merit. No, I had been terminated simply because my position was not among those included in the required complement of positions in the office of the Vice Chancellor. Each of those positions was an item in the annual budget that was justified by the specific duties necessary to permit the office to function. Unfortunately, my job was a surplus position remaining from an activity and department that had been discontinued. The work I did was peripheral to the University's academic programs, the main thrust of the Vice Chancellor's office, and surplus positions were highly vulnerable in the budget cuts.

Now that the programs I had designed were operational, any number of people could administer them; my absence would put the office at no disadvantage. Indeed, it was arranged for the young woman whom I had hired as an assistant to do that job. I was fifty years old and as I looked back on my professional life I could not ignore the fact that this latest event was not unique. It was part of a pattern. Budget cuts or realignment of funds had been significant factors in my leaving WQED, Captioned Films, and now SUNY. At the State Education Department I had indeed occupied a line item position, and was secure for life, but I found the work demeaning and without challenge and many professional acquaintances across the country agreed with me. I did not like being a bureaucrat, which was what I had become, and rather than continue to do what I considered meaningless work, I accepted a job in Washington. Had that been a mistake? I had a need to do something, anything, that was meaningful and despite the difficulty I had experienced in my attempts to obtain security and professional recognition, I was a risk taker. I had assumed that having attained a permanent job in a large organization, I would be able to continue to pursue my career with that kind of security. I believed I had something to contribute and so explored areas where I believed there would be opportunity. Captioned Films had sought me out and at USOE, I again had a permanent job safe from budget cuts. Line item staff positions such as the one I occupied were secure, but unfortunately, program funding was not, and I found myself with a secure position, and no work. I could have remained at USOE for the rest of my life, enjoying the benefits of federal employment, but once again, there was no challenge for the skills and talents I had to offer. The pattern of my experience haunted me. Was I simply incompetent? Certainly in many ways I must have been like the drummer boy in the parade who is out of step with the rest of the brigade and doesn't know it. I recognized that my entire life was out of phase with my contemporaries. When they were learning the social skills consistent with emerging man and womanhood, I was not part of the experience. It took me a long time to learn them. Later, when my friends were marrying and producing families, I had still not learned those skills or had the experiences others had had while still teens and young adults. And when I had finally found my métier, in television production, my lack of sophistication and political savvy had ended my progress. Despite my various accomplishments, my employment invariably involved special projects or part-time assignments. In these various temporary and part-time experiences I had learned the functional aspects of my desired profession, and despite the fact that in the aggregate they constituted a series of successes, my resume lacked the important ingredient of regular, consistent, institutional employment. Within the space of a few years, what once were my unique capabilities as an "early bird," lost their value as increasing numbers of younger people became adept at what I could do. Since these younger professionals held permanent jobs in the newly emerging industry, they earned the cachet that went with their permanent line-item positions and led to more responsible positions in administrative and creative areas.

How much my late blooming as a result of disabilities affected my subsequent development is a matter for conjecture. It was only at the beginning of my later years that I realized that to a considerable extent, as crucial as the physical disabilities that had complicated my life and created difficulties had been, it was the actual persona, the character and personality, tenacious drive, intrepid independence and social-political naiveté molded by the disabilities and difficulties, that had ultimately become my greatest disability.

Again the pile of job rejections grew. I was at this juncture competing with much younger men and women for jobs in what had now become Public Television. I signed up for unemployment compensation and each week visited the unemployment office, stood in line and answered the required questions, "Did you look for work this week? Have you searched the posted job openings lists? Have you used the computer program? Are you ready to work if you find a job?" It was the most humiliating experience to which I had ever been subjected. On one occasion, when Barbara had been called to work as a substitute teacher, I took my son with me to the unemployment office and was told by the unsympathetic clerk, "We can't pay you this week. You're not ready to work. You have a child with you!" even though there were women present in similar circumstances. That week we went without an unemployment check.

The months slipped by, a year passed. In the summer of 1977, after being unemployed for eighteen months, I received another call from WMHT. "Would you be interested in doing some consulting work for the Johnstown- Gloversville Chamber of Commerce?" My answer was obvious and I arranged to meet with the principal developer of a proposed project, Daniel Ben Schmuel, artist, sculptor, designer and new owner of the Johnstown Hotel. At a luncheon meeting, Ben Schmuel laid out the idea.

The Johnstown/Gloversville area, famous at the turn of the century for its tanning and leather mills, had come on hard times. There was little left of this industry in the area except for a few small tanners and leather fabricators, and the St. Thomas factory. Headed by local millionaire William St. Thomas, the factory still conducted a brisk trade manufacturing men's and women's gloves and wallets for better department stores across the country. The area was off the beaten track. Vacationers heading to the Lake George/Champlain area from the west, who had historically traveled through the Johnston/Gloversville area, now followed the New York State Thruway to Albany and took the new Northway in order to arrive at vacation areas in northeastern New York.

Ben Schmuel wanted to create a reason for people to come to his area. He professed that as a sculptor, he was in touch with well-known sculptors all over the world. His proposed project was the Fulton County Sculpture Symposium, patterned after the Spoleto Sculpture Symposium that was first held in Italy in 1962. A committee of recognized sculptors would invite twenty sculptors from around the world to live in the community for a period of time while creating their works.

During the period of sculptor residency, a varied program of arts activities, including seminars, lectures, demonstrations, courses and other arts-related activities, would be offered providing opportunity for public participation in the Symposium. The works created in the Symposium would be displayed in a permanent collection housed in a specially designed sculpture garden.

This process would be repeated for several years and the resultant sculpture park would become a tourist attraction. The area would develop as a new artist community that would be certain, as Daniel Ben Schmuel put it, to attract other artists, painters, dancers, potters, weavers etc. Ben Schmuel, whose own artistic talents and arrival in Johnstown had been sponsored by a local resident, had presented the idea to the Chamber of Commerce and the Chamber had formed a committee to move the project forward. What they needed was someone who could organize and implement the design, structure and operation of the project and write a formal proposal. "Would I be interested in doing it?"

I was hired for a three-month period to give the idea form and organize the project. I met with the President of the Chamber of Commerce and the organizing committee of six local businessmen and a woman realtor. My first questions were probes to learn, as best I could as an outsider, whether all of the critical power bases in the area were in accord and supportive of the proposed project. I was assured they were. In the next several weeks, in association and consultation with various members of the committee, I identified the major elements, sequenced the course of events, constructed a time line, located an appropriate site for the sculpture garden, developed a preliminary budget, and identified a number of potential funding agencies to be contacted. I advised them of the necessity, in order to justify a substantial grant, of having a reasonable percentage of the proposed total cost of the project pledged by the local community and businesses to demonstrate, to a potential funding agency, the community's dedication to the effort. The Chamber committee understood and accepted the recommendations. The next step was to identify the local community leader who would chair that effort and set an example by pledging a significant amount of money. It was decided that William St. Thomas was without question that key figure. An appointment was set for the President of the Chamber and me to meet with Mr. St. Thomas to enlist his cooperation as an active supporter and fundraiser. I had a nagging thought that if Mr. St. Thomas was so important, perhaps he should have been a member of the organizing commit-tee? I remembered how I had enticed the government training directors in Washington to buy into the secretarial training project by convincing them it was their idea. As an outsider, however, I lacked the time and the means to learn the confidential nature of the local political and social scene; I had to rely on the wisdom of the local leaders for whom I was working. Unfortunately, their wis-dom was severely flawed.

Mr. St. Thomas was indeed the informal and popular leader of the community and possessed tremendous influence. Without his stamp of approval, any large local endeavor could not succeed, and in this instance he had been neither consulted nor included as an initial contributor to the project development. In addition, he was a dedicated amateur musician active in local orchestral groups, and for reasons that were never discussed, he was not enamored of Daniel Ben Schmuel. Being unaware of Mr. St. Thomas' interests and dislikes, it was an abrupt surprise, to both the Chamber Presi-dent and myself, after we had presented the case for the Sculpture Symposium, to have St. Thomas ignore the primary purpose of the proposed enterprise, an effort to improve the economic well being of the local area, and hear him say, "A sculpture garden? Do we need a sculpture garden? What I'd like to see is a good quality music hall where we could present high quality musical performances."

To say I was dumfounded would be an understatement. I avoided looking at the Chamber's President who was aware that a tremendous mistake had been made and was now awkwardly and hastily taking his leave. I murmured a quick "Pleased to have met you" to St. Thomas and followed. It was unbelievable. How could all of these local businessmen have been so unknowing? No one had even questioned St. Thomas' support. They had taken him for granted, and he was not someone whom one took for granted. St. Thomas was obviously the single most powerful man in the community and he had been ignored until too late. Moreover, he was not a man who was going to support someone else's proposal even if it were good for the community, and particularly if he had no liking for its creator. The project was doomed. It would never see the light of day. Critical political mistakes, which I had been powerless to prevent, and the organizers of the project too unknow-ing to recognize, had been made, and I had witnessed the payoff.

••

For twenty-two months we lived in fear of losing everything as our meager savings dwindled and we lived like church mice. During this time we did not inform either my mother or Barbara's parents of our situation. There was little they could have done and there was no point burdening them with worry. Even the children, Jessica now eight and Jared, four, when they spoke by phone or saw their grandparents, did not divulge the nature of their father's unemployment, just as they never discussed his disability with nonfamily. They appeared to possess an unusual ability to avoid such matters.

Our stringent living had diminished our savings to the breaking point; our two used cars were worn out and in need of repair. I had done numerous repairs myself, scraping to buy the parts: brake linings and calipers, spark plugs, timing chain, muffler, even a replacement fender. Then once again Don Schein called. There was a new government program that would pay most of the salary of a new employee for one year and if I were interested, we might explore how we might take mutual advantage of it.

On two previous occasions, he had offered me jobs, but there was something about the man that put me off. Having conducted close liaison with him while in the State Education Department and having enjoyed a good professional relationship with him, I had shied away from working for him. Physically, barely five feet tall, soft spoken and friendly, but with a calculating manner, He seemed always to concentrate on the downside of every situation, particularly fiscal ones. I likened him to a small town haberdashery proprietor operating the town's only clothing store who was reluctant to take a chance on stocking a new line of clothes. His approach appeared to concentrate almost wholly on the financial aspect of operations rather than on any intellectual or aesthetic aspects of the medium. In retrospect, I cannot remember his ever becoming enthused about new programming in other than fiscal terms. His questions were only, "What will it cost?" and "How much will we make on it?" And while he would give lip service to any outsider who was promoting a new program idea, agreeing and complimenting what he perceived as the promoter's view of the intrinsic values of the project being presented, in private he would immediately revert to his two important questions. I perceived him, in a sense, as a disabled person, disabled by his small physical stature and his inability to reason intellectually or be affected emotionally; one who was unable to understand television programming except in terms of the balance sheet. In addition, I had the impression that he preyed on people's weaknesses and disadvantages and had gained a reputation for hiring people who were down on their luck, offering salaries far lower than the person, in a reasonable marketplace, could have normally expected. His personality was perhaps better fitted for commercial broadcasting, but he had seen his opportunity when he had moved into Schenectady, wrested control of the then budding station enterprise from the person who had begun it, and ensconced himself in what was now public broadcasting. With native shrewdness and balance sheet approach, he had parlayed a few inoperable donated television cameras into a healthy small broadcast facility and he had done it penuriously with only lip service to the idealistic reasons for which educational and then public television had been brought into existence.

I had been pleased to be able to work for the State Education Department and United States Office of Education instead of accepting his job offers. Even though it was a broadcast station and I wanted to again work in broadcasting, hopefully creating programs, I had been very hesitant about what the future might offer at WMHT. I didn't really want to work for him despite the fact that he had always maintained a professionally friendly attitude toward me. I had the feeling that my artistic and intellectual approach to television programming might not fare well over time. Nevertheless, I had no other options and my need for income was critical.

On the basis of my success at having rewritten the project proposal that was subsequently funded by the National Endowment for the Humanities, he decided to offer me a newly created position of Director of Program Development at $1,000 less than I had been making at the State University, fifty percent of which would be paid by the government grant. My prime function would be to create program ideas and write production proposals that could be funded.

I quickly learned that at best, this would be a difficult task in an organization whose general manager and president was reluctant to invest a reasonable proportion of anticipated program costs in order to justify matching funds from government and philanthropic funding agencies on the order of 1-1, 2-1, or even 3-1. The businessmen in the Johnston/Gloversville Chamber of Commerce had immediately recognized the importance of this requirement, but my new boss was reluctant to dedicate even ten percent of projected program cost and expected reimbursement for all operational costs that the station would normally incur even if it produced no programs at all. To put it succinctly, he was inordinately "tight with a buck," and motivated only by profit. He was also preoccupied with the underlying reasons for anybody's actions. His natural shrewdness compelled him to best each suspected adversary. At the same time he was habitually indecisive, always wanting to know more before making a decision. Perhaps the best clue to his character was a story he told unwittingly about himself. When a youngster in the Boston vicinity, his father had been an itinerant sidewalk photographer. During the summers he and his brother, who later became a successful film producer in Hollywood, would sometimes accompany their father as he worked on the beaches taking photographs and attempting to sell the prints. On one such occasion the two boys were exploring the beach and came upon another boy who was carrying a toy sailboat. "What is it?" He asked the boy. "A model sailboat." The boy replied. "Do you want it?" And while he paused to ask, "You mean it?" his brother said, "I'll take it" and did.

Proposal after proposal was turned down for lack of his willingness to invest in the station's own ideas, but in the process a strange thing happened. Because of my experience at the state and federal level, he consulted me with increasingly frequency on matters of production, particularly on the project for which I had rewritten the proposal. Production on that project had not yet begun and all progress was tied up in a disagreement about the contract that was necessary between the station, the filmmaker, and the academic consultant who had initiated the project. My boss walked into my office one day particularly upset. "If they don't sign this damned contract, I'm going to send the money back to the NEH." I could see that the man was sufficiently provoked at not getting his way as to actually carry out his threat. He was so reluctant to give up what he believed to be his prerogatives in the contract that he was willing to cancel the project rather than, as he perceived it, submit to being robbed. His perception of the problem was exclusively fiscal. "That would be a bad idea," I said, "That project is the first big one you've had funded and it was funded by a large federal agency that has a lot of money. If you give it back you'll be telling them that you are incapable of doing what they expect you to do and you'll never get another penny from federal agencies for production. Furthermore, if you turn it back, I might just as well begin to look for another job because once you do that I'll be dead in the water. I won't be able to get funds anywhere." Still exasperated, he paused for a moment as the full meaning of what I had said sunk in. "Then why don't you take it over and see if you can get it moving?"

I called the widely experienced and respected lawyer in New York City, who handled the station's legal affairs. "I've been asked to straighten out this contract dispute and see if we can get the project rolling. Can you please tell me exactly what provisions the station must have in the contract?" The lawyer's initial response was, "Why the hell are you getting yourself involved in this? It stinks. Even if you can straighten it out nobody's ever going to thank you for it. Do you have to do it? Why are you bothering?" To my mind $300,000 was not something to let slide. I thought it was a good project, I had a vested interest and I was hoping to generate more such projects. After some further discussion, he outlined what he considered the bottom line and then gave me what he recommended as the station's initial negotiating position. I called the filmmaker, who had a reputation for hard bargaining on film production contracts and explained that I had been asked to bring the two parties together. I asked him the same question. "What do you need to have in the contract?" He explained that the problem involved clarification of credits and also how and when money could be transferred to him on a regular basis so he could pay expenses as the filming and editing progressed. The primary disagreement lay in the fact that the filmmaker needed to have significant amounts of money in order to facilitate the filming and my boss, who trusted no one, did not want to transfer any money until the filming was done. I stated the station's position that the lawyer had provided. "If we can work out your needs," I asked, "do you think we can come together on the station's?" The possibility pleased him. "I think so," he said, "it's worth a discussion. I want to get this thing moving." Again I called the lawyer to report. "Do you think you can bring this together ?" He wanted official assurance. "What does your boss say about it?"

"I haven't told him yet, but I'll do that now and have him call you."

A date was set for all the principals to discuss the contract dispute the following week in New York and the lawyer put on the kind of performance for which he was well known in legal public television circles. With only occasional references to the documents, he verbally outlined the contract point by point, and at each objection, he negotiated the point back and forth between the parties until agreement was reached, before going on to the next item. At the end of a two-hour session, he had agreement on a contract that all parties were willing to sign and in quick order had copies reproduced for signing. The project was a go. His prediction was absolutely correct; nobody ever thanked me.

Although I wasn't aware of it, word of my success quickly filtered through the station's grapevine and there was a constant stream of people coming in and out of my office, discussing matters with me that were not within my purview. Everyone was seeking me out. On a particularly busy day, my secretary came in chuckling, "You are apparently the fair haired boy in this place. It seems everyone thinks you have the inside track to the boss and they're all trying to get you to act on their behalf." It surprised me. I was embarrassed to realize that I wasn't sufficiently astute to have figured that out on my own, but now that it had been pointed out to me, I recognized the worth of her observation. I had inadvertently and unconsciously built a power base within the station and not recognized it. Moreover, now that it had been brought to my attention, I had no idea of how to use it and make it grow. I wasn't much of a politician. My only ambition was to create fine programming and my interests were so intently focused on that process that I gave too little notice to the political environment that surrounded me. In previous situations where I had been empowered to facilitate or implement a project, I had functioned well within the limitations of that authority, but had never been able to expand my power base or to generate one when it was not given to me, either for parlaying situations or finding jobs.

On the heels of my success, I continuously cast about for new ideas for programs or series that could generate grants and be distributed nationally and one day I remembered my old friend and advisor, Charles Siepmann. I outlined a discussion program in which Charles would be surrounded by two or three guests whom he had invited—with his reputation he would be able to induce anyone in the country to participate—and they would discuss a topic that Charles would select. Charles would then expertly elicit their respective opinions and suggestions while holding forth as he saw fit with his own. The shows would focus on national personalities, be a simple production with most of the costs being guest travel and accommodations, and without question the series would be carried by every Public Television station in the country. It could continue indefinitely. I wrote a proposal outline and discussed it with my boss and as I expected, it appealed to him.

I called Charles, who had retired from New York University and was spending his time in his old farmhouse home in the small town of New Fane, Vermont, told him I wanted to visit and he welcomed me. It was summer, and we sat in lawn chairs on the grass while I presented my idea. He listened carefully as I emphasized that the programs would be his to determine the subjects and the guests, and the conversations could go wherever he chose to take them. He had a knowing look as he focused his piercing gaze on me, and he nodded and agreed that, "It might be fun." He asked about my job and well being and I related my recent years of stress and unemployment and he nodded in understanding and asked me, "And when nobody would hire you, did you begin to lose faith in yourself?" I admitted that I had and he nodded again and looking directly at me, replied, "Yes, that is inevitable, and that's exactly how I felt when I first came to this country. Nobody would give me the time of day and I was very depressed and discouraged." I was astounded. This man, sitting here with me on the lawn, without doubt the most learned and accomplished man I had ever met, was telling me he had had the same experience that I had just recently endured. "Yes," he continued, it is devastating." And we talked, for a while about how we had handled our respective situations. As the afternoon ended, and I took my leave, he thanked me for my interest, repeated that it sounded like a good idea, and asked for time to give it some thought. I was delighted.

A couple weeks later I heard from Charles, and to my great disappointment he told me that although he had been sorely tempted, he felt that he no longer had the energy that such an undertaking would require, and he shared with me a private secret. "As you know," he said, "for many years, as a promoter of educational television, I have made television appearances and spoken publicly in venues all over the country, and I have rarely refused an invitation, but each time, almost without exception, I have suffered an uncontrollable stage fright that prevented my eating and invariably resulted in physical distress. I have said what I have to say, and to repeat it has no purpose."

My tenure at the station ended at the end of 1984 and in March of '85 Charles died of a heart attack. In September, a memorial service was held at the Brookline Church in Brookline, VT following which Siepmann's wife, Jane, invited former students and friends to their home in New Fane where personal eulogies were given by Reverend William Sloane Coffin and John Houseman, both close friends. In London a similar memorial featured Alastair Cooke, another close friend, as eulogist. As I remembered my last conversation with Charles, I thought what a wonderful television series that might have been.

I experienced an almost constant sense that there was some barrier that prevented me from accumulating power, from finessing various small successes into more meaningful ones. In my psyche, perhaps conditioned by my disabilities, there had always been an indefinable point beyond which I dared not go. It was perhaps a psychological counterpart of the physical limitations that constrained my life. To dare to go beyond them would invite disaster and I remember numerous times when, given the choice of two risk-laden physical or professional options, I had taken the less risky one, frequently with the thought that "they" might not permit me, as a disabled person, to fully exercise my capabilities or acumen. Despite my outward appearance of indomitable independence, my physical inadequacies coupled with my early life experiences had undoubtedly imprinted on my psyche and prevented self-confidence from realizing its full potential. Despite my ability to defend myself aggressively when threatened, my personality did not include inherent feral aggressiveness or the gregarious offense of the "What Makes Sammy Run" would-be executive.

As the months went by, the film project began under the skillful direction of the filmmaker who, as the production progressed, played a running game of hide and seek with the Teamsters' Union that was attempting to coerce him into signing a union contract to utilize more vehicles than the production required. They were consistently one step behind in finding the locations where he was filming. Each day I received calls from the union representatives, sometimes with veiled threats as to how pressure might be exerted on the station and each time I would tell them that the station had no involvement with the production schedule and that the director was working under contract and in full charge of the production.

Spring and fall fund raising campaigns lasted for days as various station personnel and community leaders pleaded with listeners to send in their memberships in varying amounts in order to support the ongoing program service. The general manager was a superb pitchman of the doomsday variety. He called viewers' attention to the cost of each of the most popular program series and threatened that if there were insufficient support forthcoming it would be necessary to cut one or several of them. In actuality the program cost to insure a full broadcast schedule was far less than stated, and year by year the excess was added to the station's savings account until the day, several years after my tenure had ended, it became public knowledge that the "poor" station, which pleaded so eloquently for funds to enable it to continue to broadcast popular programming, had, in the 80s, actually accumulated a $4,000,000 surplus and had been paying its chief executive almost $100,000, per year, two facts which ultimately ended the reign of the general manager under questionable circumstances.

I became increasingly involved with the station's program production. Very small supporting grants from local agencies made a number of local programs possible and I was called upon for assistance, sometimes designing settings, writing scripts and eventually producing.

I was delighted to be back in a broadcast station and in the middle of the production activity that I loved and knew intimately. My title was changed to Director of Television Activity, which did not relieve me of the responsibility of writing proposals and looking for funding, but added the responsibility of overseeing all of the station's television production. I now administered a staff of some 20 persons: producers, directors, cameramen, technical directors and performers and became the station's executive producer. It was the job I had dreamed about, a job that utilized all of the skills I had developed over the years, one that called upon my imagination, creativity and theatrical skills, and it had happened almost by coincidence. It was a job that was the epitome of that for which I had so long searched and desired. Yet there was a flaw, and as the days flew by, it became a significant one.

All members of my staff were full-time employees. In addition, the station employed an equal number of engineers to operate the hundreds of thousands of dollars of technical equipment, a fully equipped studio and a remote truck, but none of it was permitted to be used to create new programming unless and until new dollars were available to pay for what was called production cost. For days at a time, staff did make-work tasks and were paid regular salaries when, for only the additional price of two rolls of videotape, they could have produced a new live show or a taped program. I tried mightily to convince my boss that the unused labor pool was an asset that should be utilized for developing new programming, that the more we produced, the better the chance that one of them could generate a sponsor or, when fully developed, be sold to the PBS network. Other stations had developed the practice of creating local shows, running them for a season while they fine-tuned them, and then selling them to PBS. "Wall Street Week," originally produced in Maryland, "This Old House" from Boston, and numerous other programs had begun as local, station-under-written programs and when fine-tuned and perfected, became national PBS sponsored offerings. Fred Roger's *Children's Corner*, after a full year at WQED as a local program, was aired on the NBC network as the summer replacement for the *Jerry Mahoney Show*. My boss could not visualize that staff and equipment was an investment when it produced shows, and an expense when it lay idle. He saw it only as a cost when used, a cost for which somebody else should pay. Seasonal schedules were therefore the same kinds of talking head shows, grudgingly produced with bare-bones budgets. At the same time, numerous potential network programs went untried. It was extremely difficult to produce a new idea, with a new face, or a new guest. The only exception to this pattern had been the daily New York State news show *Inside Albany*, winner of a Peabody Award, which WMHT had originated a few years previously, primarily because of its location in the Capital District, and then only because the other stations in the New York Network had agreed to share the production cost of the show. The fact that others underwrote this show in large part from the beginning was indeed a compliment to the boss' shrewd business sense, but the concept calcified in his mind and became the only model he was willing to accept. When new shows were initiated, budgets for making them look professional: sets, artwork, costumes, lighting, were extremely limited, and rehearsal time was grudgingly given. The prevailing idea was that all that was needed was a host who would run the show on camera, and a director who could get all the shots. The results were a series of different programs that all looked the same. Unless content alone captured the viewers' fancy there was nothing to keep them from switching channels. I was now executive producer of these programs and I worked hard with my staff to try to make each of them look interesting and different. The staff was aware of the problem and they made every effort to improve the shows. I was forced inevitably into an adversarial position with my boss, who sometimes accused me of wasting station funds and asked if I would spend my own money on such and such a program. I was unable to bring him to an understanding of how much of the station's resources were being wasted by going unused. Even bringing all my creative effort and that of my staff's to bear, it was difficult to create interesting, high quality programming. And when we did manage to be successful, when we created a good looking show which had the earmarks of professional quality, he would sarcastically inquire, "What did that cost?" On one such occasion, when the producer and talent together managed to borrow furniture and set dressings to create a fashionable set for a senior citizens' program, his reaction was, "It was opulent." which was by way of saying that it probably was unnecessarily costly. I persisted in my efforts to improve and bring variety to the local programs and slowly the quality began to improve.

Saratoga Springs, which functioned most of the year as a bedroom community for the State Capital in Albany, blossomed each spring as a tourist attraction and during the racing season from late July through August, it was the Mecca for racing fans from near and far. Just prior to the beginning of the racing season, the enormous summer homes, many built during the middle of the 19th and the early 20th centuries, after lying empty and locked up during the fall, winter and spring months, suddenly boasted new awnings, endless plantings of multicolored flowers, sparkling clean windows and trimmed lawns in anticipation of their wealthy owners' arrivals for the racing season. I had an idea that behind the annual blossoming was a story that could support a documentary that might appeal to a wide audience. I set about to produce it and was able to find a small amount of money which would permit hiring a local cinematographer to videotape and edit the show. I needed to learn more about whose houses were being spruced up and their social plans for the season. I contacted Mrs. Cornelius Vanderbilt (Mary Lou) Whitney, wife of multimillionaire "Sonny" Whitney, and Saratoga's most visible socialite. The Whitney's were year round residents of Saratoga and thus were not involved in the "blossoming" ritual, but, Mrs. Whitney suggested, via her social secretary, that if I was interested, she would lead my camera crew through her summer activities including the preparation for the highlight of the social season, the Whitney Ball at the historic Canfield Casino. It wasn't the show I had in mind, but it was an offer I couldn't refuse, and so I hired Michael Martin, a local independent filmmaker, to follow Mary Lou to the Racing Museum, the Performing Arts Center, the Saratoga Racetrack, the Museum of Dance, the horse owners' restaurant at the track, at her home preparing for a dinner party, and at the preparation for her ball at the Casino.

Mary Lou was a cooperative and generous hostess and a fine on-camera personage. Off camera, she radiated strength and directness, displaying a real estate agent's license that she kept current, joking, "Well, you never know?" She openly discussed many aspects of her life, her daughter's pending marriage, Sonny's love for fishing and picnicking, their racing stable, how she cleaned Sonny's fish at their home in the Adirondacks and her relationship with Gloria Vanderbilt. Unfortunately, when she appeared on camera, the candid Mary Lou who had related these intimate aspects of her life was replaced by the public Mary Lou, the Grande Dame of Saratoga who discoursed at length on inconsequential matters in a decidedly patronizing noblesse oblige manner which ultimately presented her at a disadvantage. It was indeed, a harsh glimpse at the persona of an extremely wealthy woman who was out of touch with the world of those who served her. I was ready to scrap the effort. I attempted to prevent airing the finished piece because I thought that Mrs. Whitney had, unknowingly, presented herself unwisely, and despite Michael Martin's best efforts, the show ended up being a hatchet job. It served no purpose to embarrass and alienate this influential, cooperative person, and airing it would result in bad public relations. I was overruled; my boss decided that the money had been spent so the show would be aired. When it was, the telephone switch-board lit up with calls from Saratoga chastising the station for presenting such an unflattering view of their most famous and generous resident and the PBS network scheduling office, although they thought the show was a devastating character study, declined to distribute it fearing repercussions.

While reluctant to invest in new local programming, my boss was always eager to explore possibilities for creating a "network" program that PBS would ultimately underwrite. In addition to my continued attempts to improve local programming in the face of his resistance, I was constantly working on funding proposals for several new programs, among them a documentary of the evolution of the amusement park, a series which addressed the difficulties of the disabled, and a series of programs which would recreate the major choreographic successes of Pearl Primus.

Following my meeting with Percy Borde in Binghamton two years previously, I stayed in touch with Percy and Pearl while I searched for a way to implement our cooperative ideas and subsequently submitted a proposal to the National Endowment for the Arts for a small development grant that had been awarded. With the funds it was possible to send a two man videotape crew to tape a special performance of Pearl's troupe at Riverside Church in New York City as a reference for the program I planned to eventually produce. I needed to find a director and called Emile Ardolino, the WNET director of all New York City Ballet television performances who recommended a former dancer, now director, Gardiner Compton. Compton, I learned, had directed a number of Jerome Robbins films plus several other films featuring recognized dancers. He was familiar with Pearl Primus' work and intrigued with the project. He agreed to meet the film crew at the church and direct their efforts. The filming went well and a month later Pearl called to invite me to come to New York to see her new dance production which was to be staged in a small theater on the west side of Greenwich Village. The theater was a small house with steep grandstand type seating and a narrow proscenium that limited large movements. Pearl's staging and choreography overcame the physical limitations of the proscenium, however, and the program was exciting and colorful. A few weeks later I was shocked and saddened to learn that Percy, after exiting the stage following the performance of a physically demanding number, had suffered a heart attack and died.

The evening funeral services were held at a small church in Harlem. Barbara was a native New Yorker, and while working on her master's degree, had attended meetings of Narcotics Anonymous in East Harlem for several months as part of a research project. I had been initially fitted with my prostheses a few years earlier on 125th street in Harlem, but neither of us was familiar with the area where the church was located, and there had been much civil unrest in Harlem in the intervening years. It was with some feelings of disquietude therefore, as white strangers in a black land, that we made our way to the church where our uneasy feelings were forgotten in the warmth of the attendees, the beautiful singing, and the eloquent eulogy given by the actor, Ozzie Davis, a close friend of Percy's.

Two venues in Schenectady's local area offered possibilities for potential network shows; Proctor's theater, a restored relic of the heyday of the Proctor theater circuit, operated as a non-profit which presented a full winter schedule of music, dance and drama programs and the Saratoga Performing Arts Center, in nearby Saratoga Springs which offered a star studded schedule of summer performances. Proctors presented Broadway road show productions, individual singers and instrumentalists, and national and ethnic music and dance troupes. PBS was by this time in the business of contracting with major stations such as Pittsburgh, New York, Boston, Chicago and Los Angeles to produce high visibility shows featuring the most popular entertainers of the day that would be used as feature attractions to generate station memberships during fund raising drives. It was not usual for a small station to produce one of these shows. Nevertheless, it was WMHT's intention to produce one or more of these programs through its local venues. A lunch was arranged with Herb Chesbrough, Executive Director of SPAC, to open a series of discussions. I was asked to follow it up

and develop the idea. I had never met Herb, but knew him by reputation to be a knowledgeable, capable administrator whose venue
was one of the most successful summer theaters in the East and
who managed with great expertise and finesse, a board of directors
that was most prestigious. Herb dealt regularly with the Philadelphia Symphony, the New York City Ballet, and a full spectrum of
top-notch artists. He knew what could and could not be done in his
theater, what it would cost, and how to go about it.

My meeting with Herb was cryptic and informative. "Look",
said Herb, "I'm going to be frank with you. I know that the idea
of WMHT producing a television program here is new to you, but
it's not new to me. On a number of occasions your boss has
advanced the idea that we should cooperatively videotape this or
that show that I've booked and I've always been cooperative. I've
taken the trouble to discuss the possibilities with artist's agents
and a few times even arrived at reasonable packaging and rights
agreements only to have him pull out for one reason or another,
usually because he didn't see any money coming to him up front.
And that's not a realistic expectation. If we produce it, we'll have
to pay for the production before we can sell it. If it's possible to
sell it before the production that's fine, but for a small upstate station to do that in the existent marketplace is a long shot. I can
make the theater available to you and if you tape a regular performance you'll also have my crew. I can also assist you in negotiating with the talent, but any production funding will have to
come from your sources. I'll work with you as much as I can and
I'll give you whatever information I have, but I won't again
attempt to negotiate unless there's real commitment from the station." There was no mistaking the circumstances and I left telling
Herb I'd take a shot at it and would not bother him unless it looked
like a live project.

Just prior to my joining WMHT Sam Francis had joined the
staff. Sam had been a volunteer with me at WQED many years
before, had stayed in Pittsburgh, secured a job at WQED, and
slowly worked his way up to become comptroller. Years later, when
there was reorganization at WQED as the result of several years of
questionable mismanagement, Sam, who had not initiated the situation, but whose involvement was inextricable, was one of several who exited the station. My boss saw an opportunity to employ

•••

someone, at a cut-rate salary, who had large-station financial expertise that had been somewhat devalued.

George Wein's *Newport Jazz Festival*, a twenty-four hour continuous jazz festival, was booked into SPAC for the 4th of July holiday and Sam was assigned, because of his previous contractual experience at WQED in Pittsburgh, to explore the possibility of contracting with Wein to tape the Festival. Surprisingly, with Herb Chesbrough's assistance, a deal was struck with Wein, and even more surprisingly a gambler's decision was made to proceed with it. Sam immediately needed a producer/director and Gardiner Compton was a natural choice. Gardiner suggested that since a twenty-four hour festival would ultimately require an unusual amount of editing, the editing options would be enhanced if five cameras were used with each camera dedicated to a separate video-tape machine that in the aggregate would produce approximately 100 hours of videotape. For such a large-scale project a remote van housing the video equipment and control room facilities was required. It was rented from WGBH-TV in Boston.

Almost overnight WMHT was into "big time" television production. This level of production was new to me. I knew the process and the procedure, but had no experience dealing with the contractual and talent liaison aspects of such projects. Fortunately Sam had been deeply involved in such arrangements at WQED as it was a major network program producing station. With one SPAC program con-firmed, we approached Herb Chesbrough with the idea that perhaps we might be able to sell the Charlie Daniels show that was booked for later in the season. Herb checked with Daniels' agent, and made a tentative deal. Sam and I put the numbers together and pitched the Charlie Daniels band to the executive producer of the specials series at WNET in New York. The response was that they would like to have Charlie Daniels, but had booked all the shows for which they had money that season. Within a few days, however, word came through the grapevine that one of the programs in the series had been canceled and the producers were scrambling to find a replacement. We called New York again and told them of the availability of Charlie Daniels with the result that an agreement was reached which made WNET the producer in association with WMHT, but WNET reserved the right to assign the director.

For a small station, the Newport Jazz Festival was an extremely large undertaking, but ultimately it played, as expected, to standing room only crowds, and was videotaped in its entirety. Gardner Compton spent the next month in New York City editing rooms working with CMX, the then new computer based editing system, and eventually produced a two-hour abbreviated jazz show that was sold to PBS as a special, and seven one hour shows of separate musical groups that were also distributed to the PBS network.

As a local station and with Herb Chesbrough's help, we had an excellent arrangement with the SPAC stagehand's union. For the Charlie Daniel's show, however, WNET's producer's and associates moved in and, ignoring our local arrangements, and flaunting their big city know-how, managed to arrange a contract with the unions for more than twice the cost of our agreement. Having been forced to accept WNET's choice of director, which turned out to be a good one, we insisted that the technical director for the show be one of our own, Mike Heftler who, despite some resistance from the big city boys, proved also to be an excellent choice. The Charlie Daniels show went off without a hitch.

In the meantime, as Pearl Primus emerged from her grief at the loss of her husband, she decided to continue with our plan to recreate her previous works. The development funds from the grant paid for the construction of a special dance floor that was laid on the studio's concrete and linoleum floor as well as for a full crew and equipment including electronic background inserts. In a production session that lasted over a weekend, with Gardiner Compton directing, Pearl's dancing and verbal presentation became the pilot for a proposed program series, which unfortunately was never funded.

The success of the two SPAC shows motivated the station manager. He had another luncheon meeting, this time with Dennis Madden, Executor Director of Proctor's Theater. I was again dispatched to confirm the possibilities and in short order we arranged three remote shows at Proctor's, each one for a pittance of what it had cost to record the Jazz Festival. Two national touring shows were available for taping and distribution: *Jury's Irish Caberet*, an Irish song and dance troupe from Dublin; and the *Romanian Folk Festival*, a troupe of ethnic dancers and musicians in native costumes. The third show was a one-man performance, *The Lincoln Douglas Debates* that featured Dick Poston, brother of the comedic actor Tom Poston. For each of these programs, the contractual terms were quite simple; for taping and broadcast three times in the local area, each company was paid a small initial fee up front. Should the program be distributed, additional fees would be paid dependent on the scope of distribution. It meant that WMHT's major costs were its ongoing labor and equipment costs plus over-time; a low risk considering the unique quality of the resultant pro-grams. With Dennis' help, agreements were signed with the three companies. Will Stone, who was Director of Engineering, and I met with Dennis Madden and his house manager and worked out the details of camera placement, power feeds and lighting. Since the shows were one-night stands and we were not paying for a camera rehearsal, we would be seeing the show for the first time as we were taping it. Camera coverage would therefore be similar to coverage of sports events that relied on the cameramen to find the action and the director to choose the shots. In short, we'd "wing it." The Romanian dance show was performing in Worcester, Massa-chusetts the night before they played in Schenectady, so my direc-tor, Lou Meyer and I drove to Worcester to see the show and take production notes. The next night, Lou did a masterful job of fol-lowing the action with the cameras.

After the show, as we were on stage wrapping up, the Chair-man of the Proctors Board of Directors, a mid-level General Elec-tric Company executive who was quite full of himself, came storming onto the stage insisting in talking to whomever was in charge. I told him I was, and in the presence of his employees and my crew, he immediately subjected me to a diatribe about how inconvenienced and distracted the audience had been by the pres-ence of cameras in the house. I held my temper and tried to tell him that all arrangements had been made in concert with the the-ater's General Manager, but he would have none of it and was unnecessarily abusive. On his departure, Dennis, the house stage manager, the lighting director and the stagehands all came to me and apologized for his actions.

In the next couple of years I was able to slowly introduce some new shows into the schedule and to initiate a few ambitious proj-ects. My staff became more upbeat, interested in their assignments and pleased to be involved in the broadening variety of different kinds of programs. The engineering staff too, enjoyed the challenge of new projects. The variety and quality of the shows improved and the on-air look of the station improved with them. But it was not done easily. Each new idea, each new show was a battle, and slowly, over the few years, my relationship with the boss diminished, aided by his unparalleled deception and divisive administrative tactics.

It was his procedure, with Sam's counsel, to have department heads execute periodic job evaluations for each of their staff members and, under his guidelines, to recommend pay raises where deemed appropriate. His strict orders demanded that performance was to be rewarded and increases given only when absolutely necessary. For three of my staff members: the station's primary on-air hostess, a producer/director, and the art director, I recommended raises that he subsequently disallowed. When they questioned me, I told them what I had done, but disbelieving me, they sought audiences with him. He shrewdly discerned their unhappiness and, not willing to admit it was he who had disallowed their pay increases, simply reversed his previous decision, and permitted the complainants to assume he was reversing my decision. The three staff members had the satisfied feeling that they had gone over my head and obtained what they wanted; he in turn had undermined my effectiveness. The episode changed three loyal employees into three staff members who no longer would trust or support me, and opened up for them and for all others, a direct line of communication around their supervisor to the top. I was irate. I attempted to explain, but it was to no avail. I thought I had understood his character and methods, but this was a new and particularly heinous action.

I realized I had a basic problem. I was charged with accomplishing certain program activities, but was not given the resources that would make it possible to achieve them. I was attempting to do two jobs, operate local program production, and raise funds for special projects. The larger producing stations with which WMHT was now in competition employed a person full-time for the former, and in some cases, two or three people for the latter. I knew too, that it was unrealistic to expect that in my role as fundraiser for program production I would provide all the funds that were necessary to produce programs and still turn a profit for the station.

The boss's penuriousness raised barriers for this effort as well. From meetings with others in similar positions at other stations, I had learned how the grant process worked. In other than the federal grants programs, grants were not generally obtained by simply submitting proposals. Rather, grant winning proposals were often written after the project had been accepted for funding following a series of meetings, luncheons and conferences with agency program administrators during which the basic project concept had been discussed, developed, revised and sometimes completely changed to conform with the interests of the funding agency. Funding developers with whom I spoke traveled constantly like salesmen, visiting funding agencies with a portfolio of potential projects, establishing relationships with grant officers and familiarizing themselves with the interests of each agency. There was a saying that most significant grants are made in drawing rooms, not as the result of proposal submission.

My travel budget was minimal. In fact I had none. Each time I had a need to travel it required a travel request which invariably required a discussion which usually ended with his question, "What do I get out of this?" which of course was unanswerable, particularly if the travel were for the purpose of exploring possible funding. The notion that other stations would pay people full-time to, as the boss saw it, just run around and have business lunches, was incomprehensible. Our relationship further deteriorated. Despite the fact that even though I had been reluctant to work for him and had accepted employment only because I had no other choices, there had nevertheless been inside me a dream that perhaps if I were able to produce a few programs of note, I would be able to parlay my successes into a similar job in a more equitable venue. That dream had now faded. I knew my capabilities, but with extremely limited resources and travel, those attributes weren't enough. I had given it my best shot, was proud of what I had been able to accomplish with minimal resources, but I had had to fight my boss every step of the way to do so, and the loyalty of my staff was now being co-opted. The next step was one I could not avoid although I saw its dangers.

It would be difficult to justify terminating a disabled executive who, on the record, had no tangible inadequacies or against whom there had been no complaints. Despite my growing unhappiness with him, I had always received a reasonably good evaluation. A specific charge would be needed to terminate me. When the program manager who, like myself, had been searching for a better situation finally found one and departed, a new staffing reorganization plan was initiated, which involved moving responsibility for local production from me to the new program manager. I would then concentrate my efforts on special projects and grant proposals under the new title of Director of Program Marketing. With no budget support to expedite the necessary travel, this translated to grant writer with little hope of success. The alternative, of course, was to resign and seek employment elsewhere. The essence of the new position was to generate funds from the sale of existing programs and the production of new ones; its tactical purpose however, was to narrow the focus of my day-to-day activities to a finite area of activity which could be chronicled and accounted. I was ordered to develop a marketing plan and to submit it for consideration by the beginning of June 1984.

The marketing of programming by public television stations had become an increasing income source for the so-called producing stations, those that regularly produced programs for sale. Stations that pursued these activities structured themselves so that all income accruing to a station from program production, sales, or rental, was automatically credited to the program marketing department. The total income, less the production cost and departmental expenses, determined the success of the operation.

I submitted a marketing plan that among other factors called for the creation of a committee drawn from the station Board of Directors who, because of their contacts and status could advise and direct program marketing in the manner similar committees currently functioned with the station's development and endowment programs. In the following months however, I was unable to schedule a discussion of my marketing plan and the recommendation for committee oversight and leadership was ignored. In addition, no authorization for the production of quality programming which would afford opportunity to compete in the marketplace was forthcoming, and several exploratory efforts were curtailed for superficial reasons. I was denied approval to attend several conferences and meetings at which marketing possibilities might be explored, and income from projects directly assigned to program marketing was not credited to program marketing. I had been set-up and boxed in. I was charged with selling, but there was almost nothing to sell. I was prevented from developing new products, and also prevented contact with the marketplace.

In the preceding season, out of personal conviction, I had pressed hard to produce a series of four television programs that dealt with the experiences and points of view of people with disabilities. I had given much thought to the fact that the larger society had little understanding of the nature of the problems that complicated the lives of disabled persons and minimized their opportunities for social and professional success. I believed the series would be worthwhile and might even be successful. I titled it *All In A Lifetime* and its four shows focused on four age groups: children, teens, working adults and elderly, and were respectively titled *Anticipation, Preparation, Participation and Reflection.* I obtained a small grant to cover the production costs and on completion sold several sets of the tapes to special education departments in schools and state agencies. I submitted the first program in the series to the Sixth Annual Media Awards of the California Governor's Committee on Employment of the Handicapped. In June of 1984 it finished among the finalists and received a Second Prize.

My personal experience clearly provided the answers to all of the questions that the programs posed and so I personally interviewed each participant. The responses elicited were taped in a manner that would permit my voice and image to be deleted in the edited program. When the taping was completed and prior to editing, I searched for a host for the series, someone who could be on camera occasionally and tie together the continuity of shows. The search was a difficult one and after a few weeks, Lou Myers, whom I had assigned to direct the project and who had great sensitivity and a fine sense of drama said, "I think you're going to have to do it." "Me? No way, I can't do it." "Well, there's nobody else and you know all the questions as well as the answers and you know just how you want the points to be made."

The thought of appearing on the show bothered me. I was hoist on my own petard. In my producer's eye this was a series about disabled people. I wasn't disabled. At least I never perceived myself as being disabled. And it wasn't generally known that I had artificial legs. Moreover, I had never associated myself with disabled people, and, I realized with considerable guilt, I wasn't particularly anxious to do so. I had been mainstreamed during all of my schooling and afterward had entered the world of work head on and unknowingly without ever acknowledging or accepting that I was disabled. After my rehabilitation I had presented myself as a normal person. In the process, my arm was overlooked. I had just forged ahead with, as I had to admit, marginal success. But host this series? It would mean admitting to the world that I was disabled. I had no idea how many people I saw every day or met for the first time knew that I was a triple amputee. I didn't mind if they knew, but I made no effort to inform them. According to Irving Goffman I was "passing" and I was very much aware of it. [15] In effect, if I hosted this show I would be coming out of the closet. I didn't like the idea at all. I thought about how the camera would see me. Would we use a close up and hide my arm? No, I couldn't justify that. It would be cheating. On principal alone, we'd have to use a medium shot. And what would I say? Would I talk about "Them?" or "Us?" Each of the people I had interviewed for the show knew of my disability. I couldn't separate myself from them if I appeared on the show. It wouldn't be fair. I didn't remember when I had been so uncomfortable. I stewed about the problem for a couple of days and talked it over with Barb. Her position, much like my mother's, was "Do what you have to do." In the end I hosted the shows, in a wide shot, on camera.

Being in front of the camera was a lot different than being behind it. For one opening sequence I had to do twenty-two takes before I got it right, and I had written the script, but Lou's recommendation ultimately proved to be correct. Publicity for the show in the local newspapers noted the fact that a triple amputee had produced the series, but I was not aware that anyone with whom I had contact thought it important.

Although I knew rather precisely, from personal experience, the nature and scope of social discrimination faced by persons with disabilities, I had nevertheless lived my life, even with disabilities, self-centered on my personal survival within the mainstream of the

---

[15] Traditionally, the question of passing has raised the issue of the "visibility" of a particular stigma, that is, how well or how badly the stigma is adapted to provide means of communicating that the individual possesses it. (Goffman, p-48)

non-disabled. I had little knowledge and no connection to the large-scale activism that sought to initiate change.

In the process of researching and interviewing for the series I met the director of the local Capital District Center for Independence, a part of the Disability Rights and Independent Living Movement.[16] Disability activists in Berkeley, California founded the first Center for Independence in 1972. In the intervening years a series of landmark court decisions and continued activism resulted in: Rehabilitation Act of 1973; Individuals With Disabilities Act of 1990; and Americans with Disabilities Act of 1990, all of which have guaranteed persons with disabilities access to their civil rights. In 1984 the Capital District Center for Independence was one of hundreds of such non-profit centers across the country whose mission providing services to people with disabilities included: a shuttle bus service; wheelchair loans; counseling on fiscal, educational and legal matters; translators for the deaf; a telephone answering service for the deaf; and later a TTD service – prior to the telephone companies' decision to provide such services directly.

Following the broadcast of *All In A Lifetime*, I was invited to join the Board of Directors of the Capital District Center and found it to be a satisfying experience to which I, as a disabled person who had made my way without assistance, could bring considerable experience and counsel. At Captioned Films for the Deaf I had worked with deaf persons who, although disabled, were college graduates and belonged to a social milieu with which I was familiar. At the Center I was made aware that there were many people with life disabilities that were much more severe than my own, whose remove from the mainstream of "normal" social and pro-

---

[16] "*Although groups and individuals have since the nineteenth century advocated for an end to this oppression, large scale, cross –disability rights activism, encouraged by the examples of African-American civil rights and women's rights moments, did not begin until the late 1960s.*" The independent living movement has been an important part of this broader movement for disability rights. It is based on the premise that people with even the most severe disabilities should have the choice of living in the community. This can be accomplished through the creation of personal assistance services allowing an individual to manage his or her personal care, to keep a home, to have a job, go to school, worship, and otherwise participate in the life of the community. The independent living movement also advocates for the removal of architectural and transportation barriers that prevent people with disabilities from sharing fully in all aspects of our society. (http://bancroft.berkeley.edu/collections/drilm/introduction.html p.1)

fessional life might not be as easily resolved as had mine, even though I didn't think mine was resolved.

In early November the axe fell. My boss informed me that he had decided that inasmuch as Program Marketing had not met the goal for the first year, my position was to be changed from Director of Program Marketing to Producer/ Marketing Coordinator. I would retain my current salary, but would report to the Program Manager who had just been promoted to Director of Broadcasting. It was a high visibility demotion, from administration to production. I was both humiliated and infuriated. I could not accept the demotion that would place me side-by-side and competing with those whom I had directed for a long time. There was nothing more to lose so I wrote a frank memo which stated in part:

"I was undoubtedly naïve in hoping that my lengthy memorandum of June 20, 1984 addressing the subject of Program Marketing would enable objective and realistic assessment of marketing potential at WMHT and provide more direct leadership and support to that function in order to ensure its success. It is now clear that is not to be, therefore I am prepared to immediately submit my resignation effective December 31, 1984."

My boss couldn't wait that long. He summoned me Friday afternoon, just two weeks before Christmas, and, while the personnel officer scurried to brief my secretary as to what was happening, he informed me that as of the moment I was terminated. I was asked for my key to the building and told to collect my personal belongings and leave. Merry Christmas!

18

Slippery Slope

The timing could not have been worse. Our daughter, Jessica, was in her junior year in high school and we had begun to plan for her college education. Jessica's academic qualifications placed her near the top of her class and her non-academic activities included drama, literature, music, dance, and school services. She was a well-rounded applicant, but given our present situation, without some kind of scholarship support, her further education would face significant problems. Barb embarked on the process of searching for college scholarships for which Jessica might possibly be eligible and organized a plan to visit a number of colleges that offered scholarship potential and were located within a few hour's drive.

I had no immediate prospects for employment. It meant beginning over again at the age of fifty-eight, but I was resolved that no matter what the consequences, I would not again submit to the unemployment payment procedure. I decided to make an attempt at freelancing as a producer/director. During my years at WMHT I had occasion to talk with a number of young men and a few women who were struggling to make careers as independent producers doing industrial documentaries and sales and marketing materials that a number of manufacturing companies and advertising agencies in the area frequently utilized. I spent several weeks researching the local area, talking to people with whom I had had contact while at WMHT. I designed and printed a single sheet folded brochure and then began to make sales calls, something which was new to me and to which I did not bring a surplus amount of either self-confidence or bravado. It was a limited local market and I quickly learned that I faced two types of competitors, the all service agencies that handled all types of media assignments, and producer-director-cinematographers who were one-man production units. Of the former, two or three organizations were in control of most of the marketplace, the leader being a company that had spun off the now dismantled General Electric Media Service, enjoyed close and intimate ties to GE, and satisfied most of GE's media needs. Of the latter, I was apparently the only one who, much older than any of them and possessing much more and varied experience, was without my own camcorder and editing facility. They were capable of going to any location, shooting quickly whatever the client requested, hurrying home and after spending the night editing, delivering the result to the client in the morning. Most of the locally produced television spots were produced this way.

What I had to offer, as writer/producer/director, was of a type and quality that most potential customers were accustomed to buying in New York or Boston where all the divergent needs of a production would be served by a single agency. I made known my availability to work in any capacity and offered myself to the major producing organizations as a writer, producer, director or production designer. Everyone was impressed with my credentials. Outside of New York and Boston, my experience far outshone, with a few exceptions, the local producers and directors. But each agency had their own dependable, predictable, proven crews with whom they were used to working and unless an unforeseen opening or need occurred, they had no need for my services.

Since her temporary substitute teaching license had expired and permanent certification required additional coursework, Barbara searched for work in the area of human services. With a Bachelor's degree in Nursing and a M.A. in Sociology, there were a variety of situations into which she might fit, but she found no openings. I applied for work as a substitute teacher in the local schools. I was called only once to substitute in a high school art class.

By the end of March, as I was beginning to call on my listings for the second time, I found my first job. Phoenix, a computer software company, had developed a unique computer program which permitted data recorded in a medical MRI to be reconstructed into a three dimensional image which could be rotated, tilted, sectioned or sliced thereby permitting a physician to study and map internal organs without invasive examination. Its capabilities were amazing. For example, the program, by absorbing a series of MRI images taken every 100th of an inch of a skull that had been fractured, could present a detailed three-dimensional image of the injury showing the exact location and number of bone fragments. For the surgeon to have such detailed imagery prior to surgery offered untold advantages. The company was in process of selling the program to every hospital in the country, but that market was not large enough to support their ongoing expensive development in other areas. They needed a documentary to sell both the medical program and their expertise to new investors.

I met the president of the company who introduced me to the company's public relations man who had written the script. I was asked to read it and work with the PR man on any revisions that the president would approve. I found the script to be a veritable jungle of technical detail that seemed to confuse more than it clarified. Experience had taught me, however, that changing a writer's script was tantamount to beating his child so I categorized my criticisms and selected one or two that I hoped might be the least sensitive in hopes that, if I was able to get beyond those initial problems, I might have a chance to chip away at some of the more important ones. It was a lost cause. The PR man believed that his was the only way the topic could or should be presented. With a change of only a few words, I was told to proceed with the taping.

I remembered the discussions with my boss at the United Nations. It was a similar kind of situation, but this time it was my client and whatever he wanted, I would do. It wasn't a big job; the total cost was only a little over $3,000. I hired a cinematographer and a narrator, shot and edited the tape and delivered it to the PR man who was pleased. I submitted my bill and waited for payment that didn't come. A few weeks later I succeeded in getting the executive on the phone only to hear him say that it was a bad script and didn't serve his purpose and he wouldn't pay for it. The fact that I had not been responsible for the script made no difference to him. I contacted a lawyer who informed me that unfortunately Phoenix had just filed for bankruptcy and the president had informed him he was in no position to write checks. It was demoralizing to have my first production attempt, on which I had labored in good faith and paid a cinematographer and narrator, be rejected with no complaints as to quality, but because of a poor script that had been given me and over which I had no control. My effort at freelancing was shattered. For weeks I just grieved: at my failure, my circumstances, and my life in general. I wrote letters of application, but had little hope that any of them would even be answered.

Barbara, deeply involved in researching the possibilities for Jessica's college education, became enthused with the field of college student personnel and enrolled in a Master's program. A bright spot that appeared on our familial horizon rewarded Barbara's efforts. In June at her high school graduation, Jessica scored a coup by garnering a collection of financial awards from the Kiwanis, the Pan Hellenic Association, the Jeanette O'Dasz Prize in Music, and the Band Award for her performance as first flute. In addition, of the eight schools to which she had applied, she was accepted by seven, each of which offered generous scholarship and work-study awards. We rejoiced in her good fortune and were relieved to know that despite our perilous circumstances, she was going to obtain an education at a good school. Her choice was Wesleyan University in Middletown, CT.

By the summer of 1986 our finances were nearing bottom. Once again our savings had been depleted and had we not lived as modestly as was our practice, it would have been worse. Having once been a state employee, I searched for possible openings in state service, but too many years had passed for the contacts I once enjoyed to be of any assistance. I managed to connect with one or two who had in effect "retired" in the state service but they were not in positions that enabled them to be of help. I also requested and received letters of recommendation from my local Democratic Party leaders and the former Lt. Governor. I remembered a former, but not close, colleague in the State University who had departed to make his way in the political world and had become a relatively close associate of the Governor, Mario Cuomo. I wrote him and then called him and explained my situation candidly. Receiving a sympathetic approach and given permission to use his name as a reference, I wrote a letter to the Governor outlining the nature of the conditions that had seemingly pursued me for so many years, stressing the fact that I was now frantically trying to prevent a disastrous slide from which I might never be able to recover. It was an anguished letter that was in effect asking for that which I had never ever asked, special consideration. I wasn't proud of my appeal; I was shamed by it. I was begging and I had never before begged, but I was frightened at a situation that was beyond my control. I was now after a political appointment and I could think of no other way, at my age and with my disabilities, to obtain work and support my family. I could explain my actions, but I could not excuse or justify them in a manner that made them acceptable in accordance with my own values. I needed a job. I would accept any job. There was no chance of my finding another job in broadcasting. But begging for help was the antithesis of everything I believed in and held dear. It was a bitter pill to swallow.

A few weeks later, the Governor's Appointment's Secretary called me and I was interviewed by the personnel manager at the Department of Motor Vehicles and introduced to the Commissioner. For a week I trembled in anticipation and then received word that I was being appointed to the position of Deputy Public Information Officer at the Department of Motor Vehicles. I began work at the beginning of September at a salary commensurate with what I had received at WMHT.

There were two Deputies: one, an intelligent and politically astute young woman who assisted the Director with press conferences and liaison with the media and other state offices, and me. My assignment was to coordinate all print aspects of the department's public relations that included numerous publications of all varieties, from posters, bulletins and informational brochures to the State's Driver's Handbook, newly edited and published every year. Several writers and two staff artists contributed to the publications. The process of creating new publications and editing and updating existing ones was unending and bureaucratically complicated. The artists were Civil Service employees; there were countless regulations that governed when and what tasks they could be required to do. Meeting a publication deadline for even a simple project required many months of planning and scheduling. Moreover, over a period of a few years there had been a number of persons in the job I now had and the artists had learned how to manage the job requirements to their own satisfaction. I recalled that, in my previous tenure at the State and Federal Education Departments, permanent employees had viewed political appointees with a certain amount of envy and distaste. "Here today, gone tomorrow," was the catch phrase.

My new boss, the Public Information Officer, was a young man who had been a local radio and television newsman and we enjoyed swapping war stories from time to time. The Department's television production work was handled in its entirety by another person with much less experience than me, but who had been responsible for this activity for several years and there was no expectation that I would be called upon to render an assist in television production.

For the first two months I concentrated on orienting myself to the massive departmental structure with its several thousand employees and the myriad levels of administrative staff with whom I had to work while at the same time sorting out the pecking order of the various regular staff and political appointees. By Thanksgiving I was beginning to think I knew my way around. Then, just before the holiday I experienced severe intestinal cramps that I knew to be a diverticulitis attack of a kind that I had experienced from time to time over several years. My usual response was to immediately go on a low residue diet and drink a lot of fluids. This time the process didn't produce the anticipated response and when the doctor had finished examining me he just shook his head. "You've been flirting with this for too many years dealing with the symptoms. Now you need to deal with the problem. I think you should have that section of your colon excised so you won't have to worry about it anymore."

I entered the hospital the following week. After a month's convalescence, I returned to work at the beginning of the year and began immediately to explore, with administrative encouragement, the possibilities for revamping the print production process into a computer dependent operation.

I found that my job benefits were an improvement over what I had enjoyed at the television station and was surprised to learn that, due to my previous state employment, I was in a benefits bracket wherein my medical premiums and retirement were paid in full by the state. In addition, the status of my job was management confidential and provided me an enhanced medical and insurance package. The job, particularly development of computer assisted printing, was interesting, but underlying my new solvency was the knowledge that I had been unable to find work in my field and had been reduced to begging in order to facilitate my current position. I was well treated in the new environment; I had reentered the comforting, protective womb of government employment, but I was not happy with myself.

Personnel management responsibilities that required every action to be examined for possible legal or union contract ramifications weighed heavily on me. My staff at the station had been people who were there because they enjoyed being a part of that kind of enterprise; the employees whom I supervised in the Motor Vehicle Department were there because they had to make a living and had become bureaucratic. Of course I was there for the same reason; I too had to make a living and had qualified for the job I held. Given the job, however, I wanted to move forward with it; my staff, over which I had no direct administrative control, was less inclined. It was like trying to fly a lead balloon. The strain took a toll on me and in May, while working in my yard planting a vegetable garden, I experienced chest pains sufficiently severe to make me stop what I was doing and return to the house. When the pain continued, Barb decided that I had better get to the hospital. The diagnosis of a heart attack devastated me. This was indeed the end of the life, good, bad and indifferent, that I had known and the independence I had enjoyed. Testing revealed that although there was no question as to the nature of the trouble, I was fortunate in that it had been a mild attack and the damage to my heart was minimal. I was sixty-one years old.

19

Siblings

There is an eight-year age difference between my brother Wayne and me. It had taken Mother that long after my birth to overcome the fear of having another child. Eight years, however, proved to be a significant separation in view of our relative and different interests, and because of my disabilities and the special care that they necessitated from my parents, notably my mother. By the time Wayne was five or six, and determinately tagging along behind me as I spent time with friends in the neighborhood, I was already into junior high school, feeling the pressures of adapting to a new and strenuous physical and academic schedule, and becoming exposed to the first glimmers of teenage behavior and development.

By the time I graduated high school, Wayne was only in the fourth grade; four years later when I graduated college, he had yet to enter high school. During the early years that I attended the Saturday morning art classes at the Carnegie Museum, Wayne was a part of the museum experience along with our mother, but the years between us unfortunately precluded development of common interests or even understandings, and although we loved one another, our lives rarely touched except in our home. Another and crucial factor separated us; whereas I was disabled and limited in my physical activities, Wayne was an athlete, swimming on the high school team, playing organized sandlot baseball, and college basketball. Dad's younger son was a reincarnation of his own athletic achievements in track and basketball in his early life, and his enthusiasm was the type seen years later among Little League fathers. Although at no time did he limit his interest, love or support for me, Dad nevertheless relived his youth in Wayne's exploits, and just as he made extensive and strenuous efforts to facilitate delivering and picking me up from school, he also rearranged his schedule to attend as many of Wayne's games as possible.

Despite possessing artistic talents and knowing intuitively and from experience how to match colors and fabrics or place mannequins in a store window, Dad's actual knowledge of the arts was minimal and he had little understanding as to where or how I might make a living in the arts. Sports however, was an area with which he was quite familiar, one to which he could easily relate on the basis of both his personal experience and his many years of following the exploits of professional players. He became a true athletic "stage father," full of pride at Wayne's athletic prowess and accomplishments. His face beamed and eyes twinkled as he watched the games. When Wayne made the varsity basketball team at Carnegie Tech, Dad was in his glory and never missed a game. To his credit, despite the intensity of his enthusiasm for sports, he showed equal interest in my accomplishments and interests, never displaying any type of favoritism. He had two sons and was equally proud and delighted with both of them.

In the years following my graduation from college I was so involved with the struggle to find work and to participate in the social life in which my friends were involved, that I saw few of Wayne's basketball games and, because he was living at school, we saw little of each other. When he eloped with his high school sweetheart, in the spring of his junior year, the family was thrown into turmoil; Mother, while accepting the inevitable with reservations, perceived the event as limiting Wayne's future as well as complicating his present life. Dad absorbed the shock and, as was his manner, concentrated on the bright side of the situation, welcoming the new bride unconditionally into his family. Wayne and his bride moved into the attic rooms, but, at the insistence of our parents, he continued to live at school during the week in order to concentrate on his studies. Their early-married life was confined to weekends. When, in the following spring, he became a father, the enormity of the differences that separated us became obvious to me. As a college graduate, I was strenuously struggling to become a part of the professional and social mainstream and find meaning in my very lonely life, hoping to meet someone with whom I might have a relationship. Wayne, still in college and eight years my junior, was already married and a father. His graduation from college a few months later and a job in a major industry 1,500 miles from home increased his separation from the family.

In the years that followed, Wayne and his wife and my parents made occasional visits back and forth between Pittsburgh and St. Louis and maintained contact as the children, now a girl and boy, grew. My struggles to survive limited my visits to St. Louis except when a business trip provided the opportunity for a stopover, and even after I had married, my limited income did not permit my visiting; it was an unaffordable expense. In those same years Wayne rose methodically through the ranks to increasingly responsible and rewarding positions and, although his increasing affluence might have permitted it, his visits were increasingly rare. In a period of almost twenty years we had visits from him perhaps three or four times. Although Dad and Mother stayed in closer touch with Wayne, periods of time, one as long as ten years, would elapse without our seeing one another or being in touch by mail or phone except at Christmas when we would gather at our parent's house.

While I struggled through the world of work managing to survive until retirement, Wayne rose to a position of high corporate authority. Two years after my marriage, when I worked in Washington, D.C., Wayne, already an experienced, hard working corporate man, was earning a salary double the size of mine. Short of having emerged from the same womb and spending our early years together under the same roof, we had little to draw us together. Our age difference was a major factor, but there were also differences in our individual characters and interests. I had inherited our father's artistic tendencies; Wayne his acuity for mathematics, but we were both endowed with our mother's pragmatism and perception. My interest was in the arts; my brother's in the sciences.

In retrospect, I am aware that the concentration of attention bestowed on me in my earlier years had resulted in less attention being paid to my brother, and that lack of nurturing had possibly had an effect on how he perceived familial relationships in general, and ours in particular. Then too, in my younger years it had been the pattern of our mother's sisters and their children to gather together frequently, almost weekly, at one or another's houses, and I had had the experience of being a part of large extended family gatherings. By the time Wayne had grown old enough for that experience, times had changed; there had been a few deaths and marriages in the family and the frequency of the gatherings decreased although the family remained closely knit.

As the years passed, separated by distance and lack of contact, we grew further and further apart until we ultimately lived in two different worlds; our interests, aesthetics, politics, activities and particularly our socio-economic status were at opposite poles. Although I cared deeply for him, I felt both neglected and dismissed. Despite distance and lack of contact, Barbara and I did have a long range relationship with he and his wife and were saddened, during one of my stressful periods of unemployment, to receive a call from them informing us of an impending divorce. A few years later, aware that my brother was planning to re-wed, I was surprised to be called and asked if I planned to attend the wedding. It was only after I gave assurance that I would be present that I was asked to serve as best man. The sequencing of the questions made me aware that there was some uncertainty as to how I perceived his second marriage, that I might possibly have disapproved of his divorce and would not attend. More importantly, however, it struck me that he did not really know me. Like my father's, my familial relationships ran deep and there was nothing that could change that. I was unhappy that we had grown so far apart and had so little understanding of what each could expect of the other.

I always hoped that we could have had closer contact, but my financial circumstances had prevented my pursuing it; and I was saddened that he had not. At a time when we had both retired, an opportunity presented itself for some initial frank discussion about how we had perceived our respective actions and reactions and I believed that a new relationship was begun that, although it could never recapture years lost as we went our separate ways, nevertheless posed hopes that might offer some limited promise that memories and feelings fostered in our youth in our house on the steep street in Pittsburgh might provide some comfort and closeness in our remaining years. Unfortunately, another decade passed without that happening, until a death in the family brought us together once again. For me, however, hope springs eternal.

20

A Passion

With only a few rare exceptions, my disabilities didn't prevent me from doing what I wanted to do. My problem was implementing the routine of my day-to-day activities. Pain from standing or walking demanded that I take roundabout means to accomplish my ends. That complicated my life and exhausted my physical stamina. As I have said, vehicles functioned as equalizers, expanding my physical, sensory, and emotional horizons by making it possible to painlessly experience some portion of the pleasure, thrill, and satisfaction that others enjoyed in physical pastimes. I developed an affinity for inanimate objects and skill at utilizing them. The skies and water offered mystical and romantic enticement and of these, boats were the most attainable. Rowboats, motorboats, sailboats, became my passion. They provided a way to have a relationship with the water otherwise denied me; a means of testing myself against the vicissitudes of the weather and facilitating family centered adventures. From early teens, boats had been an important part of my life. They gave me a feeling of going head to head with the elements and provided an opportunity to utilize physical and intellectual capabilities in a manner that I was never able to enjoy as successfully in dealings with people

I always enjoyed fishing, whether dangling a piece of baloney on a string to catch crawdads in a freshwater stream, or sitting quietly watching the bobber on my line quiver for the first time indicating a fish interested in the bait. I never caught many fish, and always yearned for an uncle, or a friend or a father who would frequently take me fishing. My dad was as attentive to my needs as could be expected, but fishing wasn't within the spectrum of his experience or interest. On occasion Mother would take my brother and me to the park and while she watched my brother on the swings, I would fish in the small lake. I lived for those days. One day in my very early teens my Uncle Steve invited me to go fishing at night on the river. I was thrilled, but when I found myself in a small rowboat out on the Allegheny River in the dark, watching enormous paddlewheel steamboats go by belching smoke and sparks and feeling the skiff bob and tilt in their wakes, I was frightened, although I wouldn't let my uncle know it. We caught a few catfish and when we returned home my uncle showed me how to drive a nail through the head of the fish and pull the skin off using a pair of pliers.

Being unable to swim never diminished my fascination with boats and when I had acquired a driver's license and some driving experience I'd drive, with a fishing partner, a hundred miles north to a lake where we would rent a double-ended rowboat with two sets of oars and spend the day fishing for perch, crappies or bass. If the wind were in the right direction at the end of the day, we would wedge one oar vertically in the bow as a mast, tie lines to an old blanket and sail into the dock. When we acquired small outboard motors, we fished broad stretches of the lake with rental skiffs.

I handled a boat naturally and well. Like driving, it became second nature to me. In a seated position I had none of the discomfort that I had when standing or walking, and boating offered a additional sense of freedom not otherwise enjoyed. In my midteens, on family vacation, we rented a skiff, attached my outboard motor and I spent every day fishing from the boat or speeding past the public docks where girls would wave and ask to go for a ride. When I drew nearer and they noticed my disabilities they would usually demure and find reasons why they couldn't go for a ride, and I learned to avoid surprising girls with my disabilities.

Flying lessons at a marina and the leisure time spent there resulted in making friends with several boat owners, one of whom had a small outboard boat, enjoyed water skiing, but had no driver. It followed that I became his driver and at the annual Yacht Club Boat Festival, I drove the boat for the star attraction who was dressed in a red and black striped, turn of the century bathing suit, and carried an umbrella.

When we first married, Barbara and I, knowing that my disabilities prevented me from participating in many of the recreational activities enjoyed by friends and acquaintances, sought other diversions. Most people we knew belonged to country clubs, played golf and tennis or spent days lazing by the pools while their children cavorted in the water. Others hiked or cycled, or worked out at spas and gyms. I was unable to participate in these activities. I was, however, an experienced camper and boater. Barbara had no experience with either of these activities, but agreed to try them and found them enjoyable. During our first two years, we rented a boat and motor and camped on the islands at Lake George. Later, with a boat of our own, all the equipment could be left in the boat between trips and I had only to carry it to and from the tent site when we made camp.

We took the boat with us to Washington, fished the Pautuxet River and the Chesapeake for perch, blues and spot, and back in Schenectady moved up to an old wooden nineteen foot outboard cruiser with a 100 hp. outboard and high gunwales. It was perfect for us. With a lot of hard work: a new coat of paint on the hull, a set of new canvas which completely enclosed the cockpit; five coats of sanded, stained and varnished bright work; and non-slip, indoor-outdoor carpet on the cockpit deck; our new floating summer cottage sparkled and shone and drew compliments everywhere we went.

Boating provided us, and later our children, the opportunity to enjoy family time together while also giving us, and particularly me, access to the water. It was important that the children learn to swim as early as possible and Barb enrolled Jess in a mom and tot class at the Y. Jared too, learned to swim early, barely out of nursery school. Boats remained the center of our family recreational activity.

Barb's first experience on a sailboat was a positive one, on a rented daysailer while on vacation. "There's no noise, no fumes," She said, "we can talk while we're sailing, and it's great fun." We talked it over on the drive home and two weeks later, on a sunny day absolutely made for selling a sparkling, newly refinished boat, we sold our cruiser for a good price, and started our search for a sailboat.

It took almost two years of looking before we decided to take a chance on what we thought was the safest, least expensive, boat we could find, a 22 ft, centerboard pop-top with a furling headsail, a small cabin with a galley, icebox, portapotti and barely enough space to sleep. We had added Jared to the family and again wanted a safe boat so Barb and the children could learn to sail and we had a couple of fun years learning to sail the boat. With the board up we were able to get into small bays where the water was only a foot deep and let Jess play in the shallow water. I rigged a hanger for Jared's baby seat and when the boat heeled his seat stayed vertical and we all got used to living in the tiny cabin.

When New York Governor Carey cut the state budget by ten percent and my job was sacrificed it was time to sell the boat. We advertised at a price our boat dealer friend thought was absurd, but since it was paid for, and sitting on a trailer in the back yard, and since we could use the money, we felt it worth a try and sure enough, that one person for whom every boat seller looks, the one who wants to buy your boat, came along and we suddenly had a handsome profit and an empty space in the back yard.

It was a long time between jobs, but as soon as we knew the new job was permanent we began searching for another boat. Now we wanted something more substantial with which we could learn to cruise, anchor out overnight, stay aboard for several days, and carry what we needed. Our boat dealer friend, Don, made us an offer we couldn't refuse. He'd sell us a new boat at his cost and if ever we had to sell, he'd sell it for us and we wouldn't lose. The price was more than we wanted to spend, but, always a risk taker, I thought that, having made the purchase at the wholesale price, if we were forced to sell, we could probably at least get our investment back, so we ordered a Tanzer 7.5 meter sloop with a double axle trailer. Pick-up would be at the factory in Montreal, Canada. I began the new job on October 4th, and found myself in Montreal taking delivery of a new boat on Dec. 22nd in order to avoid a price raise that would take effect the first of the year. The new boat was just a few inches less than twenty-five feet long with a shallow draft keel drawing thirty-eight inches, berths for four, galley, icebox, outboard rudder, dining table, bow and stern pulpits, life lines, and a host of attractive appointments to which I made a few additions. With clear weather and dry roads, the trip from Montreal was uneventful and I backed the new boat in beside the garage on Dec. 23rd just as it was beginning to snow.

After a summer on Lake George, we enrolled in our first Power Squadron course and met some big-boat sailors who sailed Lake Champlain and extolled the virtues of the lake. Their stories of anchoring out and staying aboard for a week or two motivated us to move our boat to Lake Champlain despite doubling our travel distance. We rented a slip at on the lake and continued to take courses in seamanship, piloting, sailing, navigation and engine maintenance.

Cruising Lake Champlain was everything we had hoped it would be. Each Friday evening we would settle down in the boat, enjoy the company of the other boaters, and sleep in comfort in our floating summer cottage. Early Saturday morning, as soon as the wind was up, we'd set sail to some previously selected location. In mid-afternoon, we'd find a safe anchorage, and while the children swam, we would relax. On hot days, the children would pour buckets of water over us in the cockpit, and after dinner we lounged in the cockpit and watched the fading daylight. I learned to take bearings on our anchorage and wakened during the night to be certain we were not dragging anchor. On occasion, during a weather change or high winds, I would arise, go on deck, check all fastenings and ties, pay out more anchor rode or set a second anchor. Being able to keep my family safe and secure in the face of the threatening elements provided a sense of masculine prowess I never felt in the company of men. My understanding and ability to cope with nature exceeded my skills in human relationships. It was a stimulating and enervating experience.

We sailed to different towns and marinas, anchored out in uninhabited bays and coves, and rendezvoused with sailing friends. We became familiar with the lake, its winds and desirable anchorages, learning where in a given anchorage was the best holding ground or the least danger from winds, and how to protect ourselves when the weather changed. Little by little we became experienced fresh water sailors. As happens with many new sailors, our increasing skill enticed us into thinking that our boat was too small. Our familiarity with cruising generated a desire for greater comfort and self sufficiency to permit living aboard for longer periods of time without resorting to land support.

Our marina at Westport on Lake Champlain was a stopover for world traveled cruising sailors who were making the circuit from the Atlantic up the Hudson River and the Champlain Canal, through the Lake, then down the Richelieu River into Canada, to the St. Lawrence River and down the St Lawrence to the Atlantic or vice versa. Wouldn't it be wonderful to be able to cruise like that? I wasn't ready to take on the challenge of salt water with the complications of tides and additional maintenance, but what about fresh water cruising? The Great Lakes offered a myriad of sailing opportunities and the North Channel of Lake Huron was renown as a fabulous cruising ground. Why couldn't we spend a summer cruising the great lakes, decommission the boat wherever fall found us and then continue the following summer? But for that we'd need an even better and larger boat. With visions of sailing both the great lakes and eventually the Intercoastal Waterway to Florida on retirement, we trailered our boat to a used boat show in Newport, RI, and on a rainy, stormy weekend, sold it for our asking price. There followed another two years of traveling weekends along the coast of New York, Connecticut and Massachusetts, sightseeing and searching for our ideal boat. We finally found our "big boat" sitting in a yard in Annapolis, MD, dirty and bedraggled, its hornet infested mainsail hanging sloppily from its boom, a vision of neglect. The surveyor declared it structurally sound, but it had enough repairable, do-it-ourselves, cosmetic blemishes to keep the price within reason. With some work, we could make it new again, so we made an offer and became the thrilled new owners of an unsightly and ill-maintained 1971 keel/centerboard Morgan 35 sloop, already 12 years old. It slept six, had a power water system, a 22 hp, 4 cylinder Palmer gasoline engine, five sails including a spinnaker, ground tackle, and a Tillermaster autopilot which the surveyor reported as inoperable. It also had a head with a shower and sleeping arrangements that permitted privacy. The only problem was getting it to Albany. I talked with some experienced sailors who declared that it would take a minimum of five days of hard sailing. I authorized the yard to do some specific repairs, check out the various systems, tune the engine, and launch it. In a moment of undaunted self-confidence and daring, I decided I'd ferry it to Albany myself.

Ferrying the boat proved to be more complicated than I had supposed. It became in fact, one of my most challenging adventures, the kind that most of my friends might not be quick to attempt. For me it was not only doing what needed to be done, but also the thrill of accepting the challenge. Certainly it was not the kind of behavior that a triple amputee would ordinarily be expected to attempt.

Despite having taken the Power Squadron courses on sailing and piloting and basic navigation, I had no coastal sailing experience. I needed at least one experienced salt-water hand on my crew and fortunately, a word of mouth search for a "no-pay" crew yielded Jim, a former bosun's mate on a Caribbean windjammer, and his wife, Jean. A Power Squadron friend, Howard, completed the crew. With a rental car packed tight with supplies, gear and tools, we drove from Albany to Annapolis, where the boat was in the water. After stowing food and personal gear, Howard and Jim checked running and ground tackle and I settled my account with the yard. Jim and Jean stayed over with friends and Howard and I spent the first night on the boat, awaking at six to the sound of midshipman doing calisthenics on the Naval Academy lawn.

We executed an extensive pre-check of the boat and equipment, repairing and replacing parts, checking out sails and halyards, and adjusting equipment. A yardman tuned the rigging. At one point I looked up from what I was doing and saw Jim's 6'-4" frame coming DOWN the mast, using only his hands and feet. "The jib halyard was off its pulley. I fixed it." I had the secure feeling that with Jim on board, I was in good hands.

The boat's systems left room for improvement. The VHF radio was operational; the depth finder worked, but its accuracy was uncertain; the same for the log, knot speed, and wind speed indicators. The compass also worked, but was not adjusted for deviation and variation. The oil temperature and ammeter gauges were fine. Missing entirely was a fuel indicator. The monel tank held twenty-four gallons, but was connected to the deck fill plate by a hose with a tight "S" turn making it impossible to use a dip stick to measure. Without fuel-per-hour data, it was a guessing game. I decided to lash an extra five-gallon can on the lazarette. The standing rigging was in excellent shape. The wire to rope halyards needed new splicing, but were sound. I taped the frayed rope ends. The head was operational, salt-water pump in the galley functioned, as did the new fresh water system, for washing, not for drinking. We pumped out the 40-gallon fresh water tank and refilled it. With some play in the mooring lines, I tested the transmission. In reverse at idle speed it wanted to move, but above idle speed the clutch slipped. Forward was fine, but, I reasoned, I wasn't planning on going to Albany in reverse.

We departed the yard at noon and swung into the Severn River on a brief test circuit. The boat handled well and after getting the feel of her, we returned, fueled up, kicked it in forward gear and were under way. We eased out of the Severn River and as we passed Bell Buoy 11 in the Chesapeake we set the main and No. 1 jenny and swung north ready for a good sail, but a few miles north of the Bay Bridge, the breeze died and we began to motor, moving along at about 4 ½ knots under a clear sky and a hot sun. As afternoon wore on I began to be concerned about how much fuel remained so we headed for a charted marina on the eastern shore. On approach it was obvious that it was the remains of a sizeable marina, its docks rotted and crumbling. I gingerly approached the crumbling docks, found a sturdy section, and tied up. Howard set off toward some houses with an empty gas can, and in an hour returned with a full can and carrying a quart of milk, some ice and a Baltimore newspaper. He'd hitched a ride, told his story, and was driven 4 miles to a gas station and back.

I computed our speed over the ground as 7 ½ knots, but by dusk we were 15 miles south of our overnight anchorage in the Sassafras River. With dusk came my first experience at being overtaken, in short order, by a 150' workboat to starboard, then to port by an ocean going container vessel and finally by an ocean going tug carrying fifty or sixty large containers headed South. Two more hours of first-time, nighttime piloting finally brought us to our anchorage. The night was quiet and the sky filled with stars.

By 9:00 A.M. we were sailing on a very light breeze managing to make headway up the Bay. With Jim at the tiller the boat slowed, turned to port, and stopped. We were aground. We tried the usual maneuvers, moving weight forward, then aft, swinging the boom amidships and shifting weight to starboard. I tried the engine in reverse. The clutch slipped. Help arrived in the form of a 26' single engine cruiser whose skipper noticed our maneuvering and offered to help. We rigged a girdle from the bow cleat running along both sides below the toe rail to distribute the strain and with a towrope the good Samaritan pulled us off. After providing local advice as to the location of the channel, and accepting with reluc-

tance a donation to his fuel budget, our rescuer went his way and
we headed north, motoring.

At a marina near the mouth of the Bohemia River there were
a number of sailboats in a moorage west of the entry. I approached
cautiously, dead slow across the moorage area, but before we
reached the first moored boat, I felt the dragging. I immediately
put it in reverse, but of course the clutch slipped. We were aground
again. We didn't see anyone on shore, but the gas pump was visible. Almost in the next second I heard a splash and looking forward saw Howard, his 6' 2" frame standing in water up to his chest.
"Enough of this damned stuff. I'm gonna push it off." And he tried,
standing at the bow, pushing one way and another, but a six-ton
boat doesn't move easily when its keel is in sand and mud. At that
point, Jim jumped in. I started the engine, put it in reverse and holding it just at idle to prevent slippage, the hull came free. We were
afloat again. With crew back aboard and engine at idle, I backed
away from the moored boats into deep water and then made
another try going in at a right angle to the shore with Jim sound-
ing with an improvised lead line. We made it to the gas dock without a hitch and Howard and Jim were able to hose off at the dock.
Cold drinks and ice were available and we fueled up. I computed
the hours motoring and the fuel consumed and found that we used
1 ½ gal. per hr. as a conservative fuel consumption rate.

Once safely through the Chesapeake and Delaware canal, we
headed down Delaware Bay in hopes of making Cape May the
same day, but tide and wind were against us and it was clear we
weren't going to make it. An enormous, empty Panamanian flag
oil tanker overtook us a quarter mile to port and seemed to blot out
the entire Bay. As she passed, about 6:30 P.M., we switched to the
contingency plan, to anchor in Cohansey Creek on the east side of
the Bay.

Darkness was upon us before we reached the entrance to the
creek, and I had forgotten a high powered searchlight. I misread the
light tower position and after almost ramming the embankment,
was able enter the winding creek in the black, moonless night. With
Jim on the bow taking soundings and Howard watching abeam, we
slowly made our way up the invisible waterway. Two thirds of the
way up the creek, following one hairpin turn after another, we
smelled something burning. Howard took one look and announced

it was the generator belt. He tried soaping it to reduce friction, but it was too late. It broke. I elected to keep going as long as possible. As we made the next turn there was a faint glow in the sky outlining the shore. A second turn revealed the dock lights and boats at Hancock Harbor near Greenwich, MD, a few hundred yards ahead. Relieved, we glided into the gas dock of the deserted marina and tied up. I apologized for having almost run us aground and we drank a beer and unwound.

Daylight brought welcome sunshine. Howard installed the spare belt and we dropped the lines and headed down the creek, seeing it now for the first time. Following its twisting course I realized that the combined knowledge and efforts of my crew had avoided serious trouble the previous night. When I looked at the marker light tower in daylight, I shuddered. It had been close.

We raised sail, dropped the centerboard, the boat settled in, found its comfortable spot and just stayed there, shrouds singing and whitecaps splashing. For the first time there was a real wind in the sails and feeling the boat's power was exciting. In the six hours sail, we trimmed sails several times as the wind shifted and increased to 28 knots. At 3:30, we dropped the main, motored into the Cape May canal and tied up in Cape May at the South Jersey Marina where hot showers were more than welcome. I was pleased with the boat's performance, but I had cause to think about that day's sail later.

We departed Cape May at 6:15 A.M. and set a northerly course following the buoys paralleling the coast. With no wind, the swells coming from the southeast under the starboard quarter required constant sawing back and forth on the tiller to hold a steady heading. Jim hauled out the automatic pilot and took it apart; finally deciding it needed only a fuse. Finding one that seemed to fit, he plugged it in and we had an autopilot. With knowledge gained from the Power Squadron courses, I located our position by plotting running fixes, set a compass course that agreed with my charted course and set the Tillermaster. It was just in time. Within five minutes we were enveloped in thick fog. As I watched the compass I could see that the autopilot was holding course within two degrees either side, better than we had done when manually steering. This coastal fog brought with it a feeling of helplessness that was less than enjoyable, but it burned off in an hour and we found ourselves on course approaching the next marker buoy. In late afternoon, having motored all day without wind, we were undecided whether to proceed on through the night to New York or find a place to anchor. We were approaching Barnegat Bay, which I had heard had a tricky approach. I called the coast guard at Barnegat on the radio, told them I was unfamiliar with the harbor, and asked if it was safe to come in. The answer was affirmative so in we went, negotiating a right-handed dogleg, then a short straight leg followed by a sweeping turn to port. Tying up at nearest marina, we relaxed, fueled, had dinner, strolled the docks and got a good night's rest.

The next morning there was fog, but a lot of traffic, fishing boats moving out to sea, most with radar dishes mounted topsides. I decided to head on out, believing I could follow one of the local boats, so we left the dock, and got in the procession of boats heading seaward. We rounded the big turn, lined up in the straight section and approached the dog leg only to discover eight foot swells coming into the channel. The boat I was following suddenly disappeared in the impenetrable wall of fog ahead that also made the dog leg invisible. It was too thick to chance continuing. I negotiated what I thought was a careful 180 degree turn to port in the midst of the high rollers, and as I came back on my reciprocal course the tiller jammed 5 degrees to starboard. I could move it to starboard, but not to port and only barely to center. Fortunately, there were three factors in my favor, and quick thinking saved the day. The jammed rudder position made the boat want to go to port; and I wanted to go straight. With the tide running against me, the pressure of the tidal race against the port bow counteracted the rudder that was set a few degrees to port and I was able to use to keep the boat pointed straight ahead, holding just enough power to make headway. As I swung into the port curve I used the tiller and the current to turn the boat to port so that by the time we got to the dock we were approaching at a 45-degree angle, but unable to center the rudder and straighten out. Howard and Jim were in the bow and fended the boat off, made a line fast, and I just about collapsed in the cockpit. Howard made a dive to check the damage and found the lower end of the rudder bent eight inches to starboard. The boat had bottomed out in one of the high swells. The ferry trip was over for the time being.

Locating a yard that could fix the damage, having the boat towed and hauled and renting a car for the trip home took the better part of two days. Repair would require a new rudderpost and a rebuilt rudder, bushings and labor. Fortunately, I had had the foresight to attach a ferry insurance rider to the boat insurance policy. The repair time was three weeks.

Three weeks later, with Jim unavailable for the second leg of the journey, my neighbor, Gary, volunteered. Howard's position was "I started this and I'll see it finished." The boat was ready on the hoist when we arrived and as soon as we had inspected the work, they launched it. They had done an excellent job, on time and on budget.

On the advice of the owner of Mariner's Marina, we waited for the morning high tide, then crossed Barnegat Bay and started down the snaking, winding channel to Barnegat Light. Four-fifths of the way down, with fishermen anchored on both sides and traffic in the narrow channel, the engine stopped. Gary, a mechanic, dove into the bilge and managed to start it before the boat lost way, but it stopped again, and then ran unevenly until we tied up at the same dock into which we had limped three weeks previously. In the next few hours, Gary disassembled the carburetor, cleaned the filthy filter, checked the gaskets, and generally improvised. By 3 P.M. he had the engine running and we decided to head north instead of laying over another day. We proceeded past the fearful dogleg to the outer marker and then north up the coast. In a light wind from the south, we hoisted sail, tacked on a Genoa and had an easy sail until almost nine o'clock in the evening when we found ourselves boxed in by the worst land-based storm system along the eastern seaboard that year. Far to the south there were occasional flashes of lightning. To the north there were similar flashes. By the time we'd heard the revised weather forecast after leaving Barnegat that afternoon, the lightning was already visible to the south and it was too late to turn back. We'd discussed our options earlier and agreed to sail through the night so I'd set a sailing pattern paralleling the coast six miles out, far enough to stay clear of shoreward obstacles and not far enough to put us in the shipping lanes.

The light breeze dropped off and I asked Gary and Howard to drop the Genoa and the Main. The Genny came down quickly and was secured and the main followed. As I started the engine and

Gary and Howard returned to the cockpit the wind hit us and the rain came in torrents. We were six miles off New Jersey headed for New York Harbor and directly in front of us a series of parallel line squalls was moving in a southeasterly direction intersecting our course on a 45-degree angle. Wind and rain were hitting the port bow, sheets that seemed to be poured from buckets. Lightning now lay across the bow a few miles ahead and there was more lightning to the west and the south. It was my first experience at coastal sailing and I was ferrying my first big boat, a trip I'd expected to take five or six days. It was now the ninth sailing day.

The line squall to the west passed to the south; the one to the north was an unknown factor. I huddled under the dodger, holding the tiller and staying out of the downpour. Gary and Howard broke out foul weather gear, and we crowded under the dodger congratulating ourselves on having dropped the sails in time. I headed northwest on the reciprocal of the southern edge of the next approaching squall. Since the storms were land based and we were only six miles out, there was only a three or four foot chop and no major wave action. Lightning continued to spew from the leading edge of the storm that now thundered past just north of us. I eased the throttle and awaited its moving out to sea. When it did, I again swung northward, parallel to the shore. Through the pouring rain the shore was illuminated for miles, like a dazzling string of sparkling jewels. Suddenly, a flash of chain lightning—like fine Irish lace— filled the sky as far as I could see from north to south, accompanied by an instantaneous thunder clap that shook the boat. It sent icicles down my spine and in for just a brief moment I wondered why this triple amputee was in this situation. Then I saw a micro-montage of the numerous times that someone had studied me closely and in a split second decided that I was unable to perform the task in question. I knew that, despite disabilities, I was able to perform anything to which I set myself. And I knew my limitations. If I wasn't certain I would succeed, I didn't attempt it. I never took undue risks. Now here I was, offshore New Jersey at night in my well worn boat in a pouring rain, watching the lightning, and enjoying every minute.

As the initial wind and torrential rain eased, and the line squall passed out to sea, we motored north behind it, keeping an eye out for the next one. It became my plan for continuing up the coast with the primary concern that I might not go far enough north and thus get hit by the northern edge of the storm behind us, or go too far north and get into the storm ahead of us, and there was no assurance that there was enough space, if any, between them.

For the next few hours, traveling at five knots in a continuing rain, the squalls swept in from the northwest and I throttled down until they crossed our path, and then increased throttle and followed the same procedure with the next one. Lightning marked the leading edge of the storms. It was after midnight when we sighted Ambrose light outside of New York Harbor and the flashing red 4-second bell buoy at the entrance to Sandy Hook Channel. As I followed the channel markers westward in outer New York Harbor one magnificent flash of chain lightning lit up the sky directly overhead for a distance of ten or twenty miles north and south with a simultaneous clap of thunder. Then, as I throttled down to enter the narrowly buoyed and unlit channel into Greatkills Bay at the southern end of Staten Island, the engine, after running beautifully for six hours, suddenly stopped. In a flash, Gary had the hatch up and had it running again. I eased the boat past the sandbar at the harbor entrance and pulled alongside the marina dock and we just looked at each other, heaving sighs of relief. It was 3 A.M. and the rain had stopped.

Next morning it was thrilling to sail up the harbor and under the Verazano Narrows bridge and, after dropping sails, motor past the Statue of Liberty and Ellis Island, a wonderful sight from the deck of my own boat, and then eastward, avoiding the fast moving Staten Island ferries, to pass close under the fantail of the aircraft carrier Intrepid, enjoying an impressive view of that enormous ship. By evening we were at Peterson's boatyard at Nyack, where Barbara, our children, and Howard's wife, Janet, met us. Gary drove Barbara's car home and our wives and the children accompanied Howard and me on the rest of the journey.

Cruising up the Hudson we noted Anthony's nose, West Point, Harriman Park and Bear Mountain. We lunched on the hatch cover and picnicked up the Hudson and overnighted at Poughkeepsie. The next day, south of Saugerties, a Republic Seabee four passenger, amphibian aircraft made a forced landing on the river. As he drifted into hailing distance we asked if he was in trouble and he said yes. Did he want a tow? Yes. We circled and threw him a line and were soon towing an airplane up the Hudson.

What does one do with a towed seaplane? Where does one take it? The problem was solved when we spotted a coast guard crew engaged in river buoy maintenance and when the pilot dropped the tow line he was, as a vessel in distress, their responsibility. Twenty minutes later, the roar of the Franklin engine resounded as the plane came past us, twenty feet off the water, waggled his wings and climbed to altitude. We learned later that the pilot was also on a ferry trip and that had been his seventh forced landing that day, caused by a dirty carburetor. Birds of a feather.

At the boat club just south of Albany we used the club's jinn pole to lower the mast, secure it on deck and coil the shrouds and lines. On the last day we traveled past the Port of Albany and through the lock at the Federal Dam. On the way, I went forward to secure the lines we'd use going through the locks to the Mohawk River. I grasped the Sitka spruce mast spreader that, with the top of the mast forward, was lying thwart ships. It fell off the mast, completely rotted. It was the only real structural damage on the boat, missed by the surveyor, and had been held in place only by the compression of the shrouds that attached to the spreader's outer end. My mind flashed back to that sail down Delaware Bay, with the wind at 25 knots and white capped seas. How narrowly we had missed being dismasted.

When we exited the last of the flight of five locks into the Mohawk River we were on home ground and thirty-five minutes later we tied up our "big boat" at Blain's Bay Marina, our winter base, a bit poorer, older, much more experienced, and absolutely convinced we had the best boat in the world. Of course, it would need a bit of work.

21

Resolve

I had never contemplated failure of my physical body. For 61 years I had repeatedly invented ways to overcome most of its inadequacies and I was surprised that it had lasted as long as it did, but the heart attack was a serious blow to my independence. This new irreparable condition now loomed as an insurmountable problem that, added to my congenital disabilities, posed a set of circumstances so extensive that my ability to cope was strained to the utmost. The future just disappeared. The drive and motivation that had been the source of continued strength through the years vanished. I was totally humbled and depressed. I knew not what would come next and wasn't interested. I spent my days grieving, resting, and worrying that the next few minutes would bring on a second and final heart attack. I joined that legion of heart attack survivors who are convinced that their next movements will prove too strenuous and their lives will come to an abrupt end.

Returning to work held no interest for me. I was content to just sit on the patio in the sun until my life ended. Although the heart attack was adjudged to have been minor, the doctors recommended I take an extended convalescence. Fortunately, the health insurance benefits of my new job provided such coverage so I applied for disability leave and it was granted. At the doctor's urging, I enrolled in a bi-weekly monitored post-heart attack exercise class at the nearby rehabilitation center and as I began again to use my body on the treadmill and rowing machine while wearing a heart monitor, I began to regain some confidence that I might still be active if I kept my physical efforts within the limits of my minimally reduced capacities. In addition to exercise, Barb and I began a low salt, low fat, no red meat diet and I walked a little bit each day in the neighborhood.

••

My depression persisted. Barbara urged me to seek a therapist's help and I was soon engaged in a cathartic exercise that purged some of the hurt, worry and anger that I had carried as baggage for many years. Foremost in my mind was how to continue to provide for my family. Our needs for the moment were met by disability payments and as months wore on I wondered if perhaps an early retirement might be possible. The thought was appealing. I had never thought about retirement, nor prepared for it. During the last ten years of my working life I had been unemployed for almost forty-five months. My working career had been so disjointed and discontinuous that my only concern had been finding work, not retiring from it. As I reflected on my problem, I remembered how I had concluded early in life that I would never marry and have a family, and had also believed I would never be able to retire. I would work until I died. But I had married and had had a family. Might I also be able to retire?

At the State Education Department and continuing through several subsequent jobs, fees had been deducted from my pay for a retirement plan that I never expected to use. I contacted my retirement plan and the Social Security Department to learn the monthly amounts I could expect to receive and how to initiate retirement. The totals heartened me. Although modest, they would be sufficient for us to live simply. After discussion with Barb I submitted an application for disability retirement to Social Security, sweated through the weeks required to process the request and was pleased to receive the notice of approval. I then activated my retirement payments and was suddenly a retiree.

My heart attack resulted in changing our plans to sail the Great Lakes; with a weakened heart I was no longer willing to risk sailing a big boat, and discretion being the better part of valor, we sold our boat taking a sizeable loss in a bad market. By-pass surgery two years later improved my condition and stabilized my health and we were again able to go camping, this time in a small travel trailer. Being able to fish from our lightweight, unsinkable canoe was, like the big boat had been, the subject of an "interesting adventure," perhaps the last assertion of my high-risk independence. I was seventy at the time and the memory remains fresh.

Barb and I had driven the little used dirt road in remote upstate New York to the Salmon River. It had rained and the water was twelve to eighteen inches higher than the last time when my friend, Phil, caught a fat, 22 inch brown trout and I was eager to beat his record.

Barb dropped me off with the canoe 11 A.M. "Pick me up here at 5:00 P.M." I told her. "I'll motor one hour upstream and then drift back down." With Barb's kiss and a "Be careful" I started the motor and headed upstream to catch some trout before the season closed.

On this cool September day the temperature was in the low 60's. The sun was out, offsetting the chill air, but clouds were building. Foliage was still green, no touch yet of fall color. Trees and bushes grew to the water's edge, deadfalls and occasional boulders rose above surface of the water. Clear enough to see bottom in most places, the river was a mixture of boulders and snags. In the ten-foot canoe were rods, lunch, fishing gear and oars (the canoe had oarlocks). I was warmly dressed in a chamois shirt, sweatshirt, personal flotation vest and a blue peaked baseball cap.

A pleasant aura of isolation and solitude surrounded me as the tiny motor drove the canoe up the twisting river that varied from 12 to 50 feet wide and six inches to six feet deep. Through the trees, the sunlight reflected on the dancing riffles like twinkling stars. The motor moved the boat through the fast water, around a narrow turn through a configuration of enormous boulders, and into a placid stretch. For the next half mile, in water eighteen inches to three feet deep, I steered around submerged logs, branches and rocks.

About 11:20 I approached a sharp turn in the river, thirty-five feet wide at that point. Deadfalls from either shore angled downstream, leaving only a narrow V shaped opening through which the current poured. I eased into the current, grabbed a tree branch to hold position and killed the motor to study the situation. Continuing required crossing the stream to the left and making a 180-degree right turn through the narrow opening between the deadfalls. Since underwater branches could foul the propeller, it necessitated driving the canoe into the downstream leg of the V, killing the motor and then man-handling the canoe around the narrow bend of the V. Once clear of the deadfalls on the upstream side, I'd restart the motor. When fishing with Phil, we had negotiated such situations numerous times, but that was with the leverage of two in the canoe. Could I do it alone?

Releasing my hold on the deadfall, I allowed the current to wash the canoe downstream. Then, restarting the motor, I headed back upstream, attempting to get as far up into the V as possible without fouling the prop in the underwater branches. I cut the motor, and with a stevedore's hook, grabbed a deadfall, holding against the current. I pulled the canoe into the V, moving quickly with the hook from one purchase point to the next. Releasing my hold on the port side, I quickly leaned over to starboard for the next one, forgetting that the weight of the motor was on that side. Too late. My "untippable," unsinkable canoe was upside down and I was in the water, headfirst. It was not a dire situation for an able bodied swimmer; but for a triple amputee with two below-knee prostheses and a right arm terminating at the wrist it was a calamity. In addition, I was 70 years old, had had a heart attack and a by-pass, and most importantly, I couldn't swim.

The water was a bit over six feet deep, the current strong, and the bottom treacherous with branches. The life vest brought me up. I grabbed the canoe. The water was cold, but after the initial shock, bearable. My first thoughts were: Can I right the canoe and get back? What about my heart condition, hypothermia? My left foot found an underwater log, but the water was still chest high. I was unable to get purchase with my right foot and then realized that my right prosthesis had come off and was floating upside down next to my chest. I grabbed it with my right arm. Luckily, it was still in my pant leg, which had prevented it from floating downstream. It was not good situation. With only one leg, I had no stability to manipulate the canoe or even help myself in the water. I held on to the canoe which appeared to be stuck in some way. Although the water was flowing past forcefully, the canoe wasn't moving. I leaned against it and it didn't move, so I leaned hard on it, and with the water at my chest, raised my right leg up out of the water, pulled up the pant leg and forced the prosthesis on. Now I again had two legs and as I stood on the underwater log holding onto the canoe, my position was, for the moment, stabilized, but I was in trouble.

I made a quick inventory. I still had my glasses, and looking around, noticed that twelve feet away, there was a back eddy that captured debris floating down stream. Floating in it was my half-filled gas can, a cushion, the thermos and one of the oars. Some-

thing bumped against my chest. It was my rain gear pouch. I picked
it up, let it drain and threw it over with the other floating things in
the hope that I'd recover them later.

The steep and thickly forested surrounding terrain didn't make
hiking a preferred choice. The canoe was the only realistic way
back. Feet tenuously planted on the log, I tried to right the canoe.
It barely moved. I realized that, amid the tangle of underwater
branches, something was holding it firmly in place. Peering under
the canoe, I saw that the inverted motor was hung up on an underwater branch and the current was holding everything in place. To
right the canoe, it would be necessary to jettison the motor, so I
slid down in the water up to my neck and, reaching under and
across to the other side of the canoe, located the clamp that held the
motor to the canoe. I slowly loosened it until the motor fell off the
boat. Immediately the canoe had more buoyancy, and lifting the
upstream side, I turned it over and hung onto it in the current.
Although filled with water, it floated. I pushed it back into a crotch
of the deadfall. Filled to the gunwales, the canoe now rested on the
branches just as solidly as on a beach. Inside it were the second
cushion, the ice chest, one oar, a fishing rod and a wooden seat.
My bailing scoop was visible underwater fifteen feet downstream,
beyond reach. I opened the ice chest intent on using it to bail and
discovered a small plastic container, much more easily handled. I
lifted the upstream side of the canoe high enough to drain sufficient water to gain an inch or two freeboard. Then I started bailing
and in a short time had the canoe completely afloat. As it gained
buoyancy, I kept wedging it tighter in the crotch of the deadfall.
Then, holding on to the stern, I got my right leg over the gunwale
and rolled in. Now I knew that I would get back down the river. I
took a breather, but now out of the water and in the wind, I felt
chilled and began to shiver. The sun came out and the shivers dissipated.

The anchor line floated in the stream within reach. I hauled in
the slack and secured the canoe to the deadfall. I crawled to the
bow and could see the motor four or five feet down amid the tree
branches. I weighed the alternatives of attempting to recover the
motor or getting back downstream as quickly as possible to cut the
risk of hypothermia or heart attack. The sun was still out. I wasn't
shivering and was calming down. I decided to take the risk.

The motor lay with the shaft and propeller downstream. Retrieving the rest of the anchor line, I saw that it went down to the top of the motor. As I tugged, the motor moved. A few more tugs and the line came loose. Seconds later the small collapsible anchor was on board, but the line was still fouled somewhere under the boat. Looking down again at the motor, I could see my extra coil of rope lying at the downstream end of the motor shaft, near the propeller. An extra coil of rope might come in handy so I carefully lowered the anchor and luckily hooked the coil. As it came up, it became tangled in the propeller of the motor that was also coming up far enough to allow me to secure a grip on the prop. Wonder of wonders! The motor was now upside down in the water, but still snagged below. Taking a couple of extra turns around the propeller I tied it off to a branch at the surface. I was so busy I didn't realize that the clouds had covered the sun and now I was shivering again. But I was so close. I had to make another try, shivering or not. I couldn't leave that motor lying at the bottom of the stream.

Moving to the stern, I paid out line so the canoe could move forward, then crawled to the bow and threw the anchor ahead and upstream to hold the bow steady. Tightening up the bow line moved the canoe forward a few feet, held fast bow and stern, cross-stream. Now the position of the motor was downstream, amidships on the port side. With another grip on the propeller, and fearful that it might slip, I jiggled the motor up and down. Suddenly it broke free and I hauled it in over the port gunwale being very careful this time to keep my weight to starboard. I was elated, and shivering. Now I had to get out of there. But what about my other gear?

Again I crawled to the stern line and paid out line, then back to the bow to tighten up on the anchor line, thus moving the boat further forward and closer to the eddy in which the gear was still floating. Laying down on the bow and, reaching out with the oar, I secured the second oar, the gas can, the cushion, the rain gear pouch, and finally the thermos. There was now a pile of wet gear in the canoe. Moving on all fours with prostheses is exceedingly difficult and awkward, so I removed both prostheses and on hands and knees, organized the boat, replacing the stern seat, remounting the motor, and arranging the gear. Then I sat back in the stern seat and re-donned my prostheses. The sun came out and I started to feel good. I was ready to cut loose when I noticed the tip of a fishing rod sticking up out of the water. I retrieved it. Just under water on a branch was my heavy wool shirt, held fast by the current. I pulled it aboard. The tip of my third fishing rod was bobbing up out of the water, just out of reach. Paying out some more line and dropping the canoe downstream a foot or two, with the oar I moved the rod tip close enough to grasp it. With all three rods retrieved, only my knapsack with the fishing gear was still missing and I was amazed to find its strap caught on a pulley I used for sailing. My only losses now were the bailing scoop, which could still be seen, but wasn't worth bothering about; the anchor, also within sight, but after several tries unable to be freed a second time, and my hat, which was nowhere in sight. The sun was gone, the sky was cloudy, the wind was blowing and I was shivering. I put on the wet woolen shirt and raincoat to cut the wind, bailed the remaining water from the boat, put both oars in the sockets, cut the mooring lines fore and aft, allowed the current to wash the canoe into the main stream, and started to row to warm up. It was 12:30. It had taken an hour and fifteen minutes to fall in, jettison the motor, right the canoe, get out of the water, and retrieve the motor and the gear. I was pleased at how I had handled the situation, but concerned about the weather and the temperature.

I had to return and to stay warm until 5:00 P.M. when Barbara would pick me up. As I alternatively rowed with the current to stay warm, and then drifted, I planned my next moves. I spotted a bright blue object caught in the tangle of a fallen tree downstream, and guiding the canoe close, picked up my hat as I drifted by. At 1:30 I was back at the pick-up point, warm and comfortable after the rowing. Beaching the canoe, I unloaded everything, removed the woolen shirt (a mistake as it helped to cut the wind) and re-donned the raincoat, spread out the chamois and the wool shirts on the grass, and dragged the canoe out of the water. The sun was gone, the wind was blowing about 8-10 knots and I was shivering. I had to get out of the wind. Tilting the canoe on its gunwale and propping it in place with the oars formed a windbreak. I retrieved the two pair of rubber pants from the raingear, stripped off my dripping pants and underwear and donned both pair. I lay down under the canoe and covered up with the two wet shirts, but now the sun was gone and the chill was increasing. Then I remembered the gas can. I started walking along the dirt road to get warm, collecting firewood, uncertain as to how I'd get a fire started but knowing I had to keep warm until 5:00 P.M. I kept hoping there would be some reason for my wife to come early. At 3:00 P.M. I heard a car. It was Barbara, two hours early, planning to relax, walk the dog and read the newspaper. ESP? Luck? It's anybody's guess.

******

Retirement slowly induced a peace and tranquility. It was necessary to closely curtail expenditures, but for the first time there was no worry about losing a job or searching for another. With that enormous load lifted from my shoulders, life, even in a diminished state, began to again to look hopeful. When I had asked Barbara to marry me I told her, "I'm never going to make a lot of money, but I think I can promise you an interesting life." On a few occasions Barb had said to me, "Please, enough interesting life." But the interesting life was far from over. With our daughter doing well in college, our son was encountering problems.

Every bit as capable and intelligent as his sister, our Jared had encountered difficulty reading in the early grades until he was placed in the class of a perceptive teacher who permitted him to read independently at his own pace. In that year he moved from the second lowest reading level to the highest. With math, he could perform all the required computations, but did them slowly, and when he moved to middle school was mistakenly tracked into a slow math class until, on the basis of high testing scores, Barb appealed to the Vice Principal who placed him at a more suitable level. In high school he began each semester with high grades, which then dropped precipitously as the semester progressed. His guidance counselor warned that unless his grades improved, his chances of entering a four-year college would be limited. We knew that Jared marched to a different drummer and when questioned, he expressed his dislike and unhappiness with the school. Most of his friends from elementary school were involved in sports; he was not an athlete. Socially and academically he was becoming an outsider; he didn't enjoy being there. With resources almost nonexistent, we nevertheless determined to find a solution. We scouted several preparatory schools and interviewed the headmasters, telling them frankly of both Jared's need and our current situation.

••

The Darrow School Headmaster responded immediately with an offer of a generous scholarship if we could manage to pay monthly installments. With no assurance that we could meet that requirement, or how, we immediately accepted and with effort, managed to meet the obligation. Jared prospered in the new environment and two years later, at his graduation, was class valedictorian, winning a generous tuition support package from his chosen college, Connecticut College, in New London, Connecticut.

My working years had not been easy and my job security had always been tenuous, but with exception of my final job, I had always been fortunate in being able to work at things I enjoyed. On balance, I had perhaps been more fortunate than many workers. I had begun life at a place and time when many disabled persons were publicly subjected to the stares and curiosity of unthinking and insensitive individuals, asked personal and impudent questions, verbally and physically accosted, or all too often hidden from the public out of shame and embarrassment simply because of being different.

I had experienced such public abuse for thirty-four years and to accepted that, because my outward appearance was unusual, my capabilities were perceived to be less. In puberty and early adult life, as I remembered it metaphorically, I was ill matched in the physically oriented competition between the sexes as they searched, a la Darwin, for the superior specimen with which to mate. When the pairing off trickled down from the highly prized specimens at the top of the spectrum of eligible participants to the lesser desirable at the bottom, those like myself were few, and ultimately excluded from the process. And yet ultimately, I had the good fortune to find a life partner from the very top of that spectrum.

Experience in the world of work taught me that it mattered not what one was capable of doing, but what one appeared to be able to do. Irving Goffman in "Stigma" suggests that society first determines the role of the deviant and then requires that the deviant adopt the prescribed role. Deep in my innermost being I knew and understood that I possessed serious physical disabilities, but I never accepted that because of them I was unable to do what I wanted to do. I had totally and continually ignored society's unarticulated dogma. Ignoring it, however, didn't make it go away. Experience taught me that if one could not satisfy the physical demands of the lowest levels of the career ladder, one had little hope for rising to higher levels, and although these requirements had constituted barriers for me at various times, I nevertheless had, on numerous occasions, experienced the happiness of overcoming them and achieving success.

At a time when incarceration of the disabled was still in vogue, my mother had never hidden me, but rather had encouraged me to face life directly and independently. Accordingly, I had pursued every possible opportunity, using whatever skills and experience I could bring to bear, switching direction when the road closed before me, attempting new options, and constantly driving forward with all my strength to survive and prosper in the available situations. Although for thirty-four years almost every day was spent in pain, I managed to do what was expected of me, and what I demanded that I do for myself. In the process I had found approval, and pleasure, and enormous self-satisfaction.

When the miracle of my rehabilitation occurred and I was relieved of pain and was no longer the object of comment and derision, I found it unbelievable that I could walk down the street and not a head would turn. My newfound anonymity was a profound change from what I had previously experienced. In the years that followed, however, I valued that anonymity so much that I protected it more and more, fearing that if my disabilities were disclosed, I would again become that object of curiosity and pity that I had been for so many years. In so doing I had inadvertently self imposed limitations on myself similar to those from which I had miraculously escaped.

I have walked more miles and for more years with prostheses than I walked on my congenitally malformed feet. I experienced numerous lows in my life, times of total despair. I was at times convinced I would never again overcome inertia and develop momentum, but in retrospect I can count equally as many highs as I proved to myself and others my creative, intellectual and sometimes even physical capabilities. I demonstrated tenacity in clinging to my dreams, and constantly pushed forward in an unending search for survival, acceptance and recognition. As concerns my rehabilitation, there is no way to know with certainty the reactions of casual acquaintances to my good fortune.[17]

Following my rehabilitation, I received numerous expressions of happiness at what was perceived as my good fortune, which it was, and complimentary remarks of my "great courage" which in actuality was merely a pragmatic decision to prevent major physical and medical problems from developing in the future. The downside risks, in retrospect, had been minimal, and the rehabilitation, of course, had been most successful, and the transformation quite dramatic, but there had been little room for indecision at the time. Despite the pragmatism, it was always, for me, a miracle.

A dear friend told me, "I was thrilled. It was a very unusual happening and to see it unfold was absolutely thrilling." Another said, "When I learned of your surgery I suddenly realized how difficult your previous condition was. You had a presence that made people who knew you discount your disabilities and I realized I hadn't fully understood your situation. And when I saw you with the new legs I could hardly believe the transformation of your appearance, yet you didn't seem changed a bit. Having known you before, I didn't think there was as much change in my perception of you, as probably there was in your perception of yourself. Perhaps, when we make our judgments about people, we tend to conserve our image of them as a constant. Your previous ability to distract others from your disabilities was, of course, now considerably enhanced. After the surgery, I would suppose that people who met you for the first time (except for little children), failed initially to notice that you had only one hand. Your surgery was enormously successful, but I would suggest that for those who knew you previously it did not significantly change their image of you."

From a friend to whom I had written in despair during my last period of unemployment that followed my having "come out" to serve as the host of a television series of programs on people with disabilities, I received this response, "…I have read your letter a number of times and have thought about it for a few days. The paragraph that shines most brightly is the one in which you say that you have finally accepted the fact that you are disabled. I think

---

[17] "…It seems that persons who suddenly find themselves relieved of a stigma, as in successful plastic surgery, may quickly be seen, by themselves and others, to have altered their personality, an alteration in the direction of the acceptable, just as those who have suddenly acquired a defect may relatively quickly experience a change in apparent personality…" Goffman, p.132.

I can understand how much harder it has been for you to come to
this latter realization than it is for the garden variety of drunk like
me to accept that he is an alcoholic. If I had not accepted that years
ago, I would have been dead years ago, but the thrust of your life
has been to minimize your disability... Remarkable as it all has
been (and I knew you before), I think I can appreciate the psychological complexities of what you have been living through since
that day, and possibly even understand them. Let's just say that it
is evidence of maturity, a state to which we all aspire but not all of
us achieve. You have also been visited by the Gods of Lousy Luck,
as have I...There is nothing that one can do about these particular
gods, because they are busy spreading their mischief throughout
the world. What I try to do is concentrate on those few times when
the Good Luck deities throw a bone or two my way...At our age,
and we are "of an age," we do indeed get depressed and angry and
at times lose faith, because of the world we never made and the
things we did not do, and now, of course, it is too late. I imagine it
all has to do with the realization, at our stage in the game, that we
have used up most of our time without accomplishing what we
wanted to do in the first place, especially when we read the obitu-
ary columns and see those around us drop away from the court."

In the aggregate, my life has not been too dissimilar from the
millions of persons who, for various reasons did not fulfill their
dreams. Such fulfillment is given to only a very few. My disabilities have obviously been a deterrent in my life and the experience
of living with them molded a character and personality that contains flaws that in some measure became additional disabilities.
During a life begun at the level of simple, working class people, I
struggled mightily to pursue education, improve my values and
behavior, even my dress, and to make my life meaningful and complete. Although in numerous ways I am unusually successful by
just surviving, and also in having a career, (some say it was a successful one), in my view I never accomplished my dreams and my
socio-economic status has not changed significantly. My still recur-
rent dream is to be able to comfortably afford to invite my family
to dinner at a good restaurant and have everyone order from the
left side of the menu, something we have never done.

I have witnessed changes in society's view of the disabled,
even though the changes are still, in my opinion, only token. I am

satisfied that I have been able to survive in the face of the impersonal barriers that society placed before me. After having been convinced, early in life, that I would never have the opportunity to have a "normal" life, I have in important ways experienced the best that life has to offer, the satisfaction of having survived, and having the opportunity to enjoy the experience of being a loving and beloved husband, father, and late in my retirement, a grandfather. As I promised my wife at the outset, I've taken her on an interesting journey that's been at times meaningful, productive, frightening, satisfying, and enjoyable. I'm not certain I understand the whys and wherefores of my life and I still have unanswered questions, but I'm still here and ready for whatever comes next.

Acknowledgements

I am thankful and indebted to many, some of whom appear in my story, who took the time to read my manuscript, confirm its accuracy, and contribute their thoughts.

Among the many readers whose generous contributions and advice were of utmost assistance were Statton (Buzz) Rice and Cate McMahon, Gilbert Delgado, Klaus Lohman, Dale and Martha Stein, Ron and Judy DeWitt, Phyllis Rutigliano, Dr. Anthony Grieco, and Theresa Capporossi. In addition, Don Ferguson willingly shared his expertise and Dr. Ronald Legum's comments as a physician were of great value. Nancy Hoffman's penetrating critique resulted in major changes and improvement of the manuscript. Names of some who appear in the story have been changed to protect their privacy.

I am grateful to several individuals, now deceased: Robert Lepper, Charles Siepmann, Richard Goggin, John Gough, William Hoddapp, William Wood, Barbara Yanowski, Muriel Green, Dr. Donald Dowie, and George Gordon, who were empathetic and helpful along the way; and to Dr. Allen Russek who had the vision and the dedication to create what for me, was a miracle.

Our children, Jessica, and Jared, for whom this book was begun so that they might be aware of my journey, both made immeasurable contributions to the effort. My deepest regret is that Jessica, who was lost to breast cancer in 2011, was unable to enjoy its completion.

A major influence in my life was my father, whose unlimited love, devoted assistance and enduring optimism sustained me. I credit my ability to survive and to enjoy a number of small successes, however, to two people; my mother, who gave me free rein, taught me to see beyond my disabilities and to be what I could be, and my beloved wife, Barbara, a continuing bastion of strength and hope, who has not only supported my efforts every step along the way but has also contributed her critical perceptions and editorial skills to this effort.

NORBERT NATHANSON, July, 2013

Made in the USA
Charleston, SC
29 July 2013